Social Control
3rd edition

Social Control

An Introduction

3rd edition

James J. Chriss

polity

First edition published in 2007 by Polity Press
Second edition published in 2013 by Polity Press
This third edition published in 2022 by Polity Press

Polity Press
65 Bridge Street
Cambridge CB2 1UR, UK

Polity Press
111 River Street
Hoboken, NJ 07030, USA

ISBN-13: 978-1-5095-3949-9
ISBN-13: 978-1-5095-3950-5(pb)

A catalogue record for this book is available from the British Library.

Library of Congress Control Number: 2022930578

Typeset in 11 on 13pt Swift
by Fakenham Prepress Solutions, Fakenham, Norfolk NR21 8NL

The publisher has used its best endeavours to ensure that the URLs for external websites referred to in this book are correct and active at the time of going to press. However, the publisher has no responsibility for the websites and can make no guarantee that a site will remain live or that the content is or will remain appropriate.

For further information on Polity, visit our website:
politybooks.com

Contents

Tables and Figures

Tables

Figures

Preface and Acknowledgments

While swimming in a pool in the jungle of Nool, Horton the elephant heard a small voice. Kangaroo is the matriarch of the tight and well-maintained social order of Nool. She is depicted as straight-laced and traditional, dripping with conservative "family values." For example, she proudly proclaims that her son, Rudy, is "pouch-schooled."

Horton is viewed by Kangaroo as far more than simply eccentric – in fact, he's downright dangerous – for holding to and spreading his ridiculous belief that he heard a voice coming from a small speck on a clover. Horton insists there are people living on that speck, and he goes about protecting it with every fiber in his being. Kangaroo casts Horton as a weirdo and possibly deranged, certainly a destabilizing influence in Nool. She says, "If you can't see it, feel it, or hear it, it doesn't exist." In no uncertain terms, these sorts of beliefs will not be tolerated in the jungle of Nool. Horton says in his defense, "A person's a person, no matter how small."

As Horton continues to maintain that the speck has life on it, which is his duty to protect and preserve, the dour Kangaroo makes a public case against Horton that he is deranged and deserves to be punished. Most of the jungle caves in to Kangaroo's view, and Horton is successfully made a pariah (except for a few close allies). Being deemed deserving of scorn and ridicule, Horton is harassed and treated shabbily almost until the end of the story.

This is the film adaptation of the classic Dr. Seuss children's book, *Horton Hears a Who!*, but it has profound implications for social control.[1] After being immersed in the study of social control and having committed a good deal of effort grappling with it through these three editions of the book, I am not sure at all if the scholarly writings – and they are voluminous, as attested to by the bibliography – are much better on the subject than this simple, elegant Dr. Seuss tale. I believe that the further you get pulled into deviance and social control, you start realizing it is something akin to a bottomless pit and there is really no way out. There are no happy endings here. Horton did okay by the end of the story because, well, fairy tales are supposed to be uplifting for young and curious minds just starting on their long trek into the heart of the social system. But the stark reality is that this is really dismal stuff, and it will keep getting much worse before getting better, if it ever does.

This sour tone may reflect close to two years of hell dealing with a crazy virus and people losing their minds over politics. This book was delayed because of the strangeness of 2020 and most of 2021. Even under the best of circumstances, it is not easy to wrap your head around the endgame of social control, but with all the noise and cacophony and angst and turbulence and desperation and madness and anger and hostility and sanctimoniousness and virtue-signaling and punitiveness and prudishness and symbolic inflation and superciliousness and faddishness and querulousness – and so on and so forth – the task is nigh hopeless. I truly believe whatever order is created and maintained is pretty much arbitrary, and any order will do. The only thing you can really do is lay low and cover your ass, because the system is just a big grinder moving people and pieces around here and there according to the whims of those who are temporarily in charge. Yes, the only thing to look forward to is knowing that the assholes in charge won't be there for long, because there is a restlessness and the political system plays gotcha games for those ignorant enough to enter the arena.

This restlessness does not lead to the Marxist permanent revolution but to PISS, the perpetual investigative state squared. We are now at the point where we might as well pass a law that all elected officials will from day one have a special counsel assigned to them so that they can dig into their finances and private lives and affairs flush with unlimited cash. You know, the whole "indicting a ham sandwich" thing. And then when they are caught, they will play the silly game of the public confessional where they will grovel and claim trauma or addiction – sex is the juiciest one of course – and that having gone through the ordeal they'll be better and healthier persons for it. And all the while the social media mobs armed with their virtual torches and pitchforks and smartphones are out chasing Frankenstein's Monster into the night serenaded by wolves howling at the moon.

I want to thank my wife Mandy and my daughter and son, Ariana and John, for helping me get through the ordeal of writing this book over these past few years. The editorial team at Polity has been a delight to work with, including most prominently Karina Jákupsdóttir who was understanding about all the delays. And Ian Tuttle did a magnificent job with the copyediting.

Speaking of which, the world of books and publishing provides slivers of light in the vast darkness. You can escape to your favorite authors and spend time with them and learn from them. I have been spending some time with the great Giambattista Vico and thinking a lot about his eternal cycle of history.[2] I could not figure out a way of working it into the book, so I will take this opportunity to share my take on his description of the rise and fall and rise again of civilizations through the three great eras of gods, heroes, and men.[3]

The ancients needed gods to bring them out from the caves, out of super-stition and animal lust, and so the Word was brought to the people and enforced with rapaciousness into the era of heroes, where a myth arose that the lowly masses yearned for leaders to lead them out of the wilderness. The age of heroes delivered the fables and tales of heroic protagonists fighting evil and deadly sins, and on their backs kingdoms were built and defended in the earlier, absolutist version of government (the kingship model). Such king-gods became heroes and also appointed themselves as such through such cultural innovations as the divine right of kings, but, with the dawning of the age of enlightenment, the people – the humble citizens of the sovereign state – started growing restless and challenged the unquestioned rule of leaders and sought to share power with them. The toppling of kings and the ushering in of democracy gives rise to the era of people (men), and as satisfaction of wants and desires are met more systematically with the advent of labor-saving technologies along with the rise of the service city and numerous helping professions (medicine, psychotherapy, and social work to name a few), persons lose tolerance for even the small aches and pains of life, while at the same time demanding that the government protect them from the profanations of a hurdy-gurdy, dangerous world. Although launched in the antiquity of cosmological and theological speculation, this escape from the state of nature, which ushered in civilization along with the belief in a growing chasm between the animal and human, becomes a core cultural feature of modernity even as ecological movements emerge – hearkening back to the ancient Greek Cynics – which direct true believers to reject the distinctiveness of human beings in favor of a unitary theory of nature and life.

Along with this, the self, which used to be shored up through close and personal relationships with friends and family, now becomes a focal concern of governments as well, and subjectivity is mined further and deeper to protect fragile self-esteem and punish those who would violate it. In addition, the health tag, initially applied to the body and later to the mind, is continually extended and now we can talk about public health, behavioral health, family health, immigrant health, pet health, prisoner health, adolescent health, friendship health, and the real biggie: sexual health. With sexual health, eroticism is sought as an end for and of itself, the feeling part carved out of the functional aspect of sex, which is of course procreation. Of course, Lester Ward noted long ago that humanity slowly and inexorably circumvents and ensnares nature's method, producing an artificial human society alongside the state of nature from which humanity had continually worked to escape.[4]

But the focus on satisfying wants – erotic and otherwise – becomes a runaway norm, because human appetites are insatiable and, without suffi-cient constraints in place to moderate them, the pursuit of gratifications will bring a collapse to social order and return men to the caves – to animal or bare life – once again.[5] And then at some point, lost in the wilderness, grunts and utterances will attain the minimal level of symbolic significance made intelligible to those particular human beings in that particular setting – the early poetry of the rude races – once again giving birth (or rather, rebirth) to the gods. And so, the cycle churns on.

Soon after the era of gods comes the era of heroes, the first attempt to inject humanity into the grandiosity of the cosmos and the mysteries of life that confront primitive minds just escaping savagery and barbarism. The early epic poetry of Homer and Virgil are well known, but we will move ahead to the late medieval period, specifically the early fifteenth century, where an unknown (perhaps Scottish or English) author wrote the poem 'The Alliterative *Morte Arthure*', in which the goddess Fortuna makes an appearance in a dream of Arthur's.[6] As a genre of classical heroism, King Arthur is invested with the power of Alexander, but Arthur's campaign against the Roman emperor Lucius would aspire to avoid the bad fate (or the bad repetition) that befell the latter. In the dream Arthur finds himself in a forest filled with savage beasts but escapes to an earthly paradise replete with vines of silver, grapes of gold, fine fruit, and colorful birds.[7] After this, Lady Fortune descends from the heavens on her bejeweled wheel which contains eight of the Nine Worthies. All the riders on the wheel are kings or great military leaders, among whom are Alexander, Hector, Julius Caesar, Judas Maccabeus, Joshua, David, Charlemagne, and Godfrey.[8] After several of them fall, Fortuna places Arthur on the wheel, giving him a scepter, diadem, and a "pome" or "orb engraved with a map of the world."[9] Originally quite taken by Arthur, by midday Fortune's mood changes and she crushes Arthur under the wheel.

After awaking, Arthur consults a trusted confidante to interpret his dream. This philosopher – in the poem, clearly playing the part of the medieval moralist – tells Arthur that his time has passed and that he should prepare for death. With the appearance of Fortuna in the dream, Arthur was not able to escape the tyranny of repetition after all: Arthur's initial escape to paradise from the terrors of the jungle was a repetition of Alexander's arrival at his own earthly paradise after successful military campaigns. In that paradise Alexander was given a stone by his own philosopher – Aristotle – which has the extraordinary property of outweighing everything in the world. This wonderstone is Alexander, whose presence in the world outweighs history and time. As Lee Patterson explains, "Alexander received an object that marked the limits of the very sovereignty it was supposed to acknowledge, just as the Earthly Paradise itself stood as an impassable limit to his geographical conquests."[10] Likewise, Arthur's demise after briefly being placed in the company of the Nine Worthies ends in darkness and tragedy, yet the saving grace here is that it is only a dream.

We can dream and dream we shall!

PART I
UNDERSTANDING SOCIAL CONTROL

Chapter 1
What Is Social Control?

Introduction

What are we to make of Stanley Cohen's assertion that social control has become a "Mickey Mouse" concept in sociology and the broader social sciences?[1] What Cohen meant by this is that, because it is used so extensively to cover so many things, the concept "social control" has no clear meaning at all. It is simply a catchall phrase for explaining all the ways conformity is induced in human beings.

That there is a vast array of mechanisms and procedures in place for attempting to do just that – to extract compliance of individuals or groups to some ideal standard of conduct, whether this takes place at home, in the factory, in school, within personal relations, at the doctor's office, while driving a car or at the stadium watching a ballgame – is undeniable. Indeed, as anthropologist Siegfried Nadel argued, "In this sense control is simply coterminous with society, and in examining the former we simply describe the latter."[2] The study of social control is the study of how society patterns and regulates individual behavior.[3] So, in response to Cohen, why should the extensiveness of a procedure, practice, or process render the study of that procedure, practice, or process somehow problematic or even futile?

I would argue that even given its vastness and ubiquity, social control is very much a viable concept for sociology and other social and behavioral sciences. The study of social control can be managed by keeping in sight its basic forms. These three basic forms, which will be expanded upon throughout the book, are legal, medical, and informal. This book may profitably be used at the undergraduate or beginning graduate level, in a wide variety of courses, including of course social control, but also deviance, juvenile delinquency, criminology, criminal justice, sociology of law, corrections or the sociology of prisons, the sociology of policing, and the administration of justice. It should also be noted that the topic of social control brings together literatures from a number of fields including history, social psychology, medical sociology, anthropology and linguistics, political science, economics, geography, sociological and criminological theory, law, criminal justice, and sociology more generally. As a consequence, the bibliography is quite large, and should be a useful reference to scholars in many of the disciplines and fields of study listed above.

Part I of the book lays out the groundwork for understanding the concept of social control, including its history and usages. As discussed later in this chapter, the early American sociologist Edward A. Ross was the first person to investigate, in sustained fashion, something called "social control," beginning with a series of articles he wrote on the subject in 1896. Indeed, without Ross there is no social control. It should be pointed out that, unlike Ross, most of the authors we will be investigating in this book did not set out to study social control per se. That is, a number of philosophers, theologians, political theorists, and social scientists from antiquity onward have written about the relationship between the individual and society, and in most of these instances, although the term "social control" may never have been explicitly invoked, there nevertheless was a concern with how the individual is held in check by wider social arrangement or structures, whether in the form of the state, the family, the community, the economic system (the explicit focus of Marx's politic philosophy, for example), the group or tribe, or some other regulative mechanism.

After establishing the threefold typology of social control in chapter 2, separate chapters are devoted to issues and controversies associated with informal control (chapter 3), medical control (chapter 4), and legal control (chapter 5). These five chapters will provide to the student a rigorous understanding of social control as it is typically used and applied in sociological and social science analysis.

Part II is dedicated to critical case studies in social control. Chapters 6, 7, and 8 build upon the basic groundwork established in chapters 3, 4, and 5 respectively. For example, while chapter 3 lays the foundation for an understanding of informal control, chapter 6 provides critical case studies of informal control. Because it continues to play a prominent role in modern society, race and race relations is the theme connecting the three case studies in chapter 6, as well as those of chapter 8 (on legal control). The case studies of medical control in chapter 7 focus primarily on the control of youth and adolescence.

Chapter 9 focuses exclusively on terrorism since it is the most pressing concern of Western democracies today. Finally, chapter 10 ponders what the future of social control may hold in light of the challenges to the social order which such problems as terrorism, pandemics, or political upheavals – for example, revolutions or the rise of authoritarianism – have wrought. In examining these broad cultural, political, social, and historical trends, we are in a position to better understand how states attempt to blend medical and legal controls to shore up the social order, and how and to what extent such formal actions either strengthen or weaken the informal controls taking place among friends, families, small groups, religious congregations, communities, and so forth.

At the end of each chapter, I provide an annotated bibliography consisting of five books which are strongly recommended to readers seeking more in-depth information about the topics and issues treated therein. I also provide five discussion questions pertaining to the material covered in each chapter.

The Covid-19 pandemic

On December 31, 2019, Chinese authorities alerted the World Health Organization to a number of pneumonia-related deaths of unknown origin, with the epicenter of the illness located in Wuhan City in Hubei province. It turned out to be a new strain of the coronavirus – which belongs to the same family as the common cold and various influenzas for which vaccines have been developed – and now identified as Covid-19. Since Covid-19 was a new strain of the virus for which a vaccine had not yet been developed, the world could only look on in horror as illnesses and deaths mounted as the virus was carried from China to other parts of the world. By early April 2020, the worldwide death toll from Covid-19 stood at almost 37,000 with the number of infected just under 770,000. And by March 2021 the US figure alone had climbed to over 500,000, with worldwide deaths topping 2.5 million.[4]

Because of how rapidly and easily the virus is spread from person to person, in the United States and elsewhere many group activities – including sporting events – were shut down and persons who had to be in public (to get food or for health reasons) were told to practice "social distancing," that is, as much as possible to stay at least six feet away from others.[5] This also meant closing down many "nonessential" businesses such as malls, hair salons, bars and taverns, and the restaurants that remained open could only serve takeout or via drive through. This of course had serious economic ramifications, as jobless claims skyrocketed to a level not seen since the Great Depression, while the stock market and other financial institutions took a historic beating. (The stock market later rebounded, however.) In addition, schools and universities shut down and classes were converted to online instruction. Retail giant Macy's announced they would be furloughing 130,000 of their workers, producing a ripple effect of bad economic news across many sectors of society.

There was early speculation that Covid-19 emerged from wet markets in Wuhan, which are open-air markets where customers can shop for fresh meats, vegetables, and dairy products. But the wet markets per se were not the problem. Instead, there was some mixing of legitimate wet market activities with illegitimate wildlife market activities, whereby exotic animals like snakes and bats were introduced into these markets and infected some of the personnel and products that were otherwise legitimate.[6] There has also been growing evidence that the virus may have originated in a lab in Wuhan, specifically, the Wuhan Institute of Virology, which was conducting gain-of-function experiments allegedly funded on some level by the National Institutes of Health (NIH).[7] President Trump had made this claim at the beginning of the pandemic, and public health officials and the mainstream media treated such claims as wildly speculative conspiracy theories, and any mention of the lab leak theory was blocked by social media companies and the accounts of some of these "offenders" were suspended.[8]

The Covid-19 pandemic is a good example of how social problems can spread rapidly and go global. The attempts to respond to conditions on the ground as they emerge in each local community create a patchwork quilt of social control policies whose interventions target social, legal, and medical aspects of the pandemic. For example, on the social or inter-actional level, federal and local government informed persons that they should stay home and, when out, engage in social distancing. They should also wear masks, wash their hands thoroughly (for at least 20 seconds), and use (if available) hand sanitizer. On the medical side, public health officials scrambled to provide medical guidelines regarding symptoms, where to go to get tested, and describing the most vulnerable populations (the elderly and patients with underlying medical conditions). Finally, the legal side of control is made operative in a major way, mainly through disaster declarations, decisions to quarantine, and other powers vested in the executives at various levels of government, for example, requiring businesses to shift production and engineering capabilities to produce more protective gear for medical personnel but also ventilators for critically-ill patients.

Lockdowns and executive orders

Stay-at-home orders promulgated by executive fiat raise anew questions concerning the constitutionality of such orders, especially as they necessarily curtail personal liberties in the name of public safety. As lockdowns continued through December 2020, many persons became restless and started staging political protests, while others opened their businesses in defiance of executive orders that shuttered such nonessential businesses as barbershops, hair salons, gyms, restaurants and bars, and furniture and clothing stores.[9] When the governor of Wisconsin attempted to extend the stay-at-home order he had originally declared in March 2020, the Wisconsin Supreme Court declared the extension to be an unlawful restriction on personal liberties.[10] Additionally, in late 2020 the US Supreme Court ruled that New York Governor Andrew Cuomo's restrictions on in-person religious gatherings were unconstitutional because such restrictions were harsher than those of comparable gatherings without providing the legal reasoning for such exclusivity.[11] The ruling amounted to the unconstitutionality of the executive order because of the way it violated the First Amendment rights of religious worshippers, and that there are limits to the restrictions than can be placed on lawful activities even during a pandemic.

This issue of executive orders, especially when they involve the curtailing of liberties in the name of public safety or health, gets to the heart of conceptualizing and analyzing social control in its various forms. Decades ago, German political theorist Carl Schmitt defined the sovereign (or the executive) as "he who decides on the exception."[12] So, this gives the executive an extralegal and even extraconstitutional avenue for acting unilaterally, even while other branches may move to check the emergency declaration (such as happened in 2019 when President Trump diverted money to build his wall on the southern border, claiming it to be an emergency).

For example, as it relates to lockdown decrees issued by executives at various levels of government (state, county, or municipal) to slow the spread of the coronavirus according to recommendations of public health officials, such stay-at-home orders are basically house arrest. Under normal criminal justice procedures, house arrest is the punishment for someone already convicted of a crime. But a stay-at-home order is a proactive strategy that doesn't require a crime; indeed, it is close to the pre-crimes conceptualized by Philip K. Dick and made into the movie *Minority Report*. People could easily make this out to be yet another version of totalitarianism, of a Big Brother, nanny state curtailing liberties for the sake of public health, public safety, or whatever (as depicted in Orwell's *1984*). Both sides of the political aisle can claim totalitarianism. It speaks to the existence of a hyperpartisan political divide in which persons of one political persuasion (whether Democratic or Republican) are likely to view the actions of the executive from the other political party as an unconstitutional power grab. Hyperpartisanship, especially as it has operated in the United States beginning with the 9/11 terror attacks and continuing on through the Trump era and into the current Biden Administration, is reflective of Schmitt's idea that the political, in its most basic or essential form, is always "friends vs. enemies."[13]

Toward social control proper

The study of *social control* – namely, all those mechanisms and resources by which members of society attempt to assure the norm-conforming behavior of others – is almost as old as the discipline of sociology itself.

If we mark the beginning of scientific sociology with the publication of Lester Ward's *Dynamic Sociology* in 1883, social control did not appear as a specific and sustained focus for sociological analysis until about 13 years later, in 1896. In that year, Edward A. Ross published the first of many articles on the topic of social control in the *American Journal of Sociology*. Although Ross is credited as being the innovator of the study of social control within sociology, by no means did he create this subfield out of whole cloth. Rather, like the great majority of intellectual innovations, Ross deftly synthesized pertinent aspects of the extant literature that dealt with the relation between the individual and society, as well as with the problem of social order more broadly.

Shortly after the establishment of the study of social control by Ross, Ward, and other early American sociologists by the late 1800s, a group of European classical sociologists provided contrasting approaches to social control. The two most prominent of these European thinkers are Emile Durkheim in France and Max Weber in Germany. Although this overview of the thought of Ross, Durkheim, and Weber will provide a solid foundation for conceptualizing social control, in later chapters additional theoretical background will be provided as particular substantive phenomena are introduced, including norms, sanctions, socialization, groups, culture, the professions (especially medicine), and the criminal justice system (police, courts, and corrections).

Ross and social control

Edward Ross's first article on the topic of social control appeared in the *American Journal of Sociology* in 1896 and was titled, appropriately enough, "Social Control."[14] Following the position of Lester Ward,[15] Ross argued that the true constitution of human society is to be found somewhere between the lone individual and the social group or collectivity. How do we make sense of this twin reality, that is, the reality of the individual and society? For Ross, there is good evidence of the existence of a source of influence whereby individuals are transformed into social beings. Rather than a mere random assemblage of individuals, there exist distinct resources or social forces that create patterns of association between members of society. These resources and forces, which (ideally) bind persons together in shared projects and understandings, are various aspects of social control which collectively contribute to social order.

Ross was concerned not only with describing social control but also shoring up the foundations of social order in the face of the appearance of rampant individualism in the transition to modernity. For much of the early history of human civilization, human beings were held in check by the powerful forces of kinship and small, tight-knit communities where everybody knew everybody else and shared the same experiences, beliefs, values, and aspirations. In essence, for eons the group reigned supreme over the individual. But somewhere along the way this changed. Certainly the breakdown of feudalism contributed to the demise of group control, as persons were now free – as individuals – to offer their services to anyone who would hire them in newly burgeoning capitalist markets.

Additionally, the Enlightenment affected the way social thinkers began talking about human society. For example, beginning in the mid- to late 1700s, utilitarian thinkers such as Cesare Beccaria and Jeremy Bentham conceptualized human beings as rational actors who seek to maximize pleasure and minimize pain on an individual basis. Here, the individual is released from the constraining pressures of the group or the collectivity, and this loss of informal social control is one of the factors that explains rising rates of criminality and deviant behavior, especially beginning in the 1800s across Europe and in the United States. Indeed, these observations and concerns contributed as much as anything to the beginnings of criminology as a field of study.[16]

The forces of industrialization, migration, urbanization, and secularization were in effect releasing the individual from group control, and by the late 1800s criminologists and sociologists were theorizing how such changes were affecting the relationship between the individual and society. For Ross specifically, the question was "What is the nature of social control in today's society, and how does it differ from the past?" Following Ward, the major social force impelling human beings to act is feelings, desires, or passion. But with the advance of human society, actions based on raw passion give way to "reasoned" or "rational" actions coinciding with the evolution of the human brain and the upgrading of the intellectual faculty.[17] The growth of reason also coincides with the growth of human population and the simple fact that with more anonymous others around with whom one must interact on a routine basis, more care, restraint, and calculation is needed in dealing with them.[18] Hence, in answer to the question posed above, Ross suggested that the feelings and desires of individuals are continually and in innumerable ways being shaped by the community of fellow human beings with whom they live and associate.

Here Ross distinguished between social coordination and social control. *Social coordination* consists of the rules and procedures for ordering a society's activities so as to avoid mutual interference between its various parts. An example of social coordination would be traffic regulations. Since everyone is on the road for ostensibly the same reason – to get from point A to point B – the ends that actors pursue in this case are harmonious. Rather than controlling, traffic regulations merely coordinate the combined activities of the multitude of individuals using public thoroughfares. *Social control*, on the other hand, seeks to harmonize potentially clashing activities by checking some and stimulating others. According to Ross, social coordination adjusts the essentially harmonious actions of society, while social control regulates incompatible aims and actions.[19]

The distinction Ross made between social coordination and social control is no longer prevalent in the social sciences, having been erased in favor of a more expansive notion of social control which replaced social coordination with a specific type of social control, namely informal control. At the same time, the other side of Ross's distinction, social control, was more apt to emphasize the coercive forces of the state and other collective entities such as organizations and institutions that set rules for its members to follow or face consequences. This systematic coercion enforced by special agents is described as formal control (whether legal or medical), while informal control operates through the influence of agents of socialization (friends, neighbors, parents, siblings, and so forth).

By the 1930s the new expansive understanding of social control – which now incorporates social coordination along with cooperative bases of control (such as the development of transportation systems that facilitate myriads of travelers moving from one point to another) – was established. This was best exemplified in a book on social control published in 1939 by sociologist Paul Landis, who stated:

> This analysis takes into account not only the conscious deliberate attempts of society to regulate its members, but also those subtle, unconscious, latent, underlying factors which operate in group situations. For this reason, it holds that social control embraces not only such agencies as law, authority, punishment, codes, and creeds, but also mores, customs, traditions, the subtle influence of group expectancy, and other such factors.[20]

Additionally, although Ross did not follow Herbert Spencer's terminology of referring to human societies as "social organisms," he did utilize Spencer's idea concerning social structures, which carry out vital functions for society analogous to the way this occurs in individual organisms. Specifically, Spencer argued that organisms and societies evolve specialized structures devoted to sustenance, distribution, and regulation.[21] Organisms must *sustain* themselves by finding food and converting it into energy through digestion, and likewise societies set up operations for extracting resources from the environment and turning them into products which members of societies can consume or utilize (e.g., by way of farms, grocery stores, and utility companies). *Distribution* is the process of getting valued resources to different parts of the body (i.e., blood carrying nutrients to all parts of the body through the vascular system), or to society (by way of road and railway systems over which needed supplies are transported). And most directly for our purposes, for individual organisms the function of *regulation* is met by the nervous system whereby sense organs send information to the brain which stimulates appropriate muscle responses (e.g., fight or flight depending on the circumstances of the situation). And with regard to society, the supreme regulatory system is the political and military assemblages through which offensive and defensive state actions are pursued (through law enforcement, legislation, protection of borders, and occasionally warfare).[22]

Although French classical sociologist Emile Durkheim did not focus as explicitly as Ross did on social control per se, his observations on the changing nature of society nevertheless continue to inform contemporary understandings of and research on social control. Let us examine the ideas of Durkheim in somewhat more detail.

Durkheim: From mechanical to organic solidarity[23]

In his *Division of Labor in Society* (first published in 1893), Durkheim argued that earlier forms of human society (e.g., hunter-gathering, horticultural, pastoral) are characterized by a mechanical solidarity where everyone is held in check through likeness and day-to-day familiarity with everyone else in the community. Hence, in primitive, preliterate, or preindustrial societies, the basis of social solidarity is cultural homogeneity, to the extent that all members share a common set of understandings, beliefs, symbols, and life experiences.

Since folk societies tend to be small, attachments between members are deep and abiding, grounded in large part along kinship lines and secured via a shared understanding of the sacred. In this *mechanical solidarity*, group cohesion is strong; indeed, the group takes precedence over the individual in virtually all social settings. Because of this, individuals are held in check because violations of the normative order are interpreted as an assault on the collective conscience of the community, and hence punishments against violators tend to be harsh, public, and focused on the body.

With the advent of industrialization and the democratic revolutions occurring across Western society beginning in the late 1700s, central cities experienced increases in population density as productivity increased and as more and more persons immigrated to these cities in hopes of finding work in the newly burgeoning industrial economy. As populations grow denser, the social solidarity previously ensured through likeness, familiarity, and face-to-face contact is imperiled as the urban metropolis now becomes characterized by anonymity as well as temporal, spatial, and social distancing between its members.

Durkheim was worried that in this new associational society, the quality and quantity of attachments would become increasingly superficial and impoverished as persons are set adrift in a sea of faceless and anonymous others. Especially as exhibited in his book *Suicide*, published in 1897, Durkheim's pessimism about modern society was fueled by data, already well documented by the late 1800s, which indicated that social pathologies

– suicide, divorce, poverty, homelessness, mental illness, crime, violence, and drug use and abuse – were occurring at higher rates, per capita, in these urban, metropolitan communities. The assumption was that the city was a dysfunctional place that threatened the socialization process, the unity of the family, the routine commitment to civic participation, and the development of secure and stable attachments to others.

In this new situation of heightened individualism and aggrandizement of the self, what would be the basis of social solidarity? Durkheim argued that it is the division of labor, as well as the increasingly prominent role law would play in adjudicating conflict between an increasingly disparate citizenry.[24] Hence, the nature of social solidarity changes from mechanical to organic. Instead of likeness and cultural homogeneity, the modern society is characterized by anonymity, cultural heterogeneity, and a vastly expanded division of labor where tasks become increasingly specialized. Because of this increased task specialization, persons are no longer self-reliant. They must turn to others for their day-to-day necessities, whether it is figuring out taxes, getting a medical checkup, buying a house, or even attending to one's mental wellness. In this new *organic solidarity*, social integration is assured as a result of the heightened interdependence between citizens of the community.

Concomitantly, whereas in earlier times the group was everything while the individual was nothing, in modernity the individual attains prominence over the group. Indeed, because of the increasingly divergent characteristics of inhabitants of the modern metropolis, the last remaining thing we all share is our humanity. This abstract ideal becomes further embodied in the activities of the democratic welfare state, which remains further and further committed, through the creation of welfare legislation and other provisions, to protecting its citizens against accident, injury, illness, and death.

Table 1.1 provides a summary of Durkheim's distinction between mechanical and organic solidarity. It should be noted that since Durkheim's time a number of social scientists have gone beyond the two-era classification – that is, an earlier primitive era of humanity (coinciding with mechanical solidarity) contrasted with a later modern era (coinciding with organic solidarity) – and have begun speaking of a third, so-called postmodern era.[25]

Where modernity emphasized centralized authority and operations, in postmodernity decentralization is emphasized (e.g., the use of police mini-stations under community policing, as well as the rise of community corrections). In modernity, there were sovereign nations with well-defined borders, while under postmodernity there is a collapse of such distinctions with the new realities of deindustrialization, globalization, and shifting or disappearing national borders. And whereas in modernity there was trust in the grand narrative of science and Enlightenment reason, in

Table 1.1 Mechanical vs. Organic Solidarity

Area of application	Forms of social solidarity	
	Mechanical	Organic
Type of society	Small, rural, agricultural, culturally homogeneous (familiarity and similarity)	Large, urban, industrial, culturally heterogeneous (anonymity)
Basis of evaluation	Ascription (who you are)	Achievement (what you do)
Basis of recognition	Family (primary groups)	Work (secondary groups)
Prevalence of law	Low (disputes handled informally)	High (needed to adjudicate conflict between increasingly disparate citizenry and to enforce contracts)
Punishment	Harsh, focused on the body (public)	Rehabilitative and restitutive, focused on the mind (private)
Division of labor	Not a great deal of task specialization	High task specialization
Education	Informal (family and church)	Formal (esoteric knowledge and the rise of professions)
Nature of social bonds	Strong and abiding	Weak and shallow
Source of social solidarity	Collective conscience	Division of labor and law
Societal focus	The group	The individual
Sense of self	Weak or nonexistent	Strong (flowering of personality with multiple cross-cutting affiliations)

postmodernity there is a fragmentation into a number of discourses (scientific and otherwise) that compete for attention. This idea of a "postmodern" condition, and how social control is conceptualized and operates within it, will be returned to occasionally throughout the book.

Social control as regulation

Both Ross's and Durkheim's work place emphasis on the idea of social control as regulation. The organization of human society is simultaneously both unity and regulation. In escaping the lawlessness of the state of nature, the social life of human society comes to be characterized as a *nomic* life, and hence society is a state of *nomia* (the Greek word for law or rule).[26] This amounts to the idea that within society, a system is in place to deal specifically with the sanctioning or punishment of individuals who do not comply with the rules, that is, with social norms. Norms provide guidance for behavior. For example, because of the operation of the shipboard rule "women and children first," women and children indeed were more likely to survive the sinking of the Titanic than other categories of people. In a life or death situation, many have suggested that morality is thrown out of the window as people fend for themselves in order to survive. This indeed may be the case, yet, even in the desperate case of the sinking of the Titanic, females were significantly more likely than males to survive the sinking, while those traveling with children under 17 were also significantly more likely to survive. Additionally, social class mattered: those traveling in first class were much more likely to survive than those traveling in second or third class.[27]

The starting point for any system of control is *socialization*, which can be defined as the learning of a culture. Because human infants are helpless at birth, ideally there should be competent adults – usually their parents – available to supervise children's activities and provide to them their physical and emotional needs as they mature. Beyond the provision of food, warmth, clothing, shelter, and emotional nurturing and support, agents of primary socialization also provide to the growing child a set of guidelines for proper conduct. These guidelines can be thought of as a moral template, the contents of which are drawn from the prevailing cultural traditions of a society.

According to Sigmund Freud, Talcott Parsons, and others, the ultimate goal of socialization is the production of self-controlled individuals.[28] Children will typically be rewarded by parents and other agents of social-ization – teachers, priests, friends, and other family members to name a few – for good behavior and punished for bad behavior, thereby compelling individuals to comport their behavior to the expectations of the group.[29] That is to say, if socialization works properly, individuals will choose to act in norm-conforming ways because the costs and pains associated with deviance or non-conformity are simply too great. Equally important, however, is that once individuals take the position that deviance is too costly to engage in, they have in effect internalized society's standards of what is fair, proper, just, appropriate, normal, ethical, or lawful. In this way, socialization assures the production of self-controlled individuals, insofar as persons are held in check by the threat of external sanctions as well as by internal feelings of blameworthiness, guilt, disgust, shame, embarrassment, chagrin, sorrow, self-loathing, or regret whenever they do something that does not meet the approval of significant others in society. No society can properly be maintained merely by way of external constraints such as those embodied in the legal system and its system of sanctioning.[30] The internalization of the moral code of a group by way of socialization is typically a far better mechanism for ensuring social control (as we shall see in chapter 3).

Although this point cannot be discussed in detail in this chapter, it should be noted that a seemingly growing number of persons believe that today's youth are not being raised properly and lack a conscience, that is, an internal voice that tells them right from wrong. This again is reflected in Freud's notion that stunted or incomplete socialization is likely to produce individuals whose personality is characterized by an overdeveloped Id (where raw passions hold sway) or an underdeveloped Superego (where moral conscience is not fully formed). News accounts profiling cases of children acting badly and for inexplicable reasons – such as the infamous "wilding" incident in 1989 where six boys attacked a woman jogging in Central Park just for the "fun" of it, or the string of school shootings that have occurred sporadically across America since 1999 – are especially likely to prompt observers to suggest that the socialization process is in decline and perhaps irreparably damaged.[31]

Moral panics and social media

This reflects how public opinion and group sentiment can affect public policies even when it can later be shown that the original sentiments stirring such changes were wrong or misguided. Indeed, many public policies, especially those that are related to social control – whether legal, medical, or some combination – can be understood as arising as a result of *moral panics*, namely, widespread concerns which focus attention on a person or group who are believed (rightly but more often wrongly) to have created harmful or deteriorating social conditions.[32] Members of society can thereby focus moral outrage on the person or group allegedly causing problems in the first place and, through this process of scapegoating, society-at-large can take comfort in identifying and punishing trouble-makers who throughout history have variously been tagged with such pejoratives as demons, devils, witches, hooligans, vermin, rats, or worse.

The Central Park case, mentioned above, is a classic example of a moral panic.[33] A white female who was jogging in New York's Central Park in 1989 was allegedly attacked and raped by seven youths. The youths were reportedly part of a larger group of youths who were out of control and assaulting people for no apparent reason. The lead detective on the case, Robert Colangelo, reported that some of the youths arrested later and brought in for questioning claimed that the random assaults were part of an activity they called "wilding." This report of wild and out of control urban youth randomly attacking people was the sort of sensational crime story that the news media thrives on, and of course the news spread like wildfire.

Initially seven youths were charged with rape, assault, and attempted murder. Later, charges were dropped against one youth while another turned state witness. Although acquitted of the attempted murder charges, the remaining five youths were convicted on some combination of the rape and assault charges and given sentences ranging from five to fifteen years. The youths came to be known as the Central Park Five. All of them were Black or Hispanic, and their race and socioeconomic status played into ugly stereotypes about urban "superpredators" terrorizing public spaces and neighborhoods.[34] However, in 2002 a serial rapist, Matias Reyes, who was serving a prison sentence at the time, confessed to the assault and rape which later DNA testing confirmed.[35] The youths who had been falsely imprisoned were released, and from that day forward an even bigger story began unfolding about the perniciousness of moral panics and racism in the criminal justice system.

It should also be noted that moral panics and the work of moral entrepreneurs need not eventuate in official actions of the state (that is, formal controls), but can be dispersed across society more or less randomly by individuals or groups in the form of mob violence or vigilantism more generally (which are more akin to informal, "off the books," or non-state controls). The increasing presence and availability of social media can now link disparate persons, who otherwise would never have met, into concerted action across neighborhoods or communities, some of which could be described as moral panics. Social media is particularly adept at spreading fear.[36] These social media platforms – Twitter, YouTube, Facebook, Reddit, TikTok, and Pinterest to name a few – allow focalizing of concerns over such things as pedophiles in the community, human trafficking, cruelty to pets or animals, and many others.[37] Indeed, the mob has gone digital, whereby persons can use social media to shame, humiliate, and release private information – so-called "doxing" – about those targeted for denigration and attack.[38] Jeremy Weissman believes that things have gotten so bad that government needs to step in to protect persons from social media mobbing:

> I argue a new apparatus of surveillance and control is being generated that threatens individual freedom through a coercion of the will by an anonymous and interconnected crowd. I conclude that we must urgently assess how to protect individuals from a social tyranny of the public enabled by these new technologies while effective measures can still be taken to mitigate their dangers.[39]

As David Altheide notes, social media technologies have the ability to expand, for good or bad, the informal social controls available at the level of everyday life (the lifeworld), in effect amplifying them according to users who come together on various platforms and who share abiding interests on specific issues.[40] Even before the advent of such communications technologies, however, sentiments had arisen that not only are children in crisis, but so are families, schools, neighborhoods, and civic participation, the traditional sites and activities of informal control. These sentiments of crisis or deterioration – noting full well that such sentiments may not be accurate and shot through with distortions such as racism, sexism, xenophobia, transphobia, and so forth – inexorably lead to some version of the story being told that the mechanisms of informal control can no longer be trusted to assure the production of self-controlled individuals. When this happens, formal mechanisms of control are turned to with growing frequency. This growth of formalism, especially the growing reliance on law in modern or postmodern society, is one of the key elements in any overview of social control. On this topic, the thought of Max Weber is especially helpful.

Weber on power, domination, and the rise of the state

Oftentimes within social relationships actors will be guided to act based upon the belief of the existence of a *legitimate* order.[41] For example, a member of a firing squad aims and fires at the person sentenced to death because he or she believes in the legitimate authority of the state to impose death sentences in certain cases.

The concept of legitimacy is closely connected with two other concepts: power and domination. *Power* is defined by Weber as "the probability that one actor within a social relationship will be in a position to carry out his own will despite resistance." And *domination* is "the probability that a command with a given specific content will be obeyed by a given group of persons."[42] For all practical purposes Weber understood "domination" to mean "authority," and he employed an ideal type methodology to specify the types of legitimate domination (or authority).

There are, according to Weber, three ideal types of authority.[43] *Legal authority* rests on the belief in the legality of rules and the right of those in positions of authority to issue commands. In the case of legal authority, the validity of the claims to legitimacy is based upon rational grounds. The member of the firing squad mentioned above is acting on the basis of the perceived legal authority of the squad leader to give the order to fire.

Traditional authority rests on an established belief in the sanctity of long-standing traditions and the legitimacy of those exercising authority under them. Traditional authority is often vested in the eldest members of a group because of their intimate and longtime familiarity with the sacred traditions of a culture. It may also be vested as a result of inheritance, as for example in patriarchalism, where males are designated as heads of households. Members of societies in which such systems of traditional authority operate give their obedience to the masters (elder tribal leaders and fathers in patriarchal society), not to any enacted regulation.[44]

Finally, *charismatic authority* rests on devotion to the exceptional qualities or exemplary character of an individual person. A charismatic person is said to be endowed with supernatural, superhuman, or exceptional powers or qualities that distinguish him or her from ordinary persons. Oftentimes these special powers or characteristics are understood as being magical or of divine origin. As Weber explains, "In primitive circumstances this peculiar kind of quality is thought of as resting on magical powers, whether of prophets, persons with a reputation for therapeutic or legal wisdom, leaders in the hunt, or heroes in war."[45]

Notice that, although a head of household exercises domination over other members of the household, he or she does so more or less as a solitary individual in that under normal circumstances there is no executive staff assisting the head. Domination and authority can be extended, however, beyond the situation of individuals or small groups, especially in the case of a political authoritarian association. The rise of the modern state is one such political authoritarian association. Weber defines the *state* as "an institutional enterprise of a political character, when and insofar as its executive staff successfully claims a monopoly of the legitimate use of physical force in order to impose its regulations."[46]

A state, then, seeks to maintain the integrity and viability of its regulations over a specified geographical area by the use, or the threat of, physical force by its executive staff. Further, the systems of orders emanating from the state and embodied in its executive staff are considered legally binding over all members of the state, namely citizens, who obtain membership typically through birth within the state's territorial borders.[47] These points are consistent with the earlier work of Franklin Giddings, who argued that the primary purpose of the state is to perfect social integration by way of the maintenance of armies to protect against external threats and tribunals and police to enforce peace within its own borders.[48]

States may vary with regard to the distribution of power in society. Some states are autocratic or totalitarian, meaning that power is concentrated in the hands of a single ruling elite (such as a king) or a small ruling class (such as the mullahs of Iran), while other states, such as constitutional democracies or republics, disperse power more evenly across the citizenry, guaranteed (ideally) by a Bill of Rights, including the right to vote.

Beyond the case of complete and utter domination of the citizenry at the hands of a dictator, most states maintain regulations within a sovereign territory via a combination of what Jürgen Habermas calls facticity and validity.[49] *Facticity* reflects the reality of laws as a "social fact," in Durkheim's words, to the extent that laws are codified in writing and are backed by the state's monopoly on legitimate force to compel citizens to align their conduct to its prescriptions and proscriptions. *Validity*, on the other hand, refers to the state's concern with legitimating its rules and regulations in the eyes of the citizenry.[50] Ruling is made easier if those being ruled assent to the system of regulations being imposed. Ideally, then, states seek to administer a citizenry which obeys the law not only because of the threat of punishment, but because it is the "right thing to do."

Socialization is the single most important and efficient mechanism by which moral and legal rules are inculcated in and internalized by citizens. These rules are first those of the family, but then continue to expand outward as children encounter other spheres and activities of social life as they mature, such as same-age peers, education, the church, the public sphere, business, and so forth. The sum total of these activities adds up to the state's efforts to maintain both moral and legal regulation over a specific political territory, utilizing both facticity and validity in the ways described above.[51]

Rationalization

The rise of the state leads to concentration of power through bureaucratic control, while the modern trend of secularization wrests power away from competing sacred institutions. For Weber, rationalization is the master trend marking the rise of the state specifically and modern society in general. He described the rationalization of action as "the substitution for the unthinking acceptance of ancient custom, of deliberate adaptation to situations in terms of self-interest."[52]

Here, Weber applies the profit motive of the economic sphere to all other areas of social life. This means that the process of rationalization affects both the system (the state, social institutions, and organizations) and the lifeworld (friends, family, community, church, and so forth), that is, both the formal and informal realms and their respective systems of social control. For example, with the waning influence of a religious worldview and the rise of secularism, there was simultaneously a premium placed on greater predictability and efficiency through bureaucratic control and legal order. The social control function of rationalization is placed into the hands of specialists overseeing particular domains of social reality, and as Barry Glassner observes: "Scientists oversee nature, lawyers administer justice, critics orchestrate taste, physicians regulate health, and so forth."[53]

Rationality became especially prominent in the *Occident*, that part of the world located to the west of Asia, specifically Europe and the Americas. Consistent with this idea of the rise of Occidental rationalism was the emergence of the Enlightenment beginning in the eighteenth century in Europe. Massive changes in Western society before and up to Weber's time signaled to him the continuing march of the Enlightenment ethos of rationality, especially with regard to measurement, systematic observation, and calculation in human affairs. On all sides, then, traditionalism is under assault, and in its place are the specialized knowledge and values operating within particular spheres which, in total and ideally, deliver to society and its inhabitants the "best bang for the buck." The scientization of more and more areas of life; the rise of bureaucratization; the increase of textualization in law, religion, business, and family life – that is, putting more things to paper and relying less on tacit agreement – patterns of immigration to central cities for better paying jobs; and even art criticism and the growth of fad and fashion cycles, are all part of rationalization.[54]

The creation of surnames

Weber's main task with respect to the issue of rationalization was to examine those aspects of economy and society that gave rise to and were characteristic of Occidental rationalism. For early colonial powers especially, the centralization of power was not only a crucial consideration, but a manifest strategy in attempts to expand political control over wider and wider territories. A good example of rationalization has to do with the general projects of standardization and legibility carried out by state governments. In some instances, states have engaged in the enforcement of naming practices on its citizenry. As James Scott argues, the invention of permanent, inherited patronyms (taking the last name of the father) was the last step in establishing the necessary preconditions of modern statecraft.[55] With the rise of the state, administrators felt the need to identify citizens unambiguously, whether for purposes of taxation, tithing, census-taking, the maintenance of property rolls, or conscription lists. In earlier human societies it was not uncommon simply to use first names for purposes of identification. In such informal settings, this simple system of naming could be used and understood by members of kinship groups and the local community.

In England in the fifteenth century, only wealthy aristocratic families had surnames. These were often designated according to families' places of origin in Normandy (e.g., Baumont, Percy, Disney). For the rest of the population, naming was limited to linking fathers and sons (but not daughters). For example, William Robertson's male son Thomas might be called Thomas Williamson (son of William), while Thomas's son in turn might be called Henry Thompson (Thomas's son). Such naming practices based upon local logic and practices worked for the immediate needs and understandings of members of the community, but it made more formal tracing of descent by outside observers difficult.

As populations grew denser, it was less likely that the government would know or be able to identify individuals by sight or kinship affiliation. The development of the personal surname (the last name, usually a family name) went hand-in-hand with the development of written official documents such as birth, marriage, and death certificates, censuses, tax and land records, and travel documents such as passports.[56] Such official records were necessary to the conduct of any administrative exercise involving large numbers of people who had to be identified for various state purposes.[57]

States that oversee colonial populations are especially concerned with legibility. When the Philippines were a Spanish possession (from 1565 to 1898), Filipinos were instructed by the decree of November 21, 1849 to take on permanent Hispanic surnames. Up to that time Filipinos generally lacked individual surnames, as the local naming custom involved drawing from a small group of saints' names. This caused Spanish administrators "great confusion." The remedy was the *catalogo*, a compendium of personal names as well as "nouns and adjectives drawn from flora, fauna, minerals, geography, and the arts."[58] The authorities used these to assign permanent, inherited surnames. These names were divvied up by alphabetical order to populations in particular areas of the Philippines.

The "confusion" was of course from the perspective of administrators and tax collectors. The colonial subjects had a perfectly workable naming system in place, internal to the particular logic and way of life of the people. Western ideas and practices of rationalization were especially well represented in the use of universal last names, which facilitates the administration of justice, finance, and public order. The ultimate goal of these state builders was a complete and legible list of its subjects.

We see, then, that universal last names are a fairly recent historical phenomenon, beginning near the end of the eighteenth century with the expansion of the Western European colonial powers (especially England, Spain, and France). The surname was the critical first step in making individual citizens officially "legible." Additionally, the types of rationalization forced upon colonial subjects by largely white, Western, male administrators has been the focus of recent withering criticism under the guise of postcolonial studies.[59]

Gift-giving

Another example of rationalization, this time in the informal sphere, is how gift-giving has been transformed and made more rational. Traditionally, gifts were offered in celebration of persons experiencing some important life event such as marriage, the birth of a child, birthdays, graduation, a job promotion, and other types of good news. The gift itself was not really the focus, but rather the sanctity of the gathering as persons come together in solidarity and goodwill to celebrate important life transitions. Indeed, there had always been a guiding motto that, with regard to the gift, it is the thought that counts. That is, the sentiment lying behind the gift, and the willingness to be with others in a show of solidarity and support, is more important than the gift itself.

It had always been considered gauche or even vulgar to give a gift of cash, for how much thoughtful planning does it take to grab some bills from your wallet and stuff them into an envelope? A level of informal social control discourages gift-givers from doing so. Hence, more acceptable gifts were usually in the form of tangible items which reflected some level of thought and creativity on the part of the giver. There was also always an element of surprise and uncertainty, as there was no way to predict whether the recipient would like the gift or be assured that the gift would not merely duplicate something already owned by him or her.

This problem of receiving duplicate or unwanted gifts is especially prominent in the marriage celebration, which brings together relatives and friends who may have not been in meaningful contact with the new bride and groom for quite some time. And with the continuing expansion of the therapeutic ethos, gift-giving itself may be interpreted more and more in relation to therapeutic notions of uncertainty or even trauma, in which trying to decide what to give the couple may be viewed as debilitating and fraught with fitful contemplation. A socially accepted solution to this dilemma is the gift registry, whereby the couple can register with a retail establishment and provide a link in their wedding invitation to allow guests to access the list of possible gifts along with their costs.[60] This is the epitome of rationalization, which appears to be a win-win for all sides: The wedding couple assures themselves that they will receive gifts they want while avoiding duplicates, and gift-givers can be relieved of stress knowing that whatever they choose will be welcomed by the couple, all the while staying within their budget.

Gift cards are connected with gift registries in terms of this process of rationalization. For example, because some evidence of planning and thoughtfulness is associated with choosing a gift card in the amount desired and with regard to the products associated with the business, the gift card shields the giver from the crassness associated with gifting cold hard cash. It also provides the recipient the freedom to choose items according to his or her own tastes, needs, or desires.

Conclusion

Although the theoretical work of Ward, Ross, Durkheim, and Weber greatly contributed to the establishment of social control as a distinct object of study within sociology, in actuality this classical phase of the project represents merely a beginning. In the next few chapters other prominent thinkers, both classical and more contemporary, will be brought into the discussion to help flesh out and bring to life the tripartite classification of social control (to be presented in the next chapter) which will serve as the conceptual guide for the remainder of the book.

SUGGESTIONS FOR FURTHER READING

Emile Durkheim, *The Division of Labor in Society* (1984)
    This book, which evolved from Durkheim's 1893 doctoral dissertation, contains a complete elaboration of the transition from mechanical to organic solidarity, as well as the rise of restitutive (or civil) law within modern society.
Erich Goode and Nachman Ben-Yehuda, *Moral Panics* (2009)
    A useful compendium on moral panics utilizing the interpretive or social construction approach to social explanation. Topics include the role of media in

defining and disseminating moral panics; moral panics as a form of collective behavior; drug abuse panics; feminist anti-pornography crusades; and the institutionalization of moral panics.

Don Martindale, *Institutions, Organizations, and Mass Society* (1966)
This is the single best treatment of social control after Ross's groundbreaking work on the topic. Martindale dedicates individual chapters to conceptualizing social control; social control and the community; social control in the United States; large-scale control organizations; and socialization and its relationship to social control.

Edward A. Ross, *Social Control: A Survey of the Foundations of Order* (1901)
The definitive early statement on social control, which established an agenda for its study within sociology and other social sciences for decades to come. A reprint edition was published in 2009 by Transaction Publishers, containing a new introduction by Matthias Gross.

Max Weber, *Economy and Society* (1968)
Weber initially prepared this material in 1920 and it was later translated into English and made available in this edition in 1968. These writings represent the leading classical sociology statement on the nature of the state and associated concepts such as power, authority, and domination.

DISCUSSION QUESTIONS

1. Were the Covid-19 lockdowns constitutional, or were they a fundamental violation of First Amendment rights – especially freedoms of assembly and association – guaranteed by that same constitution?
2. Discuss the key contributions of early American sociologist Edward Ross to the study and understanding of social control.
3. What are the implications of Durkheim's distinction between mechanical and organic solidarity for understanding social control in the modern world?
4. We discussed how concerns over wilding and superpredators evolved into moral panics. Give an example of another crime story or media event that could be described as a moral panic and provide evidence for it.
5. In the chapter we discussed Weber's concept of rationalization and how it is related to gift-giving and the creation of surnames. Provide other examples of rationalization and explain how and why they came about.

Chapter 2
A Typology of Social Control

Introduction

The idea of social control is often associated with the physical or coercive powers of the police. It is certainly true that police force is an important and prominent example of social control, which as defined in the previous chapter consists of all those resources – both material and non-material – available for ensuring the norm-conforming behavior of members of society.

Yet social control is much more than police control. In everyday life, for example, individuals you know exert pressures on you to conform to their wishes and expectations. Some of these methods are subtle, while others are flagrant and meant to be noticed by all present. For example, when a husband tosses his cell phone out the window in exasperation because his wife just called to say that she will be late home from work and will miss their son's cello recital, that is a form of informal control. Or when a professor is scolded in front of the entire faculty for not having the minutes ready from the last department meeting, that again is a form of informal control. And when a complete stranger glares at you because she is offended by the slogan on your T-shirt, that, too, is an example of informal social control.

In addition to police (or more broadly legal) control and the types of informal control exerted in everyday life, there is also a form of control that arises in those cases where someone has done something that, although not necessarily illegal, is nevertheless seen as threatening, scary, weird, strange, bizarre, or just downright senseless. Medical or psychiatric control, then, is a catchall category that straddles the borders between informal or everyday control, on the one hand, and legal control, on the other.

The main goal of this chapter is to introduce a typology of social control consisting of three main types: informal, medical, and legal control. The three forms of control amount to a range of normative prescriptions and proscriptions covering the areas of interpersonal relations and group living (*informal control*), behavior more generally irrespective of the nature of the ties between persons in interaction (*medical control*), and the law and legal systems (*legal control*). These three areas of the human experience – relationships, behavior, and the law – have associated with them the three respective systems of control that comprise our typology.

We will also examine a number of concepts closely linked to social control, including norms, sanctions, and the nature of social order, and how key thinkers, both classical and contemporary, have used these concepts to explain the ways in which order is maintained in society, but also under what circumstances this order may break down. In addition, we will briefly consider how social control is typically conceptualized within social scientific research. For example, some researchers seek to explain how various factors lead to or produce social control (that is, social control as a dependent variable), while other researchers seek to explain how social control itself, in its various guises, gives rise to various social outcomes or processes (that is, social control as an independent variable).

Conceptualizing social control: an example

As we begin our discussion of social control and its three major forms – informal, medical, and legal – the category of medical control needs to be dealt with somewhat carefully. It is important to understand, for example, that in our routine, everyday lives, we are quick to use phrases such as "You're crazy!" or "How weird!" or even "What have you been smoking?" when someone does or says something that is seen as unexpected or somewhat out of the ordinary. But just so long as the societal reaction to the act in question remains at the level of comments of this sort, without further formal actions being taken, then this counts as a form of informal control. In other words, any disturbance that is handled within the context and boundaries of everyday life, where no official or quasi-official representatives of the government or medical community are brought in to assist those witness to the bizarre or odd act, remains at the level of informal social control. Informal control is *mano a mano*, being between two persons face-to-face who handle things by the seat of their pants, and which typically does not involve the intervention of third parties. These sorts of "off the books" actions, namely self-help, are the epitome of informal control.[1]

Conversely, the intervention of third parties, whereby a person or persons intervene in some way between two potentially conflicting parties, typically introduces more formality whether being overseen by medical personnel (that is, medical control) or legal practitioners (that is, legal control). The introduction of third parties, however, does not always lead to greater formality, and in such instances informal control is maintained. For example, friends, neighbors, relatives, work associates, passersby, or even strangers can be brought in as third parties under particular circumstances, and these may never spill over into the formal realm. Indeed, the outcomes of third-party interventions are of three basic types, namely, *partisanship* (lending support to one side of the conflict), *inaction* (not getting involved), or *settlement* (acting neutrally toward both sides such as in mediation or arbitration).[2] The various combinations of third-party interventions can lead to social control outcomes that are characterized as formal or informal based upon the peculiar circumstances of the event and its social history.

An example may help to clarify the boundaries of the three basic forms of control. Suppose you are eating in a fast food restaurant and someone a few tables away is staring at you, perhaps grinning wildly but saying nothing. You could simply ignore him, or move to another table, or even hurry up your meal and get out of there as quickly as possible. If any of these options are taken, the disturbance remains in the realm of informal control. In this case informal sanctions – specifically, avoidance – were applied against the person for his perceived deviance. What if, on your way out the door, you tell the manager about the "weird" guy disturbing the customers? Here's where things can get interesting. If the manager decides to go over and ask the guy to leave, as far as our categories of social control go, there still is "no harm no foul." In other words, at this point the manager has decided that the disturbance can best be handled informally and, by politely asking the fellow to leave, he is attempting to avoid a scene. His hope is that the person will get up from the table and walk out voluntarily. The condition of informal control still applies.

But what if the confrontation between the manager and the guy at the table does not go this smoothly? What if the person starts complaining loudly, perhaps cursing at the manager, showing signs of being prepared to make a very big scene? At this point, although the manager could take it upon himself to lay his hands on the individual and forcibly wrestle him out the door, he probably will not do so. He has probably already decided that the guy is just too dangerous, too out of control, or at the very least the manager simply has no idea where he is coming from. If this scenario unfolds, very likely the next course of action is for the manager to threaten to call the police. This may in fact do the trick, in that the mere threat that the police will be summoned may be enough to convince the fellow to vacate the premises. Although the disturbance has certainly escalated, if it ends here it is still resolved by means of informal social control. The guy goes away and everyone gets back to their normal activities as best they can.

But what if the threat to call the police does not work? What if the guy remains at the table, daring the manager to make the call? Very likely the next step is for the manager to make good on his threat, and he calls the police. At this point, when a police report is made and a squad car is dispatched to the scene, we have now entered the realm of legal control. Indeed, in most jurisdictions when a manager of a business establishment asks a patron to leave and he or she refuses to do so, a criminal trespass has occurred.

Being now convinced that a call has been made, perhaps the fellow bolts the premises in hopes of avoiding a confrontation with the police. But even if he gets away safely, the manager will have a description of the man to give to the police once they arrive, and it will be up to the discretion of the responding officers to either pursue or not pursue the case further. If, for example, they find out that police headquarters has received similar complaints from other restaurants in the area about a guy matching the suspect's description, they may indeed continue to pursue the case (and such charges as disturbing the peace or menacing could apply).

If, on the other hand, the fellow decides to stay even as the police officers are arriving at the restaurant, we have a full-blown legal control situation. It is very likely that once at the scene and face-to-face with the suspect, the officers will not mince words. They will ORDER the suspect to come along with them, telling him that "we can do this the easy way or the hard way." The easy way is simply escorting him out of the restaurant, with the suspect providing little or no resistance. The hard way would amount to yet another, even more severe escalation of the confrontation, if the man decides not to come along peacefully and forces the officers to handcuff him and drag him away.

In any event, the legal control scenario may well end with the arrest of the suspect, who could get cited for anything from disturbing the peace, trespassing, criminal menacing, or resisting arrest, to a whole slew of even more serious charges, depending on what happens between the suspect and the police. It is hard to say how this case would eventually be disposed of, owing to the myriad of possibilities with regard to the suspect's past record, the nature of the police report, the suspect's own demeanor while in police custody, and so forth. But one thing that could happen touches upon the third realm of social control, namely medical control. Somewhere along the way, the judge may request that the suspect be given a psychological examination, based upon the somewhat bizarre nature of his actions in the restaurant. For example, if it is discovered that the man has a history of being angry and confrontational with others, the judge may order him to attend anger management counseling as a condition of his probation, assuming he is not incarcerated.

In many situations, then, medical social control occurs only after legal control has been brought to bear against a suspect. Here we may think about the social conditions necessary to call forth medical personnel as the primary agents of control, rather than legal officials. First, disturbances involving those who are known to one another are more likely to call forth medical forms of control than disturbances involving strangers. In other words, the more intimate the gathering, the more likely a breach of propriety will be viewed as a medical issue rather than as a legal issue (assuming it has already progressed beyond the level of informal control). Second, the social class of the participants involved in the disturbance often affects the nature of control responses. Higher status offenders and victims will tend to seek medical or therapeutic remedies for their problems, while lower status offenders are more likely to be dealt with by the police or other representatives of legal control.[3] The poor typically do not have the funds or resources available to reach out to mental health professionals, and in times of crisis they are likely to come to the attention of the police rather than psychiatrists, social workers, or psychologists. When police are summoned to deal with difficulties besetting the urban poor – especially those that may later be defined as mental health issues – they enter into a "gray zone" of uncertainty and ambiguity because the actual conduct that is raising alarm may not be technically illegal.[4]

Let us return to our example of the person in the fast food restaurant staring at fellow patrons. Imagine this exact same behavior occurring in an exclusive dues-paying dinner club. Because of its exclusivity and high cost, member rosters are likely to be relatively small, and there is a very good chance that on any given night patrons of the club will know most everyone in attendance. A person engaging in this sort of behavior will probably first get the attention of the host or hostess, who most likely will recognize the individual. If the person is unresponsive upon further discussion with the host or head waiter, he or she will likely have a phone number of a wife or an acquaintance who could be summoned to come pick up the offender. Having arrived at the club, the friend or family member may whisk the person away, saying something to the effect that "Dr. Long is not feeling well." Here instead of a police officer, we have a friend, family member, or perhaps even a family physician or psychiatrist intervening as a therapeutic agent.

The idea of intervention, whether by a sworn law enforcement officer or a therapeutic agent, is the key to distinguishing between informal and formal control. In informal control, disturbances are dealt with by persons acting only in their capacity as fellow human beings or citizens. This means that rarely are external third parties brought in to ameliorate this class of disturbances.[5] Formal control on the other hand, whether of the legal or medical variety, always involves the intervention of a third party, while under more limited circumstances third parties may also intervene in events that remain at the informal level (as discussed above).

Drift and techniques of neutralization

David Matza's concept of *drift* helps explain how and why disturbances in everyday life, which is the province of informal control, may follow trajectories into higher or more formal levels of control whether medical, legal, or some combination.[6] Armed with tacit notions of propriety delivered through socialization and the "ought" of morality, all of us monitor others for the extent to which they are abiding by such tacit norms of good conduct. A person who gives some indication of straying from group expectations alerts those with whom he or she is associated that "something is up."[7] This concern that the person may be drifting into untoward conduct ignites societal reaction, first in the form of questions or discussion ("Why are you doing that?), and then, in order to stem the tide of possibly further, more serious deviance, the application or threat of informal sanctions (such as the silent treatment, withdrawal of expected rewards, degradation ceremonies, grounding, or even threats to call the police). Indications of a drift into deviance is the first line of defense for maintaining the viability of the group, and any informal sanctions which are applied are an attempt to bring the person back into conformity so as to stave off more serious trouble for the individual and his or her associates. Erving Goffman – whose ideas will be examined more closely in chapter 3 – described this movement or drift into trajectories of higher-order or formal systems of control as follows: "Persons who come to the attention of a psychiatrist typically come to the attention of their lay associates first."[8]

Further, it should be noted that when persons are caught in deviance the impulse is to disavow it, to ignore concerns about it, or to shift the focus to those who are raising concerns. Indeed, these and other sorts of neutralization are a pervasive tactic employed by those who are accused of misconduct.[9] Sykes and Matza have referred to such strategies of containment and management as *techniques of neutralization*.[10] The authors initially formulated this idea within the context of delinquency – misconduct of persons under the age of 18 – but it can be generalized to all instances of deviance regardless of the status of the offender. The five techniques of neutralization, consisting of rationalizations or excuses for offending conduct, are discussed below.

First, there is *denial of responsibility*, the assertion that the deviant act was accidental or beyond the control of the individual. This also helps reduce self-blame, which staves off internalization of a negative self-concept. Second, there is the *denial of injury* whereby, even if the accused admits some responsibility for the bad act, a claim is made that no one was really hurt and that any threatened sanctions are out of proportion to any harms caused. There can also be attempts at redefinition by the accused, for example, that vandalism is merely mischief, or auto theft is merely borrowing, or gang fighting is nothing more than a private squabble, or looting is a form of civil disobedience.[11]

Third, there can be *denial of the victim*, which goes beyond denial of injury in the following way. With denial of the victim, the accused admits both that he or she is responsible on some level and that indeed some persons suffered harm as a result, but that those injuries were not wrong or blameworthy under the circumstances. In this way, persons accused of deviance set themselves up as avengers who are retaliating against the provocations of those claiming victim status. Examples provided by the authors include assaults on suspected homosexuals, vandalism of schools in retaliation against unfair teachers, and thefts from a crooked store owner.[12] Additionally, those caught in deviance and who clearly were the aggressors in a situation may claim victim status for themselves, such as in the case of violence which the perpetrator explains was provoked as a result of being bullied.[13]

Fourth, there can be *condemnation of the condemners*, which makes the case that the entire regulatory system is corrupt from top to bottom and that those standing in judgment of others are "hypocrites, deviants in disguise, or impelled by personal spite."[14] It has been standard practice since the institutionalization of metropolitan policing in the early 1800s for suspects who are detained or arrested by the police to make claims of their improper conduct, including claims of use of excessive or illegal force. These claims, which sometimes grow into concerted social movements and protests, such as what happened during the summer of 2020 after the death of George Floyd while in police custody in Minnesota, are as much as anything rebukes of previously unchallenged or tacitly accepted governmental authority in general and police authority in particular.[15]

A fifth technique of neutralization involves *appeals to higher loyalties*. Here, someone who is caught in deviance justifies it by claiming that an additional set of principles beyond those recognized by the group or by the society-at-large were more important to honor or abide by in that specific instance than the other principles that typically prevail. For example, a father who is aware of some misconduct by his son, even perhaps illegal activities, may choose not to report it to the authorities in order to maintain the honor of the family. Or someone who bombs an abortion clinic may claim that God's word trumps mere manmade law, the latter of which maintains that abortion is legal and hence does not amount to the murder of innocent human fetuses.

The derivation of the three primary forms of control

The three primary forms of control – informal, legal, and medical – are derived from Egon Bittner's discussion of the functions of the police in modern society.[16] Drawing from Max Weber and other sources, Bittner argues that the capacity to use force is the essential characteristic of the police role. Yet, as was pointed out above, police use of force does not exhaust the management and organization of responsive force in modern society. In most types of human societies, three distinctive forms of responsive force are viewed as legitimate given the right set of circumstances.

First, societies authorize the use of force in cases of *self-defense*. Self-defense, or self-help, is synonymous with informal social control. Over the course of human history self-help, based originally in kinship or clan systems, has been the predominant mode of organizing responsive force and settling disputes. But with the rise of modern legal systems, it is no longer acceptable to "take the law into your own hands," which is now often condemned as vigilantism. Indeed, except in those cases where self-defense is recognized as a legitimate action by the courts, vigilantism is itself a crime. Those who claim to be victims of a crime are legally prohibited from meting out justice on their own. Rather than victims pursuing justice against offenders, it is the state that steps in to prosecute cases against criminal defendants. All forms of informal social control are examples of self-help, and only the small percentage of cases which raise the issue of the legality of self-defense ever come to the attention of the courts.

Second, there is a form of coercive response which authorizes certain agents to enter specifically named persons into a *custodial* arrangement, for example, the involuntary or voluntary admittance of a person to a mental hospital for tests, observation, or simply for his or her "own good." The nature of such custodial arrangements runs the gamut from extremely formal (e.g., a judge involuntarily committing a first-time DUI (driving under the influence) defendant into a drug or alcohol rehabilitation program), to less formal (e.g., a disruptive student in school being diagnosed with attention deficit disorder (ADD) or attention deficit hyperactivity disorder (ADHD) by a school physician and placed on a drug regimen, typically Ritalin), to nearly informal (e.g., a married couple seeking counseling for various problems in their marriage). Custodial arrangements, where a third person (a therapeutic agent) is brought in either voluntarily or as a result of some prior or impending legal action, are synonymous with medical social control.

Third, legitimate responsive force can take the form of military (in the case of a sovereign nation) or *police* (in the case of a state or municipality, or an administrative or governance body) actions. This represents the realm of legal social control. As Bittner explains, "Contrary to the case of self-defense and the limited authorization of custodial functionaries, the police authorization is essentially unrestricted."[17] Police and military personnel are authorized to use whatever force is necessary to enforce laws or pursue combat objectives, up to and including the use of deadly force.

For a growing number of citizens, however, the sentiment is that the state should not be in the business of killing its citizens, neither with regard to lethal police shootings nor the enforcement of the death penalty as a penal sanction. As discussed earlier, this represents a continuing lack of faith in and critique of governmental authority, and such killings are now likely to be described as state-sanctioned murder or violence.[18]

Bittner clarifies his position by noting that police coercive powers are *essentially* but not completely unrestricted. There are three limitations on police use of force:

- In most jurisdictions the *use of deadly force* is authorized in only a limited number of cases (e.g., against an armed suspect or someone threatening imminent harm);
- Police may use force only in the *performance of their duties*, and not for personal reasons or as private citizens; and
- Police may not use force in a *malicious or frivolous* manner (the problem of police brutality).[19]

The police and other agents of formal control are entrusted with enforcing legal norms (or laws), while the norms of everyday life are enforced by private citizens. It is important, however, to explain how norms arise in the first place, and this will be the focus of the next section.

The emergence of norms

If it is not apparent by now, our discussion of social control relies heavily on the concept of norms. It is now time to define this concept more explicitly. A *norm* is a rule for behavior, a guide to conduct. In essence, norms are statements that regulate behavior.[20] This is the epitome of social control as regulation, as discussed in the previous chapter. Even so, norms need not be explicitly stated or codified. Indeed, many norms, especially those operating in the realm of everyday life, are not manifest or overt or committed to paper. Rather, many norms are part of a group's tacit understandings of the proper way to act given certain conditions or situations, and these norms are passed on more or less informally through socialization and other means available to group members.

Where do norms come from? How do they arise in society, and why do different societies, and even different groups or subcultures within the same society, have different norms? Early American sociologist William Graham Sumner provided the classical explanation, as he employed an evolutionary approach to explain how norms arise slowly and incrementally over time, moving through an early phase of tacit folkways, then a middle phase of more formalized norms called mores (e.g., taboos), and then on to the full formalization of norms through their textualization into laws and statutes.[21] Sumner argued that the folkways are the most important operation by which the interests of the members of society are served, and that sociology ought to take folkways as its core concept or primary object of study. As Sumner stated, "The life of society consists in making folkways and applying them. The science of society might be construed as the study of them."[22]

More recently, Christine Horne and Stefanie Mollborn have developed an integrated model of the emergence and formation of norms and how they change over time.[23] Importantly, and going somewhat beyond the initial efforts of Sumner, they argue that norms have implications for two major issues studied by sociologists and other social scientists, namely, order and inequality. For Horne and Mollborn, norms consist of group-level evaluations of behavior, that is, approval or disapproval of certain types of behavior. But in addition to approval or disapproval, norms also consist of sanctions for punishing or rewarding members of the group consistent with the extent to which their conduct is approved or disapproved. This complex of norms and sanctions, understood and internalized by the individual members of society, ideally produce social order – including most importantly predictability – at the group or collective level.

The authors subscribe to a *consequentialist* argument for explaining the emergence of norms. Consequentialism is the idea that when an actor's behavior has consequences for others, those others have interest in, and pay attention to, their actions. As an initial or starting condition, namely, being alive to the actions of others, persons are inclined to negatively evaluative behavior that harms them and positively evaluative behavior that benefits them. Norms are *conjoint* when everyone in the group experiences similar consequences as a result of members' behavior. Norms can also emerge when persons' actions affect others indirectly (which are *disjoint* norms), as in the example of norms that have evolved over the harm of second-hand smoking.[24] Additionally, inequalities emerge because not every person or group holds to exactly the same set of norms. And with these different interests, some groups may benefit from certain norms more than others. For example, people and groups holding more socially-valued resources (money, status, power) are better able to enforce the norms they prefer, thereby either shutting out disadvantaged groups from receiving rewards for conformity or punishing them more severely for their deviance.[25]

Statistical rarity

As both Sumner and Horne and Mollborn argued, because human beings are not solitary but involved in various types of association with fellow members of their group, they are also likely to share their observations and experiences with others. This means that in addition to the consequentialist approach to norm-formation discussed above, norms are also *relational*, that is, they emerge out of the relationships persons form with others. Across these networks of relationships, persons use their senses – predominantly those of vision and hearing – to monitor physical and social environments and report back to others. The most basic and consistent basis for alarm and heightened concern among members of a group are rare events or characteristics of persons and places. Odd or rare events or traits "stick out like a sore thumb," that is, they attract attention, and people are prone to taking a cautious and even fearful stance toward them merely because they are rare, unknown, or novel. Lacking a basis for predicting what will happen when dealing with the new or the novel, persons learn to be cautious or to avoid them altogether. In this sense, the earliest and most profound basis of deviance or abnormality is statistical rarity, which constitutes "extremes of behavior that seldom occur in the general population."[26]

Indeed, random preventive patrols that take place in most municipal and suburban police departments typically assign officers to a regular beat or sector, the logic of this being that officers will come to know the regular features of the neighborhood and the typical characteristics of the residents of the area. Officers are especially keen to notice things that do not fit or that appear "out of place."[27] Courts generally side with the police regarding the use of such "out-of-place" considerations as a component of reasonable suspicion for stops or searches. The authorization for allowing officers to consider whether a motorist is out of place "is the recognition that good police work frequently requires officers to be observant of outliers."[28]

Over the course of human history examples abound over the tendency to punish and/or stigmatize persons merely for odd, strange, or rare behaviors or characteristics. The Trobrianders, a primitive tribe living in northwestern Melanesia, viewed albinos (persons lacking normal skin pigmentation) with disgust and deep disdain, judging them to be barely human.[29] Throughout history many societies have stigmatized persons who are too short or too heavy, although more recently such ideas as "fat-shaming" have emerged to contest such deviant attributions.[30] All things being equal, ugly persons tend to get fewer breaks in life and are treated more harshly for misconduct than better-looking and even average-looking individuals, which vividly illustrates the importance of looks in everyday life.[31] And even left-handedness, which occurs in about 14 percent of the population, was broadly condemned across early human history, and in some places it still is.[32] There is a tendency for human societies to develop a preference for the right hand and to associate more positive attributes toward it while simultaneously condemning left-handedness as "dark" or "evil." In the vast majority of societies there is cultural evidence – especially religious and linguistic – of positive bias toward the right and negative bias toward the left.[33] For example, to be correct is to be "right," and the right hand is used exclusively for saluting, shaking hands, and making the sign of the cross in the Christian religion. Overall, the judgment that statistically rare events or characteristics are dangerous or pathological is part of the natural folk psychiatry that persons utilize in monitoring the stability of the environment along with the humans who populate it.[34]

The unique or the rare, then, are generally discomfiting, while conversely most persons prefer the predictability of the average or the mean. The whole idea of norms – central to many conceptualizations of social control discussed throughout this book – derives from tacit notions of the normal and of the predictable. For many persons, it is reassuring and comforting to be located squarely within the golden mean of the normal or Gaussian curve, where sameness and familiarity win the day much like was the case for Durkheim's mechanical solidarity.

But the movement of modernity has seen a shift away from that earlier solidarity to a new, organic solidarity characterized by diversity and heterogeneity rather than likeness and homogeneity. Indeed, across politics, culture, academia, and media there has been a growing denunciation of the normal because of the way those who are labeled as pathological, delinquent, deviant, or abnormal are also systematically excluded from social participation and, hence, suffer diminution of their life chances. This new way of seeing things makes the argument that those who fall outside of the mainstream and who are punished for their status deficiencies by way of informal, medical, or legal control, are being discriminated against. Discrimination against alleged deviants is especially likely to garner media attention and public scrutiny when those being punished occupy minority statuses whether on the basis of race, ethnicity, religious affiliation, gender, sexual orientation or identity, or being an undocumented immigrant.

This coincides with the rejection of dualistic thinking such as good/ bad, moral/immoral, normal/deviant, healthy/sick, or even legal/illegal in favor of a continuum or a spectrum – that is, shades of gray – whereby the variety of the human condition must be tolerated and accepted for what it is while attempting to avoid the invidious labeling of persons falling on the disvalued side of the old dualisms. For example, persons who have the temerity to describe someone as fat may well be accused of fat-shaming, while new ideas of fat acceptance and positive body imaging regardless of size are flourishing. So, too, the idea of mental illness is being replaced by a softer, more inclusive notion of neurodiversity, as embodied in the new spectrum system of DSM-5 (for more on this, see chapter 7).

Unilever, one of the largest personal care product companies in the world, recently announced that it is taking the word "normal" out of its advertising and off its product labels altogether. Flagship haircare, beauty, and skincare products such as Dove, Lifebuoy, and Axe will remove references to "normal" so as to champion a new era of inclusivity and diversity and to challenge now outdated notions of beauty. Indeed, there is an explicit attempt, as corporate policy, to "work towards helping to end discrimination and advocating for a more inclusive vision of beauty."[35] Here, we see Unilever overtly and purposely linking normal with discrimination. If there is no longer a consensus over what constitutes the normal, or if the sentiment prevails that punishment or differential treatment is *ipso facto* discriminatory, then the concept of social control is rendered precarious because all normative prohibitions are deemed illegitimate or potentially so. This culminates in a "death of deviance" movement, the sentiment of which has been growing since the early 1990s across law, politics, the social sciences, and media and corporate cultures.[36] This broad rejection of the normal is related to the fact that at various times across human history, atrocities have been perpetrated in the name of defending the normal (read as the "status quo"), including such policies, programs, or laws as eugenics, slavery, lobotomies, and sterilization. These and related phenomena are described by Kathrin Braun as the "injuries of normality."[37]

The concept of neurodiversity shows up in the sociological literature as *neuroplasticity*, meaning that the brain is not simply hard-wired and relatively immutable by age eight or so – with the development of the self – but is continually subject to modification throughout the life course as stimuli from the social and physical environments dictate. Within this burgeoning field of *neurosociology*, there is also an acceptance of Freud's idea of the unconscious and how it is connected with the conscious brain, and this is why much attention has been devoted to rooting out the evils of implicit bias and other subtle aspects of the human condition.[38] These pursuits are an extension and updating of Robert K. Merton's earlier work on the sociology of unintended consequences of purposive action, and the question of how best to deal with the statistically rare as a policy matter.[39]

Perspectives on social order

Sumner's theory of the rise of norms, laws, and values is reflective of a consensus theory of society. The *consensus theory* originated in the seventeenth century with utilitarianism and the classical contract theories of Hobbes, Locke, and later Rousseau. In short, the theory states that the unity of social life is a matter of agreement and understanding between individuals.[40] With the rise of evolutionary theory in the nineteenth century, contract theory was merged with the so-called organismic theory – the idea that society is or is like an organism – whose various parts were held together as functional elements in the broader social system.[41] This newer consensus theory was initiated by Herbert Spencer in sociology and picked up by both Sumner and Emile Durkheim, and even later by functionalist sociologists such as Talcott Parsons, all of whom argued that shared norms and values are the key element in the maintenance of a stable and orderly society.

Conflict theory, influenced by the writings of Karl Marx, suggests on the other hand that rather than being maintained by a voluntary consensus of the citizenry, social order is just as likely to be maintained by advantaged groups whose members use their privileged positions in society to dominate and oppress members of less powerful (often minority) groups. In this sense, laws do not reflect the general will; instead, they reflect and protect the vested interests of the powerful, who through the law systematically cast the powerless into the class of the criminal, the deviant, the deranged, and the unfit. The central focus of conflict theory is criticism of capitalism because of the way it emphasizes profit as an end in itself which leads to atomistic individualism as persons compete with others in the struggle for status, power, and wealth. Capitalism is also criticized for choosing winners and losers, thereby increasing inequality and setting the stage for endemic class conflict, while those in the middle and upper classes can stigmatize the poor by labeling them dangerous, deranged, and criminals.

Capitalism is so all-encompassing – indeed, it has gone global – that partial adjustments will do little to make it fairer or more humane. Critical theorist István Mészáros, who wrote a Marxist-inspired treatise titled *The Necessity of Social Control*, argued that "nothing less than a radical transformation of our whole 'manner of being' can produce an adequate system of social control."[42] Only after capitalism is defeated in its entirety can socialism deliver genuine human emancipation and with it, a system of social control that somehow produces liberation rather than repression.

A third perspective on social order is represented by *interpretive theory*. The main goal of interpretive theory (examples include symbolic interactionism, phenomenology, dramaturgy, and ethnomethodology) is to learn how persons make the social world meaningful. Interpretive theorists assume social phenomena are fundamentally different than natural phenomena, and as a result sociology requires distinct methodological and explanatory approaches from those found in the natural sciences. Rather than seeking to discover the timeless laws of the social universe, interpretive theorists emphasize the importance of meaning and the subjective orientations of persons as they do things together. Additionally, the interpretive approach "does not seek an objective truth so much as to unravel patterns of subjective understanding."[43]

Whereas consensus theorists assume that social order arises from the fact that persons will seek agreement and understanding between one another in order to avoid what Hobbes called the "war of all against all," interpretive theorists make no such assumptions regarding the basis of social order. Instead, following George H. Mead, social order and hence social control is explained as a result of persons taking the attitudes of others with whom they interact in everyday life.[44] Social control is not imposed from above, but instead negotiated between real flesh-and-blood human beings who develop selves through everyday social interaction and shared activities. From the interpretive perspective, social control is not a timeless "social fact" but rather a phenomenon to be explained on a case-by-case basis taking into account the peculiar set of circumstances and conditions facing members of a society in any given situation.

The nature of sanctions

As we have seen, norms are rules for conduct. Norms aim to guide behavior via a system of *sanctions*: those who comply with norms are rewarded (positive sanctions) while those who violate them are punished (negative sanctions). When we talk about norms and sanctions, we generally assume that it is individuals who are either rewarded or punished for complying with or violating norms. But there is also the possibility of *collective sanctions*, namely, a situation in which a group is punished (or rewarded) for the actions of one or several of its members. In boot camp, for example, if a recruit is caught using a light to read after lights out, the whole unit may receive a punishment, for example, lights out an hour earlier for the next week or 50 push-ups. Systems of collective sanctions create especially intense pressures for members to conform to group norms.

In reality, however, sanctions are rarely purely individual or collective. This is because individuals are not isolated units, but are members of groups and thereby interdependent on others. For example, if a man who is married with children is sent to prison for embezzlement, not only is he being punished, but so are his wife and children, who now must find other sources of material, social, and emotional support.[45] Another point to consider is that, contrary to utilitarian perspectives which assume that human beings rationally calculate the costs and benefits of any line of action and adjust their behavior accordingly (a forward-looking version of social control), in reality actors often have no (or merely partial) knowledge of the long- or even short-term consequences of their actions. Rather than forward-looking actors who possess complete (or nearly so) information about the gains and losses associated with any possible course of action, actors rely more on past experiences to judge to what extent negative or positive sanctions may apply to current situations. This means that the system of norms and sanctions operating in most human societies aptly may be characterized as *backward-looking social control*.[46]

Sanctions may also be either centralized or diffuse. The most obvious and important form of *centralized sanctions* is the legal system of a nation-state supported by formal agents of control (police, courts, corrections, and so forth). Social order may be seen, then, as a problem of collective action, and the classic dilemma is how to motivate enough people to contribute to the production of this shared or public good (in this case, social order). In the collective action "game" of human society, centralized sanctions must be available to apply against "free riders," namely those who do not contribute to the public good, either through their overt violation of the social order (*meat eaters* who directly engage in criminal or deviant behavior) or through their failure to sanction other violators (*grass eaters*).[47] On the other hand, *diffuse sanctions* are rewards or punishments meted out by individuals or organizations on a local, informal basis against violators (either individuals or collectivities). By "local" is meant the more or less informal realm of face-to-face behavior, including small groups, neighborhoods, and communities.

So far we have covered the distinctions between positive and negative sanctions, collective and individual sanctions, and centralized and diffuse sanctions. Centuries ago English jurist and philosopher Jeremy Bentham worked out a general theory of sanctions which still rings true today.[48] This general theory of sanctions was the bedrock for developing his utilitarian or deterrence theory of punishment, namely, that punishments ought to be just severe enough to offset the pleasure derived from criminal or deviant acts. Bentham suggested that the four basic types of sanctions or punishments which operate in all human societies are physical, political, moral or popular, and religious.

Travis Hirschi and Michael Gottfredson have provided a useful discussion and extension of Bentham's original theory of sanctions.[49] First, however, they changed the terminology slightly. They refer to Bentham's category of physical sanctions as natural sanctions. Bentham's political sanctions are referred to as legal sanctions. Moral sanctions are referred to as social sanctions. And, finally, religious sanctions are referred to as supernatural sanctions.

Following the terminology of Gottfredson and Hirschi, *natural sanctions* are negative, harmful, or painful consequences of operating within a natural environment, such as the dangers associated with heat or fire, animals, diseases and similar factors affecting human health and well-being, or even other human beings. The idea of natural sanctions places great emphasis on evolutionary learning, and stresses, for example, that the most important thing parents and other competent adults do is protect children from such sanctions. *Social sanctions* are a product of human society, such as the pains associated with a friend's withdrawal of friendship, being expelled or isolated from a group, or the expression of disappointment or anger from a parent. Whereas natural sanctions are automatic and direct, social sanctions require the presence and participation of other human beings.

Legal sanctions are the penalties provided by the state for violations of the criminal, administrative, or civil law. Today legal sanctions are confined to fines, imprisonment, and a range of intermediate sanctions, but in earlier times they included flogging, transportation, bodily mutilation, and various forms of torture (see chapters 5, 8, and 9). Finally, *supernatural sanctions* are rewards or punishments individuals receive upon their death. These supernatural sanctions, such as the belief that one will go to Hell for breaking a religious commandment, are ostensibly geared toward shaping the behavior of individuals in this world, in the here and now.

Hirschi and Gottfredson further argue that the four sanctions can be ranked according to the time that elapses between behavior and the receipt of sanctions.[50] Natural sanctions are the most direct and certain, followed by social sanctions, legal sanctions, and finally supernatural sanctions, the consequences of the latter of which can never be known for certain and must remain an article of faith. According to these authors, the history of human society has been a slow and inexorable adding on of the secondary sanctions (supernatural, social, and legal) to augment those natural sanctions which are primordial and most immediate.

Social control as a dependent or independent variable

Scientific explanation typically involves stating the relationship between two or more variables or concepts of interest. For example, a researcher studying juvenile delinquency might argue that religiosity – namely, the intensity of one's relation to the sacred – is related to rates of juvenile delinquency. Further, the nature of the relationship would be assumed to be causal, meaning that changes in religiosity are associated with changes in delinquency, and that because religiosity occurs in time before delinquency, changes in the former "cause" changes in the latter. (Indeed, it would not make much sense to say that one's delinquency causes one's religiosity.) Simply stating that "as x changes, y changes," however, says nothing about the direction of the relationship. It simply states that changes in x (the independent variable) are somehow related to changes in y (the dependent variable). In order to bring more precision into scientific explanation, it is usually desirable to state the direction of the relationship as well. A better hypothesis, then, might state "As religiosity increases, delinquency decreases." In plain language, this hypothesis asserts that as the intensity of one's orientation toward the sacred increases, the likelihood of being delinquent decreases.

Traditionally, social scientific explanations have tended to view social control as a *dependent variable*. This is due to traditional conceptualizations of social control as reactive: a person is robbed at gunpoint and calls the police; a woman is mad at her husband and gives him the silent treatment; a person seeks counseling for a gambling problem. In other words, various forms of deviance or criminality are conceived as igniting social control responses. This relationship may be stated in the form "as deviance increases, social control increases."

The labeling perspective

Treating social control as a dependent variable certainly does not exhaust the possibilities for its conceptualization, however. The labeling perspective – a theory within the interpretive paradigm – suggests that social control leads to deviance, or at least certain types of deviance. In this sense, social control is conceptualized as an *independent variable* (see figure 2.1). Beginning with the work of Frank Tannenbaum in 1938 and continued by David Matza, Howard S. Becker, and Edwin Lemert during the 1950s and 1960s, the *labeling* perspective takes the position that societal reaction to deviance can produce further deviance because of the difficulties and strains persons encounter as a result of being labeled criminal, delinquent, mentally ill, strange or weird, or any other negative characterizations.[51]

Consider the example of a person (call him Bob) who has spent seven years in federal penitentiary for armed robbery, and is being released upon completion of his sentence. Even as he leaves the prison a free man, the label of "ex-con" will follow Bob around wherever he goes. Labeling theorists argue that, once applied, such labels are "sticky" and difficult to shake. With whatever money he had before his incarceration or accumulated during his stay in prison, Bob would likely try to rent an apartment, apply for a job, and meet new people. But it is equally likely that he will be rebuffed at every turn: employers are unlikely to hire him because of his felony conviction; the apartment complex will reject his application either

Figure 2.1 The Labeling Perspective

because his credit rating is too low or because of the negative information contained in the background check; and most persons are simply leery about befriending someone fresh out of prison.

The stickiness of the label makes it difficult for Bob or anyone for that matter – save for high-profile celebrities such as Martha Stewart or Tiger Woods – to reintegrate into conventional society. Left with few alternatives, Bob may end up engaging in petty theft or other street crimes to make ends meet, or at the very least going back to old haunts and acquaintances, thereby falling back in with the very same crowd that helped get him into trouble in the first place.

Labeling theorists are not so much interested in *primary deviance* – Bob's original criminal act which brought the attention of law enforcement – but in *secondary deviance*, namely, the deviant behavior that occurs as a result of the affixing of a stigmatizing label. According to labeling theorists, the high *recidivism* (or repeat offending) rate that afflicts the correctional systems of the United States and western Europe is indicative of this labeling process and the incidents of secondary deviance. The results of a 2018 study found that roughly 68 percent of those released from state prisons between 2005 and 2014 were arrested within three years after release, 79 percent within six years after release, and 83 percent within nine years after release.[52]

Punishment is supposed to instill prosocial adjustment in individuals and, if calibrated correctly according to utilitarian theory, because the pains of punishment outweigh the pleasures of the disvalued act, the expected outcome is that the punished person decides "I'm going straight." Hence, under ideal conditions, punishment produces conformity. Labeling theorists, however, argue that under certain specifiable conditions, punishment *amplifies* deviance rather than reducing it. Specifically, when persons feel they are being treated unfairly, for example being singled out and punished even as others are doing the same thing but receiving no sanctions, such persons are more apt to become agitated or defiant, thereby amplifying deviance as a result of the punishment or label. Indeed, one of the general risks of imposing negative sanctions on persons – regardless of whether or not the punishments are deserved or proportionate – is the possibility of backfire effects. This occurs because of the strong aversion most people feel when coerced into doing something, especially when it involves pain or loss of autonomy.[53]

Likewise, persons may become angry or defiant if they believe they were punished excessively, that is, that the punishment did not fit the crime.[54] Indeed, false accusations in general may lead to persons lashing out at the system because they feel that the deck is stacked against them and that they will never get a fair shake. And this can start early in life, such as when youth or adolescents are labeled as "troublemakers" by teachers, school administrators, parents, or others in positions of authority in the community.[55] Such negative labels can stick with a youth through his or her formative years and may even lead into more serious deviance and criminality in adulthood.

In this way, the affixing of a stigmatizing label can amplify deviance which, according to labeling theorists, is synonymous with secondary deviance. Connected with this problem of amplified or secondary deviance, Jason Ditton suggests that, rather than focusing on crime, which is of course the traditional approach in sociology and criminology, what should be the focus instead are the control attempts embodied in societal reactions to perceived deviance. This approach Ditton has aptly called *controlology*, or the study of control.[56] Individual intentions and acts are irrelevant (or at least unworthy of scientific scrutiny) without societal reactions to those acts. Indeed, a "crime" is never committed in and for itself. For something to be labeled a crime, it must be reported or detected, and the person alleged to have committed the act must be tried in a court of law and found guilty. This shifts the focus from individual *responsibility* to societal *response ability*.[57]

As discussed above, persons who have been incarcerated and who are released after serving their time face numerous obstacles to full reintegration into society. The stickiness of labels such as ex-con are particularly evident when persons so labeled seek employment. In order to facilitate successful reintegration with an eye toward reducing recidivism, some communities have instituted a *ban the box* policy. This policy limits employers from asking job seekers about their criminal history, thereby eliminating the social stigma associated with a criminal record.[58]

A ban the box law was implemented in Hawaii beginning in 1998, and research was conducted to ascertain whether it accomplished the desired effect of reducing recidivism in areas where it was put into effect. Statistical tests were utilized to compare Hawaii's recidivism rate before and after the implementation of ban the box. The results were that "the ban the box law lowered the odds of repeat offending by 57%."[59] This is a robust finding which supports key elements of labeling theory.

SUGGESTIONS FOR FURTHER READING

Egon Bittner, *The Functions of the Police in Modern Society* (1970)
> Bittner's sophisticated analysis of police operations and organizations contributed immensely to scholarship in the field of police studies. His argument that the core of the police role is the distribution of non-negotiably coercive force in modern society is still very much on the mark.

David P. Farrington and Joseph Murray (eds.), *Labeling Theory: Empirical Tests* (2017)
> This is an edited volume containing investigations of various aspects of labeling theory, including a history of the concept; experimental evidence of the predictive value of labeling, defiance, and restorative justice theories; the role of labeling in juvenile justice processing; and the effects of official intervention on later offending.

Stefanie Mollborn, *Mixed Messages: Norms and Social Control around Teen Sex and Pregnancy* (2017)

Mollborn provides an analysis of how family norms emerge and are contested in the special case of the control of teen sex and pregnancy, tracing out how communities and schools affect negotiations between parents and their children regarding what is allowed or disallowed, that is, what is considered normal or deviant.

Colin Sumner, *The Sociology of Deviance: An Obituary* (1994)

Sumner argues that the study of deviance within sociology was launched with Durkheim's *Suicide* in 1897, but that the project became moribund over time – largely because social control is an unmanageably broad and amorphous concept – and is now knocking on death's door. Consistent with critical and labeling approaches but in ways even more radical, Sumner believes the sociology of deviance will be replaced by a sociology of censure, that is, being alive to how derogatory categories (defective, dependents, delinquents) are themselves versions of moral panic.

William Graham Sumner, *Folkways* (1906)

Sumner, an early American sociologist, provided one of the first systematic treatments of the evolution of norms and values in society. Even today, more than 100 years later, the book is still an engrossing read.

DISCUSSION QUESTIONS

1. Explain the difference between folkways and mores and give an example of each.
2. Describe under what conditions a system of collective sanctions is likely to arise.
3. Identify and discuss the four basic types of sanctions first developed by Bentham and later modified by Gottfredson and Hirschi.
4. Compare and contrast the concepts of primary and secondary deviance. Which of these are labeling theorists more likely to focus on, and why?
5. Techniques of neutralization often arise when people are caught in deviance. Describe an incident in your own life where you utilized one of these five techniques in an attempt to neutralize claims of deviance. Did it work? Why or why not?

Chapter 3
Informal Control

Introduction

When we are born, we arrive at a time and place, in a particular society, that is not of our own making. For most of us most of the time, there is hardly any thought of problematizing or questioning this "natural surrounding world" which we have come to know and within which we operate.[1] It just *is*. It is a stubborn reality. It is the pre-given social reality that we come to know and accept, the taken-for-granted background for virtually everything we do. It is the world of everyday life.[2]

As a *social* world, as distinct from a physical world or the subjective world of our own thoughts and reflections, it is populated by other human beings, some of whom are very close to us – our mothers and fathers, aunts and uncles, brothers and sisters, good friends – while others we know only in passing or not at all. The human condition is the condition of association, of living among fellow human beings, however distant or near they may be relationally. Indeed, it is very rare to find a truly isolated person or group.

Although human beings are carbon-based life forms operating and moving about in a physical world and thereby subject to the same physical laws as are other objects whether animate or inanimate, it is quite limiting to think of the human condition in only this physicalist or objectivist sense. This is because with the rise of human society, something has been added to the physical conditions of existence which characterize the situation of all lower life forms. Because of the superior intellect of the human being in comparison to other animals, the continuity of human groups is predominantly cultural and historical. Since the dawn of the human species, knowledge and ideas have grown slowly but surely, and the most useful of these have been maintained and transmitted across human groups. As Charles Ellwood explains,

> In this way man gradually builds himself up out of the perceptual world, the world of objects, with which he began, into an ideational world, the world of culture. As the social tradition grows in bulk it increases in influence. Men

now come to live, not so much in a world of objects, as in a world of ideas – of pattern ideas – which immediately control their adjustments both to the objects of nature and to their fellows.[3]

Informal social control consists of all those mechanisms and practices of ordinary, everyday life whereby group pressures to conform are brought to bear against the individual. Beginning in the 1930s, concepts such as group "culture" and "climate" were being developed and tested by various researchers. These studies documented the ways in which groups regulate, modify, and sometimes distort the judgment and actions of individuals.

Before examining these studies, however, we will first summarize and reiterate the importance of socialization for the understanding of informal social control. Any understanding of informal control and the role of socialization in assuring social order must be squarely grounded in the social psychological literature on the nature of groups and group living. Within informal control with its emphasis on group pressures to conform, a variety of agents of socialization carry out the tasks of maintaining social order and producing predictable (that is, norm-conforming) behavior. After examining these various agents of socialization, a somewhat extended overview will be provided of the dramaturgical theory of Erving Goffman, whose ideas regarding the nature of face-to-face interaction amount to a general theory of informal control.

Agents of socialization

Socialization, or the learning of a culture, begins at birth and ends only with death. A person learns the rules and cultural traditions of a society through routine contact with various other persons and groups throughout his or her life. There are eight basic *agents of socialization* that help steer persons toward norm-conforming and away from deviant behavior. Seven of these basic sources of socialization, to be covered below, are the family, the community, peers, school, work and consumption, religion, and public opinion and mass media.[4] (The legal system will be covered in more detail in later chapters.)

The family

In the earliest stages in the development of the human species, men did not take on traditional fatherly roles, but were more concerned with gaining access to females for purposes of sexual consummation. This meant that it was mothers along with other women of the clan who had to band together to raise children. This meant also that the earliest human societies were likely matriarchal, with descent being traced through the mother's line since biological fathers were invariably absent and could not be relied upon for support.[5] Somewhere along the way, however, fathers started becoming more or less permanent fixtures within kinship systems, as human populations increased and group norms began developing with regard to greater accountability in the areas of sexual and procreative behavior. Moving beyond the original primitive stage of human existence, then, the collective wisdom has been that children ought to be raised in the most stable environment possible. This stable environment was (and still is) the family, a supportive infrastructure consisting of a mother, a father or close male relative, any children, as well as extended kin (aunts, uncles, grandparents, and so forth).

Parents, biological or otherwise, have traditionally taken on the societal responsibility of caring for young children as well as instructing them about the rules of their society. As George Hillery has pointed out, "primary responsibility for imparting the tradition of the village to its new 'recruits' rested with the family."[6] Hillery notes further that although families are the primary agents of socialization of children, in no known society do parents perform this task alone. Families are typically located within broader social settings known as communities.

As noted above, not just in the family but in many other areas of life, there is movement toward greater diversity and heterogeneity in both form and function. In the nineteenth century Herbert Spencer predicted precisely this, arguing from the theory of evolution that matter "passes from an indefinite incoherent homogeneity to a definite coherent heterogeneity."[7] In the transition from an agrarian to an industrial society, the family has moved from being primarily a production unit (e.g., the small family farm) to a consumption unit. And the modern family also displays enormous diversity in its form, ranging from the traditional heterosexual nuclear family of husband, wife, and any children, to single-headed households (usually mothers) with children, to blended families (including stepfamilies or multiple generations of kin living in the same household), and even to families consisting of same-sex marital or domestic partners with or without children.[8] Within this great diversity there have arisen various strategies for monitoring the activities of family members, the purposes of which are to keep them safe and to provide for their physical and emotional well-being. But it is not only family members watching over each other (that is, informal control). For example, juvenile courts monitor the activities of wayward youth (legal control). Likewise, pediatricians and medical personnel in schools and elsewhere check on the health status of children under their supervision, while also assessing the extent to which parents or legal guardians are providing them adequate levels of care (medical control).[9]

The community

In 1995 Hillary Clinton published a book entitled It Takes a Village.[10] The main thesis of the book is that, although parents are important in imparting societal norms and values to their children, socialization is complete only when parental oversight is supplemented by a supportive community – the "village" – consisting of safe schools and neighbor-hoods, caring teachers and neighbors, churches, civic organizations, and other private and public institutions. In smaller, tight-knit communities characterized by mechanical solidarity, it is indeed the case that many community members beyond those of the immediate kinship group are actively involved in the instruction and guidance of youth.[11]

With increasing modernization and the advent of organic solidarity, however, community standards of behavior play a less direct role in assuring the conformity of youth. Because of this loss of informal oversight and regulation with advancing modernity, both on the parts of families as well as communities, more emphasis is placed on the work of formal agencies and agents of control, including the criminal justice system and medical oversight of youth in the guise of social service and public health agencies, as well as medical and therapeutic personnel employed in the schools. This is why the recent trend in municipal governance has been the systematic attempt to bring the community back in, whether in the form of community policing, family and community preservation, alterna-tives to traditional punishment which include heavy doses of community sanctions, and a concern with shoring up "social capital," namely, the collective resources arising from close and sustained social relations between members of a community. (We will return to these issues in chapter 6.)

Peers

Because schooling is emphasized in advanced industrial societies, and because children are being placed into formal education at younger and younger ages, children are spending much of their time in the presence of same-age peers. Although schools provide the primary context for peer socialization, the influence of peers can also be felt in the community, in homes with siblings, and in more general social settings. The idea of *peer pressure*, namely, intense social influences exerted on young persons by their close friends, can indeed lead them into making bad decisions or engaging in delinquent conduct. However, the negative outcomes associated with peer pressure have been somewhat overblown and exaggerated, because there are countervailing tendencies for friends to keep young persons in line and out of harm's way. In short, conventional peers and the youth cultures arising from shared activities and orientations exert strong pressures to conform, even as deviant peers and deviant youth subcultures may produce strong inducements toward deviance and delinquency.[12]

Although it has long been felt that parents are the single most influential agents of informal control for assuring the norm-conforming behavior of youth, a growing number of observers believe that other agents of control, especially same-age peers, exert as much or even more influence than parents. Indeed, psychologist Judith Harris argues that the nurture assumption – that parents and especially mothers have the most direct bearing on how their children turn out – is wrong.[13] According to this line of thinking, because children are now spending more time than ever before in the presence of other children, whether at school, in daycare, or in other settings, parents have been dethroned as the frontline agents of socialization.

School

The primary function of schooling is to impart the knowledge that youth will need to take on adult roles, especially in the areas of work, citizenship, family, and community relations. In school, youth are confronted with an array of rules and regulations, and this early exposure to authority figures beyond those of the household is considered to play a crucial role in the moral development of youth. The major agents of socialization in school are of course teachers, while other agents include school administrators, school medical personnel, and of course fellow students.

Because the trend in modern society is to place children into formal education at younger and younger ages, a battleground of sorts has developed as families are increasingly pitted against schools for the souls and minds of children. From the perspective of schools, parents are mainly to blame for the underachievement and/or misconduct of their children both within and outside of school settings. As schools attempt to take more complete control of the lives of youth – because of the assumption that parents are failing in their roles as agents of socialization – parents demand more accountability from schools, thereby producing more strains and antagonisms on all sides.

One important manifestation of this conflict between schools and families is that traditional parental authority is diminished, to the extent that the local culture and knowledge of the family (as in "family values") are replaced by the more cosmopolitan and "modern" values of the school system. The authority of the school system is presumably based not on status (e.g., the father as the unquestioned head of the patriarchal household), but on impersonal and universal knowledge which transcends local knowledge and circumstances.[14]

Another important aspect of informal control in schools is the various extracurricular activities offered to students, including those of organized sports. In high school especially, traditional team sports such as football, baseball, and basketball provide important sources of identity for, and solidarity among, team members. In high school and extending into college, student-athletes (so-called "jocks") attain a relatively high status within the school or university.

There has been a longstanding assumption that participation in youth sports is positive because of the things you need to be good at to help the team: cooperation; practice and repetition (a desire for continuous improvement); attention to detail; physical training and skills acquisition; mutual respect among players and obedience to coaches; time management; loyalty; altruism (putting the team ahead of yourself); multi-tasking (juggling student and athlete roles); motivation (in order to keep playing the sport, you need to make decent grades); and character-building (learning how to be a "good sport" as well as learning how to manage both winning and losing which prepares athletes for the ups and downs of real life). There is also the idea that because youth playing team sports are supervised by competent adults (managers, coaches, and staff) and are kept busy with practice and games, they have less time available for unconventional activities which could get them into trouble. In short, like other extracurricular activities, the sentiment is that participants in team sports ought to be less deviant than those who do not participate.

However, the exact nature of the relationship between sports participation and deviance is murkier and less certain than the above assumptions would suggest. One way of examining this issue empirically is to make a distinction between different types of sports to see if participants are more or less deviant across these categories. David Maume and Michael Parrish examined data from the *Study of Early Child Care and Youth Development*, a longitudinal study of children's social, physical, and cognitive development.[15] Mothers were recruited into the study after giving birth in 1991, and both they and their children (when they were old enough, of course) were interviewed over the years until the study ended in 2006. The authors examined self-reports of the children from ages 12 through 15 (as noted, the study concluded when all children turned 15). By the end of the study, 974 youth remained in the sample.

The youth self-reported on their participation in violent and property crimes from ages 12 through 15. Parents also reported on the types and amount of sports activities in which the youth participated during the same period. The authors hypothesized that the nature of the sport may have something to do with any possible correlations to delinquency or deviance, and they made distinctions between the sports based upon level of contact with other players. This produced three categories of sport: *non-contact* (swimming, tennis, golf); *semi-contact* (soccer, basketball, baseball, softball); and *heavy contact* (football, wrestling, hockey, lacrosse). The authors found no relationship between delinquency and participation in non-contact or semi-contact sports, but they *did* find that participation in heavy contact sports was significantly related to both violence and property crime.

Another study looked at high school sports participation and later deviance without controlling for the type of sport. The authors (Douglas Hartmann and Michael Massoglia) came up with a mixed or bifurcated result: High school sports participation *increased* the risk of drunk driving later in life, while it *decreased* the risk of shoplifting later in life.[16] Findings from both these studies reflect the rather complex issue of the relationship between sports participation and deviance and invites further exploration (including replication and validation studies) into this dimension of informal control.

Finally, there is a raging debate around public schooling and homeschooling. Many critics of homeschooling argue that children educated in this way lose meaningful attachments to same-age peers and are limited in their understandings of the increasing complexity and diversity of the broader social realities existing outside of the home. Many homeschooling parents reject public schooling, citing such reasons as the poor quality of public schools; the political or ideological values embedded in public education; the stultifying nature of bureaucratic control of public schools; and the presumed dangers of public schools, especially larger schools in urban or even suburban settings which are overrepresented in the school shooting data. Some even argue that forcing children to attend public schools is unconstitutional. As Milton Gaither has noted, "Most people who use their homes to teach their children still do so as a form of protest against public education."[17] Many of these homeschooling controversies subsided or shifted focus during the Covid-19 pandemic as children were stuck at home and schools were shuttered as part of broader lockdown mandates, but they promise to be reignited as things return to normal.[18]

Work and consumption

Although schooling prepares individuals to join the adult labor force with the hopes of their becoming relatively self-sufficient and productive members of society, persons must still "learn the ropes" once they become members of a work organization. In other words, whether entering the workforce for the first time, changing jobs, or reentering the workforce after a period of idleness, persons must learn the particular norms, values, rules, and history of the place of their employment. This learning process, often referred to as *organizational socialization*, consists of several domains.[19] Such socialization attempts to instill in workers a tacit sense of what is expected of them at work and the forms of discipline – which amount to projects of behavior modification – which could be implemented.[20]

First, there is *performance proficiency*, which simply refers to the learning and mastery of tasks associated with one's position within a work organization. Second, there are other *people* within the organization that workers must learn to adjust to in order to do their jobs effectively. In the modern workplace, this ability to deal with others – often referred to as *soft skills* – is considered to be nearly as important as traditional performance proficiency.

Third, there are *political* considerations, in terms of being aware of various aspects of the organization, specifically (1) who the politically powerful actors are (on the formal side), but also (2) the nature of the informal networks which are vital for general information and as sources of social solidarity. Fourth, workers must learn the special language or *argot* that is used within their particular line of work. Fifth, workers must be familiar with the organization's *goals and values*, represented in the rules and principles – both formal and informal – which (ideally) help to maintain the integrity of the organization. Finally, persons are expected to be familiar with the *history* of the organization within which they work. In this sense, organizational history includes the traditions, customs, myths, and rituals used to transmit cultural knowledge to organizational members.[21]

In capitalist society there is an ethic ingrained in persons from a very young age that in order to get ahead in life, one must work hard to gain the valued resources which allows one to attain and maintain a middle-class lifestyle. This reflects the idea that society is a *meritocracy*, that is, that persons are rewarded in proportion to the effort they put forth. Whether or not a meritocracy even exists, or if it does exist whether it is good or bad, is a contentious issue in public deliberation, academia, and elsewhere. For example, Paul Kingston finds support for the meritocratic ideal in American society: economically valued positions are allocated more on the basis of educational attainment, cognitive ability, and personal character-istics (such as a conscientious work ethic), than on ascribed characteristics such as race, gender, or family background.[22] Therefore, in capitalism there is an emphasis on economic competition and productivity, and those who are most successful – those who produce the most within any particular work area – are typically the ones who maintain higher levels of consumption and desired lifestyles.

On the other hand and in separate analyses, both Robert Frank and Michael Sauder reject the idea that there is a clear path running from early socialization in stable homes and on through to success in the educational system which then sets up those who play by the rules of the game to be rewarded with a job delivering the promise of a middle-class lifestyle or better.[23] This version of meritocracy is more fictive and mythical than real. Even more important than the steps to success, which are marked out and available for anyone to follow, success or failure has more to do with chance, fate, and dumb luck, but sometimes also knowing the "right people" who get you a foot in the door which could send you on your way to later success. Although conservatives are generally correct that cognitive competence and a steadfast work ethic are valuable in attaining status and standing, liberals are correct as well in noting that there are multiple impediments blocking attainment of the American Dream including race, gender, disability, the quality of schooling, exposure to trauma, community disorganization, health, and so forth.

The economic boom of the 1950s led to heightened levels of consumerism in American society. As more and more persons were in a race to "keep up with the Joneses," conspicuous consumption increased and persons took advantage of the newly burgeoning credit system which allowed them to have the outward appearance of success – a brand new car, a nice home in the suburbs – all the while dealing with growing debt which would need to be paid for somehow down the road.[24] With the transition from mechanical to organic solidarity, families and communities became more fragmented and personal identity shifted from the cozy, expressive bonds of primary groups to the more calculating and instrumental contexts of secondary groups. This also meant that, to a significant degree, the locus of informal control shifted from friends and families to more distant and impersonal settings, most importantly the work setting but also the mass media providing images and information about identity based upon one's personal patterns of consumption.

The bottom line is that, across most Western societies, the fields of business and commerce play increasingly prominent roles in social regulation. As Richard Adams states, "the market is a primary center of decision making in these [industrial] economies."[25] This is consistent with the earlier writings of Herbert Marcuse, whose primary thesis was that within industrial capitalism consumption becomes the dominant impulse in society. This impulse toward consumption becomes so strong and abiding that it produces a "one-dimensional man" hell-bent on acquiring the latest products, gadgets, and technologies without a clear understanding of why they are sought in the first place. Following Karl Marx, this is a new form of alienation to the extent that identity is now connected to success at acquiring valued resources – whether acquired legally or illegally – and not much else. As Marcuse argues, "They find their soul in their automobile, hi-fi set, split-level home, kitchen equipment," and that "social control is anchored in the new needs which [these commodities] produce."[26]

Religion

No one knows how far back in human antiquity religion began, or for that matter what form or forms it took. There have been plenty of theories developed concerning the origins and functions of religion, and there is simply not enough space here to do justice to them. Several, however, can be mentioned. Herbert Spencer believed that the earliest religion appeared in the form of ancestor worship arising naturally from the fear of the dead.[27] Consistent with the evolutionism of Spencer, Edward Tylor believed religion begins with a belief in souls or ghosts, evolving from the most primitive form, namely magic (shamanism), into later forms in the order of animism, pantheism, polytheism (the believe in many gods or deities), and finally monotheism (the believe in one true god).[28] And both

Sigmund Freud and Emile Durkheim viewed totemism as the earliest form of religious expression.[29]

In earlier societies characterized by mechanical solidarity, shared orientations toward the sacred provided the groundwork for truth, knowledge, and wisdom concerning all matters religious and secular. Indeed, religion was one of the first systematic forms of social control, and as Charles Ellwood argued,

> The religious sanction for conduct, being a supernatural sanction, all human experience shows, has been one of the most effective means of controlling the conduct of normal individuals. The desire to come into right relations with a deity, who represents in the earlier stages of [societal] development the ideal of personal character, has been an effective means of preventing too wide a variation in conduct in individuals.[30]

Religious socialization is the process by which important principles of a religious belief system are transmitted to new members across generations.[31] Religious socialization is especially concerned with the collective solidarity and identity of a group of true believers, otherwise known as the church or congregation. Harry Alpert has summarized the four primary functions of religion according to Emile Durkheim, these being:

- *Regulation and discipline* – All religions promulgate a set of rules for living in this world which prepares true believers for attaining salvation or grace in the afterlife. These uncodified rules (e.g., taboos) are directives for abstaining from certain types of behavior. As forms of social control, these rules or directives remain in the informal realm in the sense that religion is practiced among a group of like-minded individuals sharing a particular orientation to the sacred. (Later of course, with the advent of written language, these folkways may become mores, and some of these religious customs may later inform more formal systems of understanding such as law.)
- *Cohesion and solidarity* – Following from the last point, religion and its elaborate rituals and ceremonies bring persons together and bond them strongly to each other, forming an ongoing and persistent set of shared beliefs and activities. The church embodies this form of religious solidarity or cohesion. It is interesting to note that the Greek word for society is κοινωνία, which literally refers to people and their customs. And the religious ritual of taking communion, known as Holy Communion in the Greek Orthodox Church, is also called κοινωνία. Hence, the concept of "society" is likely derived from the original forms of solidarity arising within the church or religious congregation, where true believers partake in important shared rituals such as communion.
- *Revitalization* – One of the important ways religion maintains strong solidarity among a group of like-minded believers is by telling and retelling stories about the origins of humanity as well as its place

in the cosmos. The rituals practiced by true believers transmit these important understandings and traditions across time and generations. The partaking of these rituals serves to revitalize and sustain the most essential elements of the collective consciousness of the group, thereby linking the past to the present and beyond.

- *Inculcation of a sense of well-being* – In providing a sense of belonging, or so-called "we-feeling," to a group of true believers, members of the church are endowed with a sense of well-being or even euphoria. This produces a sense of security among true believers, comfortable in the knowledge that they are among friends and that god or the gods are watching over them. Religion, then, serves an important psychological or tension management function, in that whatever calamities may befall them, persons of the faith are reassured that in the end all will be well.[32]

Especially as represented in a church whose members are bonded together via their shared orientation toward the sacred, religions also create the groundwork for the earliest notions of a systematic surveillance society, as members watch each other carefully – not only face-to-face when attending church services, but also generally in the community – to assure their actions comport with the teachings of scripture.[33] This is a powerful social innovation, one which speaks not only of all members of the faith being always and eternally visible to God, but also visible to all other members of their faith.

Mass media and public opinion

In modern society, entertainment and news media – television, film, radio, music, newspapers, magazines, the Internet, and mass-marketed video games – provide a tremendous range of information and images which are consumed by a mass public with varying results. Some observers believe the effects of the mass media on the public are generally bad, while others believe that various types of media can have a positive impact on society.

For example, because television news is in the business of maximizing viewership and ratings, the crime stories they choose to cover tend to be more sensational, bizarre, and violent than the typical crime. This then distorts the picture of crime that the average citizen receives, thereby also fueling higher levels of fear of crime among the citizenry than is warranted. Additionally, many observers believe that the generally high levels of sex, violence, and depiction of deviant behavior in films, cable television, and video games leads to a host of behavioral problems among younger members of viewing audiences. One study, for example, found that adolescents who are exposed to high levels of sexual content in television, movies, magazines, and music are more sexually promiscuous than youths who are not exposed to such content.[34] On the other hand, in countries that provide citizens only a narrow range of media (such as China and Iran), the Internet is considered to be an important source of democratization to the extent that totalitarian states are less able to control access to, as well as the content of, this particular communications medium.[35]

Historically there existed an ethic of value-freedom and impartiality among journalists, whose professional duties amounted to delivering the facts of a particular crime story or event. However, more recently journalists have taken on advocacy roles, not only reporting on the news but also providing commentary and opinion with a decidedly political or ideological bent. Indeed, some journalists do not even try to hide who they are pulling for in delivering the news about crime, especially those that involve innocent victims (see the related discussion of expressive justice in chapter 8). This tendency is what David Altheide has described as *gonzo justice*, which is

> the use of extraordinary means to demonstrate social control and moral compliance, often through rule enforcement and punishment designed to stigmatize publicly, e.g., the mass media, and to demonstrate the moral resolve of those mandating the punishment.[36]

Closely related to mass media and communications technologies is *public opinion*, which can be defined as the extent to which individuals in a society hold the same or similar views about issues of the day. The idea of public opinion is captured in closely related terms such as "social mind," "general will," "public sentiment," or "national character." It is the idea that otherwise disparate and distinct individuals hold to certain beliefs, attitudes, or opinions shared in common by a large segment of the society.[37] In 1920, British sociologist Benjamin Kidd predicted the rise of scientific techniques for measuring public opinion and how control of such information would become useful to governments and private interests alike. As Kidd explained,

> It is clearly in evidence that the science of creating and transmitting public opinion under the influence of collective emotion is about to become the principal science of civilization to the mastery of which all governments and all powerful interests will in the future address themselves with every resource at their command.[38]

Since Kidd's time there has arisen the modern "information society" made possible by the invention of computerized information technologies including the Internet. In his work on the topics of the information age and network society, Manuel Castells argues that power and wealth are rapidly becoming products of knowledge, information processing, and symbol manipulation, while the Internet itself represents the restructuring of cultural and political power relations.[39] The labor force recruited to service and manage the new information technologies is increasingly characterized as technocratic, meaning that the bulk of their training is concentrated in "harder" technical studies such as engineering, computer and information systems, and organizational and systems management, with less emphasis placed on the "softer," traditional humanities curriculum. There is also a concomitant diminution of localistic ties and knowledge in favor of a cosmopolitan orientation, which is part of the historical tendency toward increasing interdependence of the information labor force on a global scale. This new workforce, then, is comprised largely of the technologues of Alvin Gouldner's New Class.[40] As Castells explains, this trend is accelerated via three mechanisms:

> global employment in the multinational corporations and their associated cross-border networks; impacts of international trade on employment and labor conditions, both in the North and in the South; and effects of global competition and of the new mode of flexible management on each country's labor force. In each case, information technology is the indispensable medium for the linkages between different segments of the labor force across national boundaries.[41]

In various of his writings during the 1970s, Gouldner pointed to these and other aspects of a second "communications revolution," one which is altering human social relations just as profoundly as the emergence of written language and the invention of the printing press did during the first communications revolution.[42] Although his writings on the topic predated by several decades the birth of the Internet, Gouldner nevertheless understood the enormous ramifications of the establishment of computerized mass information systems, which near the end of his life were looming just over the horizon. As Gouldner states,

> We are presently at the early stages of a radically new communications era in which computerized information storage and retrieval systems will be integrated with "cable" television. The computer console will control the computer's information storage and order it to produce selective bits of information, making them directly available in offices and homes via television scanning through cable television, or through specially ordered print outs.[43]

As more and more persons are drawn into intimate contact with the mass communication technologies of cable television and the Internet, they are less likely to meet face-to-face – such as in the "liberal" public square of bygone days – to discuss and hammer out shared visions of the "good life" or the just society.[44] The mass production and marketing of stereophonic sound equipment and the television beginning in the mid-1950s gave rise to the "home entertainment" system, a panoply of sight and sound that was only the beginning of what is today the near total immersion of modern citizens in a mass popular culture, the values of which may be only dimly recognized or understood by them. Contrary to talk of objectivity among the technologues – or the technical intelligentsia – of the New Class, new technologies often contain distinctive sets of values that reflect the wishes, aspirations, aims, or desires of those persons and organizations that produce or make possible these technologies in the first place.[45]

As Gouldner explains, as a result of the burgeoning of mass media and communications technologies "the shared beliefs people define as true and worthy could now be controlled from a remote distance, apart from and outside of the persons sharing the beliefs."[46] As entertainment values replace news and other civic values, public rationality is undermined, thus threatening the public good. Gouldner's observation made in the 1970s – that the increasing numbers of isolated hearers and speakers busily consuming predominantly entertainment values is fueling an inexorable decline of civic engagement in the public sphere – is virtually the same point that Robert Putnam has gotten so much mileage out of with regard to the thesis of declining social capital.[47]

It should also be noted that social media giants like Facebook, Twitter, YouTube, and Instagram are becoming increasingly influential agents of social control through the promulgation of various content moderation policies. The revelations that Russia and other nations attempted to interfere in the 2016 presidential election – where Republican Donald Trump defeated Democrat Hillary Clinton even as polling data had predicted an easy Clinton victory – led to concerns that such online disinformation campaigns posed a serious threat to democracy.[48] For example, a study on how information is disseminated on Twitter found that fake news travels six times faster than real news. Although there is a saying that truth is stranger than fiction, apparently the fictional travels much faster than the real.[49]

There are claims that social media platforms should merely make available the technologies and the meeting places for bringing persons together to openly and freely discuss issues of the day, but when they restrict content and sometimes even suspend or ban accounts – as Twitter, Facebook, and YouTube did to President Trump after the siege of the US Capitol in early 2021 which, they claim, was instigated, at least in some measure, by him – then they are violating rights to free speech, and often doing so in a biased manner. Concerns over media censorship of conservatives and Republicans led to House hearings in February 2021, but there was little in the way of legislative or policy recommendations resulting from them.[50]

On the other hand, others argue that even though lying and prevarication are generally considered forms of constitutionally protected speech according to the First Amendment – save for such utterances or writings that could be shown to be defamatory or libelous in a court of law, or of course lying under oath in a court proceeding which could bring a charge of perjury – the lies and disinformation spread across social media platforms which reach potentially millions of users, constitutes the kind of threat which social media corporations have an obligation to curtail.[51]

This is similar to the imbroglio that has erupted over the promulgation of speech codes to reduce or eliminate the problem of "hate speech" and other forms of discrimination in business and educational settings. How far organizations – particularly those located in the United States where hate speech is not officially recognized as a justiciable element of law – can go to control offensive speech, including the sanctioning of offenders, is still an unsettled question.[52] (For a summary of agents of socialization and the nature of social control associated with these domains, see table 3.1.)

An understanding of the nature and function of agents of socialization allows us to connect back to classical theorists such as Herbert Spencer, Lester Ward, Franklin Giddings, Emile Durkheim, and Georg Simmel, all of whom documented the fact that society exists to the extent that people are aggregated together and associate with one another across space and time. Because they do things together in groups, persons are allowed to do certain things and constrained from doing others. By the 1930s this insight began to be formalized by a number of thinkers in psychology, sociology, and social psychology. For example, Kurt Lewin asserted the existence of a group "climate" which was a key factor in shaping and directing group outcomes. In his Robber's Cave study, Muzafer Sherif also posited the importance of group culture in the creation and resolution of intergroup conflict. And a few years later sociologist William Foote Whyte showed

Table 3.1 Agents of Socialization and Types of Control Exerted

Domains of socialization	Agents of control		
	Informal	Legal	Medical
Family	Mother, father, siblings, and extended kin	Social workers	Family physician, health visitors (UK)
Community	Neighbors, local businesses, community organizations	Municipal planning, social and welfare services	Public health initiatives, community nurses
Schools	Students, teachers, PTAs, and other school personnel		School nurses and other school health professionals
Peers	Friends in schools, communities, day care, etc.		
Work	Coworkers, managers and supervisors	Administrative rules and regulations, e.g., legal department staff	Employee Assistance Programs (EAPs), and related organizational health professionals
Religion	Priests, members of the congregation		
Mass media	Music, film, television, and sports celebrities, as well as expert "talking heads" who form reference groups for some viewers		
Legal system		Police, judges, lawyers	

how status hierarchies in groups are formed, and how in turn such structuring impacts not only the group's culture but also the personal identities of its members.[53]

Solomon Asch: how groups shape individual conformity

The groundwork laid by Lewin, Sherif, and Whyte, among others, paved the way for even more sophisticated studies of the ways in which groups shape, modify, and sometimes distort the judgments of individual members. Solomon E. Asch published a paper in 1951 which reported on a series of experiments investigating the effects of group pressure upon the judgments of individuals.[54] Research subjects were asked to look at two cards. One card contained a single line, and the other card contained three lines of varying lengths. The subject's task was to judge which of the three lines (A, B, or C) on the second card was closest to the length of the line on the first card, and to proclaim his or her judgment publicly (see figure 3.1). Unbeknownst to the subject, however, all the other persons in the room who were given the same task were confederates of the experimenter. In this particular version of the experiment each of seven bogus subjects gave an obviously wrong answer when it was their turn to judge the length of

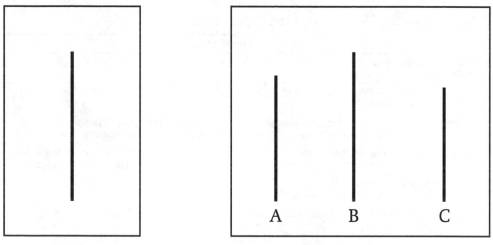

Card 1   Card 2

Note: Research subjects were given Card 1 and asked to judge which line in Card 2 matched the line in Card 1. Here, B is clearly the correct answer. However, confederates in the experiment were instructed to always give the wrong answer, either A or C. The experiment examined the effects of the erroneous majority on the subject's judgments. Adopted with modifications from Asch (1952, p. 452).

Figure 3.1 The Asch Experiment

lines. The research subject, who was always called on last, faced the difficulty of having to decide whether or not to go along with a group of people whose judgments were obviously in error.

Even though the errors made by the bogus subjects were large (ranging from ½" to 1¾" differences in the lengths of lines which they declared to be equivalent), 32 percent of the naïve subjects still went along with the majority. What Asch demonstrated in this experiment is that a surprisingly large number of persons will go along with the majority even when they are clearly wrong. In variations of this experiment, Asch reduced the number of bogus subjects from seven to three. The question was: Would a majority of three persons offering erroneous judgments be as effective as a majority of seven? The answer was yes. The probability that a naïve subject will go along with the judgments of a mistaken majority is not increased significantly as the size of the majority is increased beyond three members. Indeed, a majority of three is much more powerful and persuasive than a majority of seven with one dissenting vote. This finding supports Georg Simmel's theory that the effects of group size are not altered appreciably beyond the level of the triad or the three-person group.[55] In other words, the crucial effect of group size is found in the transition from the dyad to the triad. All things being equal, then, not much changes when a group grows from three to four, five, or more members.

Another point illustrated in Asch's experiments is the importance of *social support*. A lone dissenting voice against a majority of three or more is not very effective. However, add just one person who supports the lone dissenter, and the effects can be profound, even against a much larger majority. When a person acts or thinks in ways that go against group consensus, the dissenting person is seen as, and often labeled, strange, weird, odd, sick, or deviant. Persons generally conform to group expectations, then, simply to avoid being labeled as defective or deficient by others. Nevertheless, persons who are able to find others who act or think like them can mitigate somewhat the negative sanctions imposed by a group against non-conformers. As Cass Sunstein has observed, such dissenters can counter the "conformity effect" that groups typically impose on their members.[56] In summary, new information may indeed lead to legitimate belief change, but an even more important factor leading to changing one's stance on an issue, as seen in recent experimental research on mock juries, is the effect of normative influence, that is, the pressures groups exert on persons holding minority positions.[57]

Later research on conformity and obedience

In documenting the ways in which groups structure conformity in individuals, and how in turn individuals may resist social control measures, especially when various forms of social support are available, Asch's work paved the way for more sophisticated research and theorizing in the social psychology of conformity, deviance, and social control. For example, a few years after Asch's conformity experiments began appearing, Stanley Milgram, a student of Asch, began his own series of experiments on the nature of obedience.[58]

Milgram's Obedience Experiments

In a series of famous experiments, Milgram told research subjects that they would be participating in a learning experiment in which they would be instructed to give an electric shock to other subjects whenever they did not provide the correct answer in a paired word test. The cover story was that the experiment was designed to examine the effects of punishment on memory and learning. The true aim of the experiment, however, was to see how far research subjects would go in delivering shocks to other research subjects. The research subjects who were receiving the shocks were not true research subjects, however, but confederates of the researcher. And the "shocks" being delivered by the naïve subjects were not shocks at all, only elaborate-looking devices that made it appear as if other research subjects were receiving sometimes high voltage shocks whenever a button was pushed or a lever was pulled.

The naïve subjects were the ones delivering the shocks at the prodding and prompting of experimenters. Milgram varied a few things in the experiment to ascertain under what conditions subjects would deliver the maximum voltage shocks, even as those receiving the shocks were sometimes screaming in pain or begging the research subject to stop. For example, Milgram discovered that subjects were more likely to deliver the maximum voltage shock when the experimenter was standing next to them in the room, rather than giving orders from another room. In the 1963 experiment, 26 of 40 test subjects (or 65 percent) did indeed deliver the highest shocks on the generator, which was a complete surprise both to Milgram and to outside observers after the results of the experiments were published.

The issue of obedience to authority became a pressing issue especially after World War II and the discovery of the Nazi atrocities at Auschwitz in which some six million Jews were exterminated between 1933 and 1945. Many persons asked how it was possible that Nazi soldiers and other functionaries of Hitler's regime could follow orders to kill on such a widespread and grotesque level. Beyond trying to explain how a genocide of this magnitude could occur, however, Milgram also faced the realization that with the rise of the professions in modern society, more and more persons routinely were turning to a variety of "experts" in various fields including medicine, law, business and finance, education, but also in the burgeoning "helping professions" such as social work, marriage and family therapy, mental health counseling, public health, and so forth. The proliferation of experts across growing expanses of everyday life pointed to something like a willing acquiescence on the part of citizens to this growing legion of perceived authority figures, a cultural trend that seemed to be verified in the Milgram experiments.

A theoretical perspective known as dramaturgical theory, developed by Erving Goffman beginning in the 1950s, is one of the best single perspectives for anchoring understandings of what goes on in face-to-face interaction, the realm within which much informal control is accomplished. We turn next to an analysis of the key concepts and ideas of Goffman.

Erving Goffman and dramaturgical theory

At the frontispiece of his 1971 book *Relations in Public*, Erving Goffman quoted Herbert Spencer at length on the topic of his concept of "ceremonial institutions." Here is part of what Spencer had to say:

> If, disregarding conduct that is entirely private, we consider only that species of conduct which involves direct relations with other persons; and if under the name government we include all control of such conduct, however arising; then we must say that the earliest kind of government, the most general kind of government, and the government which is ever spontaneously recommencing, is the government of ceremonial observance.[59]

Goffman found Spencer's insight useful because it lends strong credence to the idea that the kind of things we do to extend courtesies and considerations to others in face-to-face engagements is the most ancient of all forms of social control and the foundation for other, more formal types which later arise. Without identifying it as such, Spencer's concept of "ceremonial control" is what we have been calling informal control throughout the book. Spencer is arguing that even the most primitive human groups display forms of deference and accommodation to others, and that these displays predate later formalized or institutionalized controls such as those of religion and law. As Spencer explains,

> A political system or a settled cult, cannot suddenly come into existence, but implies pre-established subordination. Before there are laws, there must be submission to some potentate enacting and enforcing them. Before religious obligations are recognized, there must be acknowledged one or more super-natural powers. Evidently, then, the behavior expressing obedience to a ruler, visible or invisible, must precede in time the civil or religious restraints he imposes. And this inferable precedence of ceremonial government is a precedence we everywhere find.[60]

We will see this attention to the ceremonial and ritual aspects of face-to-face conduct scattered throughout Goffman's work.

Erving Goffman received his Ph.D. from the University of Chicago in 1953, an institution that already had a well-established tradition of personal ethnographies of the city (primarily of Chicago itself) conducted largely from a situational or interactionist perspective. Even so, the interpretive or symbolic interactionist strand of Goffman's thinking was counterbalanced by a strand of thought heavily influenced by functionalist anthropology (e.g., Durkheim, Malinowski, and Radcliffe-Brown) as taught by Chicago anthropologist W. Lloyd Warner. Indeed, it was Warner who sent Goffman to the Shetland Islands to collect data for his dissertation "Communication Conduct in an Island Community," one of the first glimpses into Goffman's developing dramaturgical perspective.

In his dissertation, Goffman argued that face-to-face interaction represented a domain of activity that deserved to be studied in its own right. He called this domain the "interaction order." Some 30 years later, in his presidential address to the American Sociological Association, Goffman described the *interaction order* as the relatively stable sequence of events and activities that is generated whenever persons enter into each other's immediate presence.[61] When in each other's immediate presence, whatever joint activities are to be undertaken – whether talking with a friend, asking the time of day from a stranger, playing a game of baseball, working in an office, or sitting at the dinner table at home with the rest of the family – are understood on some level as always involving risks or at least uncertainties. These risks and uncertainties are of course always assumed to be minimized or held in abeyance when interacting with members of primary groups or in locations that are familiar and cozy – such as in one's home or, say, the front yard of a neighbor – but on some level occasions for face-to-face gatherings always expose our bodies and minds to vulnerabilities. As Goffman explains,

> So there are enablements and risks inherent in co-bodily presence. These contingencies being acute, they are likely everywhere to give rise to techniques of social management; and since the same basic contingencies are being managed, one can expect that across quite different societies the interaction order is likely to exhibit some markedly similar features.[62]

These "techniques of social management" amount to all the ways that persons in their everyday lives present themselves before a group of others. In other words, persons are always concerned about the figure they are cutting before a group of co-present others, and they comport their actions to fit with the expectations of this perceived moral universe. The *presentation of self* – which was the title of Goffman's first book[63] – is one of the overriding preoccupations of individuals (and of groups as well).

In some ways Goffman's dramaturgical theory is consistent with Shakespeare's assertion that "all the world is a stage." Like the theater, persons in everyday life perform on the *front stage*, and steal away to the *backstage* to rehearse for their public performances or simply to kick back and relax. For example, a professor who is delivering a lecture to his or her class does so on the front stage, and his or her audience are the students. And the professor prepares his or her lecture backstage, either in his or her office or at home away from the spotlight of the front stage. Because persons are concerned with self and team presentations, they are always alive to the nature of the audience in front of whom they are acting or performing and seek to come across as well-demeaned individuals or groups. A professor giving a lecture, for example, seeks to fulfill the tacit expectations of a competent performance, which involves having a command of the material, engaging in "free" talk rather than scripted talk, being able to use jocularity in appropriate ways, speaking clearly and varying the tone and tempo of his or her speech, and so forth.[64] Likewise, even though they are not likely to admit it, people at the swimming pool are alive to how they look to others, and will generally pick the most flattering swimsuits to accentuate the better parts of their bodies and hide the worst parts.[65] (For a summary of how the theater compares with real life, see table 3.2.)

An important and omnipresent strategy within self-presentation is *impression management*, which is simply the effort by individuals in inter-action to put their best foot forward. This amounts to emphasizing the positive aspects of self while downplaying or minimizing potentially discrepant information about oneself. For example, persons on first dates usually invest a good deal of time preparing for the date, which may include buying a new set of clothes, getting their hair done, tidying up their car or apartment, and rehearsing points of discussion – including flattery – all of which are calculated to make the best first impression possible. Will Rogers' famous saying is apt here: "You never get a second chance to make a good first impression."

The important thing to keep in mind is that impression management is not reserved only for first dates, job interviews, or other key events in a person's life. It is a pervasive feature of everyday life. For example, even among our family and closest friends, impression management through self or team presentations occurs with regularity. Even that most intimate act that takes place between a man and a woman, sexual intercourse, is a staged performance. Note also that most persons most of the time act with civility and decorum even among perfect strangers whom they are likely never to see again. Those that do not – panhandlers, prostitutes, the homeless, criminals, the mentally ill, and other assorted street characters that are a fixture in most urban industrial societies – are cast into the realm of the deviant, the disreputable, the incompetent, or the criminal.

Human beings have a range of tools in their interactional repertoire by which they can convey to others that they are not a threat, are "normal" according to the expectations of the situation, and are competent role

Table 3.2 Goffman's Dramaturgical Theory

Real life	The theater
Persons	Actors
Performing in roles	Playing parts
In a social setting	On a stage
Before a group of others	Before an audience

performers who can carry out their self or team presentations without a hitch. One such class of role resources for maintaining decorum and normal appearances are *interaction rituals*, which are sometimes fleeting or perfunctory acts by which persons convey to others in interaction that they are ratified participants in whatever activities are the focus of attention.[66] For example, when conversing with someone, the person who is in the role of listener will usually provide a steady stream of ritual support for the speaker in the form of nods of the head, a visible focus of attention such as maintaining eye contact, and verbal utterances such as "uh-huh," "yeah," "Oh really?," and "I hear you." Another kind of interaction ritual that is used in public places is the nod of the head or the perfunctory "Good day" whenever persons pass each other on the street or sidewalk. Notice also that most persons will greet even very casual acquaintances with a "hello" and often a "How are you doing?", even though the person asking the question may not really care at all how the person is doing.

Why would most persons be prompted or feel compelled to display these interaction rituals almost always and without exception? The reason is that persons are desperate to convey to others that they are well-demeaned individuals who are deserving of the kind of ritual support and consideration that they have offered up to others through their own displays of deferential and accommodating conduct. This aspect of propriety in interaction is especially noticeable in two other types of management devices, namely civil inattention and role distance.

First, *civil inattention* (or studied nonobservance) is the practice of acting as if you didn't see something when you really did.[67] Like interaction rituals, civil inattention is pervasive in everyday life. Consider the following example. One of the tacit norms of party-going is that you shouldn't be the first to arrive. Being first on the scene may display an unhealthy eagerness to have a good time, implying that you are lacking in this department on some level in your own life. Being aware of this, as you set out for the party, you look for signs that guests have already arrived, such as the number of cars parked in front of the host's house. When you arrive and do indeed notice few if any cars parked in front of the house, you are likely to simply drive past and occupy yourself with other things for the next 20 or 30 minutes.

When you arrive back at the house you are relieved to find that a number of additional cars are now parked in front, signaling that it is safe to make your appearance. You ring the doorbell, the host greets you and lets you in, and everything is wonderful. It looks like it's going to be a great party. But unbeknownst to you, the host happened to be looking out a window and spotted you driving by the first time. The host does not tell you of course, because to do so would be a breach of the framing rules of civil inattention.

Civil inattention is often invoked whenever territories of the self are brought into play, for example, when a person has a brief lapse in control of his or her own bodily functions. The classic example is the fart: The tacit norm for dealing with an audible fart on the part of the perpetrator is to admit to nothing, while those co-present others who heard the fart are expected to act as if they didn't hear or smell it either. Indeed, it would be a breach of civil inattention to say "Excuse me" after farting, for even the mere acknowledgment of the fart would bring embarrassment to all those assembled there. (Notice, however, that when someone belches at the dinner table an "Excuse me" is often permitted and expected, which points to the fact that different aspects of the territories of self have different interactional norms corresponding with them.) Embarrassment is contagious and can spread like wildfire, thereby posing one of the greatest dangers to the viability of face-to-face gatherings.

A second interactional resource, aligned somewhat closely with civil inattention, is role distance. *Role distance* is the tendency to place distance between one's authentic self and one's virtual self-in-role in particular situations.[68] An *authentic* self consists of all those attributes that a person can be shown to actually possess, while a *virtual* self consists of imputations made about a person, gleaned from the immediate situation, before verification can be made as to the accuracy of those imputations.[69] For example, persons confined in *total institutions* such as asylums, prisons, monasteries, boot camps, and similar types of all-encompassing organizations are often stripped of personal identity and made to conform to various forms of stigmatization as mandated by the organization, stemming largely from custodial arrangements concerning dress, behavior, communication, the types of recognition afforded to inmates, and so forth. Although some patients or inmates certainly acquiesce to the identity being foisted upon them by the institution, many rebel against the stigmatizing label however they can. Granted, they may give lip service and "play the game" as they comport their behavior to the expectations of line staff – this being their virtual self – but deep down they retain some fundamental essence, some conception of who they "really" are and bide their time until or when they can more fully utilize and present their authentic self. In the novel and movie *One Flew Over the Cuckoo's Nest*, Chief Bromden posed as a deaf and mute person while within the confines of the asylum, but he could actually hear and speak. This illustrates a radical divergence between the virtual and authentic self.

Role distance is not confined, however, only to the situation of inmates or to custody arrangements more generally. It is also a technique for managing interactional difficulties in everyday life. One day in a hotel lobby I noticed a young boy – perhaps no more than five or six years of age – being led by the hand into the women's restroom by a woman I presumed to be his mother. The boy was whining and resisting slightly, but when he saw that I saw him, he became more agitated and tried to break free from his mother's grip. She eventually dragged him into the restroom literally kicking and screaming.

A few minutes later I saw the boy and his mother emerge from the restroom, and I glanced away quickly so as to afford the boy as much civil inattention as possible. Out of the corner of my eye, however, I saw the boy approaching, and when he reached me he said, "Uh, mister, my Mommy needed help with something and my Daddy wasn't around."[70] This was a remarkable display of role distance, insofar as the boy was attempting to distance himself from the "virtual" self he was identified with by way of the bathroom incident. The human condition, then, is rife with various types of repair work, invoked whenever selves are in jeopardy, to uphold the definition of the situation, or to preserve the sanctity of social gatherings.

Conclusion

Goffman's dramaturgical theory is the premier theory of informal social control. Through careful study of face-to-face interaction over a career spanning some 30 years, Goffman identified a wide range of folkways, mores, and ceremonies by which persons attempt to maintain and preserve local social order. The lesson to be learned from Goffman's insights is that the social order of everyday life is fragile indeed, and this is why persons tend to go along with prevailing group sentiment. Absent good reasons to do otherwise, persons are inclined to not rock the boat, to go along with the group, to work hard to maintain normal appearances, to send clear messages to others that they are sane and can be trusted, and to control information with the aim of presenting the most flattering self-image possible.

Notice, however, with all this attention to self-presentation, impression management, and information control, persons also possess the ability to present distorted and even inauthentic images of themselves and their plans of action.[71] In other words, persons who are competent in the knowledge of a culture's folkways and mores regarding proper conduct in interpersonal relations can use this knowledge to fabricate frames of deception, dissemblance, or outright fraud. In this sense, secrecy is as important as open and honest communication.[72] The folkways of everyday life both enable and constrain the realization of the good life or the just society.

SUGGESTIONS FOR FURTHER READING

Marek Bugdol, *A Different Approach to Work Discipline* (2018)
Although there are many legal aspects of control of employee behavior in the workplace, for any organization to function smoothly there must exist a critical mass of "off the books," tacit, or informal understandings which constitute the organizational culture. Bugdol provides a systematic overview of informal systems of control operating in the workplace, including the nature of discipline and other forms of behavior modification and control.

Robert H. Frank, *Success and Luck: Good Fortune and the Myth of Meritocracy* (2016)
Frank argues that although hard work and ability are important in attaining the American Dream, it is also the case that those who have done well for themselves are reluctant to admit the extent to which chance and luck delivered the good life to them. Although meritocracy may not be a pure myth, it certainly has mythical elements which keeps reasonable policies from being implemented, such as progressive consumption taxes which would benefit everybody, including those who have done well for themselves.

Erving Goffman, *Presentation of Self in Everyday Life* (1959)
This book contains Goffman's earliest formulation of the dramaturgical theory of action, which is one of the most useful perspectives for understanding the world of everyday life, and especially of informal social control.

Georg Simmel, *The Sociology of Georg Simmel* (1950)
Simmel was one of the founders of German sociology and did most of his writing on sociological topics between 1890 and his death in 1918. This book, published in 1950, is one of the best compilations of Simmel's thought. In developing a perspective on sociology that emphasized the forms of human association, Simmel was one of the pioneers of the study of groups and group relations.

Cass Sunstein, *Conformity* (2019)
Sunstein summarizes and discusses literature from economics, sociology, psychology, and law on the various social influences which produce conformity. Also included is a timely chapter on group polarization, which in the political realm appears as hyperpartisanship (Schmitt's friends vs. enemies). Political partisanship became particularly acute and divisive during the Trump Administration.

DISCUSSION QUESTIONS

1. According to most sociologists, for better or worse, individuals are strongly influenced by their close relationships and associates. Is this correct? That is, maybe sociologists have overstated how much groups actually do control or influence their individual members. Give some examples of how individuals may, if they so choose, strike out on their own and reject the influences of primary, secondary, or reference groups.

2. There is a debate over the role of social media in influencing growing legions of users of these various platforms. Is this influence good, bad, or indifferent? Provide evidence to back your position.
3. In today's society are parents still the most important agents of socialization for youth? If not, why not? What has changed?
4. The popularity of homeschooling continues to grow. Take a position on homeschooling versus public schooling, explaining why one is better than the other.
5. Is participation in sports effective in keeping youth from engaging in delinquency or criminality later in life? Summarize at least two studies on this topic beyond those highlighted in the chapter and report your findings.

Chapter 4
Medical Control

Introduction

In 1851 Samuel A. Cartwright, a respected Louisiana physician, published a paper in *The New Orleans Medical and Surgical Journal* in which he claimed to have discovered a new disease which he called "drapetomania." At the time in southern states like Louisiana it was legal to own slaves, and drapetomonia was supposedly a condition which caused slaves to run away from their masters.[1]

Cartwright provides one of the earliest modern examples of *medicalization*, which is the process by which personal and social problems are redefined as psychiatric or medical problems. Medicalization is one aspect of *medical social control*, which may be defined as

> the ways in which medicine functions (wittingly or unwittingly) to secure adherence to social norms – specifically, by using medical means to minimize, eliminate, or normalize deviant behavior.[2]

Medical terminology, discourses, and ways of thinking are pervasive and omnipresent especially in Western society, due largely to the high status physicians enjoy relative to other occupations or professions. As Renée Fox has argued, doctors are imbued with a "cloak of competence" that sets them apart from most of the other learned professions, including law, education, and even the clergy.[3] Medicine acts powerfully as a normalizing discourse, and medical practitioners – as well as a growing legion of non-physicians who have adopted medical discourse and terminology as their own – speak authoritatively about such things as disease, illness, pathology, syndromes, health, wellness, and pathogens, to name a few.[4]

As discussed in previous chapters, the earliest human societies relied on informal methods of control. In the most primitive hunter-gatherer stage, humans relied largely on superstition and tribal customs to ensure conformity of its members. With the rise of the early Greco-Roman city-states (third-century BC), the legal and ethical philosophies of thinkers such as Plato viewed most social ills – including crime and vice more generally – as arising from ignorance. As Williams and Arrigo explain, "More precisely, virtue is knowledge, while vice is ignorance."[5]

By the early Middle Ages, philosophical inquiry was replaced by theological speculation. The earlier "crime as vice" perspective, which was inferred from the determination of the virtuous life as formulated within the context of ethical and political theorizing, was replaced by a "crime as sin" perspective fueled by the growth of Christianity, and especially of Catholicism. Even as this transition from "crime as vice" to "crime as sin" occurred between the Greco-Roman era and the Middle Ages, both of these eras were similar in that small groups such as the family, clan, or tribe effectively held individuals in check. This system of collective responsibility for the control of deviance and the maintenance of social order Michel Foucault has aptly described as the *many watch the few*.[6] The "many" refers to society-at-large, while the "few" refers to those persons, infrequent in number, who dared violate the normative order. If only a few persons are deviating, this means that the system of informal, group-based control was effective. With crime rates low or nonexistent in early societies – indeed, in these early societies there likely was not even a distinct criminal law – there was very little thought given to the need for experts or specialists who would carry out control duties for society.

As Michel Foucault and others have argued, in the transition from the primitive to the modern era, societal perspectives on deviance have changed as well.[7] The earliest societies (from human antiquity through the 1600s) tended to view deviants as ignorant (lacking ethics or virtue) or *sinful*; the era of early modernity (from the 1600s through the mid-1800s) tended to view deviants as *bad*, rooted either in bad genes (the biological explanation) or because persons simply choose to act in non-conforming ways (the utilitarian explanation); and in later modernity and postmodernity (from the mid-1800s until today) deviants tend to be viewed as *sick* and in need of treatment or rehabilitation rather than punishment. (As we will see in chapter 8, however, since the 1970s rehabilitation as a goal of the criminal justice system has declined in favor of harsher and more punitive sanctions such as incarceration. Nevertheless, the therapeutic ethos remains a prominent feature of Western societies outside of the context of formal corrections.) It is this latter stage of development of modernity within which medical social control rises to prominence, concomitant to the growth of medicine and allied professional and occupational groups. Although medicine competes with law for dominance in the realm of formal control, as we shall see, it is often complicit with law as well.

This chapter is concerned with providing a comprehensive overview of the nature of medical control. We begin with an overview of Talcott Parsons' concept of the sick role. Parsons argued that illness is a type of deviance which calls forth particular agents of social control, namely, physicians and other healthcare providers. Indeed, for Parsons the sick role is merely one aspect of his functionalist theory of society. Even as the most influential American sociologist through the mid-1960s, Parsons was at times far too naïvely optimistic and uncritical concerning what he took to be the high levels of professionalism and altruism of physicians as they dutifully tend to the sick and needy.

Although the contemporary trend is toward a continuing growth of medicalization, the introduction of such concepts as demedicalization, remedicalization, and biomedicalization will illustrate that medicine acts in neither a unitary nor unidirectional fashion with regard to its control function. Even so, one thing that continues to facilitate the growth of medicalization is the therapeutic ethos of modern Western societies, a cultural orientation which places great emphasis on the self and self-fulfillment, and especially on the emotional and physical well-being of its citizens. Further, we will examine to what extent medical control impacts men and women differently, if at all. Lastly, we will discuss the problem of the exclusion of evil as it relates to medical control.

Parsons' sick role

Talcott Parsons developed a functionalist theory which conceptualizes society as a social system composed of various interrelated parts (e.g., major social institutions such as the economy, the government, the family, the medical profession, and so forth). Just as the various parts of the system are interrelated, there also exist functional relations between individuals and society. As discussed throughout the book, the various mechanisms of social control act to induce or compel persons into norm-conforming behavior. Likewise, the primary function of medicine is to help persons cope with illness or sickness, and medical interventions are geared toward returning persons to a state of health.

The traditional understanding of deviance is that because persons who come to be labeled deviant chose to violate the moral or legal order, they deserve to be punished. But since illness is not typically volitional or planned, for this type of deviance, therapy or treatment is favored over punishment. Just as the role of the physician in modern society is institutionalized, so too is the role of persons who are ill. Indeed, according to Parsons, those who are ill play the *sick role*, which represents a bundle of institutionalized actions and expectations informing the behavior of the ill as well as understandings for how to respond to and deal with them.[8] There are four basic elements of the sick role corresponding with the four functional requisites of any social system (designated as AGIL: adaptation, goal-attainment, integration, and latent pattern maintenance). These are as follows:

- Sick persons are exempted, at least temporarily, from normal social role responsibilities, which represents the *behavioral* dimension of the role (fulfilling the function of *adaptation*);
- For persons to be temporarily exempted from their normal activities at the behavioral level, there also must be a higher level institutionalization of norms and values which specifies patterned and predictable responses by both the ill and medical personnel; this is the *institutional* or structural dimension of the sick role (fulfilling the function of *integration*);
- There exists a prevailing, generally widespread and accepted definition of illness as undesirable, which represents the *cultural* dimension of the role (fulfilling the function of *latent pattern maintenance*);
- There is also placed on ill persons the responsibility to seek competent professional help, which represents the *motivational* dimension of the role (fulfilling the function of *goal-attainment*).

This is all well and good, but wittingly or unwittingly Parsons established a tradition within medical sociology which tended to view sickness as an institutionalized condition of society requiring the generally unchallenged and taken-for-granted expertise of doctors, whose duty it is to restore their patients to health. Because the condition of wellness is so highly valued, the power of doctors and everyone else claiming some form of medical or therapeutic expertise increased accordingly, or so the sentiment goes. For better or worse, it is this sentiment which underlies the ideas of medicalization and the growing prominence of medical social control in modern society.

Medicine and social control

In his article titled "Medicine as an Institution of Social Control," Irving Zola provides one of the earliest and clearest statements on the growth of medicine and its role as a social control agent in modern society. As Zola explains,

> [M]edicine is becoming a major institution of social control, nudging aside, if not incorporating, the more traditional institutions of religion and law. It is becoming the new repository of truth, the place where absolute and often final judgments are made by supposedly morally neutral and objective experts. And these judgments are made, not in the name of virtue or legitimacy, but in the name of health. Moreover, this is not occurring through the political power physicians hold or can influence, but is largely an insidious and often undramatic phenomenon accomplished by "medicalizing" much of daily living, by making medicine and the labels "healthy" and "ill" *relevant* to an ever increasing part of human existence.[9]

Over the last 40 years social policy and law arenas have reflected the continuing concerns that nation-states have with regard to the health and well-being of its citizens. In concert with the insurance industry, unprecedented steps have been taken to minimize losses due to accidents, illness, and death. These health policies and initiatives, incorporated into civil, criminal, and administrative law at the federal, state, and municipal levels, operate at both the group and the individual level. The two branches of medicine that are particularly well-suited to taking up and overseeing the health of the citizenry are psychiatry and public health.

Psychiatry functions primarily at the individual level, insofar as the aim is to instill prosocial adjustment in persons who are suffering from any number of recognized mental illnesses as documented in the *Diagnostic and Statistical Manual of Mental Disorders* (or *DSM*), the "bible" for psychiatric and mental health practitioners. In this sense, psychiatrists have purview over the medical aspects of the mind, subjectivity, and social behavior, just as doctors for many years have held a monopoly over the medical aspects of the body. Both psychiatry and regular medicine employ a case-method approach, seeking to return to health individual minds or individual bodies.

At the group or societal level is the *public health* approach or model, which may be defined as the "art and the science of preventing disease, prolonging life, and promoting health."[10] Through routine surveillance of populations or segments of populations that are considered to be at risk, data is gathered for purposes of ascertaining which antecedent factors are associated with unwanted health or behavioral outcomes. Based upon these data, interventions are implemented which presumably reduce or eliminate the social harm connected with these unwanted activities or processes. Some of the better known public health programs that have been initiated over the years include the campaign to reduce smoking; battles against infectious or noninfectious diseases such as typhoid, heart disease, cancer, and arteriosclerosis; removal or reduction of environmental hazards such as asbestos or lead paint in homes, businesses, and schools; needle-exchange programs to combat the transmission of HIV; and condom distribution in schools to reduce both unwanted teenage pregnancies and the spread of venereal disease.

We will examine the public health model more closely in a later chapter, but here it is important to note that successful public health campaigns against infectious diseases and other medical conditions have emboldened proponents of public health to expand their mandate to include a variety of social problems. Instead of medicalization, in this context we may suggest that a sort of *hygienization* or even *public healthification* is occurring.[11] For example, the continuing concern over obesity has led to the healthification of school lunches, whereby traditional foods such as chicken nuggets or french fries are being replaced by food items with lower salt and fat content, while whole milk and soda are removed as drink options.[12] This embodies the rise of the "food police."

Relational disorders

It should also be noted that psychiatrists are attempting to expand their mandate beyond the treatment of sick individuals. Instead of diagnosing only individuals as suffering from mental disorders, some prominent members of the American Psychiatric Association are urging the establishment of a new category of mental illness that pertains to groups such as families, peer groups, work groups, or even terrorist organizations. If accepted for inclusion in the next edition of the *DSM*, this new class of "relational disorders" would view otherwise healthy individuals as "unhealthy" within the context of certain relationships or group settings.[13]

Relational disorders have shown up provisionally in *DSM-5* under the category of *V codes* which are listed as "other conditions that may be a focus of clinical attention." Even so, there is a further provision that warns that "these codes are **not** mental disorders" (emphasis in original document). A number of V codes for relational disorders dealing primarily with families are listed, including:

- parent-child relation problem
- sibling relation problem
- upbringing away from parents
- child affected by parental relationship distress
- relationship distress with spouse or intimate partner
- disruption of family by separation or divorce
- high expressed emotion level within family
- uncomplicated bereavement.[14]

There are parallel movements within law to shift away from liberal assumptions about human beings as autonomous, independent, and rational in their consideration of the costs and benefits of any line of action, and toward a relational view which emphasizes that no person is an island, meaning that selfhood is a product of society and not independently produced or developed.[15] That is to say, it is only communitarianism that gives rise to a true self – a relational self – as opposed to the hollowed-out, atomistic self of liberalism.[16]

Additionally, under the assumptions of laissez-faire liberalism from Adam Smith and J.S. Mill forward, governments took a "hands-off" policy toward individuals and intervened only when there was compelling evidence that their actions caused harm to others.[17] With the establishment of criminal law across Western societies, and especially with the advent of municipal policing in the 1830s, the category of "victimless crimes" – such as prostitution, drug use, public drunkenness, gambling, and suicide – emerged as well.[18] These special categories of self-harm launched a protracted tug-of-war between proponents of medicalization on one side and criminalization on the other, while a large group of persons in the middle held to a purer libertarian view that such self-harms should be left to the indignation of the community or to charitable work, that is, to morality and informal control.

The proponents of medicalization view these kinds of self-harm as illnesses that should be dealt with by the formal and institutionalized systems of medicine, including those of public health, while proponents of legalization (or criminalization) argue that they are crimes that are within the purview of the criminal justice system and its legal practitioners – police, prosecutors, lawyers, and judges – who can safeguard the due process rights of the accused even while convictions or other legal sanctions are sought. The heavy drinking of alcohol (or substance abuse with or without verified addiction) has been a key focal point in ongoing battles between medicalization and criminalization and recently, in an effort to extend the logic of relational disorders even further, there has been a shift away from viewing problems with alcohol as merely self-harm and toward viewing it as *harm to others*. This perspective emphasizes how the self-harm of inebriation often leads to broader social harms perpetrated by the drunk or inebriated. The four major categories of harm to others linked to substance abuse are violence, family deprivation, crime, and neglect and abuse of children.[19] Two of these categories (violence and crime) are clearly criminal justice matters, while the other two (family deprivation and child abuse and neglect) are more apt to come to the attention of social workers and psy-complex practitioners such as clinicians and counselors. Overall, women are two-and-one-half times more likely than men to suffer severe harm from known or unknown drinkers.[20]

There is also growing attention to the likelihood that inebriated persons run a higher risk of being harmed by others, to the extent that while under the influence of alcohol or other substances they have diminished mental capacities and are unable to think clearly about what is going on. This could increase the risk of being taken advantage of, including sexual assault or rape.[21] Even though this represents the crime of assault for which legal control has first rights, whenever diminished capacities are involved, there is the potential for medicalization, the discussion of which will continue in the next section.

Medicalization, demedicalization, and remedicalization

Although medicalization refers to the process by which a growing number of social and personal issues are converted into medical problems, by no means is the growth of medicalization unidirectional or unilinear. Medicalization is more aptly described as growing in fits and starts, with some areas of society falling under the auspices of medical control faster than others.[22]

Occasionally areas that were previously the province of medical expertise and intervention are *demedicalized*, meaning that medical understandings and treatment of the condition no longer apply or take precedent. A prime example of both medicalization and demedicalization is homosexuality.[23] Even as great pioneers of psychiatry such as Sigmund Freud, Carl Jung, and Alfred Adler viewed homosexuality as a mental disorder, by the 1960s this scientific consensus began eroding and was eventually rejected. Interestingly enough, this changing perception of the status of homosexuality as a mental illness was due not to dramatic new breakthroughs in the scientific evidence concerning this "disease." Rather, external factors such as changing social mores concerning the acceptability of homosexuality (as a concomitant to the sort of political activism embodied in the gay rights movement of the 1960s) were much more decisive. When the third edition of *DSM* was published in 1980, homosexuality was dropped for good as a category of mental illness. Just like drapetomania a century earlier, homosexuality disappeared from the official lexicon and imagination of medical practitioners. The immediate consequence of this demedicalization of homosexuality was that it was left as an issue for other realms of control, most notably those of everyday life and of law and politics, to grapple over, define, and respond to. Even so, in the early stages of the HIV/AIDS epidemic, there was a brief remedicalization of homosexuality to the extent that it was considered a "gay disease."[24]

Other examples of demedicalization include the continuing expansion of the availability of over-the-counter drugs which no longer require a doctor's prescription; a more inclusive or tolerant view of sexual practices that previously were viewed as "kinky" or pathological; a return to prominence of non-medical views of lactation; and new cultural attitudes toward the normalization of persons who are overweight and rejection of the stigmatizing clinical label "obese."[25] With regard to the latter, there are new concerns over fat-shaming and a greater tolerance of diverse body shapes and sizes. Nevertheless, there is currently much confusion and conflict over whether and under what circumstances medical concerns with obesity are accepted versus newer cultural attitudes toward fat acceptance. For example, even as President Donald Trump was widely criticized for his demeaning attitudes towards women, the disabled, immigrants, and other groups, there was widespread and acceptable versions of fat-shaming directed toward Trump himself in seeming retaliation for his own fat-shaming of others.[26]

Biomedicalization and "selling sickness"

Medicalization occurred largely as a result of the massive expansion of medicine between 1890 and 1945, including the professionalization of medical practice and innovations in pharmaceutical technologies along with advances in knowledge of human biology and physiology. This constituted the first great transformation of medicine.[27] The second great transformation began after 1945, as continuing advances in science, technology (especially computer technology), and pharmaceuticals have given rise to innovations such as molecular biology, biotechnologies, genomization, transplant medicine, cloning, and the extension not only of life expectancy but also the quality of life to levels never before imagined.[28]

The term for this transformation is *biomedicalization*, which inexorably renders less relevant the human element in medical care and treatment while elevating to prominence the use of technological and pharmaceutical interventions. For example, more than 30 years ago Henry Gadsen, the head of Merck, one of the world's largest drug companies, told *Forbes* magazine that he would like to expand his clientele beyond just sick people to include virtually everybody. Indeed, his dream was to market and sell drugs to everyone.[29] With the continuing rise in prominence of the medical and allied professions, the acceptance and use of the disease metaphor in everyday life, the near obsession with reducing risk and harm by governments and everyday citizens, and the emphasis placed on "quality of life" in public health, medicine, and even community policing, that dream of Gadsen's has come true. Human beings are turning with increasing regularity to the use of drugs for the minor aches and pains associated with modern living. This is at the heart of biomedicalization, an increasingly prominent form of medical control.

Connected with biomedicalization is the observation that medicalization is spurred on not so much by the purposive efforts of self-interested doctors and allied health professionals. As Frank Furedi argues, medicalization is no longer a top-down phenomenon (if it ever truly was), but instead a grass-roots phenomenon being prodded along by growing legions of "patients" who insist on medical interventions for a variety of everyday difficulties.[30] And given the presence of this growing number of savvy and informed individuals clamoring for medical and drug treatments, drug companies have been more than willing to oblige them in their quest to become – and remain – patients. Hence, "selling sickness" has become big business, and a sort of *disease mongering* has arisen, a situation whereby individuals are informed about and seek drug treatments for such things as male pattern baldness, erectile dysfunction, social anxiety disorder, emotional trauma, as well as a growing list of addictions and phobias.[31] This is the general problem of overdiagnosis – for example, ordering more medical tests or screenings for relatively harmless conditions or "just to be safe" in the unlikely event that the patient actually has an illness.[32] And as we will see in chapters 7 and 10, overdiagnosis and disease mongering are part of a broader cultural trend toward what Orrin Klapp calls the "inflation of symbols," or the proclivity to turn "nothing into something, or at least little into much."[33]

Public health and criminal justice

With the rise of the nation-state and the concept of citizenship, human beings began to be assessed and understood more and more in economic terms, that is, in terms of citizens being "resources" that the state may use to pursue collective political and social goals. It begins with such things as taxation (forced payments to the state to offset operating expenses) and conscription (forced military service), but then expands into more areas of social life, including the idea that persons ought not do things that jeopardize their own or others' safety. Since medicine had already been on the scene to provide authoritative pronouncements about the nature of human health and illness, it was only natural that the professional complex of medicine would be placed in the service of the state, largely through the granting of licenses for the provision of medical services, but also for informing legislative bodies about the health risks citizens faced.

In the United States the history of public health initiatives was at best haphazard and sporadic at least through the early twentieth century. In the southern United States especially, public health initiatives were not embarked upon in any systematic fashion until only after full-blown health crises emerged. For example, it was not until the 1870s that full legislative efforts to implement public health measures were enacted, this in response to a deadly plague of yellow fever which had been introduced through the port of New Orleans and which had spread as far north as Ohio.[34] By an act of Congress the port was eventually quarantined, in stiff opposition to local politicians and citizens who saw it as an unwarranted intrusion of federal authority and control. During the Progressive Era, attempts to establish a national health department failed, even as a Committee of One Hundred on National Health was convened in 1908 to examine the possibility of assembling a cabinet-level bureau of health. Yet, even with the support of President Theodore Roosevelt and later President William Howard Taft, states' rights advocates along with the American Medical Association – which was reluctant to cede professional authority to a new government bureaucracy – effectively thwarted the initiative.[35]

Nevertheless, precedents established in law tend to take on a life of their own, and over time more and more federally-mandated medical interventions emerged, based on the success of many such programs implemented in the southern United States and elsewhere. Unlike the uneven and erratic impetus toward public health law that emerged in the United States, however, England's public health initiatives happened earlier and on the whole were better planned and managed. The Public Health Act, passed in England in 1848, was in response to

> the gross damage to human life engendered by the industrial revolution. To seek work and financial security, there was mass emigration from rural into urban life. The towns were not prepared for this and the consequent

overcrowding, squalor and poverty created serious misery and disease affecting a large proportion of the working population. Over time, this threatened to engulf English society as a whole as disease spread across the poverty line into "polite" society.[36]

Some of the earliest mapping of cities occurred in Britain, as citizens and especially city administrators increasingly became concerned with the public health of industrial cities. In 1842 Edwin Chadwick, secretary of the Poor Commission, published a detailed map of cities such as Leeds and Bethnal Green (in London), indicating by color "less clean houses" (in brown) but also outbreaks of diseases such as cholera (in blue). Authorities could, in effect, exert social control through political surveillance of cities, keeping tabs not only on publicly avowed health issues, but also enabling "cartographic surveillance of centres of social radicalism."[37]

The successes of modern public health campaigns has led to a call for the criminal justice system to become more proactive, that is, to stop bad things before they even have a chance to start, rather than simply reacting to them after-the-fact. This idea of making criminal justice more like public health has accelerated since the terror attacks of 9/11.[38] This means also that the public health value of utility would displace the traditional criminal justice value of technical justice, and public safety is more likely to be defined as the leading criminal justice mandate (as seen especially in the case of post 9/11 policing). And indeed, the Covid-19 pandemic effectively merged the utility values of public health and public safety as local governments mandated lockdowns of the citizenry to act proactively to ward off spread of the disease.[39] Where public safety and public health effectively merge, there is no meaningful distinction between curtailing citizens' liberties because a terrorist might detonate a bomb or someone may be infected with the coronavirus.[40]

This conflict between the values of utility and justice returns us once again to the issue of victimless crimes, which are criminalized by way of *mala prohibita* laws which are laws that make things illegal by decree, that is, by passage of an ordinance specifying which acts are considered to fall under the jurisdiction of legal control. *Mala prohibita* laws are contrasted against *mala in se* laws, the latter of which are laws which make illegal a range of acts which presumably most reasonable persons can agree are bad in and of themselves, including things like murder, rape, assault, robbery, and theft. The point is that unlike *mala in se* crimes, *mala prohibita* or victimless crimes do not have a high level of citizen consensus regarding the extent to which such acts are truly criminal in nature.

Crimes that can be characterized as *mala prohibita*, such as drug use and sexual deviance, are more likely than other crimes to be caught in a tug-of-war between proponents of medicalization on the one hand, and criminalization on the other. For example, is drug use a crime, a sickness, or perhaps both? Is the best response to drug use the public safety response which seeks to treat offenders rather than punish them? This might mean a complete circumvention of their due process rights in favor of fast-tracking them into drug treatment "for their own good." Or is the best response the standard law and order and crime control responses of the criminal justice system, where drug defendants are tried as criminals for their drug-related behaviors, but who also are afforded the full gamut of legal protections by the state which must bear the highest level burden of proof, namely "beyond a reasonable doubt"? Which forms if any of "deviant" sexuality are we willing to criminalize or medicalize, and how far should it go? For example, should prostitution best be viewed as a crime, an illness, or neither (such as the case of decriminalization of prostitution in certain counties in Nevada)?

The debate over medicalization versus criminalization could become entirely moot if societal attitudes toward *mala prohibita* crimes continue tipping toward the position that many acts currently classified as criminal should be redefined as illnesses. For example, the "psychopathology of crime" perspective argues that all forms of crime and deviant behavior fall under the category of psychopathology insofar as crime or deviance is not "normal" whether in a statistical, moral, or legal sense. In this most radical version of the argument, treatment tribunals would replace judges and criminal courts, culminating in what many refer to as the therapeutic state.[41] In the next few sections we will examine the idea of the therapeutic state – and the ethos or culture lying behind it – in somewhat more detail.

The therapeutic ethos

It was mentioned earlier that medicalization proceeds and is prodded along largely at the behest of persons who do not themselves hold medical degrees. However, it is not only in the areas of service provision in business and other major institutional settings that we see a proliferation of quasi-medical personnel in support of legitimate medical personnel. The cultures of modern Western society – especially those of the United States and the United Kingdom – are also thoroughly suffused with the language, terminology, and epistemological assumptions of sickness, disease, wellness, rehabilitation, and recovery. James Nolan has referred to this as the *therapeutic ethos*, a cultural orientation in which, in their interpersonal dealings with others, persons are apt to interpret and act upon situations in terms of the assumptions of mental health, emotivism, developmentalism, and a "confessional" mode of problem-solving which emphasizes the talking out of feelings or other presumably private, internal matters.[42]

In earlier times, when the church was the leading source of morality, wisdom, and truth, priests tended to the spiritual needs of true believers through the private confessional. This normalizing discourse has of course over time been transformed into the normalizing discourses of medicine and psychiatry, where persons put themselves on public display through the sharing of feelings and emotions, especially when untoward activities are associated with an individual. Indiscretions by public figures, such as the sex scandals of pro golfer Tiger Woods and Democratic Congressman Anthony Weiner, led to both making public admissions of the wrongfulness of their behavior and checking into rehabilitation clinics for "sex addiction." Making a clean break of things in the therapeutic culture means being willing to tell others how new insights about one's self, gained as a result of mental health interventions, have transformed the individual, presumably for the better.[43]

The therapeutic ethos is also evident with self-esteem training in schools, and the assumption that children possess fragile self-concepts which must be protected against the profanations of a rough-and-tumble world. For example, in organized sports it may now be deemed illegitimate to lump children into the categories of "winners" and "losers," because being labeled as such for being on the losing team damages fragile self-esteem. This means that it is more important to attend to feelings, emotions, and the shoring up of fragile self-esteem than it is to maintain the integrity of competition in sporting events. As a consequence, some schools have moved toward a policy of not keeping score of games, at least not among the younger age groups who are felt to be too immature and emotionally incompetent to handle the pain of defeat.[44] Paying homage to feelings in this way is the hallmark of the therapeutic culture.

Additionally, in a modern, enlightened and technologically-advanced society, there is a strong belief that many of the bad things that happen in life – accidents, disease and sickness, death, broken hearts, unsatisfying marriages, uncertainty, being bullied, feeling sad, anxious, nervous, jittery, stressed out, or traumatized – can be reduced or even eliminated with the proper application of cutting-edge scientific, medical, social scientific, or behavioral science knowledge. Modern nation-states have a vested interest in the maximization of the life chances, productivity, and happiness of its citizens, primarily through the private business sector's ability to create such life-enhancing products and services for those among the middle class who can afford them.

Those who cannot attain the ideal of a middle-class lifestyle are serviced by the welfare apparatus of government, and although for many years welfare programs have been run by the rather sober logic of economics and policy analysis, more recently even welfare has become medicalized. Whereas historically the goal of welfare policy has been to help those receiving assistance to become job ready so that they can enter the workforce in relatively short order, more recently, instead of nuts-and-bolts educational and job-training programs – the so-called "hard skills" of training and job competencies – under increasingly medicalized welfare-to-work programs, welfare recipients are more likely to be given "soft skills" training, namely, behavioral "tips" or guidelines for fitting into the social relations of the workplace.[45] Whereas previously welfare caseworkers acted more like employment counselors or "job coaches," they now act more like therapists involved in intensive case management of "patients," assessing and monitoring their progress toward integration into the workplace.

Social workers are often the front-line agents in the medicalization of welfare, and therapeutic governance is directed and kept alive through their work. Avihu Shoshana's study of Israeli welfare policy finds that social workers in Israel operate similarly to their United States counterparts, but that they work with a unique client population which has not been formalized in US policy.[46] This special population consists of prisoners' wives, and social workers act to ensure that throughout the duration of their partners' incarceration, wives of prisoners are obliged to attend therapeutic sessions with designated social workers as a condition of receiving any financial benefits of the program. This illustrates the concept of *therapeutic expansion*, namely, that DSM categories of mental illness are extended to prisoners' wives even as most of them do not have a diagnosed mental illness. This also reflects the operation and application of the concept of relational disorders.

Trauma and PTSD

Perhaps the biggest growth area of the modern therapeutic state are the issues of trauma, stress, and anxiety. Specifically, post-traumatic stress disorder has become the highest profile form of stress in media, policy, and legislative circles. It originated from the ongoing effort to comprehend the Vietnam War experience by many of the veterans of that war.[47] Many Vietnam veterans were having trouble adjusting to normal routines and social activities upon returning from the war, and as they were appearing in greater numbers at veterans hospitals and mental health clinics complaining of a range of symptoms – restlessness and sleeplessness, aggressiveness and proneness towards violence, inability to sustain close relationships, suicidal thoughts, drug and alcohol use, isolationism, panic attacks, and mistrust towards others – psychiatrists and psychologists began taking notice. A set of diagnostic criteria for a new mental illness, post-traumatic stress disorder (PTSD), was soon developed and first appeared in DSM-3 in 1980. Since that time, however, application of PTSD to a widening array of complaints and conditions – not just to war-related trauma – has grown exponentially. The condition now has such prominence that June 27 has been designated National PTSD Awareness Day.

One area in which the discourse of PTSD has been most noticeable is natural or human-made disasters. Although today it is commonplace to assume that persons who have experienced such disasters – such as Hurricane Katrina in 2005 which devastated portions of Louisiana, Mississippi, and Alabama – often show classic symptoms of PTSD, this has not always been the case. As Frank Furedi has argued, until the 1980s the British people faced disasters with stoicism, rugged determinism, fortitude, and a "stiff upper lip." After the Aberfan disaster of 1966, an industrial tragedy that took the lives of 116 children and 28 adults, there was no talk of psychological distress among the survivors. Indeed, within several weeks the surviving children of the town resumed their education, and first responders and others at the scene noted that the children seemed normal and well-adjusted. The villagers had in effect managed the situation well with little help, and without much hand-wringing over the grief and trauma that may have lingered afterwards. As Furedi cogently observes,

> Today, such a response to a major disaster would be unthinkable. There would be an automatic assumption that every survivor in the area was deeply traumatized and inevitably scarred for life. Sending young pupils back to school so soon after a tragedy would be scorned as bad practice. The very attempt by the community to cope through self-help would be denounced as misguided since such victims could not be expected to deal with such problems on their own.[48]

Interestingly enough, in today's world, where disorders like PTSD are the analytical frames for understanding or making sense of the aftermath of disasters, reactions to disasters like the one that occurred at Aberfan simply cannot be accepted. Organizations like the National Center for PTSD have a "psychological first aid" manual ready to be distributed to survivors alongside life essentials such as food, clothing, temporary living quarters, clean water, getting electricity and sewage systems back on line, and preparing for physical reconstruction of the area.[49] Indeed, there is quite a bit of revisionist history going on with regard to Aberfan, as researchers are "helping survivors to reinterpret their experiences through the language of trauma."[50]

Celebrities and other public figures are also more likely to divulge that they have suffered from PTSD, and this is part and parcel of the growth of the public confessional concomitant to secularization and the decline of the private confessional. For example, in 2016 Lada Gaga told the world that she was raped at age 19 and had suffered symptoms of PTSD ever since.[51] In 2021 the Inspire Malibu website ran a story titled "7 Famous People and Celebrities with PTSD."[52] The celebrities listed were Whoopi Goldberg (who witnessed a midair plane crash); Monica Seles (who was stabbed in a tennis match in 1993); Mick Jagger (who developed PTSD symptoms after a girlfriend committed suicide); Darrell Hammond (who was severely abused as a child); Jacqueline Kennedy Onassis (who as First Lady witnessed the assassination of her husband, President John F. Kennedy); Alanis Morissette (due to her sudden fame after the release of her album *Jagged Little Pill*); and

Barbara Streisand (who for years struggled with intense stage fright after forgetting the lyrics of a song she was singing during a live performance at New York's Central Park).

Another area where trauma discourse has taken hold is the relationship between humans and their pets – now often referred to as "animal companions" – especially in the aftermath of their death, which may produce extreme feelings of grief or distress similar to PTSD. Historically, after the domestication of dogs, cats, horses, and beasts of burden (oxen, asses, and so forth), there was a tendency for bonds of affection and loyalty to form especially for those animals that were brought into the home or kept around the yard. For example, a typical domestic scene would be a father training his dog to bring him his slippers or the morning paper, and a treat would be given on completion of the act.

Dogs have also been used in war, to retrieve prey in hunting, and in police work to help capture suspects or to sniff out bombs, drugs, or cadavers. These K-9 unit dogs have even been elevated to near human status insofar as the killing of a police dog could bring charges of murder of a police officer, and state funerals with full honors may be held for them. Animals have also been kept on farms and other facilities for food production, but this is such a sore subject among pet enthusiasts that it occasionally has converged with militant animal rights activists who view the taking of life of any animal as murder. Such sentiments are typically attached to the politics of veganism.[53]

People are also investing more in their pets than ever before. For example, during the Covid-19 pandemic with many persons stuck at home unable to work, more Americans were willing to pay for a range of services for their animal companions including food as well as medical and grooming services. The American Pet Products Association estimates that in 2021 alone Americans will spend upwards of $99 billion on their pets, an indication of the explosive growth of the pet industry.[54] All things being equal, people spend far more on dogs than cats, and this has much to do with the folk wisdom that "dogs have masters, cats have staff." Specifically, the level of attachment to and investment in pets is associated with the perceived ability to control the animal's behavior, which means that persons take much greater psychological ownership of dogs than of cats.[55] Additionally, there is growth in the area of use of service animals and legal questions, especially of compliance with the Americans with Disabilities Act (ADA), concerning the circumstances under which schools, workplaces, restaurants, and transportation systems are required to accommodate access to persons requesting animal assistance or accompaniment.[56]

In general, then, we have moved beyond the instrumental use of animals to get things done – helping a blind person navigate the streets of the city, detecting cancer or the onset of a seizure[57] – and are now using them for emotional support both inside and outside the home. In many respects as well, domestic pets have been elevated to the level of fellow human beings, with the sentiment being that they should be afforded personhood status. Because dogs and cats have relatively short life expectancies in comparison to humans, and as the therapeutic ethos becomes the primary frame through which understandings of our relations to pets are filtered, we have set ourselves up for serial grieving and trauma whenever old age, illness, or injury takes our beloved Fido or Fluffy. Indeed, psychotherapist Katherine Compitus, reflecting on her own trauma after her dog died, had this to say: "The traumatic loss of my dog made me aware of my own reliance on my pets as therapeutic objects, a realization that greatly transformed my interests and goals."[58]

This is consistent with diagnostic inflation and expansion, trans-mitted via mainstream media and social media reports to mass publics concerning a growing array of afflictions including PTSD (this issue will be returned to in chapter 10). Indeed, there is now serious talk of entire populations of persons suffering from PTSD because of overt and increasingly more subtle forms of racism (e.g., vicarious or second-hand racism, microaggressions, and implicit bias).[59] The evidence of historical and current mistreatment of racial and ethnic minorities across Western society – part of the broader concept of the "wounds of history" – has led to something akin to "victimhood nationalism" in which the illness of cultural trauma, transmitted across the generations, must now be confronted by those with privilege – whether racial, socio-economic, or gender – and cured not only for the benefit of the afflicted but for society as a whole.[60] This is another version of the redemption narrative which Christianity perfected centuries ago.

Gender and medicalization

If indeed, as the medicalization thesis suggests, medicine has grown more powerful as a narrative or discourse for defining and regulating social behavior, does medicalization impact men and women differently? We would expect that in patriarchal societies, where males tend to garner the lion's share of valued social resources at the expense of relatively deprived and oppressed females, medical control would be directed more at women, and have a more profound impact in terms of regulating and circumscribing women's lives. Although this thesis has a certain intuitive appeal, it is not quite this simple or straightforward. For a more nuanced account of the impact of medicalization on women, let us look at the work of Elianne Riska.[61]

Riska argues that, beginning in the 1970s, the impact of medicalization on women has passed through three phases or stages. The first phase was *gender neutrality*, meaning that in its earliest stages medicalization proceeded in a general fashion without necessarily acting in a way that discriminated against women. For example, the precursor to the modern medicalization thesis was the antipsychiatry movement of the 1950s and the 1960s, which was a broad-based critique of the practice of warehousing social misfits – males and females alike – in total institutions such as the insane asylum. In the asylum, psychiatrists were criticized for being able to pass judgments – often uncontested – on the alleged problematic behavior of persons being confined there. In addition, advances in medical technology had produced a range of drugs that acted to facilitate behavior management and modification, and since psychiatrists and physicians were the only ones who could legitimately prescribe such drugs, their power increased accordingly with only minimal checks in place. In addition, patients in these asylums were exposed to degrading and dehumanizing conditions, including the stripping of personal identity, isolation from the outside world, being confined in close living quarters with other patients who were sometimes violent, and exposure to drug regimens and surgical procedures (such as lobotomies or electro-shock) the aims of which were to pacify and stultify patients even at the expense of their health.

The growth in the number of mental illnesses appearing with each new edition of the *DSM* was another point of criticism among proponents of the medicalization thesis; yet again early on, these criticisms rarely focused on gender issues per se. For example, in the therapeutic state behavior modification and control through drug treatment continues to be emphasized, and as more and more drugs are linked with the treatment of specific unwanted behaviors, there is a concomitant growth of *DSM* categories of mental illness. Among schoolchildren, fidgeting, inattention, hyperactivity, and not paying attention may lead to a diagnosis of attention deficit hyperactivity disorder (ADHD), and the drug of choice for treatment of this "disease" is Ritalin. There is also explosive growth in the diagnosis of depression, which is treated by a number of antidepressants including Zoloft, Prozac, Paxil, and Wellbutrin. Indeed, the diagnosis of depression and its treatment by prescription drugs is now so common and widespread that physicians have lost the ability to distinguish true clinical depression from the everyday blues. Allan Horwitz and Jerome Wakefield have aptly described this state of affairs as the "loss of sadness."[62]

It was not until the second phase, which Riska refers to as *women as victims*, that explicit attention to gender issues began appearing in the medicalization literature. Much of this was tied to the second wave of feminism which began in the 1960s and which made inroads into academic writing and spawned a vast feminist literature by the 1970s. Examples of topics appearing during this phase include:

- the medicalization of childbirth, whereby the largely male-dominated medical specialty of obstetrics displaced the traditional methods of prenatal care and birth delivery, such as midwifery, which were female-dominated;
- the explosive growth in plastic surgery, performed by male surgical specialists on a predominately female patient population;
- maladies such as pre-menstrual syndrome and surgical procedures such as hysterectomies, which pathologized the normal bodily processes of females.

Here, feminist critique merged with the critique of medical control embodied in the medicalization thesis, making problematic in more specific and focused terms the control of women's bodies and lives by a male-dominated medical profession.

Riska refers to the third phase as the *revival of reductionism*. In the early stages of the growth of medicine as a profession, the great majority of research studies on a variety of medical conditions used male subjects as the test population. This meant that medicine developed presumably general and universal understandings about illness and disease which were based on an invisible male standard. In some sense, then, the first phase of gender neutrality was reductionist in that it reduced all categories of persons to the invisible male standard, even as medicine was claiming the generalizability of its findings to all members of the human population. With the second phase of medicalization, the phase that raised the "women's issue" and tended to view women as "victims" of male-dominated medicine, the invisible male standard was shattered whether explicitly or implicitly.

But since this second phase, where so much attention had been devoted to women's health issues as well as critiques of the male-dominated medical establishment, there is now more explicit attention being devoted to men's health. For example, public health advocates have raised something that might be called the "men as endangered species" hypothesis.[63] This is generated from the reality or the perception that certain diseases or conditions are unique to, or disproportionately affect, males. In most human populations, for example, males have lower life expectancies than females. Coronary heart disease is much more prevalent in males as well, and at least initially this was traced to stress and the fact that as breadwinners in a patriarchal society, males are forced to compete with other males for the economic security of their families. This gave rise to the theory of the Type A personality – the hard-working male breadwinner – which effectively medicalized the moral aspects of heterosexual masculinity.[64] Also, with so much new focus on men's sexuality, especially with regard to sexual functioning (e.g., heightened awareness of male impotence, made famous by Bob Dole's "erectile dysfunction" commercials, as well as media sensationalism over the drug Viagra), men's health issues tend to be viewed not as social or psychological issues, but as biological issues.[65] This marks a reintroduction of reductionistic biological thinking, but instead of operating with an invisible male standard, it has now been made explicitly biological.

A brief look at transgender issues

Beyond Riska's analysis, there is a new dimension in the discussion of gender and medicalization, and this is the increasingly high profile of what used to be called transsexualism and what is now referred to as the transgender phenomenon. For many years psychiatry has operated with a classification of mental disorder associated with the discomfort some persons feel with their own body or biological sex. This concept is *gender dysphoria*, which refers to the discomfort felt when one's birth sex does not align with one's gender identity.[66] Because there is a relatively small group of people who develop this view of how sex or gender relates to the self, it was easy for the medical community to affirm that the condition is rare and even abnormal. Hence, there was no "medicalization" of the condition per se, because gender dysphoria was assumed to be real, and hence pathological, because of how rare it is and how palpable the negative consequences are for persons so afflicted.

The point is also made that those who can be described as *transgender*, namely, those whose biological sex does not align with their gender identity, do not necessarily suffer from gender dysphoria, and hence do not meet the clinical conditions for the illness. If this is the case, then the claim can be made that an illegitimate extension of the medical view of pathological sex is occurring in those cases where transgender persons are not presenting with symptoms of gender dysphoria. It is in these cases where the criticism of medicalization would come into play. Concomitant to this, there has been a movement for gender-affirming care for transpersons so as to resist their pathologization in clinical settings.[67]

There are many types of gender expression, that is, the various ways persons may present their gender to the world, and that gender expression is not the same as gender identity. Gender identity is typically formed beginning at birth, and by age two or so most persons arrive at a stable sense of their own sex, and for the vast majority of people their gender identity fits neatly into the slots of "male" or "female," which from the critical perspective represents the dreaded "gender binary." Indeed, one of the first things young children learn about themselves is that they are boy or a girl, and this cultural "truth" has been imported into medicine and has emblazoned the cisgender as normative while viewing the transgender as deviant.

This reflects the powerful operation of culture and socialization for determining expectations for conduct and assigning categories of understanding to the normal and not normal. However, concerns have arisen that what is really operating here is a tacit or invisible middle-class standard of propriety which recognizes a relatively narrow range of activities or characteristics as "normal," which then lends itself to an easy and typically unquestioned pathologization of everything else falling outside the ideal. More recent concerns arising over transgender health are that medicine unduly pathologizes transpersons from the beginning because of their relatively small numbers – estimated to be about 0.06 percent of the US population[68] – and that health initiatives for this population are a work in progress coinciding with the dynamic nature of the phenomenon.

The term "transgender" itself is akin to a moving target, first showing up as "transsexual" and now moving into more diverse nomenclature including "transgender and gender diverse people" (TG/GD), "non-binary," or simply "trans."[69] Why, for example, was the transition made from the original "transsexual" to "transgender"? A useful explanation is provided by Randi Gressgård:

> The term transgender came into usage in the late 1970s and early 1980s by people whose personal identities fall somewhere on a spectrum between transvestite and transsexual and who were reluctant to be categorized as either transvestites or transsexuals.[70]

This move represents fluidity and a rejection of immutability. It provides real flesh-and-blood human beings the ability to decide for themselves how they will understand and present themselves to the outside world, and it is also a challenge to traditional modernist tendencies toward dichotomous, "this or that" thinking, which conveniently places persons into readymade categories, presumably for purposes of predictability and ultimately social control. This also emphasizes a more open "spectrum" concept – as briefly discussed in chapter 2 and which will be taken up again in chapter 7 – rather than the discreet categorization into dichotomies of earlier approaches to medical diagnosis and social explanation. The spectrum idea emphasizes continuity between seemingly disparate cases or traits; hence, newer terms such as gender expression, which tolerates a wide range of activities and self-presentations, gets us away from dichotomous categories which inevitably have value labels attached to either side of such dualisms, such as in the standard case of normal being seen as "good" or "healthy" while the abnormal or rare is seen as "bad," "suspect," or "unhealthy."

We have warned in various parts of the book to not automatically equate social control with dominance or with the sure and inevitable diminution of life chances for those who are targets of control attempts. For example, Jodie Dewey and Melissa Gesbeck worry that transgender people are not receiving the same level of compassion, dignity, and professional competence from medical practitioners in the provision of care typically afforded to cisgender persons. They state, for example, that although the relabeling of gender dysphoria in *DSM-5* is a step in the right direction, their research indicates that "these changes will not be enough to alter the underlying structure of social control and power that diagnostic categories have over transpeople and their providers."[71] However, such concerns may be exaggerated and not accurately reflect the current state of transgender medicine. Granted, there is indeed a status incongruity in the doctor–patient relationship, whereby patients, lacking the professional expertise to adequately deal with their own health conditions, place themselves in the hands of trained physicians or clinicians whose educational and disciplinary credentials feed into a "cloak of competence," which renders their assessments of the patient's situation to be more or less authoritative.[72] Even so, doctors also adopt a universalistic orientation toward their patients, ideally not altering judgments or treatments on the basis of their particular characteristics be it gender, race, sexual orientation, or gender expression. Hence, studies have found that transgender adolescents receive the same level of care as cisgender adolescents, and in some instances the former receive even better preventive health services than the latter.[73]

Conclusion: medicalization as the exclusion of evil

An area in which medicalization is at least partially culpable is the problem of the *exclusion of evil*.[74] In earlier times, when religion was the leading source of truth, wisdom, and goodness, deviant acts were understood as sinful or evil. The religious worldview provides an unshakable moral template grounded in the word of God or the gods, and as a consequence the world is seen in black and white, as a struggle between good and evil. There are no shades of gray. But with the rise of Enlightenment thought and the deterministic explanatory systems of science, secular explanations were sought for all sorts of phenomena, including social behavior. If people's actions are caused not by God or by evil forces, they must originate in the person, or chemicals, or the environment, or society more generally, or some complex combination of worldly elements. If crime and deviance are illnesses, it makes no sense to say that such behavior is evil or that the person willingly engaged in the act. Excluding evil in this way is a logical extension of the scientific worldview, which suggests that all phenomena have worldly causes, thereby denying the metaphysical speculation that the human species may still harbor deep and dark – indeed evil – aspects even in an age of enlightened reason.[75]

This sentiment appears whenever human beings perpetrate horrendous and gruesome acts against one another. A lay sentiment toward serial killers, for example, is that no "sane" person would do something like that. We may attribute the acts themselves as evil, but still maintain that the person perpetrating the acts is "sick." Although the general public is fascinated with serial killers and they garner disproportionate attention in mass media, film, and TV, the reality is that in any given year serial killers are responsible for less than 1 percent of all murders.[76] The general attitude that serial killers are sick is driven by sensationalistic portrayals of them as sexual sadists who derive pleasure from inflicting physical or psychological suffering on their victims before killing them, all to satisfy demented sexual fantasies.[77]

Although it is true that violent sexual fetishism accounts for some proportion of all serial murders and that in such cases some attribution of sickness may be appropriate, it may also not be off base to say that they are simply evil and leave it at that. But as a therapeutic society, we cannot stop there. We want to dig deeply into the "tormented" minds of serial killers so that we may discover the "true" reasons impelling such bizarre behavior, with an eye toward eventually curing this illness once and for all. Resigning ourselves to the fact that evil still exists in the world is simply not an option.

SUGGESTIONS FOR FURTHER READING

Giorgio Agamben, *Where Are We Now? The Epidemic as Politics* **(2021)**
Agamben, a prominent Italian philosopher, has written a courageous reflection on the Covid-19 pandemic and has sought to understand the convergence of factors that are producing new ideas regarding the limits – or lack thereof – of government restrictions being placed on citizens, including lockdowns and the shuttering of schools and "nonessential" workplaces in order to slow the spread of the virus.

Bradley Campbell and Jason Manning, *The Rise of Victimhood Culture: Microaggressions, Safe Spaces, and the New Culture Wars* **(2018)**
This is one of the first comprehensive studies of microaggressions, those small, seemingly benign slights that majority group members direct toward minority group members (especially those identities of race, gender, sexual expression, and social class). This became a moral issue as modern societies experienced a transition from earlier dignity and honor cultures to a new victimhood culture. The authors utilize concepts from Donald Black's pure sociology to explain the emergence of microaggressions on the basis of underdiversity, overstratification, and other key processes.

William C. Cockerham (ed.), *The Wiley Blackwell Companion to Medical Sociology* **(2021)**
Cockerham is one of the leading scholars in the field of medical sociology. As editor, he has brought together an interesting and provocative set of papers covering such topics as the sociology of the body, stress in the workplace, sickness and wellness in an era of globalization, the sociology of bioethics, medicalization and social control, and the social organization of the health professions.

Martin Halliwell, *Therapeutic Revolutions: Medicine, Psychiatry, and American Culture, 1946–1970* **(2013)**
Halliwell presents an intellectual history of the state of medicine between World War II and the early 1970s. The normative model of medical science that

prevailed in the earlier period was challenged by developments in humanistic and transpersonal therapies during the 1960s, and this conflict between the two cultures of treatment has yet to be resolved.

P.J. McGann and David Hutson (eds.), *Sociology of Diagnosis* (2011)

This is volume 12 in the series *Advances in Medical Sociology* published by Emerald. Topics include post-traumatic stress disorder, biological reductionism, the pharmaceutical imagination, diagnosis as social control, and diagnosis in the transgender rights movement.

DISCUSSION QUESTIONS

1. How does Parsons' concept of the sick role relate to both medicalization and medical social control?
2. Many observers believe that criminal justice should operate more like public health. Explain why or why not this is attainable or desirable. Here, you would need to think about how crime and illness are either similar or different in terms of targeted interventions.
3. Give some examples of how drug companies, as well as everyday citizens in the role of patients, continue to engage in "disease mongering."
4. In the chapter we examined the concept of demedicalization as it relates to homosexuality. Give another example of a condition or behavior which has been, or is likely in the future to be, demedicalized. Provide reasons why this demedicalization has taken place or will take place.
5. Is erectile dysfunction a disease? If so, why did it take so long to be diagnosed as a legitimate illness? If not, what are the social and cultural circumstances giving rise to this way of thinking about men's sexuality?

Chapter 5
Legal Control

Introduction: the criminal justice system

Among the three major forms of control – informal, medical, and legal – it is the latter which captures more of the public imagination, is depicted most prominently in popular culture, and which people share stories about with each other in their everyday lives. The lynchpin of legal control is the *criminal justice system*, comprised of three major subsystems, namely, police, law and the courts, and corrections. The criminal justice system of the United States is huge and costly. For example, in fiscal year 2016, federal, state, and local governments spent nearly $296 billion on criminal justice functions, with nearly $143 billion spent on police protection, nearly $89 billion on corrections, and about $65 billion on judicial and legal activities.[1]

In this chapter we will examine the operation of the criminal justice system as it relates specifically to the issue of social control. The police, the courts, and corrections each has its own unique issues of control that are connected with how these subsystems operate within the broader system, and what major functions each serves. To simplify a very complex and expansive process, the *police* detain suspects and make arrests, the *courts* pass judgment on whether or not a person actually committed the crime or crimes with which he or she is being charged, and the *corrections* system punishes those convicted of crimes in criminal court.

Law and morality: where is the dividing line?

Before we embark on our overview of legal control, we must spend a few moments covering an area of contention that has been much discussed over the course of human history across such fields as theology, law and jurisprudence, philosophy, ethics, political science, economics, and sociology. This contested area encompasses the question: What is the relation between law and morality, and can a dividing line be established between the two? In terms of our three basic types of social control, the home base for morality would be informal control, while for law it would of course be legal control. Morality represents the idea of the *ought*, namely, the things one ought to do or not do as a member in good standing in one's community. We learn morality through socialization, and various agents of socialization (see chapter 3) help us to distinguish right from wrong and, in so doing, ideally instill in us a sense of obligation or duty concerning the good, the just, the fair, and the proper.

Whereas morality seeks to guide conduct based upon some notion of obligation handed down to us and enforced informally by all competent members of a community, law goes beyond the ought of morality to direct conduct toward the *must*. This means that law requires us to refrain from certain acts that are identified as illegal or face potentially serious legal sanctions. Since law commits these proscriptions (what NOT to do) and prescriptions (what to do) to paper, as embodied in legal statutes and codebooks, only those things explicitly addressed and identified as requirements of law form the basis of compulsion by the state. That is to say, everything falling outside of explicit legal articulation are "off the books," so to speak, and hence fall under the realm of the ought of morality. This is the idea that you can be subject to criminal charges only for violating a law already on the books. Hence, many acts that are morally repugnant will not put the actor in legal jeopardy.[2]

Let us look at an example of this distinction between the ought of morality and the must of law. Over the past 50 years in the United States a political tradition arose whereby candidates for president voluntarily made their tax returns publicly available. However, when he ran for president in 2016, then-candidate Donald Trump announced that he would not be releasing his tax returns, thereby bucking the trend toward voluntary disclosure of presidential candidates' tax returns. Trump realized that there was no legal mechanism for compelling him to release his taxes, because it was not one of the enumerated legal requirements for running for the office of president. It was merely voluntary, part of the public morality of presidential politics. And indeed, after Trump broke this tradition, a growing tide of sentiment arose that a law needed to be passed requiring presidential candidates to publicly release their taxes.[3] In this particular case, there is no legal remedy available for what some might view as Trump's deviant or delictual conduct. Instead, it is left to the individual morality and political will of citizens to decide whether or not to vote for such a candidate. And as we saw in the results of that election, Trump's decision not to release his taxes did not keep him from winning the presidency.

Sometimes the merely morally offensive or repugnant can become objects of government regulation, and this process is typically set into motion by well-placed moral entrepreneurs who publicize some social condition which, it is claimed, threatens the well-being of the broader society.[4] In the United States, for example, the nineteenth century witnessed the temperance (anti-alcohol) and abolitionist (anti-slavery) movements, both of which were launched by groups of moral entrepreneurs. As we saw in previous chapters, concerns over vice and depravity, activities which are for the most part victimless, have nevertheless also fallen under the sway of moral regulation, the consequences of which throw into disarray the distinction between morality and law.[5] Indeed, with continuing litigiousness, growing numbers of persons articulate the sentiment that "There ought to be a law!" This has the effect of shrinking the scope and impact of informal control while extending the reach of formal control (legal and medical).

The history of criminal justice: from informal to legal control

In England up to 900 AD, the maintenance of the social order was the responsibility of persons in their local communities.[6] By the time of the Norman Conquest in 1066, however, a sort of community policing known as the *frankpledge* system emerged. This was a system in which citizens formed volunteer teams with nine other neighbors, and this ten-member team would watch over each other to ensure everyone stayed out of trouble. This surveillance-based form of discipline worked because of the incipient forms of solidarity already found in the village or folk society as a result of the likeness and familiarity between its members. If a member of a frankpledge group observed a law being broken, he or she would engage in *hue and cry*, namely, yelling out to other members of the community that a violation had occurred.[7] All able-bodied persons would then be expected to respond to the hue and cry.

However, because frankpledge was more often than not based on neighborhood ties rather than on kinship ties per se, it was not a purely informal system of control. A level of formality was introduced, especially with the requirement that members of frankpledge teams provide a *tithing* or a payment, which created a pool of funds that could be drawn on to pay to the court or, more frequently, the constable or sheriff of the district to help offset whatever damages were caused by wayward members of the team. This form of collective responsibility represents a transition point between the pure forms of informal control based in kinship and primary groups, and the later formal systems of control represented by criminal justice.[8]

This system of control, marked by group surveillance based on neighborhood solidarity and tithings paid to sheriffs for infractions committed, remained in place in medieval England with only slight variations for the next five centuries. (At the time the position of sheriff was unpaid, hence tithings helped remunerate them for their services.) Members of local communities acted as their own police forces, and sheriffs acted more or less merely as figureheads for the king, the latter of whom wielded unbridled power over the various shires of his kingdom. For the most part, misbehavior in the community was handled informally, led by male heads of well-established families of yeomen or resident gentry. By the 1300s, however, the frankpledge system was augmented by *leet courts*, lesser public courts which rested upon presentment juries comprised of 12 or more men – generally no women were allowed to serve – who were sworn to present a collective report regarding problems of interest to the community.[9] Complaints making their way to these early leet courts included such things as scolding (a broad category of offenses, often charged against women, which included malicious gossiping, backbiting, and spreading rumors), eavesdropping, nightwalking, sexual misconduct, disorderly alehouses, "evil reputation," poverty, and illegal gaming.[10]

This system of control began breaking down with calls for law reform in England beginning in 1620. The main focus of these law reforms, in England as well as in New England in colonial America, was bringing to an end the Tudor ideology of the divine right of kings.[11] One of the most radical manifestations of this attempt to end the English monarchy was the execution of King Charles I in 1649. The execution of King Charles is notable to the extent that it serves to illustrate the way persons routinely tolerated what would today be considered gross violations and incivilities in the areas of aesthetics, human relations, and the value placed on human life.

Up to this time and at least into the late 1700s, at which point various writers began criticizing the practices of capital punishment and making a public spectacle of punishment in general, how a person died was important. As Donald Siebert explains, "It was expected that good people would die well, and that the good *and* great would die greatly."[12] The day of his execution, the king dressed warmly to guard against shaking from the cold, which could give the impression that he was afraid. When King Charles faced the executioner, the first thing he asked him was "Is my hair well?" The king looked at the chopping block and reprimanded the executioner that "you must set it fast" and that "it might have been a little higher." The king also showed the executioner the hand signal he would give to deliver the fatal blow, to which the executioner replied "Yes I will and it please your Majesty." When the signal was given with one blow the king's head was severed from his body, the head was held up and shown to the crowd, then place in a casket with the body and put into a coffin covered with black velvet.[13]

The execution of King Charles I was a symbolic and dramaturgical event, one that displayed the triumph of popular justice over royal majesty.[14] Although still under British rule, the colonial Americans attempted also to implement aspects of popular justice even while necessarily borrowing a number of features of British law. For the Puritans of the Massachusetts Bay Colony, the law was designed to ensure public and private morality.[15] Consistent with Durkheim's conception of mechanical solidarity, offenses against God such as blasphemy could bring the death penalty, both for the Puritans as well as the Quakers of Pennsylvania. Punishments were overwhelmingly punitive and repressive, because deviance and crime were seen as abominations in the eyes of the Lord. As a result brandings, mutilations, and public whippings were common forms of punishment. Public humiliation was also important. We have already seen that executions were highly public performances, and pillories and the stocks were used for this purpose as well. The collective, open, and public nature of punishment in colonial times served to identify offenders to the entire community. Unlike the modern impulse toward rehabilitation as a goal of punishment, there was no pretense of changing offenders in colonial America.[16]

The American colonies declared themselves independent from England in 1776, and from that time until 1781 the Americans engaged in a desperate war against the British crown for their own liberty and freedom. British criminal justice was monarchical and authoritarian, and the king was considered the "fountain of justice." But for Puritan leaders and others in the American colonies, this was a flawed idea. Rather than the king, it was God who was the ultimate source of justice. As vigorously as America repudiated England's royal theory of justice, it nevertheless maintained a major feature of English law, and this was the common law.[17]

There are several characteristics of *common law* worth noting. First, under the doctrine of the supremacy of law, no one is above the law, not even the king. Second, common law is law based on precedent, that is, on past court decisions. This is the doctrine of *stare decisis*, meaning "stand by the decided matter." Third, in keeping with the spirit of popular justice embedded in common law, criminal cases may be and often are decided by a jury of one's peers. Fourth, unlike other legal systems, common law places great emphasis on the spoken word.[18] As discussed previously, the criminal trial is an adversarial system in which two sides – the state as plaintiff and the criminal defendant and his or her team of defense lawyers – argue their cases before a presiding judge (bench trial) or a jury. In order to win a conviction, the state must prove its case beyond a reasonable doubt, the highest burden of proof among all forms of legal trial. Hence, much emphasis is placed on the oratory skills and knowledge of the law of lawyers, while the judge acts as a "referee," making sure that rules of procedure (or procedural law) are followed throughout the trial. Judges do not like having the decisions of their court overturned on appeal.

The Enlightenment, and changing ideas about justice and punishment

The *Enlightenment* was an eighteenth-century philosophical movement that emphasized the application of reason, experience, and the scientific method rather than dogma (religious or otherwise), superstition, or other such speculative and untestable ideas in the explanation of the physical and social world. The Enlightenment's triumph of science and rationalism pushed the search for universal laws of natural and social phenomena, including within the social realm, procedural and substantive law founded on precedents established in judicial decisions. The notion of the "universality of law" meant that treatment of persons under the auspices of the criminal justice system was supposed to be equal, fair, and transparent. Instead of the rather arbitrary and oftentimes harsh and brutal treatment of criminal defendants characteristic of earlier times, the Enlightenment ushered in new ways of thinking concerning the punishment of prisoners.[19]

By the middle of the eighteenth century in Europe a *Classical School* of criminology found its beginning in the writings of such thinkers as Cesare Beccaria, Jeremy Bentham, and John Howard. Firmly located within the Enlightenment movement of thought, these and other thinkers emphasized the importance of reason and experience while denigrating theological forms of reasoning.[20] Let us first turn to a brief summary of Beccaria's thought.

Cesare Beccaria

This new impulse toward penal reform was initiated by Italian lawyer Cesare Beccaria, who published *On Crimes and Punishment* in 1764. Beccaria was appalled at the harsh and brutal punishments characteristic of European and American penal systems, including capital punishment, torture, banishment, transportation, and exorbitant fines out of proportion to the seriousness of the offense. As it was being practiced up through the middle of the eighteenth century, punishment was irrational in that it was arbitrary, often left to the whim of the sitting judge or to more informal systems of control such as vigilantism, mob rule, blood feuds, lynchings, and even remnants of oaths and ordeals. Punishment was also irrational because it was excessively cruel and inhumane. This led Beccaria to suggest that capital punishment ought to be abolished, and that incarceration or imprisonment should replace many of the "irrational" punishments mentioned above. He further argued that rather than the severity of punishment, what should be emphasized is the certainty of punishment. If certainty of punishment is to be achieved, this would require systemization, upgrading, and expansion of resources in all areas of the criminal justice system, not just corrections.[21] These changes promised not only to make punishment more rational, but the use of planning, science, and measurement with respect to crime and deviance would increase general societal happiness as well, culminating in the utilitarian goal of assuring the greatest good for the greatest number of people.[22]

Jeremy Bentham

A contemporary of Beccaria was British philosopher, economist and jurist Jeremy Bentham. Unlike most of the thinkers of his time, Bentham believed that the common law was deficient because of its conservatism. Since common law relies overwhelmingly on the past decisions of judges, the doctrine of precedence is stultifying in that law changes only incrementally, if at all. The traditionalism of common law stands in the way of developing a truly scientific theory of law and legal process. For Bentham, a truly scientific approach to law would be grounded in the basic forces impelling human beings to act, namely pleasure and pain. According to Bentham's notion of the *hedonic calculus*, persons will act to maximize their pleasure and minimize their pain. The scientific approach to law, then, would incorporate this basic insight into human behavior, and hence the best laws would be those that ensured the greatest good for the greatest number of people. We see, then, that Bentham made explicit the utilitarianism already contained in Beccaria's thoughts on penal reform.

For Bentham, the quality of law is to be judged on its *utility*, that is, its ability to secure the greatest good for the greatest number of persons. This emphasis on utility, rather than on justice per se, led to the later medicalization of law, especially with regard to the value of public health or safety as discussed in the previous chapter. During Bentham's time, however, the penal goal of rehabilitation had not yet been formulated or made explicit, yet we can see its beginnings here.

By 1791, Bentham had conceptualized a new prison design which he called the Panopticon. The *Panopticon* was a prison envisioned as a circular structure with jail cells running around the circumference, while the jailers would be positioned in an elevated spire or steeple in the middle of the structure. From this middle, elevated position the jailers could easily monitor the activities of all the inmates. Further, the jailers' quarters would be constructed in such a way that the inmates could not tell if the observation tower was occupied. Because they had to assume they were being watched, inmates would in effect engage in self-control, which contributed to the prison's goal of assuring social control through the willing compliance and docility of the inmates.

Bentham hoped that the Panopticon design would catch on in all future prison construction, but it never really did. In 1794 a bill passed the British parliament to build such a prison at Battersea. Insufficient funds and the landowner's resistance to selling the land upon which the prison was to be built effectively scuttled the project.[23]

John Howard

Movements of thought such as the Enlightenment ideal that social progress was attainable through the application of the scientific method, as well as humanitarian and religious impulses toward the amelioration of human misery, had by the last quarter of the eighteenth century led to some laws being passed in the area of prison reform represented in the efforts of Beccaria, Bentham, Elizabeth Fry, William Blackstone, and others. For example, in 1773 Parliament authorized magistrates to appoint chaplains in their jails.[24] There were also arguments made in favor of the abolition of solitary confinement, the education of prisoners, and other general improvements in the incarceration conditions of inmates, some of which were implemented into law as well, but on a limited and sporadic basis.

John Howard, an English philanthropist who was a contemporary of both Beccaria and Bentham, attempted to move the agenda of penal reform even further. When he was appointed high sheriff of Bedfordshire in 1773, he began the routine practice of visiting gaols (jails), prisons, and other correctional institutions with an eye toward ascertaining prevailing conditions in these facilities. In 1777 he published *The State of Prisons in England*, a report on these visitations. Howard was shocked by the conditions he saw in prison, especially in the jails, which were rife with corruption (especially in the fee system by which jailers got paid), and general levels of filth, squalor, and unhealthiness. The momentum from this book, as well as Howard's earlier testimony before the House of Commons on the conditions of jails and prisons, led him to draft a "penitentiary act" which he hoped would be seriously considered by members of the British Parliament.

The draft included several principles which Howard felt needed to be implemented for any meaningful prison reform to occur. The first things Howard proposed were improved sanitary conditions of living quarters, as well as improvements in the quality of prison food. He also believed that the current fee system, where prisoners were responsible for paying for their own incarceration with fees going to their jailers, should be abolished. Additionally, Howard believed that prisons could be used to reform, and since many prisoners were being held because of drunkenness, he argued that no liquor should be allowed in jails and prisons. Howard also urged the classification and segregation of prisoners by sex, age, and the types and severity of crimes committed. Further, Howard argued that idleness was a cause of criminality, and urged that prisoners be taught "industriousness," although he did not advocate compulsory prison employment. Finally, due to his deeply religious convictions (he was a Baptist), Howard believed that religious instruction was crucial for the reformation of inmates.[25]

Howard's draft document, along with the efforts of other prison reformers such as William Eden and Sir William Blackstone, led to the British Parliament passing the Penitentiary Act of 1779. This represented the most extensive and far-reaching change in law regarding the practice of state-sanctioned punishment in the Western world up to that time. For example, shortly after passage of the Act, use of capital punishment declined, the transportation of prisoners to the American colonies diminished considerably, and the use of imprisonment as a primary sanction increased significantly.[26]

Consolidation of state power and the emergence of policing

In America by the early nineteenth century similar changes in law, policing, and corrections were underway. After gaining its independence from Great Britain, the United States experienced substantial population growth. For example, in 1790 no American city had more than 50,000 inhabitants, but by 1830 almost half a million people lived in urban centers of that size or greater.[27] After 1830 industrial development and manufacturing grew as well, and would continue to expand after the Civil War, marking a so-called Gilded Age of economic affluence for owners of industries in steel, transportation, rubber, and oil.

During this time immigration increased as well, initially primarily from Anglo-Saxon countries such as Ireland, Germany, and Great Britain, and many were arriving to seek employment opportunities in the newly industrializing areas of the American northeast. However, there was also the beginnings of a westward expansion, as Americans and others newly arriving to the country were attempting to settle the western frontier in search of gold, land, and whatever other opportunities awaited them there. Obviously, there was much lawlessness on the Overland trail, and the California gold rush of 1848 produced some extreme forms of violence, malfeasance, and organized criminality.[28]

Even so, forms of self-help such as collective violence, rioting, and vigilantism were not confined to the western frontier. Beginning in the 1830s, riots became commonplace in America, especially in the east, growing both out of class antagonisms fueled by a growing disparity between the haves and have-nots in early industrial America, but also because of the political instability produced as a result of newly gained independence. During the Jacksonian era, the balance seemed to swing away from the sovereignty of the individual (embodied in the idea of rugged individualism and the Protestant work ethic) and toward the growth, centralization, and consolidation of state power. Even though America was a society of laws, there was nevertheless a strong current of public scorn toward the law and toward lawyers specifically. In his *Vice Unmasked*, a book written in 1830, P.W. Grayson wrote about the uneasiness with law that ran throughout life in Jacksonian America. According to Grayson, although the United States had brought an end to tyrannical rule, the legal system that survived nevertheless still harbored elements that impeded human freedom. Grayson's main indictment was the way the rule of law had injured humanity's moral essence, that is,

> the way it debased man's sense of self and social responsibility by turning him from his high moral potential to a tricksy tailoring of conduct to avoid legal prosecution. In short, law was generally a tool of the cleverly vicious, a snare for the simply virtuous, and a burden on everyone, crippling human decency and progress.[29]

It was within this play of factors – increasing centralization of state authority, the real or perceived rise in unlawful and criminal activities (predominantly public order offenses), and growing class antagonisms in an era of industrial expansion – that impetus grew for the establishment of a paid, professional police force. As was the case for both corrections and the law, the American municipal police would be based on a British model as well, that of the "new police" of Sir Robert Peel.

Peel's "new police"

Robert Peel, a Tory politician, was appointed Chief Secretary for Ireland in 1812. The Irish government was especially concerned about a group of agrarian terrorists called the "banditti," who through collective violence sought to lower rents and tithes. Rural law enforcement in Ireland was magistrate-based, but when uprisings of the sort the banditti were fomenting occurred, there was little officially that could be done. Indeed, by the time of Peel's arrival, many of the local magistrates had abandoned their posts. Peel believed rather than suppressing violence and crime, more emphasis needed to be placed on prevention.

In order to solve the problem of agrarian violence, Peel established the Peace Preservation Force, a more coercive response to the problem than previously attempted.[30] Through the employment of the coercive powers of the members of the Preservation Force as well as the implementation of a fining system which placed hardships on those communities within which the disturbances were occurring, Peel was successful in quelling banditti violence, although by 1817 he had abandoned the fining system in favor of a shared responsibility arrangement where England would bear two-thirds of the cost of Preservation Force operations while local communities would pay the other third.

Successful in this venture, Peel returned to England in 1818 and began thinking about implemented such a system of policing in his home country. What Peel had accomplished in Ireland was taking law enforcement out of the hands of amateurs and placing it in those of the professional.[31] Peel worked for the next decade on putting his vision into practice, and in 1829 Parliament passed the Metropolitan Police Act. The Police Act placed 3,000 police officers under the control of the Home Secretary. This was the first full-time, paid police force, modeled largely after features of military bureaucratic organization, including a rank system for purposes of hiring and promotions, as well as a chain of command. Officers would wear uniforms, and each was readily identifiable by a copper badge worn over the left breast. The "new police," sometimes referred to as "Peelers" or "bobbies," were expected to walk a beat to ensure close familiarity between patrol officers and members of the local community. Further, officers were not equipped with handguns, although they did carry truncheons or "billy clubs." Finally, police officers had broad powers of investigation and arrest, and were entrusted with high levels of discretion, ostensibly because of their status as full-time government employees and upstanding members of the community.

Policing in America: four eras

The United States soon followed the lead of the British, with Boston being the first city to establish a professional police force in 1838, but it was not until 1854 that the department took on many of the characteristics of Peel's "new police." The New York City police force was established in 1844, followed later by Philadelphia in 1856, Chicago in 1861, Detroit in 1863, and Cleveland in 1866. By 1880 most major American cities had done likewise.

From the beginning of the establishment of municipal policing in America to the early 1900s, the police were as or more likely to respond to citizen demands for public order and urban social services than to actual criminal offenses. In other words, police were likely to respond in many areas beyond crime control per se, including maintenance of order and many other situations engendered by the less formal relations that existed between citizens and police in the early stages of the establishment of modern policing. For example, beginning in the Jacksonian era (which ran from 1830 through about 1850), Americans began losing faith in punishment (specifically those of the harsh and brutal colonial forms) as a way of dealing with crime and deviance, and started looking to other solutions for reassuring or reestablishing the social order.[32] This is why in Jacksonian America, almost simultaneous to the rise of the penitentiary, there was also the rise of insane asylums, almshouses for the poor, orphanages and houses of refuge for wayward or abandoned youth (the forerunner of the juvenile justice system), safehouses and shelters for women in distress, and workhouses for men who were deemed either unemployable or simply lazy, "shiftless," or irresponsible (but not necessarily criminal).[33] The emergence of these various total institutions set up ostensibly for dealing with a range of perceived social ills – but most importantly those of public order disturbances – was also reflective of the continuing centralization and consolidation of state power, including the establishment of municipal police forces.

In the earlier years of operation then, American police in particular, and the criminal justice system in general, had a diffuse focus on all kinds of people, not just criminals. As historian Eric Monkkonen explains, during the nineteenth century

> Police dispensed welfare; jails and prisons housed the insane; jails sometimes held more witnesses than offenders awaiting trial. During the first two decades of the twentieth century, the focus of the system began to sharpen. As a result, demands for organization responses to crime became more closely tied to the actual rates of crime because the system no longer attended to problems that were not related to crimes.[34]

With regard to the municipal police, then, the general trend from 1830 to the present has been the increasing formalization, bureaucratization, specialization, and (later) professionalization of its operations. Focusing specifically on developments in police operations since the 1830s, four eras or phases have been identified.[35]

Political spoils

The first phase of modern policing, running from the 1830s until the 1920s, is referred to as the *political spoils* era. Police departments that were emerging in nineteenth-century America were controlled largely by the political administration of the city or municipality that happened to be in office at the time. For example, in most large cities the chief of police was a political appointee of the mayor, and since there were no official standards for recruitment of police candidates, the mayor basically handpicked whomever he or she wanted. Oftentimes these choices were made on the basis of political loyalties, informal ties, and familiarity with either the recruit himself or his family, and ethnicity and other ascribed characteristics.

As a result, patronage abuses and corruption ran rampant largely because the ties between municipal governance and the police were simply too close and "chummy." Police were at the beck and call of powerful local political actors – the mayor, councilmen, and ward bosses – so they were available to do virtually anything that local officials asked them to do, some of it illegal. Hence, in this first era, police were generalists or jack-of-all-trades and had a broad mandate to engage in a variety of official and "off the books" activities. Even as they played the role of generalists, police were enforcing law within culturally homogeneous conditions, meaning that residents of the community shared similar characteristics such as race, ethnicity, religious beliefs, and views toward authority.

This strong bonding across the citizenry combined with high levels of similarity and familiarity between them – very close in spirit to Durkheim's mechanical solidarity – allowed police to act informally toward those who were accepted as legitimate members of the community. Conversely, for those who were different or who did not appear to accept or acquiesce to police authority – typically labeled "troublemakers" or "malcontents" – police took the prerogative to treat them with suspicion, punitiveness, and higher levels of formalism, which often led to use of coercive force against them. And protests against what later would be called police brutality were squelched or not taken seriously because meaningful citizen input concerning police practices was not yet institutionalized. Hence, during this first era, police acted with impunity and enforced a top-down, command-and-control policy reflected in the sentiment "My way or the highway!"

Reform and early professionalization

The second policing era, running from the 1920s through the 1960s, is termed professionalization. Because of the many problems associated with the previous era of political spoils, during the second era of *reform and early professionalization*, attempts were made to place more distance between city government and the operation of the police force. In most major American cities the informal system of police recruitment was being replaced by a more formal system, including written guidelines for the recruitment, retention, and promotion of police officers, but also the creation of tight organizational structures where bureaucratic control over police activities was emphasized. This involved the promulgation of many more operational rules and regulations, affecting not only the bottom rung line staff (patrol officers and administrative staff) but also mid- and upper-level management, including the chief of police him- or herself.

The ideology of professionalization also meant greater specialization, the implication of which was that police departments began defining their mandate more narrowly to include only law enforcement, while other activities that police had traditionally performed (such as maintaining order, peacekeeping, and social services) were not officially recognized. This meant that in the second era, police made the transition from generalists to specialists, and what they specialized in was crime control (but also increasingly traffic control with the mass production of the automobile by the early 1900s). Following Foucault, the gradual transition from informal control to the establishment of police vested with the coercive powers of the state meant that the conditions of control shifted from the "many watch the few" to the *few watch the many*. Here, the "many" are the growing throngs of persons labeled as deviant or criminal (represented, for example, in rising crime rates beginning in the 1960s), while the "few" are those professionals who specialize in legal control, namely the police but also key actors within the court system (e.g., prosecutors and district attorneys) and corrections.

Another aspect of professionalization was taking police officers off of traditional foot patrols and placing them in squad cars. This created greater distance between police and citizens, a situation that was perceived to be warranted given the corruption of the previous era. This second era is described as "early" professionalization because during this time there was still little thought given to increasing educational requirements of cadets or providing extensive training to them. The consensus even into the 1940s and 1950s was that, rather than being a full-blown profession, policing was overwhelmingly a blue-collar occupation that did not require formal education or the mastery of a body of esoteric knowledge. This aspect of professionalization would not be fully realized until the third era.

Near the end of the political spoils era, in 1893, the International Association of Chiefs of Police (IACP) was formed to provide a platform for municipal police departments across the United States to share information over best practices. Even as it was formed at the end of the political spoils era, its most important work was realized at the beginning of the reform and early professionalization era.[36] Since their establishment beginning as early as the 1830s, municipal police departments in America had historically acted independently due to the fragmented nature of political control resulting from the system of federalism established in the United States Constitution.[37] One way of maintaining contact between otherwise disparate and isolated municipal police departments was through the creation of police associations such as the IACP. Annual conferences of the IACP have been held continuously since 1893 (the first one in Chicago), but for our purposes we will focus on the 1919 conference held in New Orleans.

In that 1919 conference, August Vollmer, one of the innovators of the second era of policing and chief of the Berkeley Police Department, presented a paper titled "The Policeman as a Social Worker." Vollmer articulates an expansive and forward-looking vision for upgrading and reforming American policing, identifying best practices not only with regard to the organization and operation of police departments (legal control), but also recommending that officers receive more education and training to master the set of skills entailed in police work.

Vollmer also noted that although criminology was in its infancy, it had shed light on the social and financial implications of arrest, the latter being one of the main work products of law enforcement officers. Vollmer sought to expand the thinking of police administrators as well as police officers working the beat, stating that "Ordinarily, the policeman feels that his duty is well done when the offender is promptly apprehended and placed behind the bars."[38] Vollmer is warning that, although it is generally a benefit for society that criminal offenders be taken out of circulation through detainment, arrest, prosecution, and possible confinement in a correctional facility, those offenders found guilty and punished often leave behind families and other dependants who relied on them for social support whether financial or otherwise. This means that the good work of law enforcement always has a negative aspect, namely, leaving those in relationships with the person removed from society with fewer options for meeting basic needs. As a result, some of these persons will turn to a life of crime or become wards of the state, largely negating the benefits of the law enforcement officers' efforts to apprehend and arrest the "bad guys."

Vollmer suggested that police officers should work more closely with schools, social service agencies, and public health officials, and actively promote the funding of and support for so-called "character-building" community organizations such as Boy Scouts and Campfire Girls. Here, there is a glimpse of a new proactive strategy brewing, one which would go beyond the traditional reactive approach whereby police sit back and wait for calls for help before bringing to bear their formal powers of arrest or intervention. Connected with this, Vollmer stated that the police officer is "fast learning that dealing with criminals after the evil habits have been formed is a hopeless task as far as the eradication, or even lessening of crime is concerned."[39] And showing evidence of an early investment in the therapeutic ethos, Vollmer makes some wildly inaccurate statements regarding the alleged high levels of mental illness characterizing the criminal and dependent classes, stating that "we are safe in assuming that at least one-half of our criminals and prostitutes are persons suffering from mental peculiarities or abnormalities."[40]

The most important thing to take away from this summary of August Vollmer's talk at the 1919 conference of the IACP is that it reflects an approach to social control that emphasizes the interconnectedness between legal control, informal control, and medical control, although some of the claims made to justify the greater involvement of psychiatry and public health in law enforcement are more rhetorical and wishful thinking than reality. The reality that played out throughout the 1920s and into the 1960s – encompassing the second era of policing – was one in which Vollmer, his protégé O.W. Wilson (who later created a police code of ethics), and a later generation of police practitioners and scholars dropped the pretense of fashioning the municipal police as a model of wraparound therapeutic services in favor of viewing police as specialists in crime control while divesting themselves of many of the civic entanglements implied in the wraparound services model.[41] Hence, even though Vollmer's vision for a therapeutic policing did not directly impact his own era of policing, it did inform some aspects of the development of the third era of policing.

Community-oriented policing

This third era of policing, running from the 1970s to the present, is known as community-oriented or problem-oriented policing. *Community-oriented policing* (COP) and problem-oriented policing (POP) emerged out of the turbulent 1960s. The sixties was an era characterized by openly hostile relations between police and citizens, especially for those citizens involved in such social movements as anti-war protest; civil rights, gay rights, and the women's movement; as well as youth and campus protests. Much of this open conflict took place in urban metropolitan areas characterized by growing cultural heterogeneity as well as ethnic and racial diversity, and the old bureaucratic form of "professional" policing was badly out of step in its inability to understand the needs of diverse populations. Out of this came the call to increase the education and training of police candidates, but also to recruit more women and persons of color into policing so that police forces would match more closely the sociodemographic characteristics of the populations they served.

Another important element in what was to become known as community or problem-oriented policing was the effort to repair strained relations between citizens and police, hence police departments started putting more effort into getting their officers more noticeably involved in their communities, and not just as crime fighters or law enforcers. Because a better class of persons was being brought into policing – presumably better educated, more literate, more culturally aware, and better able to handle a wide range of interpersonal situations – police in this third era were expected to be multitaskers who could fulfill multiple roles in the communities that they served. In both community and problem-oriented policing, the police are acting like psychologists, counselors, social workers, and teachers as much as they are crime fighters. Examples of community policing activities include:

- Drug Abuse Resistance Education or DARE, a 17-week program taught by uniformed police officers in elementary schools (typically fifth graders);
- Gang Resistance Education and Training or GREAT, a 10-week program to teach middle school seventh graders skills of conflict resolution and how to resist peer pressure;
- Eddie Eagle Gun Safety Program, gun safety education for elementary

school children emphasizing the motto "Stop, Don't Touch, Leave the Area, Tell an Adult"; and

- Police Athletic League or PAL, dedicated to positive development of youth to prevent juvenile delinquency through supervision of organized activities.[42]

It should also be noted that another polarity shift occurred in police roles. In the third era, police shifted back to generalists (similar to their role in the first era), but this time, given the continuing growth of diversity in the urban metropolis since the 1920s, this generalist role was being applied in culturally heterogeneous communities. In this social environment, police were required to engage in higher levels of "social skills" training and additional training to service diverse populations, examples of which include cultural sensitivity training; domestic violence prevention and greater sensitivity to victims of rape or sexual assault; mental health assessment and new policies for dealing with mentally ill suspects; de-escalation strategies; and helping citizens and other stakeholders connect to community resources pertinent to their specific needs.

Post-9/11 policing

Finally, there is talk of the emergence of a fourth era of policing. This is the so-called *post-9/11* era of policing, in which police return to the role of specialists, not in crime fighting per se, but in the provision of security, including the implementation of counterterrorism measures as well as the development of emergency planning for local communities in the case of a terrorist attack.[43] Under neoliberal governance, security has become the key commodity to be bought and sold in the private sphere – the home security system being the most representative example of this – and made available to a concerned public by governments and law enforcement organizations.[44]

It should be noted also that because it operates alongside community policing in municipal police departments where both are established, post-9/11 policing does not as yet represent a truly distinct, separate era of police development. It is also the case that the levels of counterterrorist security measures being learned and actually implemented by local police departments are subject to fluctuations coinciding with the availability of Department of Homeland Security grants.[45] As such, there is as yet no orderly or predictable model for what counterterrorism strategies or policies will or should look like at the level of local police departments. Of course, this tension between federal mandates and local adoption is in keeping with the history of decentralized and fragmented American policing. (For a summary of the four eras of policing, see table 5.1.)

Table 5.1 Four Eras of Policing and Changes in Community and Police Roles

	POLICING ERAS			
	Political spoils	**Reform and early professionalization**	**Community policing**	**Post-9/11 policing**
Period:	1830s–1920s	1920s–1960s	1970s–present	2001–present
Police as:	**Generalists**, attending to broad needs of citizens and political leadership	**Specialists**, primarily in crime control	**Generalists**, boundary-spanning multitaskers serving a diverse citizenry	**Specialists**, primarily in security, counterterrorism, and emergency preparedness
Nature of community:	**Homogeneity** but appearance of incipient levels of heterogeneity and increasing social disorder	Increasing **heterogeneity** and crime rates achieving historic highs beginning in 1960s	**Heterogeneity** and diversity of community at historically high levels; crime rates decline while incarceration rates increase	Increasing **heterogeneity** and diversity of community, especially in urban areas
Prevailing conditions:	Structural transformation in the division of labor; the transition from self-help to sworn police forces beholden to local political machine	Attempts to professionalize and reform police in light of previous era's corruption (close citizen contact) and political patronage abuses	Return of police generalization, but this time in the context of community diversity and shrinking municipal budgets, where local governance seeks to extract greatest "bang for the buck" from safety forces	Top-down requirements from federal level (Department of Homeland Security) and uniformity of procedures across local jurisdictions disempower some aspects of local police–community relations emphasized in the previous era
Direction of control emphasis:	Informal to legal	Increasingly legal	A mixed format of varying combinations of medical, informal, and legal control under conditions of police–community collaboration and reciprocity	Increasingly legal and militaristic while seeking to ensure due process rights in an era of increasing citizen accountability and responsibilization

The dark side of legal control

Although the programs described above give the impression that community-oriented policing is a marked improvement over earlier forms of policing, problems nevertheless remain. These problems will be picked up in the next section, and in addition to the topics of police use of force and fear of crime, we will also examine net-widening as well as class, race, and gender bias in the criminal justice system.

Police use and abuse of force

On May 25, 2020, during the height of the Covid-19 pandemic which swept across the world beginning earlier in that year and which, by early 2021, had killed some 500,000 Americans, Derek Chauvin, a member of the Minneapolis Police Department, arrested George Floyd on suspicions of passing counterfeit money. This was no ordinary arrest, however. Floyd, a Black man, was not only arrested and put in handcuffs, but was forced into a facedown position in the street with Chauvin kneeling on his neck for upwards of nine minutes. During the ensuing minutes Floyd had complained that he was having trouble breathing and was claustrophobic, but neither Chauvin nor the other officers on the scene responded to him or eased the restraint hold. Floyd died shortly thereafter, and the United States experienced a prolonged summer of protests – sometimes breaking out into riots and property destruction – and which ignited similar protests around the world.

Chauvin was arrested and charged with second-degree unintentional murder, third-degree murder, and second-degree manslaughter. He was tried by a jury of his peers in a Minneapolis courtroom – the defense team tried unsuccessfully to change the venue – and was found guilty on all three counts on April 20, 2021.[46] The three police officers on the scene who failed to provide aid to Floyd faced federal trial for various charges. On February 21, 2022, the defense rested its case, and as of this writing verdicts were pending.[47] Floyd's death at the hands of Chauvin was an event that has been described as traumatic for African-Americans, reminding many in the Black community of the maiming, torture, and sometimes execution of Black slaves in the antebellum South.[48] A worldwide conversation has been initiated, a reckoning of sorts, not only with regard to historically strained relations between police and racial minorities and how to ameliorate it, but also rethinking modern policing entirely up to and including its defunding.

Community-oriented policing and fear of crime

Since its inception in the 1970s, community-oriented policing has experienced steady growth, and today a majority of municipal police departments characterize themselves as COP or POP departments. A typical statement on the characteristics and goals of community policing is provided by the Wheat Ridge, Colorado police department:

> Community policing is the cornerstone of everything we do at the Wheat Ridge Police Department. Our Mission Statement reads: "The Wheat Ridge Police Department is committed to providing the highest standards of service in partnership with the community," and we remain committed to achieving that ideal. Successful community policing requires a joint responsibility and commitment by both the department and the community members in working together cooperatively in solving problems, addressing quality of life issues, preventing crime before it occurs in our neighborhoods, with a great emphasis on beat officers rectifying problems with members of the

community as they occur. We realize that together, we can achieve what we cannot do alone.[49]

The above statement is typical of how cities portray the great advantages of adopting community policing strategies. Emphasis is placed on recognizing local residents as stakeholders who are invited to collaborate with the police department to fashion strategies and approaches to help fulfill its broader mission. There is also an explicit recognition of the department's commitment to problem-oriented policing, that is, solving problems in the community through best practices and with an offer of continual feedback from and to community members whose input is desired by police planners and administrators. There is also a promise that community policing will be proactive, to stop bad things before they have a chance to take root, rather than the standard reactive approach of conventional policing. Finally, the reference to beat cops solving problems as they occur indicates that such officers are trained in soft skills – or people skills, which are needed with the continuing diversity of the communities being served – and that they can resolve issues as they arise in an efficient and effective manner.

Although community policing invites feedback from citizens for purposes of planning and implementing operations best suited to the community, perhaps it is also the case that police feel that greater citizen input into daily police operations is needed in order to help legitimate police services in an era of declining crime rates and general public funding for the police. Also, are such problems as *fear of crime* really as big an issue for citizens as community policing advocates suggest it is? It might actually be the case that governments, by enumerating and making public the nature of crimes and the crime rate through official measures such as the Uniform Crime Reports, serve to instill greater fear of crime in citizens, even if the crime rate is actually in decline. Then, as disciplines such as criminology and sociology assume that fear of crime is a stable social object to be analyzed and studied in its own right, this produces a looping or feedback effect which helps perpetuate a fear of crime industry, helped along immensely of course by continuous coverage of sensational crime stories by the mass media.

Finally, police departments, and especially those employing community policing strategies, may be complicit in fomenting fear of crime by making police officers a continuing and visible presence in the community, in effect warning citizens about all the dangers that lurk just around each corner (such as the presence of police mini-stations in neighborhoods, the creation of neighborhood watch groups, or even the encouragement of citizen patrols). This appears to be the case, especially for those who are victims of violent crimes. For example, a study by Jessica Abbott and colleagues found that "greater effort by the police after victimization is related to greater fear levels for the victims."[50]

Net-widening

Even with the emphasis on professionalization and upgrading of policing and police services that began in the third era of policing, there is also the assumption that informal control systems continue to weaken, thereby necessitating the continuing growth and expansion of legal control. For example, since 1973 "the number of police in America has grown by nearly 50%, the number of prisoners by 500%, and the number of probationers by 400%."[51] Much of this has to do with the continuing growth of community-based corrections, which arose in response to rising incarceration rates and prison overcrowding problems since the early 1980s. A range of alternative or *intermediate sanctions* – such as home confinement, residential treatment, boot camps, halfway houses, shock or intensive supervision probation, and community service – are available to judges for those defendants whose offenses do not merit incarceration.

Although this appears to be a more compassionate and reasonable form of sanctioning, which also would appear to ease the problem of prison overcrowding, it has not worked out that way. This is because judges now have at their disposal this range of alternative sanctions which, because they are not as onerous in terms of their severity, are likely to be meted out simply because they are available. As the bar is lowered regarding what counts as an actionable offense, more persons are pulled into the criminal justice system, thereby contributing to the problem of *net-widening*.[52] Although net-widening by way of the use of intermediate sanctions has certainly increased the probation population – as noted above – it also has the potential to increase the incarceration rate as well. This is because many alternative sanctions have conditions attached to them – similar to traditional probation – whereby violation of the conditions of the sanction, or so-called *technical violations*, may lead to more formal and serious punishments, thus expanding legal control.

The poor get prison

This example of net-widening points out how legal control, as embodied in the organization, roles, and activities of the criminal justice system, operates in ways that is injurious to citizens, thereby exposing the injustices of legal control. Many of these injustices reflect the racism, sexism, and classism of the criminal justice system. Jeffrey Reiman and Paul Leighton, for example, have argued that because racial minorities and the poor are overrepresented in the criminal justice system in terms of arrests and convictions, the force used by representatives of the system to apprehend, prosecute, and punish minority defendants is no more justified than the force used by common criminals against their victims.

The authors go on to argue that even as police and other criminal justice professionals are supposed to protect the due process rights of those under criminal investigation and processing through the system, the desire of punitiveness in the pursuit of protecting and restoring the moral order often prevails. This means that for many poor and minority defendants, due process is more myth than reality.[53] Indeed, the values of due process and crime control often come into conflict even as the former is needed to ensure the legitimacy of the latter.[54]

Contrary to the notion that persons are equal under the law, the sad fact is that those with more money can buy a more favorable brand of justice than those who have less money. For example, poor defendants who are assigned public defenders are more likely to be given the advice to plead guilty (often to a lesser charge through plea bargaining) than are those defendants who can afford to hire their own private attorneys. This means that the poor are more likely to be convicted of crimes than the wealthy, who have the resources to fight criminal charges. And because the poor are more likely to be convicted, they are also more likely to have a prior arrest record if stopped by the police. And prior arrest record is one of the important elements that influences a police officer's decision to arrest a suspect. In other words, given the same crime and same set of circumstances at the scene, police officers will more likely arrest a suspect with prior involvement with the criminal justice system than one with no such record of prior arrests.

Some argue that persons from disadvantaged backgrounds should receive a "disadvantaged offender discount" when being sentenced.[55] Such lesser sentences for lesser economic crimes should help relieve the general burdens of poverty that wreak havoc on the poor. Along these same lines, in passing Proposition 47 in 2014, the state of California has reclassified the theft of merchandise valued at under $950 from a felony to a misdemeanor.[56] Supporters argue that this will lead to reduced incarceration costs, and the additional funds can then be used to expand mental health treatments, victim services, and other social programs. Critics argue that it will lead to a spike in shoplifting and other economic crimes, the cumulative costs of which will far outweigh any benefits of the legislation.

A study of crime data from the city of Santa Monica found that after passage of Proposition 47, there was a 15 percent increase in reclassified crimes, although no causal link was established between the law's passage and the uptick in such crimes during the observation period.[57] Other studies, however, have found that treating nonviolent economic crimes as misdemeanors rather than as felonies, especially in cases where nonprosecution is available, decreases the likelihood of future criminal justice involvement substantially.[58]

Conclusion

Proposition 47 and other local ordinances reflect the ongoing effort to establish goals of punishment – whether deterrence, incapacitation, rehabilitation, shaming, or even retribution – for purposes of reducing crime rates or reforming deviants.[59] As David Garland has argued, it is "only the mainstream processes of socialization that are able to promote proper conduct on a consistent and regular basis."[60] Formal punishment is at best a backup, a stopgap measure to be applied wherever and whenever the informal system fails to produce desired levels of control.

But what happens when a society has given up all hope that the informal mechanisms of control can do their job? For example, what happens when a critical mass of people believe that the modern family system has fallen into disrepair and likely cannot be fixed? The rhetoric of "families in crisis" and "children-at-risk" creates an opening for the encroachment of experts into more and more areas of life, to speak definitively about the ramifications of the loss of this most important and primary institution of informal social control.[61] But if indeed "nothing works" at the formal level of punishment and control, and if indeed the family is irreparably damaged as a mechanism for assuring the production of self-controlled individuals, what then?[62]

About all that is left is either (1) a full-blown commitment to governmentality and the carceral society, where the assumption is made that everyone is "bad" and thereby deserving of constant surveillance for purposes of catching and isolating those who will eventually deviate; or (2) a more vigorous commitment to medicalization, and especially to public healthification, whereby surveillance of the population is undertaken to determine the characteristics of those "at-risk" and to fashion interventions to reduce public harm accruing from their actions. Notice that these two options – governmentality and public health – converge on the technique of mass surveillance of the population.

In the next three chapters, critical case studies will be presented with regard to each of the three categories of control. The next chapter will kick things off with case studies of informal social control.

SUGGESTIONS FOR FURTHER READING

James J. Chriss, *Beyond Community Policing: From Early American Beginnings to the 21st Century* (2011)

> An overview of the development of municipal policing across modern society from the opening of the United States western frontier in the 1840s to new developments in post-9/11 policing. Chriss also presents a list of 106 "first principles" in the study of police and society.

Timothy W. Luke, *The Travails of Trumpification* (2021)

> Luke has assembled a number of his writings addressing the four years of

Trump's presidency, documenting the ways in which Trump's violation of notions of proper presidential conduct pushed democracy to breaking point. And even as Trump was defeated in his reelection bid, his influence is still felt with what Luke describes as the Trumpification of the Republican Party.

Marjorie Keniston McIntosh, *Controlling Misbehavior in England, 1370–1600* **(1998)**

A careful and thoroughgoing historical analysis of the changing nature of social control in England from medieval times to the early modern period.

Jeffrey H. Reiman and Paul Leighton, *The Rich Get Richer and the Poor Get Prison: Thinking Critically about Class and Criminal Justice,* **12th edn. (2020)**

Now in its 12th edition, this book is one of the best known indictments of the American criminal justice system's racism and classism. Although strident at times, on balance it contains more truths than errors.

David J. Rothman, *The Discovery of the Asylum* **(2002)**

Rothman's book, originally published in 1970, provides a thorough conceptualization of the rise of total institutions (such as prisons, mental asylums, and almshouses) in America from the colonial period to the late 1800s. His follow-up book, *Conscience and Convenience*, picks up the story from the Progressive Era (beginning in the 1890s).

DISCUSSION QUESTIONS

1. How and why was the execution of King Charles I in 1649 a watershed moment in the development of modern criminal justice systems?
2. Explain the doctrine of utilitarianism and the central role it played in Bentham's and Beccaria's ideas concerning justice and punishment.
3. Identify the social, political, and economic circumstances that gave rise to Peel's "new police" in England beginning in 1829.
4. The transition from primitive self-help to the later development of sworn police forces has been described as a movement from the "many watch the few" to the "few watch the many." Explain what this means.
5. Describe the Panopticon as originally formulated by Bentham and later made famous by Foucault. Why is Foucault generally critical of this particular design for watching over inmate populations?

PART II
CASE STUDIES IN SOCIAL CONTROL

Chapter 6

Informal Control: Housing Segregation, the Code of the Street, and Emerging Adulthood and Morality

Introduction

In this chapter we will explore a range of issues in the theory and conceptualization of informal control. Specifically, a select group of sociological and criminological theories are discussed to illustrate how informal systems of control – those associated with the socialization process and with group pressures to conform in everyday life – are often imbedded in and play an important role in theories of legal control. By examining such theories, we are in a better position to understand the linkages between informal and legal control. Marcus Felson and Rachel Boba explained this connection well when they stated that "crime carves its niche into everyday life."[1]

A basic insight to keep in mind is that, as persons age over the life course, the nature of informal control – but also legal and medical control – changes as well.[2] As discussed in chapter 3, from early childhood into the teenage years the primary agents of informal control are parents, schools, and peer groups, while the dominant institution of legal control is the juvenile justice system. For example, even controlling for such factors as the quality of the school and students' age, race, gender, and socioeconomic status, delinquent students are much more likely than nondelinquent students to be held back a grade, have poorer attendance records, make lower grades, and receive more disciplinary actions.[3] Children experiencing such educational deficiencies typically also experience difficulties in other areas of life (in their families and neighborhoods, with same-age peers, and so forth), indicating poor social bonding to conventional institutions and individuals and, hence, the weakening of informal controls.

In young adulthood, the primary institutions of informal control shift to higher education and vocational training, work, and marriage, with the criminal justice system replacing the juvenile justice system in the legal control realm. Finally, from middle adulthood and beyond, the salient

forms of informal control are work, marriage, parenthood, and investments in the community.

The main point to take away from this discussion of the shifting bases of
informal control over the life course is the importance of persons' ties to
others, or so-called *social bonds*, first within the context of primary groups
and then expanding outward as persons age, become more autonomous,
and begin contacting a greater diversity of individuals through schooling,
work, and other activities.[4] First, then, it is important to review perhaps
the major theory of social bonding ever developed, namely Travis Hirschi's
control theory. After having established the social bond as the fundamental
element in informal control, we will then be in a position to examine
critical case studies of informal control in three areas: housing segregation,
the code of the street, and emerging adulthood and morality.

The importance of social bonds

As we saw in chapter 1, Emile Durkheim argued that social order is assured
to the extent that persons are tied or attached to others in meaningful
ways. In earlier times, social solidarity – so-called mechanical solidarity
– was assured through cultural homogeneity and the subordination of
individuals to the will of the group. But with the growth of population,
industrialization, urbanization, mobility, and increasing migration from
a variety of countries, all of which served to further diversify the United
States and European nations, attachments between individuals were
jeopardized as greater anonymity made informal group-based control less
effective. As Durkheim stated, "as society spreads out and becomes denser,
it envelops the individual less tightly, and in consequence can restrain
less efficiently the diverging tendencies that appear."[5] Even so, informal
control does not simply disappear; rather, group control is augmented by
other forms of control including medical and legal.

Durkheim's emphasis on the importance of attachments in assuring
social order is located within a tradition of thought known as *mass society
theory*. As Irene Thomson explains,

> Mass society theory saw industrialization, urbanization, bureaucratization,
> and the sheer scale of modern society as destroying the strong group ties – of
> church, clan, guild, and local neighborhood – that had previously brought
> order to society and meaningful participation for individuals. The absence
> of such ties was viewed as leaving individuals alienated and vulnerable to
> manipulation by elites, demagogues, or extremist social movements.[6]

Intimate and intermediate groups such as families, friendship groups,
neighborhoods, and community organizations provide the basis for persons
to be connected with others in shared activities, and the cross-cutting
loyalties and obligations that persons feel as members of these collectivities

effectively hold them in check, thereby reducing deviance among group members.[7] The rise of the modern urban metropolis introduced various forms of social disorganization, as new social conditions effectively cut some of the crucial linkages between persons and their support groups. Within sociology, a theoretical perspective known as *social disorganization* developed at the University of Chicago and flourished between 1920 and 1935.[8] Chicago had experienced rapid population growth beginning in the 1850s, and this previously rural community was transformed in only a few decades into a thriving urban metropolis.

From social disorganization to social control

Through their empirical research taking place in Chicago and surrounding communities beginning in the 1920s, the social disorganization theorists documented that socially disorganized communities – those characterized by economic deprivation, high population turnover, low rates of home ownership, family disruption, and the like – tend also to be plagued by high rates of crime and delinquency. Albert J. Reiss, a University of Chicago sociologist who published and researched in several areas including community analysis, family studies, and delinquency, was the first person to articulate the criminological theory that came to be known as control theory. In essence, control theory emerges out of the broader social disorganization orientation, in combination with the continuing professionalization and scientization of family studies.

Reiss set out to isolate a set of personal and social controls that, when absent or weak, is associated with higher levels of delinquent recidivism.[9] Of special interest here is the problem of control in primary groups, most importantly, factors associated with the ability of families to control or provide for the needs of their children. As Reiss stated, "Primary groups are the basic institutions for the development of personal controls and the exercise of social control over the child."[10] An important part of "family control," according to Reiss, is the ability of the family to meet the needs of its members. The types of informal or primary group controls that Reiss found most significantly correlated with juvenile recidivism (operationalized as probation failures) were:

- family economic status (as status decreases, recidivism increases)
- marital relationships of natural parents (the weaker the affective ties between parents, the higher the recidivism of children)
- moral ideas and techniques of control (parents who provide their children with non-deviant role models, and parenting styles that are neither too lax nor too authoritarian or punitive, are associated with lower recidivism)
- institutional or foster home experience (children who have been

institutionalized are much more likely to recidivate than children with no previous experiences in foster or institutional homes).[11]

Reiss and later control theorists (such as Travis Hirschi) assume that persons are "bad" and will deviate unless significant obstacles are put in their way that, in essence, keep them from deviating. This is a change from ecological and social disorganization orientations, which tended to assume that persons are "good" but can be "made bad" as a result of family or marital disorganization, bad schools, disorganized communities, difficult economic times, and so forth. In assuming people are bad, control theorists must bank heavily on those social, personal, and institutional controls in place in any society which, it is claimed, steer people toward conformity and away from deviance.

Hirschi's control theory and elements of the social bond

Indeed, consensus theorists, utilitarian and rational-choice theorists, functionalist theorists, and control theorists all posit the importance of informal ties to groups and commitment to shared norms and values as the best guarantor of social order and stability. Travis Hirschi's social control theory is in essence an extension and refinement of Durkheim's notion that persons are more likely to deviate when they are poorly integrated into ongoing group relations.[12] Indeed, Hirschi cites approvingly the following passage from Durkheim:

> The more weakened the groups to which [the individual] belongs, the less he depends on them, the more he consequently depends only on himself and recognizes no other rules of conduct than what are founded on his private interests.[13]

Hirschi further suggests that the social bond consists of four crucial elements or dimensions. These elements are attachment, commitment, involvement, and belief. *Attachment* is the emotional, affective, or expressive aspect of the social bond. It is synonymous with concepts such as the internalization of norms (Durkheim), the Superego (Freud), or moral conscience. Proper internalization of the norms of conventional society orients individuals toward a feeling of respect and admiration for, or devotion toward parents, school, and peers. Hirschi argues that one must first have such an emotional attachment – a cathexis, in Freudian and Parsonian terms[14] – toward social objects before one can accept (or believe in) the rules they promulgate or represent.[15]

This brings us to a second crucial element of the social bond, namely *belief*. Belief is the evaluative, cultural dimension of the social bond. Hirschi explains that control theory assumes the existence of a common value system within society whose norms are sometimes violated.[16]

Hirschi assumes there is variation in the extent to which people believe they should obey the rules of society. Although most persons most of the time believe they should follow the rules of their society, which in itself points to a value consensus over right and wrong, moral and immoral, and good and bad among the citizenry, some do not. The less a person believes he or she should obey the rules, the more likely he or she will violate them.[17]

Another element of the social bond is *commitment*. Commitment represents the cognitive dimension of the social bond. It is the rational calculation a person engages in concerning how much time and energy to invest in certain lines of activity. For example, presumably someone who has spent many years studying to be a doctor would be less inclined to risk it all by engaging in some form of deviance, whereas another person with lower or no "stakes in conformity," such as the unemployed, the uneducated, or the petty street criminal, has very little to lose if caught in a deviant or criminal act.[18] Hirschi invokes Freud again here, stating "If attachment to others is the sociological counterpart of the superego or conscience, commitment is the counterpart of the ego or common sense."[19]

A final element of the social bond is *involvement*. Involvement is the behavioral dimension of the social bond. The idea is that the more time people spend in conventional activities, the less time they will have to engage in delinquent or deviant activities. Hirschi's control theory is summarized in table 6.1.

In summary, then, Hirschi suggests that the more *attached* persons are to other members of society, the more they *believe* in the values of conventional society, and the more they *invest in* and are *involved in* conventional lines of activity, the less likely they are to deviate.

Hirschi devotes an entire chapter to youths' attachment to parents, and a brief summary of these findings are in order.[20] As Hirschi states, "Control theory assumes that the bond of affection for conventional persons is a major deterrent to crime."[21] Children's attachment to their parents is, according to Hirschi, one of the single best predictors of delinquency: as attachment to parents weakens, delinquency increases. Granted, being attached or bonded to a parent means that the child is likely to be more heavily supervised and more often in the presence of parents than children

Table 6.1 Elements of the Social Bond

Level	Element	Description
BEHAVIORAL	INVOLVEMENT	Time spent in conventional activities
COGNITIVE	COMMITMENT	Rational calculation of the costs of lawbreaking for future goals
AFFECTIVE	ATTACHMENT	Emotional closeness to family, peers, and schools
EVALUATIVE	BELIEF	Ideas that support a conventional orientation

Source: Hirschi (1969) and Chriss (2007a).

with weaker bonds. But delinquent acts do not take much time to commit, so this sort of "direct control" explanation is only partial at best.

At least as important, if not more so, is the *moral* element in the attachment, the idea that even though a parent may be physically distant from a child who is considering committing a deviant act, the parent nevertheless could be psychologically present when such temptations arise. A child who asks him- or herself "What will my parents think?" at the moment of temptation tends to exhibit more strongly the moral component of attachment than a child whose conscience does not prompt him or her in the same way. This sort of "indirect control" is more important with regards to the attachment element of the social bond than the direct supervision of parents seeking to restrict the activities of their children.

Another element in attachment that is important in reducing delinquency is the quality of the communication between parents and their children. So-called "intimate" communication, where children freely and routinely share their thoughts and feelings with their parents or talk to them about their future plans, or even where parents explain their actions or feelings to their children, is strongly related to the commission of delinquent acts. In sum, parent–child relationships that lack intimate communication are associated with higher levels of juvenile delinquency.

Yet another important element of attachment is child's affectual identification with a parent or parents. One item in Hirschi's self-report study of youths that was especially strongly related to delinquency was "Would you like to be the kind of person your mother (father) is?"[22] As Hirschi summarizes: "the present data indicate that the closer the child's relations with his parents, the more he is attached to and identifies with them, the lower his chances of delinquency."[23] Children who affectually identified with their parents also tend to view them as role models, which thereby reduces their involvement in antisocial behavior. Beyond the level of any single concrete family, one may also observe that across a community, as more and more families are characterized by parents acting as positive role models for their children, a sort of *collective socialization* occurs at the network level whereby communities are better able to reduce or hold in check children's antisocial behavior.[24] Social (or community) disorganization occurs, then, where such community networks are weak or nonexistent.

The move to self-control

In their *A General Theory of Crime*, published in 1990, Michael R. Gottfredson and Travis Hirschi abandoned explicit reference to social bonds in favor of self-control as the primary factor in the explanation of crime and delinquency.[25] By admission of Hirschi and Gottfredson as well as outside commentators, it appeared that the move from social control (by way of the social bond) to self-control was radical, something akin to an epistemological or analytical rupture.[26] Why was this change made? Hirschi explains that

> After examining age distributions of crimes and analogous acts, Gottfredson and I reversed my original position, concluding that these acts are, after all, manifestations of low self-control on the part of the offender.[27]

According to the original social bonding theory of Hirschi, delinquency and crime were more a manifestation of the strength or weakness of the social bonds between the offender and others than of the particular characteristics of the offender. For Gottfredson and Hirschi, the stable differences in crime rates across group and individual levels that they discovered seemed to suggest that, rather than social bonds, the strength of which can fluctuate over time and with changes in the social and economic situations of individuals, the explanation of crime would more likely be found in one's level of self-control.[28]

But where does self-control come from? Gottfredson and Hirschi admit that it begins early in life and is relatively impervious to change later in life. Indeed, the authors adopted a "child-rearing model" to account for the origins of (or conversely, the failure to learn) self-control.[29] This move places great emphasis on the importance of primary groups and especially the socialization function of the family. However, Gottfredson and Hirschi never traced out the implications of the continuing importance of the family, not only for the formation and stability of social bonds, but also for the establishment of self-control.

It is clear that in the earlier control theory of Hirschi, the concept of attachments, or being embedded in a network of relationships, is the major element protecting persons from engaging in criminal or deviant behavior. Here control is a relational concept, insofar as those who have the right relationships – secure attachments to conventional others and beliefs in the propriety of conventional institutions and activities – are less likely to deviate. The theory states in no uncertain terms that, when working properly, the socialization process and the system of informal controls guarantee social order and stability. To the extent that these systems work effectively, there is less need to call forth formal control mechanisms such as police, courts, and corrections.

In their later version of control theory, Gottfredson and Hirschi argue that attachments are less important in explaining levels of crime and deviance, because self-control is relatively invariant and, on its own, accounts for rates of offending, not just with regard to criminality but to other forms of offending or deviance as well.[30] Persons who smoke or drink to excess, who are rude, loud, and boisterous, who are physically aggressive, who get into trouble with gambling and other vices, and who commit crimes of any sort (ranging from assault or theft all the way up to murder) are theorized as having lower levels of self-control than those who do not engage in such behaviors.

According to Gottfredson and Hirschi, the following are major characteristics of people with low self-control:

- They are impulsive and seek *immediate gratification*, and criminal acts often fulfill this need.
- They prefer acts that provide *easy and simple* gratification of desires, for example, sex without courtship, money without work, and so forth.
- They prefer acts that are *exciting, risky, or thrilling*, and many types of criminal and deviant acts are of this type.
- Since they seek immediate gratification, they often engage in criminal activities that provide *few or meager long-term benefits*.
- Since crimes often cause victims loss, pain, or discomfort, persons who perpetrate these acts tend to be *self-centered, indifferent, or insensitive* to the suffering of others.[31]

Psychopathy, empathy, and oxytocin

These characteristics of persons with low self-control seem consistent with aspects of *psychopathy*, a personality disorder of individuals who are described as impulsive, irresponsible, and interpersonally manipulative, and as having shallow affectivity, lacking empathy, guilt, or remorse, and having persistent antisocial tendencies.[32] Matt DeLisi and colleagues noticed this as well and investigated how or to what extent self-control converges with psychopathy.[33] Is it possible that self-control is merely a watered-down version of psychopathy? If so, psychopathy could be the unified theory of crime that sociologists, psychologists, and criminologists have been seeking for the last 100 years.[34]

All youth receiving services in the state of Missouri's Division of Youth Services – which is responsible for the care and treatment of youth sent to the agency by state juvenile courts – were invited to participate in the study. The authors used a leading self-report measure of psychopathy (mPPI-SF) along with a scale for measuring self-control developed earlier by two of the authors (DeLisi and Vaughn).[35] Other measures included sociodemographic data (sex, race, and prior year welfare recipient), a range of behavioral controls (such as ADHD diagnosis, past year substance use, and nature of police contact if any), and self-reported delinquency and victimization.

The authors found that both self-control and psychopathy predicted serious delinquency and violence. First, low self-control did significantly predict levels of violent offending, property offending, self-reported delinquency, and victimization. Second, psychopathy significantly predicted property offending and self-reported delinquency but, somewhat unexpectedly, was less strongly associated with violent offending and victimization. Even so, overall psychopathy explained more of the variance of the outcome or study variables than did self-control. In addition, youth who measured low on self-control and high on psychopathy were strongly associated with the most serious and chronic offending.

The surprising finding that low self-control was more strongly associated with violence than psychopathy may indicate that low self-control individuals act more opportunistically toward others who are perceived as vulnerable regardless of the nature of the ties between them and potential victims. Whereas males are certainly concerned with the potential of physical assault, women are concerned not only with physical assault but also sexual assault as well as uncivil acts such as catcalls or other forms of street harassment.[36] Studies of fear of public places indicate as well that, all things equal, women have greater fear in comparison to men.[37] This is in keeping with the truism, borne out in research, that "big people hit little people."[38] This means that females are perceived as more vulnerable than males and make better targets for opportunistic violence, a leading reason being the typical mismatch of size and strength between them. This is also why, for example, female police officers are more likely than male officers to be assaulted in family conflict situations, especially when the assailant is impaired.[39] Individuals with low self-control, then, may be described as generalists, who are open to all sorts of deviance and criminality perpetrated against strangers and intimates alike.

Conversely, even with the documented high levels of violence of psychopaths, they appear to be more selective in who they single out for predation. Although psychopathy has been understood as a mental disorder since the first edition of *DSM* – when it was referred to as Sociopathic Personality Disturbance[40] – research conducted by Daniel Krupp and associates casts doubt on this position.[41] Rather than a mental disorder, psychopathy may be an evolutionary adaptation, specifically, an alternative reproductive strategy that involves persistent exploitation of those with competing bloodlines.

Psychopaths are adept at extracting material, sexual, and reputational resources through deception and coercion, they are more genitally aroused to coercive sex than non-psychopaths, and they understand social vulnerability and take advantage of it. However, they are less likely than the general population to assault their relatives even as the truly mentally ill are *more* likely to violently attack kin. Hence, psychopaths show evidence of nepotistic inhibition of violence. Stated differently, although psychopaths were far more likely than non-psychopaths to have committed sexual assault, they were still less likely than non-psychopaths to assault their own kin.

Through their ruthless violence carried out strategically with no remorse or empathy, psychopaths are in effect thinning the herd of competing bloodlines while keeping their own bloodlines intact. They are also less likely than non-psychopaths to co-reside with kin, which may be a strategy to avoid harming them or simply reflects inbreeding avoidance. Psychopathy, then, is a methodically spiteful strategy, one which targets non-kin for violation so as to promote the fitness of kin bloodlines. In summarizing their study, the authors make the following points:

- Psychopathy is not associated with neurodevelopmental deficits associated with other serious mental disorders.
- Psychopathy is positively associated with successful social exploitation.
- Psychopathy is positively associated with mating effort and related patterns of sexual behavior.
- Psychopathy shows no negative effect on reproductive success.
- Psychopathy is associated with an increased likelihood of offending in instrumental ways.[42]

This suggestion, that psychopathy is not a mental illness but rather an evolutionary adaptation for assuring reproductive fitness through violent predation of non-kin, may be understood as one instance among a range of problems sharing a similar starting point or etiology. These are the problems that arise when the young are not properly bonded to society, beginning with the most consequential bond, that of mother–infant. Evidence shows that for many mammalian species – and not merely the case of humans – mothers' inattentiveness to their infants during the first two years of life are linked to a host of negative consequences. As Cort Pedersen suggests,

> In human and non-human primates, decades of clinical experience and research clearly show that the quality of nurturing received during infancy and childhood influences the development of parental and other social skills, the capacity to cope with stress and vulnerability to mental illness such as depression that often adversely affect social functioning.[43]

Such close and intimate contact, first between mother and infant, and later between adults in sexual relations, releases the hormone and neuro-transmitter oxytocin into the brain and many areas of the body. Oxytocin is especially important for "pair bonding as well as for social attitudes and conduct."[44] There is also a connection between sufficient levels of oxytocin and the development of empathy, and of course as we have seen, persons having low self-control or psychopathy are described as lacking empathy. For example, autism represents a bundle of communicative deficits including the inability to feel what others feel, that is, affective empathy or what sociologists call intersubjectivity. Treatments utilizing nasal sprays delivering doses of synthetic oxytocin have shown some evidence of enhancing understanding of social information for persons on the autism spectrum, for example, better ability to infer mental states from facial gestures.[45] These and many other problems of living, whether or not they are classified as mental disorders, share this feature of a lack of empathy for persons so afflicted. Indeed, there has been a movement to establish a new mental disorder, Empathy Deficit Disorder, which, it is hoped by advocates, will be considered by the nomenclature committee of the APA for inclusion in the next edition of *DSM*.[46]

Although it is clear there are biological aspects of social bonding, sociologists and criminologists may be averse to framing the issue in this way for fear of engaging in "biological reductionism." If this is the case, one may simply speak of the importance of parenting for informal control and leave aside the neurochemistry of social bonds. Hence, sociological research suggests that bad parenting is indeed criminogenic, to the extent that inadequate monitoring and supervision of children, as well as a lack of positive role modeling, may produce children possessing an especially destructive combination of aggressiveness and low self-control.[47] Connected with this, Gottfredson and Hirschi have long contended that males have higher rates of delinquency and crime than females because males have lower self-control. For example, research finds that girls have higher levels of self-control because parents tend to recognize and discipline their behavior more frequently than they do for boys.[48] This provides support to Hirschi's thesis that self-control is shaped early on by the nature and extent of parental supervision and oversight in the home.

Postindustrialism and the rise of the urban underclass

The problem of the decline of informal control in communities can be tied directly to major structural changes that have occurred in the United States and elsewhere. Since the 1960s especially, the economies of the United States and western Europe have experienced a profound transition. The backbone of the industrial economy was manufacturing, with coal, steel, textiles, oil, plastics, and rubber industries leading the way. Many of America's urban metropolises, especially those located in the northeast, were built on the physical labor of blue-collar industrial workers, which, in combination with machine automation, gave rise to factory mass production servicing the needs of a growing middle class. But even with the introduction of automation in plants and factories, industrialization was always labor intensive, and one way owners of industry began cutting costs was outsourcing their manufacturing operations overseas to take advantage of cheap labor in other (often third-world) countries.

This is one among a number of factors that has contributed to the transformation of industrial economies into so-called *postindustrial* economies, characterized by a move away from manufacturing as the primary mode of production to a bifurcated system in which service and hi-tech jobs prevailed. Under industrialism and manufacturing, a person who was willing to work hard could secure a middle-class wage and lifestyle without a formal education. But with the disappearance of manufacturing jobs and the transition to a postindustrial economy, a formal education became necessary in order to acquire an income that could support a middle-class lifestyle. Since manufacturing jobs were concentrated in the urban metropolis, and since a large percentage of the African-American population lived in these urban centers, due largely to the great Black urban migration that began after World War II, the problematic aspects of the transition to the postindustrial economy disproportionately affected Blacks.

Poverty became an urban phenomenon after the 1960s, and the racial aspect mentioned above became visible with the emergence of the Black urban ghetto. In 1969, the proportion of those living in poverty in America's central cities stood at 12.7 percent, but rose to 19.9 percent by 1982, a 57 percent increase over that time period.[49] As William Julius Wilson and Robert Aponte explain,

> in urban areas "postindustrial society" occupational positions that usually require levels of education and training beyond the reach of poor inner-city residents have significantly increased. Shifts in the urban job structure have accompanied changes in the demographic composition of large central cities from predominantly European white to predominantly black and Hispanic, resulting in a decrease both in the total population of central cities and in aggregate personal income levels.[50]

As Philip Cohen has argued, in metropolitan areas where the Black population is larger proportionate to the white population, increased minority size provokes a more hostile collective reaction from whites (the *visibility-discrimination* hypothesis). Also, larger minority workforces under conditions of occupational segregation lead to lower wages for minority workers (the *crowding* hypothesis).[51] Structural changes in the economies of advanced nations indicated by a number of phenomena – the concentration of the poorest of the poor in urban ghettos; educational failure; underemployment and job insecurity; social and spatial isolation; welfare dependency; teenage pregnancy and motherhood; father absence from the home and dwindling numbers of positive male role models for young boys in these neighborhoods; racial discrimination; and a propensity to engage in criminal and disorderly behavior – have given rise to a so-called urban *underclass*. Members of this underclass – whom William Julius Wilson refers to collectively as the "truly disadvantaged" – are characterized as living in chronic poverty, with little hope of escaping from it, because of a lack of income-producing employment.[52]

Besides economic disadvantages wrought by the transition to a postindustrial economy as well as continuing racism both overt and institutional, the underclass is disproportionately Black because of, ironically enough, the end of de jure housing segregation based on race. Although de facto housing segregation certainly still exists – a point we will return to shortly – it was not until recently that middle- and working-class Blacks have had the opportunity to find housing beyond the confines of the ghetto, and those economically able to move have indeed done so.[53] As William Julius Wilson explains,

> Especially since 1970, inner-city neighborhoods have experienced an outmigration of working- and middle-class families previously confined to them by restrictive covenants of higher-status city neighborhoods and suburbs. Combined with the increase in the number of poor caused by rising joblessness, the outmigration has sharply concentrated the poverty in inner-city neighborhoods. The number with poverty rates that exceed 40 percent – a threshold definition of "extreme poverty" neighborhoods – has risen precipitously.[54]

As a result, rather than being spread out across urban areas as in the past, the poor are now spatially concentrated in a subset of neighborhood locations, thereby isolating them from the social and economic mainstream. This concentration and *social isolation* of Blacks in particular are the distinguishing features of the urban underclass.[55] Although the anti-poverty programs appearing during the Obama Administration looked promising, many of these have withered on the vine as a result of hyper-partisan bickering and legislative gridlock.[56]

Housing segregation and white flight

In everyday life persons have the freedom to associate or not associate with whomever they choose, and they need never justify their decisions to others. Indeed, avoidance is one of the most often employed strategies by which persons maintain social or physical distance from others. Because of this, it is one of the most pervasive features of informal social control.

Since in their everyday lives persons are typically not required to explain why they choose to associate or not associate with particular individuals or groups, the basis for these decisions are not readily apparent at the informal or individual level. Yet, the actions of individuals – whether choosing friends, whom to date or marry, where to live or work, which organizations to join, or who to vote for – give rise to patterns at the collective level which can become objects of analysis for social scientists and targets of policymaking among legislators, city planners, and even the federal government. Certainly some of these individual choices people make about who to associate with and who to avoid are discriminatory in intent, whether decisions are based on race, class, religion, or other sociodemographic characteristics. And it is these sort of "*individual* incentives and individual perceptions of difference that can lead *collectively* to segregation."[57]

Between 1876 and 1965 so-called Jim Crow laws were passed in the southern United States, which acted as legal forms of segregation and discrimination against African-Americans and other persons of color. In response to this, four million African-Americans left the South and migrated to northern destinations between 1940 and 1970.[58] This was known as the "Great Migration," with the great majority of the movement going from the rural South to the industrial North. This immigration of Black southerners to northern destinations led to an exodus of largely white populations from central cities into newly forming suburbs.[59] Although the rate of "white flight" leveled off beginning in the 1960s, during its height in the 1940s and 1950s, it has been estimated that each Black arrival led to the departure of 2.7 whites.

Not only did this lead to an increase in the Black population in destination cities, it also produced a large decline in the urban population (about 17 percent during this time), as well as increases in housing vacancy rates, declines in housing values, and significant cuts in funding for public schooling.[60] By the 1960s, as the rise of urban ghettos became more apparent, the federal government attempted to intervene to reduce residential segregation both in central cities and their suburbs, primarily through the passage of the Fair Housing Act and the Housing and Urban Development Act, both in 1968.[61] We see, then, how legal control can be brought to bear to address actions occurring in the informal realm which, wittingly or unwittingly, limit the full participation in society of some persons or groups.

It is also worth noting that the decision to stay in or move out of certain areas, such as the phenomenon of white flight from the city to the suburbs, can be made on the collective level rather than remaining at the individual level. Mark Mulder has closely examined particular characteristics of white flight from the Chicago urban core beginning in the 1950s and discovered that not all of it occurred on the basis of random individuals or families deciding to leave during this period. Specifically, Mulder studied the conditions under which seven Christian Reformed Church (CRC) congregations located in the Chicago neighborhoods of Englewood and Roseland moved at approximately the same time.[62]

These congregations consisted of an enclave of Dutch ethnics. These Dutch-American residents of Englewood and Roseland belonged to various Reformed church communities whose traditions were largely Calvinist. The members of these churches were strongly bonded to fellow members of the church – in social network terms, they could be described as having strong or dense ties to each other – and conversely, these members had only shallow ties to the broader communities in which they resided.

Being embedded in the dense and redundant networks of their church and congregation, devout followers of the faith "are probably more likely to possess ties they are reluctant to lose (i.e., strong ties) than are those embedded in sparse networks," and "social conformity tends to be more common in the former than in the latter."[63]

In the face of the sociodemographic changes evident with regard to the influx of Blacks to the area and the departure of whites, CRC members' relatively superficial ties to their local communities, along with their strong ties to fellow members, provided the conditions for a mass exodus of virtually all members of these congregations. Most of the members ended up resettling in the outlying locations of Evergreen Park, Oak Lawn, Orlando Park, and South Holland.[64]

The racial–spatial divide

Given overwhelming evidence that de facto discrimination against racial and ethnic minorities continues to linger, some researchers are recommending policies that go even further than currently existing anti-discrimination and fair housing laws. In their research, Ruth Peterson and Lauren Krivo claim that the single greatest factor in the overrepresentation of African-Americans in violent crime is persistent and chronic urban housing segregation.[65] Peterson and Krivo point out that the opportunity to get up and move to safer neighborhoods with better schools – that is, to utilize avoidance as an informal sanction – is not equally distributed across the population. Because of the way race is conflated with social class, the ability to get up and move is an aspect of a deeper, more profound *racial–spatial* divide between whites and nonwhites, insofar as whites are more likely to be able to afford such moves while members of racial and ethnic minorities are less able. The policy implications of this structural race perspective is that we must go beyond "liberal" policies such as fair housing laws toward more radical solutions aimed at the halting of white privilege altogether. This would involve, at the very least, new massive wealth redistribution schemes where money is taken from well-off (predominately white) communities and transferred to impoverished (primarily minority) areas. This is merely one example of a list of recommendations for community reparations "as a strategy for building more equitable residential environments for areas of all colors."[66]

Subsequent research has found general support for Peterson and Krivo's concept of the racial–spatial divide and its connection to violence. Michael Light and Julia Thomas analyzed data on race-specific information on homicide, levels of housing segregation, and additional sociodemographic characteristics of 103 metropolitan areas of the United States across five decades (from 1970 to 2010). Three notable findings coming out of this research were:

- racial segregation significantly *increased* the risk of homicide victimization for Blacks;
- racial segregation significantly *decreased* the risk of homicide victimization for whites;
- controlling for all variables, segregation remains the key factor driving Black–white differentials in homicide mortality.[67]

Although these are robust findings regarding the role of segregation in driving differential homicide risks between Black and whites, there are likely micro, situational, or interactional dynamics at work that the authors did not account for. Richard Felson and Noah Painter-Davis examined National Incident-Based Reporting System (NIBRS) data and were able to take into account the race, age, and gender of victims of assault along with offenders' use of weapons and lethal intent. This micro-dynamics of crime incidents could be an important addition to the macro-based analysis of structural and sociodemographic factors regarding connections between segregation and violence. The findings of Felson and Painter-Davis suggest that Black offenders respond much more strongly to the victim's race than white offenders, and that violent incidents between two young Black men are about *six times* more likely to involve a gun than incidents between two young white men.[68] This research documents yet another tragic cost of being a young Black male.

Informal justice: the code of the street

This summary of the economic transition which has given rise to the urban underclass, as well as the various forms of informal or "off the books" discrimination that can be perpetrated against members of this class, serves as the backdrop for examining the work of Elijah Anderson.[69] Anderson, like other researchers concerned with urban poverty and the crime and social disorganization that attends to it, is particularly interested in the problem of inner-city youth violence. Anderson argues that youth violence springs from circumstances of life among the ghetto poor, including:

- lack of living wages,
- limited public services (police, utilities, trash),
- the stigma of race,
- drug use and sales,
- fatalism, or alienation and absence of hope for the future, and
- low or no stakes in conformity.

The combination of these circumstances creates a pervasive sense of despair which in turn spawns an oppositional culture among the ghetto poor. One key manifestation of this oppositional culture is the *code of the street*, a set of informal rules governing interpersonal public behavior, particularly those relating to violence.[70] These informal rules amount to "off the books" or unofficial justice which is synonymous with *vigilantism*, such as was seen in the violence that occurred across the United States during the nineteenth century and the opening of the western frontier (the so-called "code of the west"[71]). A more recent example is the vigilantism taking place between rival factions involved in urban street crime. Because criminals typically do not receive police protection (save for the occasional police informant), they often must take the law into their own hands and dispense their own brand of informal street justice.[72]

With regard to Anderson's research, areas covered by the code of the street include:

- proper comportment,
- the proper way to respond if challenged,
- regulating the use of violence,
- if the tacit rules of the code are violated, there will be consequences, and
- ignorance of the code is not a defense.

The single most important element underlying the code is *respect*. Being granted deference, being treated "right," and being accommodated are near the top of the value hierarchy of the code. Respect is hard-won but easily lost, hence the status system generated by the code is highly precarious. A person's status, respect, and sense of self must constantly be guarded. Gaining and keeping respect is important because those who are judged to be worthy of respect within the street environment are apt not to be bothered or "dissed."

This brings us to an interesting point. Within the street environment where the code is in effect and enforced, forms of "dissing" – such as maintaining eye contact too long, not wearing the right type of clothing, passing by too closely, or engaging in verbal insults – may seem trivial from the perspective of middle-class values. But on the streets of the inner-city, "dissing" can become a matter of life and death. The idea is that in mainstream society there are plenty of places to go to get your ego stroked if someone treats you badly or calls you a bad name or whatever. But in the inner-city, since respect and status are so precarious and since there is so little of it to go around, any challenges to it, even in the seemingly trivial cases of nonverbal behavior or talk which may be interpreted as offensive, are serious and deserving of vigorous defense.

Notice also that Anderson is working with the notion of status as a zero-sum phenomenon. Conceptualizing something as *zero-sum* implies that some valued thing – power, status, or prestige, for example – is a finite resource, meaning that those who have a lot of it effectively keep others from acquiring their fair share. And among those who have very little of the valued resource to begin with – such as the inner-city poor with respect to power or respect – whatever little is available will be fought over tenaciously, with sometimes deadly consequences. The zero-sum perspective on power or status is contrasted to an alternative perspective which views these phenomena as resources which go through cycles of inflation and deflation. Following Talcott Parsons, let us call this the symbolic or *generalized medium* perspective.[73] Parsons viewed power not as a fixed or finite resource in society, but as a generalized medium seated in the polity which circulates throughout the social system. Power is in effect the instrument through which collective goals are pursued. As Parsons explains,

> Power, as a symbolic medium, is like money in that it is itself "worthless," but is accepted in the expectation that it can later be "cashed in," this time in the activation of binding obligations. If, however, "power-credit" has been extended too far, without the necessary organizational basis for fulfillment of expectations having been laid, then attempting to invoke the obligations will result in less than a full level of performance, inhibited by various sorts of resistance.[74]

The thing to be pointed out here is that those who hold to a zero-sum view of valued resources tend toward the liberal side of the ideological or political spectrum, while those who hold the generalized medium view tend toward the conservative side. In the case of respect or status, Anderson's zero-sum perspective decries the fact that persons in the inner-city, often through no fault of their own, are not given the opportunity to acquire levels of status, respect, or living wages because the means for their acquisition are blocked or absent. Caught up as they are in the structural constraints and degradations of the inner-city, some will turn to aggression and other forms of deviant behavior in reaction to their dilemma. Indeed, metropolitan areas with few quality jobs for less-skilled and less-educated workers are characterized by significantly higher rates of violent and property crime.[75] Although such individuals cannot be totally absolved of their behavior, there is the recognition that structural forces beyond the control of individuals – such as the change from an industrial to a postindustrial economy, or the reality of the racial–spatial divide – are the root cause of such unwanted behaviors.

We see, then, that with regard to the code of the street, respect is a valuable form of *social capital*, which is "the ability of actors to secure benefits by virtue of membership in social networks or other social structures."[76] Because it emphasizes relationships and the informal ties to others in the community – for example, getting a job may have more to do with "knowing someone who knows someone" rather than the technical or formal aspects of the job such as how well you scored on an entry-level examination – many observers argue that social capital is an important form of informal control which in the transition from mechanical to organic solidarity (Durkheim) has declined especially in urban communities.[77]

Within the inner-city, there is a pervasive sense that the police cannot be relied upon to maintain order and respond to citizens' calls in a timely manner. Under these conditions, where formal controls are viewed as ineffective, self-help will come to predominate. The code of the street is the embodiment of this informal system of self-help. Crucial aspects of the code are those tacit norms dealing with the presentation of self. With regard to presence on the streets, young males especially must display a certain predisposition to violence. This may involve certain facial expressions, gait, talk, the wearing of certain clothing (for gangs and street-oriented persons expensive athletic attire is preferred), jewelry, and grooming.[78] To be respected, it is vital to have the right look. Those who have the "right" appearance according to the tacit norms of the code deserve a measure of respect, while those that do not uphold these appearance conventions are likely to be deemed socially deficient and thereby subject to challenge or attack.

As Anderson argues, this becomes a vicious cycle, trapping many poor ghetto youths. Ghetto youth must constantly "campaign for respect," and this means presenting a "tough" self. They learn at an early age to socialize competitively with peers, and they learn the social meaning of fighting. Physical and verbal aggression is taught at home, at school, and in the streets. In essence, might makes right, toughness is a virtue while humility is not.[79] Additionally, individuals shore up their precarious identities by acquiring valued things. One may campaign for status by taking the possessions of others. The ability to violate somebody – to "diss" or "get in their face" – is valued. As Anderson argues, "In this often violent give-and-take, raising oneself up largely depends on putting someone else down. ... The resulting craving for respect gives people thin skins and short fuses."[80] Indeed, commitment to the code of the street and the behavioral requirements arising from it predict earlier anticipated death, which of course has serious health ramifications for communities in which the code is enforced.[81] Overall, this serves to illustrate the zero-sum nature of respect within the social system of the urban ghetto.

It should also be noted that the code of the street is not limited to the physical confines of the streets of the inner-city. It is also present in aspects of popular culture, particularly in rap music. Rap music lyrics consistently emphasize the theme of respect, asserting that violence is an appropriate and expected response and that disrespect cannot be tolerated. In this case, violence is a form of informal social control in the form of self-help.[82]

Youth and morality

Earlier in the chapter we covered the social bonding theory of Travis Hirschi and looked at how informal controls operate along the developmental pathways of all our lives. The idea is that in order to keep people in check, to assure that their behavior is predictable and meets tacit notions of propriety, there must be inculcated in each of us a sense that there is something bigger and grander which provides a context for making sense of our lives. Historically, religion has been an important mechanism of informal control, whereby individual desires or wants are subordinated to broader notions of righteousness or "the good life."[83] Likewise, the primary groups of tribes and families have always operated not only to teach their members right and wrong, but also to give them a sense of home or place. Indeed, membership in these primary groups gives to each of us a sense of identity, of who we are.

Clearly one of the most pressing projects of the social order is imparting prevailing notions of right and wrong to children. This is something that all societies contend with, and human history is replete with references to the various strategies humans have devised to control and discipline young persons. The seventeenth-century Puritans of Massachusetts Bay believed that most forms of deviance were signs of sin. In order to keep them from taking the path of moral and spiritual depravity, the Puritans instilled in their youth the fear of God through immersion in devotional activities, and disobedience was often dealt with harshly.[84] Indeed, early Puritan writers such as Paul Bunyan and James Janeway spoke directly to parents and their children about how to maintain moral and godly lives, reminding them of the terrible consequences if they strayed. In short, good children go to heaven while bad children are condemned to the eternal flames of hell.[85]

Since the time of the Puritans, concern over youthful misbehavior has been a recurring theme, as each generation promulgates its own discourses of children-at-risk and wayward youth. There is also the existence of a "generation gap," namely, the disjunction that exists between the cultural values and social experiences of parents and the modified values and experiences of their children.[86] This can produce conflict and tension between members of succeeding generations (measured as a span of a decade or two). In essence, persons born within one particular generation – consisting of a generational cohort – are typically socialized into a set of norms, values, and beliefs that are somewhat distinct from those of other generations. Generational context, then, can shape how persons view the world and how they come to define and accept what is "true" or "known."[87]

Since World War II there has arisen the practice of naming specific generations and designating time spans for them. In the United States, such generational labeling is as follows:

- Baby Boomer (1946–65)
- Gen X (1966–79)
- Millennials (or Gen Y, 1980–98)
- Gen Z (1999–2012)[88]

In addition to studying generational cohorts, which are fixed in time based upon the time span designation for each of them, there is also the possibility of studying age cohorts. Age cohort studies take a snapshot of a population at a particular time and seek to determine characteristics about persons in particular age groups, for example, all those aged 12 to 17. If a study was conducted of this group in, say, 2015, the researchers could then come back in three years and gather data from a fresh group of 12 to 17 year-olds who, three years ago, were ages 9 to 14. Repeating a number of observations of 12 to 17 year-olds over a number of years would then provide a dynamic view of persons in this age cohort over time.

Long-range planning of age cohort studies could capture aspects of generational context if this were a significant part of the research design and the questions being asked. For example, Baby Boomers could be surveyed between 1958 and 1963 when they were 12 to 17 years old, and likewise Millennials could be surveyed between 1992 and 1997 when they were 12 to 17 year-olds, and so forth. These data could then be compared to ascertain possible generational effects within specified age cohorts.

Sociologist Christian Smith and colleagues at Notre Dame University have used the age cohort design to explore American youths' views toward morality.[89] Smith argues that because of certain long-term historical and cultural trends in America, the current era of emerging adulthood – specifically, persons in the 18–23 age range – is unique in world history. The pertinent American trends are:

- the explosive growth of higher education, which ties in with changes in job markets which young persons are competing to enter into;
- the delay in marriage – age at first marriage is the highest it's ever been;
- changes in the American and global economy, especially as this concerns the decline in traditional blue-collar manufacturing work and the rise of service and information-rich occupations;
- parents are increasing and extending investments in their children, both out of necessity and by choice;
- new technologies are contributing to a fundamental altering of traditional notions of family and relationships, especially as this relates to birth control technologies, which have effectively severed the connection between sex and procreation;
- the rise in postmodern theory, which teaches that traditional ways of understanding the world have fallen into disrepair, and because there are no foundational truths to be had, what is left are cultural and moral relativism.

The latter point is emblematic of a popular ethic which took hold in the 1960s with the hippie movement, especially concerning admonitions that you should leave people alone to "do their own thing." Back in the 1960s, this cultural ethos of the hippie movement was dubbed The New Morality.[90] Writing in the 1960s, sociologist Alvin Gouldner saw this New Morality as encompassing a broader social movement than merely those freedoms of sexual liberation and drug experimentation espoused by hippies. Gouldner saw the rise of the New Left in general as a repudiation of the "establishment," including their values of hard work, delaying gratification, respect for authority, and technical efficiency. As Gouldner explained,

> The emergence of new "deviant" social types today – the cool cats, the beats, the swingers, the hippies, the acid-heads, the drop-outs, and the "New Left" itself – is one symptom of a renewed resistance to utilitarian values.[91]

Youth of the 1960s who were active in the hippie and beat scenes were (often) unwittingly recreating a Bohemianism which first appeared in France in the first part of the nineteenth century. As an artistic and existential enterprise, American Bohemianism consisted of four distinct elements.[92] One is *romanticism*, a worldview which emphasizes spontaneity and originality, while simultaneously rejecting overly strict principles for ordering reality. In the arts, romanticism gave rise to improvisation – the avant garde and haute couture – in acting, music, poetry, writing, fashion, architecture, and cuisine. Another is an emphasis placed on feelings and mood, or *emotionalism*, which demands authenticity in expression and self-presentation. A third element of American Bohemianism is *monasticism*, which refers to the tendency to form self-enclosed communities where persons of like mind can congregate and do their thing safe from the prying eyes and disapproving glances of the "squares" or "stuffed shirts" who otherwise could spoil their "scene." A fourth element is *substance*, which specifically refers to the pursuit of unconventional lifestyles or experiences. One clear application of the ethos of substance in this sense is the pursuit of hedonistic experiences (e.g., mind-expanding drugs and promiscuous sex), but also the quest for transcendence, that is, the effort to push human perception to its limits (hence, in the 1960s much was made of Eastern spirituality and mysticism).

Many of the youthful beatniks and hippies of the 1960s – and of course, of the Baby Boom generation – did eventually become more conventional in their behavior and lifestyle choices as they got older. A good number of them got married and had kids of their own (although rates of cohabitation skyrocketed beginning in the 1960s, which set the stage for what today is historically high rates of divorce). The children and grandchildren of this Baby Boom generation – many of whom are represented among the ranks of those emerging adult Gen Xers and Millennials studied by Smith and his colleagues – do not share many of the ideas or perspectives of their parents (although a few continuities between the generations will be noted below). In their own way, they rebelled, just as their parents rebelled against the "establishment" during the 1960s and 1970s.

According to the findings of Smith with regard to today's emerging adults, areas of consistency between their worldview and those of their parents are those of romanticism and emotionalism (the first two points above). In its rejection of hierarchy and control, romanticism favors an ethic of "doing your own thing" and not passing judgment on others' scenes and activities. In effect, this sentiment produces forms of cultural and moral individualism. Many of the young persons Christian Smith spoke with had trouble articulating morality or its meaning. For example, when asked where they got their ideas about right and wrong, many could not explain the sources of their ideas. Many in the group of emerging adults had trouble connecting their individual notions of right and wrong to an overarching or shared system of belief. One young woman who was interviewed about this said that she made up her own view of morality, and that her moral outlook was just something she "thought up" on her own, that "just kinda came out of thin air."[93]

Young persons today, according to Smith, are apt to view morality as something imposed on society which is largely arbitrary or capricious. Who is to say what the rules are? From the vantage point of moral relativism, each person must decide for him- or herself what is or is not moral. For example, one woman stated that terrorism may not be a morally condemnable act because the terrorists believe what they are doing is justified. And what about someone who kills "tons of people"? Well, "earthquakes kill tons of people and I'm sure some people believe that God caused the earthquakes and that means there was some purpose for them."[94]

As part of their Bohemianism, the hippies and beats of earlier generations rejected materialism. Indeed, many young persons of the New Left generation saw themselves as engaging in a revolutionary struggle against not only materialism, but also Victorianism (sexual prudishness), utilitarianism, imperialism, racism, and sexism.[95] However, the current generation of emerging adults part company with their Bohemian parents with respect to materialism. Contemporary emerging adults are, according to Smith, captive to consumerism (as we saw in chapter 3). For them, self-improvement does not come by way of a shared moral code handed down across generations (Durkheim's moral solidarity). Instead, it comes by way of having the latest technological games and gadgets. And in another iteration of the generation gap, being able to use the newest consumer technologies also marks off the current generation from "old folks" who do not have a clue about computers, smartphones, or social media. The "whatever makes you happy" ethos translates into shopping and collecting stuff for the sake of having it. This consumerist redefinition of social life has affected everything, including how young persons view a college education. Whereas previously education was viewed as a public good because of the way it contributed to the development of an informed citizenry, education is now more apt to be viewed as a private good in terms of how that educational degree connects the individual to the job market and to promised higher social status.[96] This also wittingly or unwittingly buys into the "college for everyone" mantra of neoliberalism.[97]

The purpose of life

Smith's work on emerging adults and how they make sense of morality provides useful glimpses into aspects of informal control. Although it appears to be an overall bleak assessment, a brief contrast with a later-published study finds somewhat more positive aspects of the search for meaning and the good life undertaken by emerging adult Millennials. The authors (Glanzer, Hill, and Robinson) got permission to access interviews of 230 18 to 23 year-olds conducted in 2008 as part of the National Study of Youth and Religion (NSYR).[98] The authors conducted a further qualitative analysis of the interview data, looking specifically at how these young persons articulated a sense of purpose for their lives.

The authors were particularly interested in how those surveyed responded to the "purpose" question, phrased typically along the lines of "What do you want to get out of life?" or "What is the purpose of life?" In analyzing and coding the data, the authors came up with a thematic grouping of responses. Somewhat consistent with Smith's study, 32 percent of the respondents said that they had no purpose in life, that they were drifting aimlessly through a random succession of events. This group was labeled *Directionless*. However, 34 percent of the respondents were placed into the category of *Achievers*. The biggest group of achievers reported seeking professional (or work) achievement, while a somewhat smaller group sought to achieve "happiness" in a vague or unspecified sense. And strongly contrary to Smith's findings, a miniscule number of Achievers (only 5 out of 77) sought specifically material achievements.

A slightly smaller third group, consisting of 26 percent of respondents, were labeled as *Relationalists*. These persons identified their purpose as "relating to others."[99] Two subtypes were Virtue Relationalists and Family Relationalists. The Virtue Relationalists described themselves as altruists, whose purpose in life was to help others, while the Family Relationalists saw as their main purpose in life attending to and nurturing family bonds and relationships, including plans to get married and start a family. Many of the Family Relationalists admitted to being somewhat confused about what the future holds, but that establishing and shoring up family relationships would act as a foundation for getting on with the rest of their lives.

A very small group of persons (2 percent) labeled the *Religious*, specifically mentioned God or religion as a key element in articulating their purpose in life. A comment by one respondent was indicative of the sentiments of this group: "I feel a sense of purpose but that my biggest purpose is to love God and bring glory to Him."[100] The small size of the *Religious* group is consistent with Smith's finding that today's emerging adults are simply not interested in religion, seemingly in alignment with the general thesis of secularization.

Conclusion

In this overview of informal control we have truly only scratched the surface. The study of informal social control encompasses a vast arena of human values and activities. Even more to the point, even with the rising prominence of medical and legal control across most modern societies, informal control maintains a solid presence within the social control field. This is because people must still deal with other people in their everyday lives, and in these moments of contact, persons bring to bear their own ideas and resources, uniquely configured within particular lifeworld arrangements. Although the growth of formalization, whether by way of medical or legal authority, is real and palpable, there is a limit as to how far such formalizations can penetrate into the very heart of everyday life. The question of just how far formal systems of control should steer our everyday affairs is important and far-reaching, and negotiations over visions of the good life will continue to dominate discussions in the realms of religion, politics, families, schools, government, and the mass media into the foreseeable future.

SUGGESTIONS FOR FURTHER READING

Matt DeLisi, *Psychopathy as Unified Theory of Crime* (2016)
DeLisi makes the case that psychopathy could be the unifying theory for criminology while gathering data on various aspects of it to bolster his argument. In addition to examining parallels between self-control and psychopathy, DeLisi relates a number of other established sociological and criminological perspectives to psychopathy. In so doing, DeLisi forces confrontation with sociobiological perspectives on crime, which are largely out of favor among sociologically-oriented criminologists.

Wilhelm Heitmeyer, Simon Howell, Sebastian Kurtenbach, Abdul Rauf, Muhammad Zaman, and Steffen Zdun, *Codes of the Street* (2019)
This book extends Anderson's code of the street concept to the international level, examining the specific street codes operating in dangerous neighborhoods and the youth violence emerging from them. The primary focus is on Germany, Pakistan, and South Africa.

Brian J. Jones, *Social Capital in American Life* (2019)

The author analyzed data from the General Social Survey (GSS) from the 1970s through 2008 to ascertain the conditions under which Americans reported being relatively happy and contented with their lives. Even with concerns with the general decline of social capital, Jones' careful analysis of attitudinal data from the GSS shows the potential for linking satisfactions from everyday life back to public and institutional spheres.

Richard Rothstein, *The Color of Law: A Forgotten History of How Our Government Segregated America* (2017)

This study complements Ruth Peterson's observations on the racial–spatial divide, going beyond the level of individual decision-making toward a historical examination of those US policies that effectively produced and sustained various forms of segregation.

Werner Stark, *The Social Bond*, six volumes (1976–87)

This is the definitive treatment of the social bond which took the author a decade to complete. Stretching across six volumes, topics covered include antecedents of the social bond (vols. 1 and 2); custom and law (vol. 3); ethos and religion (vol. 4); and threats to the social bond (vols. 5 and 6).

DISCUSSION QUESTIONS

1. What is the social bond, and how does it play a part in informal control? Is Hirschi's conceptualization of the social bond correct or believable? Why or why not?

2. In the chapter we saw that one of the most pervasive aspects of informal control is simple avoidance, that is, the personal freedom to associate or not associate with whomever you want and for whatever reason. Under what conditions should avoidance be brought to the attention of higher level agents of control (e.g., legal or medical)? Think about how to deal with issues of avoidance at the personal level versus the group or collective level.

3. If there has been a decline in social capital, as Robert Putnam suggests, what are some things that could be done to stem the tide of individualism and promote more social engagement?

4. Are generational labels (e.g., Baby Boom, Millennial, Gen Z) a useful way of organizing understandings of shared experiences and worldviews? Why or why not?

5. Can Christian Smith's findings regarding problems of morality and consumerism among emerging adults be tied to other trends or factors not explicitly mentioned in the book? For example, what about political correctness? Or communications technologies (such as social networking sites)? Think about how these or other factors could be related to the author's findings.

Chapter 7
Medical Control: Selective Mutism, Autism, and Violence as a Disease

Introduction

These case studies in medical social control have been chosen for the following reasons. First, autism or autism spectrum disorder (ASD) is perhaps the single best known *DSM* category of mental illness afflicting young persons today, although its diagnosis is increasing among adults who may have gone undiagnosed for decades. Because of its high profile and the wide coverage it has received in both the mass media and the medical and social scientific literatures, ASD is worth examining from the social control perspective. The Centers for Disease Control (CDC) recently reported that 1 in 54 children born in the United States is diagnosed with the condition.[1] Autism has become such a prominent medical condition that a scholarly journal, *Autism*, was founded in 1997 to explore the numerous issues – social, medical, political, legal, and psychological – associated with the illness. Second, in order to provide a contrast to this high-profile childhood affliction, I have chosen to cover selective mutism, a mental illness that although virtually unknown to the general public, nevertheless vividly illustrates the continuing expansion of categories of mental illness of young persons. Third, due largely to the success and growth of public health across Western society, many conditions previously dealt with as social problems, such as violence, are now being viewed as medical issues. The third case study, then, examines this idea of violence as a disease.

The antipsychiatry movement

In order to set the stage for this discussion, it is worthwhile to note that a number of prominent critics of psychiatry, such as Thomas Scheff, Thomas Szasz, and Erving Goffman (all of whom were pioneers in the "antipsychiatry movement" of the 1950s and 1960s) argued that mental illnesses were merely labels applied to social deviance.[2]

The 1960s was a decade marked by challenges to the political and authority structures of the Western status quo, with such social movements as civil rights, women's rights, gay rights, campus protest, and anti-war protest leading the way. Included in this critical movement were denunciations of psychiatry and the warehousing of "social misfits" into prisons and mental asylums.[3] The critiques against the psychiatric establishment launched in the 1950s by Goffman, Szasz, and others culminated in the 1960s and into the 1970s with a deinstitutionalization movement whereby large numbers of formerly institutionalized individuals were released back to their local communities. Diminished funding for rehabilitation, stricter guidelines for involuntary commitment, and the development of antipsychotic medications such as olanzapine and clozapine to control the symptoms of schizophrenia – one of the most common mental illnesses linked to violence and hence to arrests and incarceration – all contributed to further deinstitutionalization along with rising rates of homelessness in urban areas.[4] The earlier left-liberal and anti-authoritarian critique of total institutions – especially the prison and the asylum – coincided with a later conservative turn in American politics in the 1980s (e.g., the election of Ronald Reagan as President of the United States and the founding of the conservative legal organization the Federalist Society in 1982, the latter of which was handily blamed for the scourge of homelessness and community disorganization which had become palpably visible by that time).[5]

Allyson Skene's summary of the position of scholars within the antipsychiatry movement is worth noting:

> Psychiatry, they agree, is the only branch of medicine which will treat a "disease" in the absence of biological abnormality and without a patient's consent. This, combined with the fact that the primary target of psychiatric interventions is behavior and psychological states, leads to the conclusion that psychiatry is a form of social control which represses socially undesirable behaviors.[6]

Skene is correct about the general animus directed towards the field of psychiatry by these authors and others within the antipsychiatry movement. However, one need not take an overtly critical or even hostile stance toward psychiatry and its system of classifying mental disorders when pointing out the unmistakable social control function of psychiatry. The overriding concern of the discussions of selective mutism, ASD, and violence in the next several sections will be to explore how and why these particular conditions became medicalized, or similarly, why informal control of and responses to these behaviors came to be deemed somehow inadequate.

Selective mutism

According to the *DSM-5* (published in 2013), selective mutism (313.23, formerly "elective mutism" in earlier versions of the *DSM*) is listed as a mental disorder usually first diagnosed in infancy, childhood, or adolescence. The essential characteristic of *selective mutism* is the failure of a child to speak in situations where there is a social expectation that the child should speak (such as, for example, in the classroom). Additionally, the child's silence in these social settings cannot be attributed to any speech impediments (whether physiological or neurological). In other words, when a child who is able to speak refuses to do so in certain situations or social settings, the child could be diagnosed with selective mutism.

Research on the "disorder" finds that it typically begins during the pre-school ages, is more common among girls than boys, and although rare (affecting between 1 and 3 percent of the childhood population, and only 0.01 percent of the general population) is found at all levels of society.[7] Prior to the release of the fourth edition of the *DSM* in 1994 and later *DSM-TR* (or "text revision") version released in 2000, clinicians consistently found that one of the early developmental "risk factors" for selective mutism was "a history of immigration."[8] This is clearly absurd insofar as an immigrant child newly arrived to the United States (or any other host country) would likely not yet have full proficiency in spoken English (or other host tongues) and hence might very well not speak much, if at all, in a classroom or other formal setting. Here, given the social circumstances of newly arrived immigrants, the mutism or silence would be normal, not pathological. The acknowledgment of this oversight was added to the *DSM-4*. Diagnostic criteria for selective mutism include:

- consistent failure to speak in specific social situations (in which there is an expectation for speaking, e.g., at school) despite speaking in other situations;
- the disturbance interferes with educational or occupational achievement or with social communication;
- the duration of the disturbance is at least one month (not limited to the first month of school);
- the failure to speak is not due to a lack of knowledge of, or comfort with, the spoken language required in the social situation; and
- the disturbance is not better accounted for by a communication disorder (e.g., stuttering) and does not occur exclusively during the course of a pervasive development disorder, schizophrenia, or other psychotic disorder.[9]

As mentioned above, selective mutism is classified as a disorder of infancy, childhood, and adolescence because the etiology of the disorder is thought to be complex. Earlier researchers suggested that selective mutism was a motivational disorder, insofar as children were using silence as a way of manipulating persons and the immediate environment. This is, in effect, a variation of the "silent treatment," a strategy used in informal relationships, often most effectively employed by females against male friends or partners for their perceived wrongdoings. Extending this idea from the realm of informal control to that of medical control, children who choose to be silent may be understood as motivated out of the anxiety of having to face situations where speech is expected.[10] Other studies suggest family dysfunction may play a role, such as enmeshment between mother and mute child, a distant or detached father, strained marital relations, or a history of shyness in the family.

All things considered, the current consensus among psychologists, psychiatrists, school personnel, and other clinicians who deal with selective mutism on some level is that it is an anxiety disorder and should probably be classified as so. The shyness mentioned above is considered to be the major contributor to anxiety disorders that may in turn become manifest as selective mutism. In essence, we have in selective mutism the pathologization of shyness, and this has occurred overwhelmingly within the context of school assessment and evaluation.[11] Just as the use of drugs such as Ritalin to treat attention deficit disorder (ADD) has experienced explosive growth within the past two decades, so too have drugs (primarily antidepressants such as Prozac) been recommended for the treatment of selective mutism. As far as children are concerned, and especially insofar as social control within the schools is considered tenuous and in desperate need of shoring up (because of, among other things, the alleged decline of the family; the proliferation of violent television, film, and video games; the changing sociodemographics of public schooling; the diminution of teachers' authority within the classroom; and the tragic phenomenon of school shootings), the biomedicalization of youth continues unabated.[12]

Proponents of a biomedicalized view of childhood ills tend to agree on the biological, hormonal, or neurological underpinnings of various disorders, including selective mutism. The extent to which they favor drug treatments, however, depends on the ability of particular clinicians or therapists to provide drug treatments to patients or clients. Since doctors and psychiatrists own a monopoly on drug treatments, other non-medical personnel are limited to providing various types of "talking cures" such as behavioral or cognitive-behavioral therapy, social learning or self-modeling approaches, play therapy, family systems approaches, social skills training, or psychoanalysis more broadly defined.[13]

A few researchers have offered warnings about how far this pathologization and biomedicalization of youthful conduct could go if left unchecked. For example, as Neil Gordon argues,

Although elective mutism may be one end of a spectrum from shy children to those in whom there is a presumptive cause, such as immigration, unhappiness at school, or anxiety over some social disaster, it will be important to reserve management and treatment to those in whom the problem is significantly affecting the child, and or, the parents. Otherwise, as stressed by Kolvin and Fundudis, a lot of children will be labeled unnecessarily who are reacting not unreasonably to a strange situation, such as a reception class in school, and who will soon be talking normally.[14]

One of the reasons that a seemingly innocent behavior such as shyness could be interpreted as pathological and brought under the orbit of selective mutism is that a critical mass of mental health and school professionals assume that shyness itself is biologically-based. This means that when shyness becomes excessive and is deemed to "interfere" with the activities of children within (primarily) school settings, it is subject to drug treatment or other types of clinical interventions. Indeed, children who possess a "shy biological temperament" and who exhibit the various diagnostic criteria of selective mutism are apt to be viewed by clinicians and health providers as suffering from a childhood anxiety disorder that is biologically-based.[15]

For the most part, school personnel appear to be thoroughly committed to the notion that selective mutism is a "real" mental disorder and that it has a biological basis. Consider the case of a 13-year-old student who since the age of five-and-a-half had remained virtually speechless within classroom settings.[16] Early on, elementary school teachers and school psychologists had attempted to get him to speak but to no avail. He was placed in a learning disability classroom, but this did not help. He maintained his muteness. By the age of 13, teachers had become so frustrated by this student's lack of progress that school administrators threatened legal action against his parents because they would neither seek nor consent to psychological services for their son. Under the threat of legal action, the parents relented and the student was put into a multi-modal treatment plan involving therapists, school personnel, family members, and peers. After one-and-a-half years of treatment, the student began speaking and made a successful transition from junior high school to high school. The treatments were deemed a resounding success, targeted as they were to the reduction of his social anxiety which was believed to be fueling his mutism.

However, claims of the efficacy of these and other interventions aimed at "curing" the "disorder" of selective mutism need to be critically examined. First, the fact that the student graduated to high school is not necessarily an indication of the effectiveness of the treatment. Notice, for example, that throughout his school career, during which time the student was presumably afflicted with selective mutism, he still managed to graduate on time at each grade level. Second, in order to assess the efficacy of the treatments, a standard A-B design was employed, but these are notoriously problematic with regard to questions of external validity. Since no controls were utilized in the research design, there is no scientific basis upon which to assert that the intervention itself was actually what caused the student to start talking again in school settings. In other words, with no adequate controls in place, there is no way to rule out a host of other factors that could have actually brought about the desired outcome, including the very real possibility that the student was likely to start talking on his own regardless of the treatments.

The case of Seung Hui Cho

It is interesting to note that at least one notorious school shooter was previously diagnosed with selective mutism.[17] In April 2007, senior English major Seung Hui Cho opened fire on the campus of Virginia Tech, killing 32 people and wounding 25 others before killing himself. It was the single worst school-related rampage shooting in US history. Cho, born in Korea in 1984, was a sickly child. By age three, he had had numerous medical procedures for such problems as whooping cough, pneumonia, and a hole in his heart. This presumably caused the young Cho emotional trauma, and from that point on he showed signs of withdrawing from social interaction and human contact in general. As he grew older, he had few friends and was considered a loner. His family moved to the United States in 1992, and Cho's isolation was exacerbated by the language barrier. Cho spoke even less frequently with his parents and friends, and he was visibly avoiding eye contact with everyone.

When he enrolled in the third grade in Virginia, teachers noticed that Cho did not play with his classmates and remained virtually mute throughout the school day. Nevertheless, Cho made it through every year of elementary school, but by the seventh grade school personnel talked Cho's parents into having him evaluated for possible mental or behavioral issues. He was placed in an art therapy program in an effort to elicit expressions from him. At this time he was diagnosed with severe social anxiety disorder, yet there were still no reports of behavioral problems in school or elsewhere. His IQ was tested above average.

By eighth grade, however, Cho showed signs of becoming even more withdrawn and isolated. The year was 1999, which was of course the year of the Columbine High School shootings. A paper he wrote for that class made reference to the shootings at Columbine, and teachers became even more concerned. Psychiatrists from George Washington University Hospital took over his case, and because of the "disturbing" paper he wrote alluding to murder and suicide, Cho was finally diagnosed with selective mutism along with "major depression: single episode." He was prescribed the antidepressant Paroxetine, which he took for about a year through July

2000. Because Cho showed such good improvement, his doctors took him off the medication. In high school Cho was given special accommodations because of his tendency to become easily frustrated. His special education arrangement, or individualized education program (IEP), allowed him to avoid oral presentations without penalty as well as adjusting grading criteria for group participation. Cho's grades were good, but he continued to remain virtually speechless at school, and there is some evidence that he was bullied because of it.

In high school he maintained a 3.52 GPA, and his 2002 SAT scores (540 verbal, 620 math) were good enough to get Cho accepted to Virginia Tech. Counselors cautioned that Cho should attend a smaller college, yet by this time he seemed sufficiently self-directed and independent to make it work. Cho was not on medication and was looking forward to leaving home for the first time. He also no longer had special accommodations for his selective mutism. No one at the university had knowledge of this or any of his other preexisting conditions. This was consistent with state law.

The rest is tragic history. There was much hand-wringing over why the university had not acted more proactively to head off the actions of a troubled young man who, in hindsight, was a powder keg waiting to explode. Documents released after the shooting revealed that heath officials at Virginia Tech had spoken with Cho on three occasions in 2005 after concerns were raised about his behavior. Each time Cho denied having homicidal or suicidal thoughts, and on this basis the school had no legal reason to act.[18]

Autism spectrum disorder

As covered in chapter 4, the *Diagnostic and Statistical Manual of Mental Disorders* (*DSM*) is the standard reference for clinical diagnosis and treatment of mental illness. The fifth edition, first published in 2013 (*DSM-5*), shifted from a multi-axial system for classifying mental disorders used in earlier editions to a new "spectrum" concept. The use of spectrum in classifying mental disorders allows the bringing together of previously disparate disorders which often appeared together in the same patient (i.e., comorbidity). Additionally, the use of spectrum allows for the diagnosis of symptoms of some illnesses ranging from relatively mild to relatively severe. For example, if a particular mental disorder lists 11 possible symptoms, patients who are diagnosed with three symptoms could be classified as a mild case, four to five symptoms could be classified as moderate, and six or more symptoms would constitute a severe case.[19]

Autism is a developmental disorder usually diagnosed in childhood that "presents with atypical language and social behavior, along with restrictive and repetitive behaviors and unusual interests."[20] The diagnostic criteria for autism spectrum disorder is rather complex, consisting of multiple parts.[21] (These criteria refer only to children, as diagnostic criteria for adult autism have yet to be developed.)

First, a child must exhibit persistent difficulties with social communication and interaction including: inability to sustain conversations or exhibit shared interests with others; inability to interpret nonverbal behavior or sustain eye contact; lack of facial expressions; deficits in understanding and sustaining social relationships (e.g., "mindblindness"); difficulty in making friends; and absence of interest in others.

Second, in addition to the above problems with social interaction, the patient must exhibit repetitive patterns of behavior, interests, or activities in at least two of four areas: stereotyped or repetitive motor movements or speech (e.g., echolalia, or the repeating of noises or phrases that have been heard); insistence on sameness (overly wedded to routines and inflexibility regarding new things or the potential for change); highly restricted and fixated interest in some narrow area (e.g., excessive attachment to particular objects); hyper- or hyporeactivity to sensory input (e.g., adverse reactions to particular sounds or textures, or visual fascination with lights or objects).

The third element determines severity of the illness based upon evidence gleaned from the first two areas along with some additional information. The three prongs for determining severity are: symptoms must be present in the early developmental period which may be masked by learning strategies if diagnosed later in life; the symptoms cause "clinically significant" impairment in social, educational, or occupational functioning; these disturbances are not better explained by intellectual disability or global developmental delay (e.g., the level of impairment in social communication should be below the level of presented developmental level).

As is evident from this list of diagnostic criteria, autism represents problems with social interaction and communication, and children who do not understand the subtleties of human interaction (e.g., taking jokes literally or missing social cues such as facial expressions or nonverbal gestures) are seen by peers as odd and are often subject to bullying. They may also get bullied because of their repetitive behaviors or mannerisms (e.g., flapping their hands or bringing the exact same lunch to school every single day) or speaking with a robotic or mechanical sounding voice. In addition, children labeled as odd, or strange, or described as quirky or "marching to the beat of a different drum," have difficulty making and keeping friends. Indeed, such children end up befriending others who have been similarly rejected or isolated, and at school they are likely to sit at the same lunch table having been brought together under such well-meaning programs as Lunch Bunch.[22]

Because of their lack of sophistication regarding all things social, ASD children can also be talked into doing things which get them into trouble, while the neurotypical children who put them up to it are laughing behind their backs. Because ASD children tend to take things literally – indeed, even as they move into their teen years and beyond, they may be stuck cognitively in what Jean Piaget referred to as the concrete operational stage – they are trusting to a fault.[23] In addition, upwards of 90 percent of those on the autism spectrum have gastrointestinal difficulties – the problem of disordered gut microbiota – and often find themselves having to run to the bathroom unexpectedly.[24] Since this often disrupts plans, persons on the autism spectrum tend to develop a reputation of being flaky, untrustworthy, or both. Such persons would be cast in a negative light as ones who cannot even meet the minimum requirements of managing time or their own bodily functions.[25]

Since eating at home or dining out with family or friends has become a premier social activity of modern society, this area poses special difficulties for those on the autism spectrum. Many ASD children are extremely picky eaters – chicken nuggets being perhaps the single most preferred food item – and if the meal is not served exactly as expected with regard to appearance, texture, and temperature, tantrums are likely to ensue. And with regard to the newly burgeoning phenomenon of adult autism, difficulties with the social expectations of dining together can continue into later years.[26] When dining with others, adults with high-functioning autism (which used to be called Asperger's Syndrome but is no longer recognized as an official category in *DSM-5*) are often viewed as socially uninterested in their dining partners because they take the literal view that they are there first and foremost to eat, and so "small talk" and other social niceties take a backseat in the pecking order of attention. Neurotypical dining partners may come to view the "aspie" (a high-functioning ASD adult) as on a mission because of his or her singular focus on eating. Because aspies take an instrumental view toward eating, they are also often the first ones to finish, and indeed those on the autism spectrum eat significantly faster than neurotypicals, and of course, eating fast can lead to gastrointestinal difficulties.[27] In short, ASD adults dining out with others are often seen as rude, boorish, egotistical, antisocial, and seemingly oblivious to others in their company. Sensing the discomfort others feel toward them, or perhaps being informed directly about the perception of others by, say, a neurotypical spouse, those on the autism spectrum feel detached from the ongoing stream of social activity, that they are in effect "like a spectator in this thing."[28]

In addition to problems in communication and social skills generally, persons on the autism spectrum are at a higher risk than the neurotypical population for an array of comorbid conditions stemming from a dysfunctional immune system. Children diagnosed with autism are significantly more likely than those not diagnosed to suffer from allergies and autoimmune diseases including persistent inflammatory skin conditions such as eczema and psoriasis.[29] Such inflammatory skin conditions can also be indicated in a variety of gastrointestinal issues as discussed above, including acid reflux, irritable bowel syndrome, inflammatory intestinal disease, and dysregulation of gut microbiome.[30]

A persistent state of itchiness and general discomfort often causes ASD individuals to withdraw from social activities and appear to be preoccupied with themselves, all of which is compounded by heightened levels of anxiety because of an inability to interpret or accept normal or even minimal levels of uncertainty.[31] The inability to tolerate uncertainty causes debilitating anxiety for many on the autism spectrum, although more recently treatment approaches for autistic adults, utilizing personal diaries in which patients can record and learn from different approaches to uncertain situations, have shown some promise.[32] Although anxiety per se is not included in the symptomology checklist for ASD, upwards of 40 percent of those diagnosed with the illness also display comorbidity for at least one type of anxiety disorder, most often the vague, unspecified, and persistent form known as generalized anxiety disorder.[33]

For many autistic individuals, fear of the future or the unknown produces anxiety, and anxiety in turn compounds the problem of inflammatory conditions of the body linked to autoimmune deficiency. It is a vicious cycle that makes many persons on the autism spectrum feel like they are "stuck" and unable to enter the flow of normal social activities. They are trapped in a dense fog of social awkwardness which is not only social but also physical, emotional, mental, biological, and physiological.

Disvalued versus disordered conditions of childhood and adolescence

Perhaps the most enlightening discussion concerning the problematic aspects of childhood disorders like selective mutism and ASD has been provided by Jerome Wakefield.[34] According to Wakefield, the concept of mental disorder must satisfy at least two conditions: (1) the disorder is due to some internal dysfunction within the individual, and (2) a value judgment is made that the behaviors associated with the disorder are harmful to the individual or to society. Value judgments per se regarding the nature or level of harm associated with some unwanted behaviors are not problematic, insofar as the realms of law and everyday life (legal and informal control respectively) make the same sort of value judgments about social harm as well. Where the concept of mental disorder runs into trouble is the tendency to view unwanted or disvalued behaviors as indicative, ipso facto, of some underlying or internal dysfunction within the individual while lacking an independent way of verifying the latter. To restate, oftentimes disvalued conduct is taken as evidence that an internal dysfunction within the individual is driving the conduct, when in fact no such internal dysfunction is present or reasonably can be shown to exist using the methods of the empirical sciences. Even further, even if an internal dysfunction can be shown to exist in some instances, the diagnostic criteria are overly inclusive, meaning that many false positives are produced, leading to an overestimation of the extent and severity of the disorder in the population.

As Wakefield argues, especially in the case of the myriad mental disorders that apply particularly to children and adolescents – who are relatively powerless and cannot speak for themselves regarding their being labeled mentally disordered – it is simply too easy to mistake disvalued conditions for disordered conditions.[35] Getting back to the case of selective mutism, the diagnostic criteria for determining whether an internal dysfunction actually exists within the child or adolescent make it too easy to conflate disvalue with disorder. Wakefield provides a useful example:

> a girl who refuses to talk because a bully has accused her of being teacher's pet and has threatened to beat her up if she opens her mouth in class can still be diagnosed as disordered under these [diagnostic] criteria.[36]

The production of these and other types of false positives leads reasonable persons to suspect that, rather than simply diagnosing and treating real mental disorders, the socially disvalued aspects of the behavioral manifestations of these illnesses is what is truly being targeted. This raises to prominence the social control function of mental illness, especially within school settings.

The public health model revisited

One of the clearest and most forceful articulations of proactive policy is embodied in the broad public health model of social problems, which was introduced in chapter 4. To reiterate, the public health approach includes "both the art and the science of preventing disease, prolonging life, and promoting health."[37] Since violence and aggression cause or lead to injuries and death, proponents of the public health model are apt to treat violence as if it were a "disease" with identifiable stages: etiology or onset; developmental pathways of the "disease" after onset; characteristics of the population "at-risk" for "contracting" the disease; and interventions at the individual or group level that purport to reduce or eliminate the disease of youth/school violence.

From the public health perspective, both the earlier models of punishment and rehabilitation (or treatment) were reactive in that they dealt with criminals or clients only after their offending or problematic behavior came to light or was "diagnosed." Although public health proponents acknowledge that interventions aimed at rehabilitating defendants/clients who have already offended is an improvement over the criminal justice emphasis on punishment for the sake of deterrence, retribution, or justice, the treatment model does not go far enough. Rather than intervention, the public health model's primary objective is *prevention*, that is, ensuring that the disease never arises in the first place.[38] The idea that violence – school, youth, or otherwise – is a "disease" that can and should be conceptualized as a public health issue is widespread, and we will return to this issue later in the chapter.

It is especially important to examine the claims being made by proponents of proactive school policy in light of the string of highly publicized and tragic school shootings that began in earnest in 1999. As a result of these events, there appears to be a broad consensus among scholars, policy analysts, teachers and administrators, and the lay public that a "crisis" or "epidemic" of violence has descended upon our schools, and that something needs to be done quickly. It is no longer sufficient, argue proponents of proactivity, to merely react to incidents of school violence after they have already occurred. With our "scientific" (read: medical, psychoanalytical, or psychological) knowledge about human behavior firmly in hand, we should be able to construct "proactive" approaches to school violence that in effect get at the root cause (or "etiology") of school violence. In other words, by knowing the environmental conditions of schools and local communities as well as the individual traits or characteristics of perpetrators of school violence, we should be able to predict and thus reduce or eliminate its occurrence.

Although there are ongoing attempts to construct proactive risk profiles for purposes of identifying future school shooters, for the most part these have not worked. The problem is that lethality cannot really be predicted. In fact, in general the rarer the behavior, the less likely it will be successfully predicted. Indeed, risk profiles are more likely to generate many more false positives than successful identification of actual shooters.[39] Even with the knowledge of school shootings and the tragic reality that any loss of innocent young lives is unacceptable, in the big picture schools are extraordinarily safe places to be. Indeed, school homicides are extremely rare. When taking into consideration the United States and its approximately 120,000 schools, the average school will have a homicide every 6,000 years.[40]

This is little consolation, of course, for grieving families dealing with the atrocities of any school shooting. Perhaps the worst rampage shooting to take place on school grounds was in 2012 at Sandy Hook Elementary School in Newtown, Connecticut. After completing his carnage and before taking his own life, 20-year-old Adam Lanza shot and killed 20 schoolchildren and six adults. President Barack Obama took immediate action with a number of executive orders, including renewed federal funding for research on gun violence, more stringent firearm tracing measures, and improving the availability of records into the National Instant Background Check System (NICS). Such background checks would likely not have stopped Lanza, who murdered his mother before his rampage at Sandy Hook using three of her firearms which were legally purchased and registered.[41]

Rather than the overtly psychotherapeutic approach which favors personality inventories and risk profiles, sociologist Katherine Newman focuses on the organizational structures of schools that might contribute to such attacks; the "dark side" or the underbelly of the seemingly quiet and peaceful small towns where many of the school shootings took place; the social networks of the school shooters; and the nature of adolescent culture in contemporary American society.[42] Newman refers to such events as rampage shootings, the characteristics of which are that the attacks are targeted against multiple parties who are often selected at random; they tend to take place in rural and suburban schools; and the perpetrators are predominantly white boys.

Researchers from a variety of backgrounds agree that youth violence is a serious and ongoing social problem, while a smaller group view it as the single most serious and significant public health problem we face today. For this latter group of researchers, youth violence is not simply a social problem; it is a *public health* problem. It is important to make whatever persuasive appeals are necessary to sell the notion that something is a public health problem, and this is because of the higher levels of invasiveness and surveillance of the population that is implied in the public health model as compared to other models of justice or treatment. Indeed, Deborah Prothrow-Stith suggests that the first stage of the public health mission involves the setting up of surveillance systems which, in the case of interpersonal violence, means collecting data on "who is being hurt and under what circumstances."[43] The public health model, then, is utilitarian at heart, because even though stepping up surveillance of the population for purposes of monitoring and (hopefully) eradicating yet another "disease" is potentially harmful or debilitating to some groups – especially children, I would contend – in the end what counts is "the greatest good for the greatest number of people." That is, proponents of the public health model argue that whatever costs are incurred in the process of defining and treating violence as a disease are outweighed by the expected future benefits, namely, reducing or eliminating violence.

Three stages of prevention

The public health model conceptualizes a tripartite classification of prevention into primary, secondary, and tertiary stages. These three stages or strategies of prevention are summarized below.

- **Tertiary prevention** – encompasses all those strategies designed to keep persons who are already ill from becoming sicker. This is the classic "reactive" approach to social and health problems.
- **Secondary prevention** – involves the early identification of those who already have symptoms of some disease. At-risk profiles, generated from heightened surveillance of the target population, help to determine who are good candidates for early intervention. Secondary prevention represents a mix of reactive and proactive approaches.
- **Primary prevention** – focuses on stopping some problem behavior before it starts, the overall goal of which is to reduce health problems in the general population. Strategies may include educational and public information campaigns, changing the environment (or organization, or institution), immunizing potential hosts or victims, etc. These approaches are characterized as "proactive."

More recently, some have proposed the additional of a fourth public health strategy which is referred to as quaternary prevention.[44] *Quaternary prevention* is defined as "an action taken to protect individuals from medical interventions (that is, over-medicalization) that are likely to cause more harm than good."[45] This represents the awareness that any previous stage can involve some level of overdiagnosis or testing beyond what is required according to the level of risk or harm the condition poses to the patient.[46] This newest stage of prevention is emblematic of heightened self-reflexivity among clinicians and psy-complex practitioners concerning diagnosis and the underlying assumptions (largely utilitarian) about medical interventions which go largely unnoticed and unchallenged. Those practitioners who are aware of the potential of the deleterious consequences of quaternary prevention are of a similar mindset, then, to social scientists who warn about medicalization and diagnostic inflationism.

Is violence a disease?

Since the public health model views problems in society as diseases or disease-based, the three categories of prevention – primary, secondary, and tertiary – refer to the stage to which the disease has progressed at diagnosis or discovery. In this sense, tertiary prevention is the lowest level of prevention, in that it represents a state of affairs in which the disease has gone undiagnosed or unnoticed for quite some time, and has progressed to the point that the patient is seriously or chronically ill.[47] Proponents of public health argue that the typical criminal justice response represents merely a tertiary prevention effort since most of its contacts are with core or repeat offenders who come to the attention of justice officials well after the fact.[48] At this stage in the progression of the disease, the best the criminal justice response can do is attempt to treat or rehabilitate. Often, however, among hardcore offenders the disease has progressed so far that the only viable option is either imprisonment or institutionalization, that is, the isolation of such people for their, or others', own good.[49]

It is important to point out here a serious problem in this attempt to treat violence as a disease. First of all, we must attempt to clear up some confusion over the concept of "disease" itself, for it has two distinct understandings or usages, namely, literal and metaphorical. As Thomas Szasz explains, "Literally, the term *disease* denotes a demonstrable lesion of cells, tissues, or organs; metaphorically, it may be used to denote any kind of malfunctioning, of individuals, groups, economies, etc. (drug addiction, youth violence, economic depression, etc.)."[50]

Hence, over the years social scientists, physicians, therapists, and even the lay public have become accustomed to extending the criteria of disease from malfunctions of the human body to malfunctions of the human mind (in the case of mental illness) or even society (in this case, assuming that society is like an "organism" which can possess "diseased" states such as social disorganization, violence, and so forth). But conceptualizing society as an organism – otherwise known as organicism – is an ontological move, that is, a way of setting up an analytical strategy for simplifying the complexities of the human social world. Proponents of the public health model would be doing fine if they acknowledged they were using violence in the metaphorical sense to generate hypotheses or test theories about various aspects of violence. However, many such proponents continue to insist that violence is in fact a literal disease. It will be shown upon closer examination, however, that this violence-as-a-literal-disease view cannot be sustained.

One of the first things we confront from the violence-as-literal-disease perspective is confusion over who the victim is, who the carrier of the disease is, how the disease is acquired, as well as what the "risk" factors are for acquisition of the disease. As to the first point, we know that there are offenders perpetrating violence against others, and often innocent victims are injured or even killed as a result. So in the case of violence, we have a diseased person (the violent offender) causing harm to others. Fair enough. In the search for an analogy to a "real" disease that acts in a similar way, we are led to the communicable diseases. Here, a diseased person (whether infected with HIV, influenza, malaria, Covid-19, or what have you), wittingly or unwittingly causes harm to victims by passing on the disease to them. The disease is a biological or chemical agent – a pathogen – that insinuates itself into the tissues or blood of victims, slowly harming or killing them from the inside. The diseased state of the carrier (or offender) is replicated in the receiver (or victim). But does violence really act or unfold in this way?

There is one scenario proponents of the public health model might point to in an effort to maintain the violence-as-disease analogy. They could point approvingly to the literature that suggests that violence is passed down from generation to generation, for example, the finding that children exposed to acts of violence in the home (or who are themselves victims of violence) are more likely to perpetrate violence against others. This theory of the intergenerational transmission of violence also finds an ally in cultural theories of violence, namely, that America's violent popular culture instills a proneness toward violence and aggression among persons exposed to it. And as the amount of violent images one is exposed to increases, the more violent one is likely to become.[51]

The question that arises at this point, then, is this: If violence acts like a contagious disease, what is the pathogen? Certainly culture cannot be considered a proper pathogen, because everyone receives and is a bearer of culture, yet not everyone (in fact, a very small minority) becomes violent as a result of being exposed to violent images in popular media and elsewhere.

David McDonald's take on violence from the framework of infectious disease epidemiology is instructive. From this perspective, the public health model focuses on the host (the victim of violence), the agent that creates the injury, the vector/vehicle that carries or conveys the agent, and the social context within which the violent incident occurs. As McDonald goes on to explain, from this perspective

> injury is best understood in terms of the agent of injury involved, and that the agent is energy. Accordingly, injury prevention and control turned its focus from assumed inadequacies of the victim (for instance, lazy, ignorant, and careless) to the injurious transfer of energy.[52]

The very odd implication of this is that energy or energy transfer is the pathogen impelling along the disease of violence. But this again is simply logically untenable. A slap on the back for a job well done also involves energy transfer, yet by no stretch of the imagination could this act be considered violent.

James Gilligan has articulated another take on violence from the infectious disease epidemiology perspective. Gilligan argues that the violence pathogen is emotion, specifically, the experience of overwhelming shame and humiliation.[53] The author claims that violence-prone individuals lack the ego defenses that otherwise insulates "normal" persons from reacting violently whenever they are shamed or humiliated. In other words, for some reason violence-prone individuals are overwhelmingly vulnerable and sensitive to experiences of shame, and act upon these feelings inappropriately in the form of aggression and/or violence. Presumably, normal persons possess sufficient nonviolent means by which to undo or deal with feelings of shame and humiliation. From this perspective, primary prevention would be targeted to stopping all forms of shaming and humiliation that persons might experience in their lives, especially as a result of social stratification, poverty, oppressive governments, and of course the innumerable -isms (e.g., racism, sexism, ageism, lookism). In addition, primary prevention could take the form of programs to enhance self-esteem or the feeling of self-worth.

But again, it seems bizarre to liken emotions to a pathogen. How did these violence-prone individuals acquire or contract these faulty emotions in the first place? If we are trying to stay true to infectious disease epidemiology, it appears that in no way, shape, or form could emotions serve as an appropriate pathogen regarding violence as a disease. Gary Slutkin and colleagues understand this as well, and they simply point out that the outcome of violence does indeed produce the lesion of cells necessary to meet Szasz's criteria for a literal disease. They argue that violence acts like a contagious health problem, and in taking this position there is an attempt to create a seamless link between the metaphorical and literal views of disease. The authors point out that past exposure to violence is the strongest predictor that someone will become violent, and that exposure to violence, either through direct victimization or witnessing it, "increas[e] the risk of chronic violent behavior thirtyfold."[54]

In response to these authors, Michael Greene takes the position that violence is not a disease in either the metaphorical or literal sense.[55] He goes on to argue that "More importantly, we need to be clear that there are no 'violence bacteria' or 'violence viruses', no violence parasites or pathogens. Violence is not airborne or contagious by touch or breath. There is no violence 'germ' within individuals that can be suppressed."[56] Along these same lines, if violence is a literal disease, why does it not cause tissue damage in the person who has it initially? Clearly the physical assault on the victim does cause tissues damage, but the perpetrator seems unaffected. Now, maybe one could argue that the perpetrator is affected mentally and carries out a violent act. Or perhaps the perpetrator is asymptomatic and passes along an active version of the disease or pathogen to another person. But the damage done to the carrier and the victim is different, so there is no clear path forward in explaining this discrepancy as a literal disease, as Greene points out. Proponents of violence as literal disease seem to be bringing something extra into violence, that is, into the act of violence itself, without having irrefutable evidence that this internal condition or factor is actually causing the violence. This argument still seems stuck in the metaphorical side of the debate and hearkens back to Wakefield's distinction between disvalued and disordered conditions and how easy it is to confuse the two.

The search for the violence gene

Another way that violence could be considered a disease is by examining the potential genetic basis for violence and aggression, which in many ways is similar to studies of the neurochemistry of the social bond discussed in chapter 6. From the above discussion, this is a possibility that Greene entertained but rejected out of hand. The Georgia case *Mobley v. State* (1995) was the first case in which a legal defense hinged on the claim that the defendant, Stephen Mobley, possessed a genetic predisposition to violence as a mitigating circumstance for the jury to consider in trying him for the murder he committed.[57] Some background on this case, and a review of the research which gave rise to the attempted legal defense, are discussed below.

In 1991, a young college student, John Collins, was working the late shift at a Domino's Pizza delivery restaurant near Gainesville, Georgia. Stephen Mobley, a 26-year-old, entered the store with intentions of robbing it, but instead ended up shooting Collins in the back of the head. Collins died from his wounds, and the community was shocked and outraged at the senseless homicide. As Mobley was going to trial to face charges of murder and armed robbery, his defense team received notice of research being conducted by Dutch geneticist Han Brunner which claimed to have discovered evidence that mutation in the structural gene for monoamine oxidase A (or MAOA) in males was associated with the inability to regulate impulsive aggression.[58] The MAOA gene is located on the X chromosome at Xp.11.3–Xp11.4.[59]

The MAOA deficiency does not on its own cause specific behavioral variations in the phenotype – including violence – but the risk of impulsive aggression is increased in those males who do possess the gene mutation and have low intelligence (measured by IQ tests). Deficiency in MAOA reduces the ability to synthesize or control levels of dopamine and serotonin, and decreased levels of these neurotransmitter amines in the body – because of the failure of MAOA to synthesize them properly – have been shown to be associated with aggression.[60]

Getting back to the case of Mobley, his defense team had him tested for the gene mutation and it was discovered he did indeed possess the MAOA deficiency which was associated with aggression in some men. However, the judge ruled against the defense's motion to introduce the genetic evidence, claiming that the finding was too new and speculative to be tested in a court of law. The jury eventually found Mobley guilty, convicting him of murder, armed robbery, assault, and possession of a firearm in the commission of a crime, and sentenced him to death. He was executed by the state of Georgia by lethal injection on March 1, 2005.[61] The judge's denial of the introduction of the genetic evidence was consistent with Brunner's own warnings that there is not a direct link between the gene mutation on one end, and impulsive aggression leading to murder on the other. At best, there is an indirect or perhaps epigenetic link between the two. As Brunner explains, "Thus, the concept of a gene that directly encodes behaviour is unrealistic."[62] This is because genes are simple while human behavior is complex. Additionally, finding no fault on the basis of genes throws the entire philosophical discussion of free will and determinism into disarray and turns complex social problems into relatively simple biological or medical solutions backed by the presumably authoritative verdicts of legal truth finders (namely, judges and juries).

Community violence

Yet another approach to the violence-as-literal-disease argument is the notion that community violence causes both physical and psychological harm to those exposed to it, whether or not exposed persons then go on themselves to perpetrate violence. For example, Raymond Lorion argues that by shifting from an individual to an ecological perspective, behavioral scientists can begin to understand that community violence is itself a community-based pathogen.[63] From this perspective, exposure to community violence is likened to an environmental toxin that has the potential to contaminate persons and their interpersonal relationships, thereby spreading the disease of violence even further.

But does this make sense? Lorion argues that community violence is similar to an airborne toxin that can act to disrupt the emotional, physical, behavioral, and interpersonal functioning of persons exposed to it.[64] Public health proponents argue that the causes and consequences of violence are broad and diverse, touching upon virtually every aspect of daily life. Various attempts to develop a prototype indicator set of the causes and consequences of violence typically come up with an exhaustive list of indicators, some of which are:

- impact on health and function (disease), which includes the direct effects of violence, namely physical injury, death, and psychological problems;
- impact on well-being, such as fear of crime and violence, as well as restricting activities or changing lifestyles as a result of such fear;
- individual responses to violence, which include suicide and attempted suicide, rape and attempted rape, prevalence of child maltreatment, prevalence of physical abuse of women by male partners, prevalence of elder abuse, and incidence of physical fighting, weapons carrying, and substance abuse among adolescents;
- costs of healthcare associated with intentional injuries (firearm or otherwise), the number of persons in substance abuse programs, and so forth;
- social environment factors, including the concentration of poor families in geographical areas; presence of gangs, illegal markets, and availability of firearms in communities; the number of hours of violence-related programming on television; the extent of gun control laws in an area; and the availability of shelters for battered women and their children.[65]

If indeed all these activities and settings – and many more not listed – are related to the etiology of violence or its consequence, then one would easily be led into the notion that community violence acts like a pathogen fueling other "pathologies" presumably connected to violence.[66] But how can violence be both itself a pathogen – as in the case of community violence – and something caused by pathogens – as is the case, for example, in our discussion of energy transfer or emotions as the pathogens underlying the "disease" of violence?

This appears to be where the logic of the violence-as-literal-disease approach breaks down. In light of this conceptual conundrum, public health proponents have shifted their focus somewhat, arguing that violence is like a social contagion that can spread across societies and from community to community. As Jeffrey Fagan and Garth Davies argue,

> we conceptualize the rise, spread, and decline in violence rates over time as a process akin to a contagious disease epidemic and test a theoretical framework of neighborhood risk as an engine of social contagion within and between these small social areas.[67]

The reasons violent crime rates vary from place to place is that certain communities possess features which make them more susceptible to the "disease" of violence. These community "risk" factors are the same problems discussed in chapter 6, namely a weakening or absence of informal controls and anemic levels of social capital. What purpose or purposes does the rephrasing of these issues into the language of medicine, pathology, or disease serve? Since the medical concepts and terminologies per se add no value to the explanation of problems in communities – whether violence or other issues – it must be the case that such concepts are invoked because of the social control functions they serve.

SUGGESTIONS FOR FURTHER READING

James J. Chriss (ed.), *Counseling and the Therapeutic State* (1999)
This collection of essays examines the social organization of counseling and psychotherapeutic practice in modern Western society. The provision of counseling services by psychiatrists as well as a growing legion of non-physicians is testament to a psychotherapeutic culture which elevates to primacy the care of the individual and his or her psychic well-being.
Michelle O'Reilly, Jessica Nina Lester, and Tom Muskett (eds.), *A Practical Guide to Social Interaction Research in Autism Spectrum Disorders* (2017)
Because autism largely manifests itself as a problem in communication and social interaction, a large body of work from sociology, symbolic interactionism, ethnomethodology, and conversation analysis has emerged that finds application in ASD specifically. This book is useful for both researchers and theorists interested in understanding ASD from the perspective of social constructionism.
Harvey Shapiro (ed.), *Wiley Handbook of Violence in Education* (2018)
This edited volume represents some of the best research and theory on school

violence in general and school shootings in particular. What is emphasized throughout by the various contributors is the benefits to be derived from a multidisciplinary approach focusing on the context and etiology of school violence, as well as responses to and prevention of school shootings.

Ilina Singh, Walter P. Sinnott-Armstrong, and Julian Savulescu (eds.), *Bioprediction, Biomarkers, and Bad Behavior: Scientific, Legal, and Ethical Challenges* (2014)

This edited volume contains perspectives from psychobiology on the nature of violence and aggression in human societies, focusing on the prediction of violence based upon continuing research on the MAOA enzyme which is believed to be implicated in aggressive behavior. There are also reflections on legal and ethical implications for dealing with those who possess such genetic markers for violence.

Deborah Prothrow-Stith, *Deadly Consequences* (1993)

The author, a physician and public health advocate, lays out an agenda for conceptualizing violence as a disease which is particularly devastating with regard to children and teenagers. She also provides guidelines for reducing the incidence of violence and aggression in families and schools.

DISCUSSION QUESTIONS

1. How has shyness been turned into a disease, and why has it happened?
2. Identify and discuss in some detail the two conditions that must be met in dealing with legitimate mental disorders. How and why are these conditions oftentimes not met?
3. Explain the spectrum perspective for dealing with mental disorder. Is this a useful addition to *DSM-5* in the case of autism? Why or why not?
4. Do you agree with public health advocates that violence is indeed a disease? In what ways can this argument be defended? In constructing your argument, you should be able to compare and contrast the literal versus metaphorical approaches to understanding violence as a disease.
5. In March 2012, a jury in Virginia awarded plaintiffs $8 million in a wrongful death lawsuit filed against Virginia Tech for failing to do enough to thwart Cho's shooting rampage. Is this award fair? What, if anything, should Virginia Tech have done differently?

Chapter 8
Legal Control: Racial Profiling, Hate Crimes, and the Imprisonment Binge

Introduction

Although in chapter 5 we discussed some aspects of the "dark side" of legal control, in this chapter we will examine three critical issues in the modern criminal justice system in somewhat more detail. These three critical case studies – racial profiling, hate crimes, and the growth of the American prison population – respectively represent pressing concerns in policing, the courts, and corrections. It is always crucial to keep in mind that sociology places emphasis on the broader social structures which represent collective responses to social issues of the day. Keeping in mind the work of Max Weber as discussed in chapter 1, the criminal justice system represents a culmination of developments within law and the state regarding specialization of tasks (in the division of labor) and rationalization which elevates to supremacy legal-bureaucratic thinking and reasoning. This is no more obvious than in the case of municipal policing.

Contrary to the dramatic depictions of police work in film and television, for the most part routine patrol work is a rather mundane affair which is far from glamorous or exciting. This is not to say that patrol work is not dangerous, however. Rather, rounds of random preventive patrol are typified by long stretches of "down time" which at any time can be punctuated by a dangerous or even life-threatening event.

Because of the uncertainties of police work, and the extreme danger that could be lurking just around the corner, the police have to be in a constant state of preparedness to deal with such contingencies. As part of this battle-readiness, police carry around in their heads an image of the kind of person that is particularly threatening. Jerome Skolnick has called this image the *symbolic assailant*, and persons who fit this description warrant closer attention and circumspection from the police than do other individuals.[1]

As discussed in chapter 6, because of the concentration of poverty in urban inner-city areas and the perception or reality that these are high crime areas as well, police are apt to view all citizens living in these communities as symbolic assailants.[2] Because racial and ethnic minorities tend to be overrepresented among the urban poor, it is unfortunately the case that in urban America, the symbolic assailant is typically a young, Black male. Although among urban American police symbolic assailants are young males – and specifically young *Black* males – who are assumed to be the kind of persons that are especially likely to threaten the police with violence, among British police the characteristics of the symbolic assailant are expanded beyond the attributes of race and sex. Specifically, from the perspective of British police the symbolic assailant is not only one who is assumed to be dangerous (again young males), but also anyone who could challenge or disarm police authority, including lawyers, doctors, and social workers (as "challengers"), or even women and young children (as "disarmers").[3] Although the British case is certainly interesting and worthy of further discussion, in this section we will deal specifically with the symbolic assailant as conceptualized by urban American police.

According to US Census and Uniform Crime Reports data for 2019, although African-Americans comprise 13.4 percent of the American population, they accounted for 26.4 percent of all arrests.[4] This means that African-Americans as a group are arrested at a rate about twice as high as would be expected from their representation in the population. The incarceration statistics are grim as well. When considering the lifetime chances of a person serving time in prison, the chances for whites are 2.5 percent, for Hispanics 9.4 percent, and for Blacks 16.2 percent. Assuming first-incarceration rates from 1991 hold presently, more than one in four Blacks and one in six Hispanics will be incarcerated, compared with one in 23 whites.[5]

Science and race

Now, this in no way implies that African-Americans as a group are simply more criminally-prone than whites. There is plenty of evidence to suggest that the operation of the criminal justice system accounts for much of this discrepancy primarily based on the fact that racial prejudice and discrimination are still very much alive in American, British, and other Western societies. It is probably accurate to suggest that institutional racism certainly exists in the criminal justice system (as well as in most other major social institutions), but verifying to what extent, if at all, particular persons within the system act in ways that could be shown to be racist is often extremely difficult. In other words, although there are blatant and sometimes infamous cases of police misconduct – such as Derek Chauvin's knee on the neck of George Floyd for upwards of nine minutes – or judicial or prosecutorial malfeasance involving racist and/or discriminatory decisions or rulings, ascertaining how widespread such practices are throughout the system beyond the obvious cases is not straightforward.

To reiterate, the reality of the overrepresentation of racial and ethnic minorities in the criminal justice system – from traffic stops on through to citations, arrests, and sentencing disparities – is a contentious issue. Expanding on the discussion above, it is instructive to note the explanation provided by Frank Baumgartner and colleagues on the four basic approaches to dealing with the evidence of such racial disparities in the criminal justice system. These four broad approaches are:

1. documenting actual differential criminality by race in the crime data, which is connected with disparities in differential contact with the police;
2. a limited number of "bad apple" officers acting in a biased manner;
3. widely shared implicit bias among actors within the criminal justice system;
4. possible institutional bias in the operation of the criminal justice system.[6]

As to point 1, the study of differential criminality by race is what Jack Katz has termed "hot potato criminology," namely, the difficulty of studying racial disparities in involvement with the criminal justice system through merely a dispassionate assessment of the crime data.[7] Instead, authors who study racial differences in crime are also expected to take a personal stance on such issues as class tensions or racial oppression and, if they don't, they likely will be judged to be scientifically suspect, racist, or both. Indeed, merely dealing with the data – the overrepresentation of racial minorities in serious crime, or the finding of consistent IQ differences by race – is viewed as cover for a simmering or overt racial animus.[8] This actually goes back to longstanding critiques of quantitative method – represented most prominently by positivism and empiricism – for its directive to mute the authorial voice. By casting use of the personal pronoun "I" as unscientific and solipsistic while placing distance between authors and their subjects – that is, by letting the data "speak for itself" – a lack of moral sensitivity about topics being addressed is engendered, thereby impairing the ability to make meaningful contributions to social analysis. This means, for better or worse, that politics and ideology are intimately intertwined with the products of social scientific labor.

What results from this observation is that scientists are not really free to study whatever they want, especially when there are political implications on the line. Philip Kitcher articulated such a position when he wrote that "a wise society conducts its free investigations in light of the socio-political implications."[9] Kitcher goes even further than this, however, explaining that science should abandon altogether studies which examine differences between groups on the basis of race or sex, because if evidence is found that goes in an inegalitarian direction – for example, that one racial group is engaging in more crime than a comparison group – persons can use this "evidence" to discriminate against or punish the crime-prone group and, hence, systematically limit their life chances.[10] On the other hand, when certain areas of scientific inquiry are blocked and considered off limits, science becomes little more than dogma guarded by a vanguard party.[11] Rousseau viewed science as being concerned with "truth as such, regardless of its utility, and thus by reason of its intention is exposed to the danger of leading to useless or even harmful truths."[12] Science, insofar as it seeks to understand how things are and report findings regardless of their political or ideological implications, can be dangerous to orthodoxy and sacred dogmas whether religious, political, social, cultural, ideological, or otherwise.

As a result of the unpalatability of point 1, most explanations of racial differences in crime settle on some combination of points 2 through 4, namely, bad apples, implicit bias, or institutional bias. Even so, point 2, the idea that only a small handful of police officers commit egregious offenses including racial profiling, brutality, and corruption, is largely rejected because of the desire to implicate whole police departments or the entirety of the criminal justice system in the production of racial differences in crime. If this position is widely established, it may then lead to serious attempts to rethink policing altogether, including its defunding, which in turn moves closer to adopting points 3 and 4, namely, implicit bias and institutional racism, as the favored explanations. This is the context within which current concerns over racial profiling are situated.[13]

Racial profiling

One of the areas of routine police operations that has come under increased scrutiny is police stops of citizens, taking place either during routine traffic patrols or in some other context. There has been a long-acknowledged understanding among African-American men especially that police pay particularly close attention to them. Angela Davis provides the example of African-American men who can afford to do otherwise choosing to drive drab, nondescript cars instead of flashier or sportier ones so as to minimize the risk of being stopped by the police.[14] With the appearance of crack cocaine in the late 1970s and the subsequent full-scale launching of a "war on drugs," police began targeting much more vigorously the areas in which drug activities were alleged to be taking place. The focus of much of this police activity was the urban inner-city and its predominantly minority population. A number of observers of police tactics in response to the problem of drugs in urban communities have argued that racial profiling started in earnest during the 1980s.[15] Specifically, Drug Enforcement Agency as well as local law enforcement training emphasized the importance of traffic stops of persons who fit the description of someone likely to be selling or transporting illicit drugs, especially on roads known as drug "pipelines."[16]

Racial profiling (sometimes referred to as "race-based policing") refers to the police practice of making enforcement decisions, such as a traffic stop, on the basis of a suspect's race.[17] *Hard* profiling uses race as the *only* factor in assessing criminal suspiciousness, while *soft* profiling uses race as one factor among others in determining police courses of action.[18] Critics of racial profiling, especially the "hard" version that, if proven or provable, is certainly illegal, facetiously refer to those who are stopped in this manner as committing the "crime" of "Driving While Black."[19]

Veil of darkness studies

Several studies have been conducted over the years to ascertain empirically – rather than leaving it to folk wisdom or anecdotal evidence – the extent and conditions of racial profiling. One of the more innovative studies utilizes a so-called *veil of darkness* method. The authors of the initial study (Jeffrey Grogger and Greg Ridgeway) argued that, in order to target drivers for special attention because of their race, police officers intending to do so must be able to see the drivers, that is, must be able to ascertain their race.[20] This set up a rather straightforward operational approach, namely, comparing the number of complaints of racial profiling occurring during daylight hours with those occurring after sunset. If real racial profiling is going on in any police department, we would expect to find more cases of racial profiling during daylight hours and fewer after sunset.

An earlier study of traffic stops conducted by the Oakland Police Department (OPD) found that 56 percent of drivers stopped were Black even though they comprised only 35 percent of the residential population. This finding, along with accumulated cases of complaints against the department for biased policing, led to the city of Oakland entering into a settlement agreement with the US Department of Justice in 2003 whereby OPD would collect data on traffic stops on an ongoing basis. This rich source of data was available to the researchers for carrying out the first veil of darkness study.

Specifically, between June 15 and December 30, 2003, the department recorded a total of 7,607 stops.[21] Daylight was defined as extending from sunrise to sunset, and darkness extended from "the end of civil twilight in the evening until the beginning of civil twilight the following morning."[22] After eliminating cases because of missing data and other technical issues, a total of 6,563 cases were retained and analyzed. Among motorists stopped during daylight hours, 49 percent were Black, while during nighttime hours 65 percent of those stopped were Black. This finding was described by the authors as "reverse" racial profiling because it was in the opposite direction of what was expected. To reiterate, the hypothesis was that if racial profiling is occurring, we should see more Black motorists stopped during daylight hours and fewer stopped during nighttime hours. Based upon this initial study of traffic stop data covering a six-month period in Oakland in 2003, the authors concluded that evidence of racial profiling by OPD officers could not be confirmed.

Robert Worden and colleagues conducted a later round of veil of darkness tests of racial profiling in the city of Syracuse, New York.[23] The Syracuse Police Department provided the research team with data on all traffic stops conducted by the department between 2006 and 2009. Some 50,000 vehicle stops occurred during the four-year period. Most of the stops occurred during the afternoon and evening rush hours, while about one-third of all stops occurred during the intertwilight period. The inter-twilight period is marked by "the earliest time at which civil twilight ends during the year – in Syracuse, that is 5:02 p.m. in December – and the latest time in which civil twilight ends – in Syracuse, 9:23 p.m. in June."[24] (Stops during the morning intertwilight period, roughly 5:00 to 7:00 a.m., were so infrequent that they were excluded from the study.) For studies utilizing the veil of darkness method, traffic stops typically are limited to the evening intertwilight period "in order to reduce the variation in travel patterns that are dependent on time of day."[25] Within this intertwilight period and consistent with the description of stop incidents provided in police reports and citizen contact forms, stops that occur before sunset are listed as daylight stops, while those that occur after sunset are listed as night stops. The authors also distinguished between stops made by regular patrol officers assigned to the traffic division and stops made by officers assigned to the Crime Reduction Team (CRT). The CRT "focuses on reducing violent and other crime, is deployed mainly to high-crime areas, and uses proactive patrol tactics."[26]

The test of whether or not biased policing is present with regard to traffic stops during the intertwilight period is to compare the proportion of Black drivers stopped during daylight hours to the proportion of Black drivers stopped during nighttime hours. If the proportion is higher during daylight hours, a case could be made for the presence of racial profiling. The data is broken down by 30-minute periods from daylight to darkness hours, examining the percentage of African-Americans stopped across these periods. The period 5:00 p.m. to 5:30 p.m. indicates that Black drivers were slightly more likely to be stopped during daylight hours, although this difference was statistically insignificant. A similar pattern emerged from 7:30 to 8:00 p.m., also statistically insignificant. A more significant period between 8:30 and 8:59 p.m. did show a higher proportion of daylight stops of Black drivers in comparison to nighttime stops. The authors interpreted these data as follows: "The daytime–nighttime disparity in the 8:30–8:59 interval is consistent with a pattern of racial bias, but otherwise the disparities are small and several are in the opposite direction, leading us to infer that this one larger difference is a statistical anomaly."[27] Just as in the previous studies, the authors of this study could not verify that racial profiling was occurring in traffic stops.

Later research has examined more closely the findings of these veil of darkness studies, offering new insights and criticisms on the method itself and possible reinterpretations of the data. Scott Abrahams examined the reasons for conducting a vehicle stop in the first place, as well as other ecological factors, rather than simply examining the data of stops that have already taken place.[28] For example, the great majority of veil of darkness studies never acknowledged the presence of street lighting in urban areas, and some studies have found that this can indeed account for some racial profiling of Black drivers.[29] Additionally, police officers may patrol differently at night than they do in daylight, for example, by shifting more intense focus to high-crime areas which is likely to produce higher numbers of stops of minority drivers.[30] Even so, the study by Worden and colleagues did not find that CRT officers accounted for a disproportionate share of nighttime stops of Black drivers.

The Abrahams study utilized a finite mixture model, taking into account the working rules (or thresholds) officers use to stop drivers (e.g., number of miles over the speed limit) and the costs associated with the decision to stop. Abrahams developed formulas associated with two distinct officer propensities regarding stops: One officer type is more likely to stop drivers and is associated with illegitimate stops such as racial profiling, while the other type is less likely to stop in general. Even so, the high-stop officer types are not associated with any particular race, but the assumption that they are searching for contraband, when plugged into the model as an initial condition, predicts that high-stop officers are more likely to stop Black drivers than the low-stop officers. It is also the case that Abrahams used data from eight state highway patrol associations, while the great majority of veil of darkness studies utilize city (that is, municipal) police data.

Michele Stacey and Heidi Bonner conducted a meta-evaluation of a number of veil of darkness studies, and concluded that variability in sampling decisions – that is, choosing which data to include in the study – makes it hard to say anything definitive about the conclusions reached by these various studies.[31] Researchers utilizing the veil of darkness methodology should strive toward sampling uniformity in order better to understand how the many factors – whether individual bias, department orientation, tactical strategy, or the nature of the population being served – drive disparate racial impact in policing.

The veil of darkness method could also benefit from observational studies in which researchers go into the field and observe how police officers make traffic stops and understanding the decisions that lie behind them. One such approach is the study conducted by Wendy Regoeczi and Stephanie Kent in which they and a group of research assistants conducted police ridealongs in four Ohio cities, namely, Cleveland, Brook Park, Shaker Heights, and Westlake.[32] The research team collected data on citizen demeanor, citizen sociodemographic characteristics, and officer sociodemographics, with the intent of explaining how these characteristics were associated with officer decisions regarding whether or not to initiate encounters with citizens. In general, then, this was a study of police discretion. Although the study included data on officer interactions with both pedestrians and vehicles, here we are interested solely in the result of vehicle stops. Most of the vehicle stops resulted in warnings, and arrests happened infrequently; however, minority officers were more likely to give tickets than warnings. With regard to citizens' race, Black citizens were more likely to be ticketed than white citizens. Additionally, the reasons for being ticketed varied by race. Specifically, whereas white citizens were typically ticketed for traffic infractions such as speeding or running a red light, Black citizens were often ticketed for minor things such as illegal turns or headlight violations. However, minor infractions of this kind for Black drivers often led to additional charges being filed for such things as driving with a suspended license, showing no proof of insurance, or defaulting on child support payments. Indeed, the appearance of the vehicle itself, rather than the actual behavior of the driver, may have much to do with the original decision to stop, leading critics of this practice to argue that vehicle appearance is merely a proxy for biased or racialized policing.[33] The authors conclude that

> one of the causes of the racial disparities in tickets vs warnings involves a cycle of tickets and license suspensions that occurs among some black drivers. These drivers appear to become caught up in a cycle where a compilation of prior tickets from traffic infractions, driving without insurance, or defaulting on child support payments leads to high numbers of points and subsequent license suspensions. The high reinstatement fees that accompany the suspension pose significant obstacles for many citizens to have their licenses reinstated, and some citizens will continue to drive with a suspended license.[34]

Hate crimes

Although criminal profiling is certainly a legitimate police practice, we have seen how other types of profiling – whether racial, religious, or linguistic – can be problematic both with respect to imperiling the civil liberties of members of targeted groups, but also because of the confusion such profiling can generate for law enforcement since true offenders are lumped in with a much larger group of innocent persons.[35]

Whereas racial profiling has been treated as a critical case study of legal control specifically within the context of law enforcement, this next critical case study will focus on law and the courts, examining specifically the case of hate crime legislation. We shall first provide a brief history of hate crime legislation, then look at exactly what constitutes a hate crime, that is, how it is defined. Finally, current controversies associated with hate crimes will be summarized, including the Hate Crimes Sentencing Enhancement Act of 1994, which provides more punitive penalties if it can be proved that a particular crime was motivated by hate or bias toward a person merely because of his or her membership in a particular group.

A brief history of hate crime legislation

Crimes motivated by hate are nothing new. In the book of Genesis in the Bible, Cain killed his brother Abel in a premeditated act of rage and jealousy because God favored Abel's sacrifice – a lamb from Abel's flock – over his own. This first murder set a precedent for humankind, and the problems of hate and rage have been an enduring part of our human legacy, or so the story goes.

In America organized hate groups such as the Ku Klux Klan, which has been operating since the 1920s, are some of the most visible symbols of the continuing problem of hatred being perpetrated against various groups.[36] More recent incidents of hate-based crimes include the murder of James Byrd in Jasper, Texas, who was dragged behind a pickup truck simply because he was Black; the beating to death of gay college student Matthew Shepard who was tied to a fence in the desert by his assailants and left to die; and the sad case of Abner Louima, a Black immigrant from Haiti who was sodomized with a broken broomstick at the hands of a New York City police officer. (Louima survived.)[37]

With the march of modernity, the idea arose that the worst aspects of human living, especially the deliberate inflicting of pain by one human being on another, could be reduced or even eliminated to the extent that we continue to increase our knowledge of what makes people "tick." The human and social sciences, such as psychology, sociology, and criminology, very early on were dedicated in no small measure to eliminating a variety of social pathologies, thereby maximizing societal happiness and finally securing the long sought-after "good life."

The enactment of hate crime legislation is the story of a complicated convergence of social movements and interest group politics, legislative and policymaking negotiations and initiatives, interpretations by courts of the earliest rounds of statute enactment, and the eventual enactment of hate crime law with uneven acceptance and application as each state grappled with the pragmatics of policing and prosecuting cases.[38] The first hate crimes law was the Hate Crimes Statistics Act (HCSA), enacted in

1990.[39] President George H.W. Bush signed this into law after more than a decade of growing concern over the seeming growth of hate-motivated crimes being perpetrated not only against persons of color, but also against homosexuals, women, those of a particular national origin, the disabled, and those holding particular religious beliefs.

The HCSA initially was not meant to criminalize hate-based crime (that is, beyond the level of sanctions already in place for any particular criminal act), but rather to gather systematic data about the nature and extent of hate crimes. Although definitions vary based upon the kind of hate crime committed, but also because of the unique language employed as various American states enacted versions of hate crime legislation, what makes a *hate crime* is "the existence of bias or prejudice of the perpetrator who committed the crime against an individual based on the victim's real or perceived social grouping."[40]

The reporting of hate crimes varies sometimes dramatically when comparing state data. For example, Illinois reported 133 hate crimes in 1991, 241 in 1992, a big jump to 724 in 1993, and then a precipitous decline to only 19 in 1994. Alabama reported only nine hate crimes *total* for the eight-year period from 1991 to 1998. In 1992 both New Jersey and New York recorded their states' highest hate crime totals – 1,114 and 1,112 respectively – and both declined steadily over the next few years, with 1998 totals standing at 757 for New Jersey and 776 for New York.[41]

We will now summarize hate crime data for the year 2019 as reported by the US Department of Justice.[42] First with regard to who is being targeted, there were 7,103 single-bias incidents involving 8,552 victims. This is an increase from the 2018 total (7,036). The percentage of victims are reported below:

- Race/ethnicity/ancestry bias – 57.6%
- Religion – 20.1%
- Sexual orientation – 16.7%
- Gender identity – 2.7%
- Disability – 2%
- Gender – 0.9%

About 64 percent of hate crimes target persons, while 33 percent target property, and a small percentage (3 percent) are classified as crimes against society. Offender characteristics are as follows: 52.5 percent were white, 23.9 percent were Black, and for almost 15 percent of the cases, the race of the offender was unknown. In terms of state numbers, California and Washington reported the most hate crimes (1,221 and 664 respectively) while Wyoming and Arkansas (6 and 10 respectively) reported the fewest.[43]

It should also be noted that hate crimes against Muslims and Arabs increased markedly in the aftermath of the 9/11 attacks. Further, the risk of being a victim of hate crimes increased in counties in which Muslim or

Arab populations were relatively small relative to the white population. This indicates that small minority groups tend to be more visible and hence more subject to harassment by the majority population.[44] Additionally, with the Covid-19 pandemic there was a rise of discrimination against Asians in general and Chinese in particular, with some of these acts being classified as hate crimes.[45] The most targeted groups in the Chinese-speaking world were Wuhan residents, Hubei residents, mainline Chinese, overseas Chinese, and Africans in China.[46] On March 16, 2021, 21-year-old Robert Aaron Long went on a shooting rampage at three massage parlors in the Atlanta area.[47] Long killed eight women, most of whom were Asian, and many observers believed the shootings were hate crimes connected with the Covid-19 pandemic. Although as of this writing the federal investigation of the shootings was still ongoing, Fulton County District Attorney Fani Willis filed notice that she intends to seek the death penalty along with hate crime charges against Long.[48]

Penalty enhancement law

An especially controversial area of hate crime legislation is the enactment of penalty enhancement laws in some jurisdictions. In order to illustrate what this is, consider the following situation. A white and Black male are arguing about something in a bar, and as the argument gets more heated, the white person pulls out a knife and stabs the Black person, seriously injuring him. Subsequent investigations discovered that the white person felt he had been cut off in traffic by the Black person, and the two had exchanged unpleasantries out in the street before going into the bar. The Black man seemed to be egging on the white man, calling him "punk" and "chicken," and inviting him to go settle the issue "like men." They did not know each other previous to this encounter, and there was no evidence of racial animosity on the part of the white person. The stabbing was simply the result of an escalation of mutual hostilities between these two persons precipitated by the traffic altercation.

Consider now the exact same event, namely, a white person stabbing a Black person in that same bar after a heated argument. Immediately preceding the attack, the white person had exhibited visible disgust over the fact that the Black man was with a white woman, calling him the n-word and saying he needed to "go back to the ghetto" and stay away from "our" women. The woman tried to restrain her friend and suggested they simply leave, but instead he confronted the white man, telling him that "we can take this outside and settle it like men." From that point on verbal hostilities escalated, the men moved toward each other in an aggressive and menacing manner, and the stabbing occurred.

In both cases we have the same event: a white man assaulting a Black man with a knife and seriously injuring him. Yet because in the second case the white man's motivation for the attack flowed from his racist attitudes toward African-Americans, under the Hate Crime Sentencing Enhancement Act of 1994, not only could the white man be charged with assault with a deadly weapon (among other things), he could also be punished further for intentionally selecting this particular victim because of his race.[49] This seems to violate the spirit of the Fourteenth Amendment, which specifies equal treatment under the law. The law is set up to protect people from being treated differently, and in this case equal treatment under the law means that the same acts should receive the same punishments. Punishing the motivation in *addition* to punishing the act may be seen as an illegitimate attempt by the government to restrict unwanted speech or thoughts, which could be interpreted as a violation of free speech under the First Amendment.

The First Amendment was at the heart of a 1992 Wisconsin case which eventually was reviewed by the US Supreme Court a year later in the case *Wisconsin v. Mitchell*. In 1989 a white youth, Gregory Riddick, was walking by an apartment complex in Kenosha, Wisconsin, when he was attacked by a group of Black youths seemingly unprovoked. Riddick was beaten and fell unconscious, sustaining brain injuries as a result. The leader of the violent mob, Todd Mitchell, then 19 years old, had become agitated after watching the movie "Mississippi Burning," which depicted an investigation into the murder of three civil rights workers in the 1960s amidst the backdrop of racial hostility evident across the southern United States during that time. There was a scene in the movie where a white man beat a Black boy who was praying, and Mitchell reportedly asked the others who were watching the movie with him, "Do you all feel hyped up to move on some white people?"[50] Shortly thereafter the assault and battery of Riddick occurred.

In the original case, which was decided in 1992, the presiding judge interpreted Wisconsin state law as allowing the maximum sentence of two years for battery to be doubled because the evidence showed that Mitchell targeted Riddick because of his race. Although on appeal Mitchell's conviction was reversed on the basis of a violation of his First Amendment rights, by the time the case made it to the Supreme Court in 1993, the ruling in *Wisconsin v. Mitchell* reinstated the conviction of the trial court, finding that penalty enhancement does not violate First Amendment protections because the enhanced penalty punishes behavior not mere words.

Consistent with the Supreme Court's ruling, Brian Levin has pointed out that the law frequently takes into account the motivations for a criminal act and establishes severity of punishments based upon such considerations.[51] For example, if a person enters a building for the intent of taking something of value from the premises, it is *burglary*. But if the person enters the building for some other reason – for example, the person may have checked the doorknob and discovered it was unlocked, and slipped inside without specifically planning a burglary – then it is *criminal trespass*, which is typically a less serious offense. Another example is the statute operating in many jurisdictions that provides for harsher punishments for those persons who carry a gun or other deadly weapon during the commissioning of a crime than for those who commit the same act without carrying a weapon.

In short, the law punishes crimes motivated by racial hatred or other forms of bias more severely than crimes not motivated by such attitudes because the former are considered to cause more social harm than the latter.

America's imprisonment binge

Crime rates in both the United States and Canada began increasing in the mid-1960s, peaked in the early 1990s, and have fallen or leveled off ever since. Even with this upturn in the crime rate beginning in the 1960s, however, incarcerations rates had remained relatively stable for nearly 50 years during the period 1925 to the early 1970s.[52] During this time both the Canadian and American incarceration rates hovered between 100 and 110 prisoners per 100,000 population. However, after 1973 the incarceration rates of the United States and Canada diverged markedly. Whereas the Canadian rate remained at approximately the same level it had been since the 1920s, the American incarceration rate grew dramatically. Today the United States has the highest incarceration rate in the world, exceeding 700 prisoners per 100,000 population.[53]

At the end of 2019 there were just under 2.1 million Americans incarcerated in state or federal prisons, local jails, and juvenile detention facilities.[54] Along with over four million Americans either on probation or parole, this means that over seven million Americans are either imprisoned or in some other way involved with the criminal or juvenile justice systems. This "mass incarceration" has affected some groups disproportionately: "Nine out of ten prison inmates are male, most are under the age of 40, African-Americans are seven times more likely than Whites to be in prison, and nearly all prisoners lack any education beyond high school."[55] In the next section we will discuss some of the factors that have caused America's "imprisonment binge."[56]

Factors in the imprisonment binge

A variety of factors have contributed to America's "addiction to incarceration."[57] First, the previously mentioned *war on drugs*, launched in earnest during the Reagan Administration and expanded under the next three presidents (George H.W. Bush, Bill Clinton, and George W. Bush), sent an unprecedented number of persons to prison, the majority of whom were poor and/or ethnic and racial minorities. As David Rothman has noted, "Drug law enforcement and punishment are aimed mostly at minorities, and the 'war on drugs' is in large part a war on blacks."[58] The war on drugs and its aftermath almost single-handedly created the problem of prison overcrowding that wreaked havoc on the American correctional system during the 1980s and 1990s. For example, between 1980 and 1997 drug arrests tripled, and the number of people going to prison for a drug offense went up 1,040 percent, compared to only 82 percent for violent crime and 207 percent for nonviolent crime.[59]

Indeed, newer hybrid courts, such as the drug treatment court, mental health court, and teen and family courts which appeared beginning in the late 1980s, have arisen largely through the efforts of judges who became frustrated with the backlog of drug-related cases and who were seeking alternatives to traditional sanctions which otherwise would have landed these defendants back into the overburdened prison and jail system.[60]

Second, *partisan politics* have played an increasingly important role in the public discourse concerning imprisonment and the viability and necessity of its use and even expansion for dealing with the real or perceived problems of crime. Michael Tonry explains the way that crime became a wedge issue in American politics, especially after the 1960s:

> On crime control, conservatives blamed rising crime rates on lenient judges and soft punishments, and demanded toughness. On welfare, conservatives blamed rising welfare rolls on welfare cheats and laziness, and demanded budget cuts. On affirmative action, conservatives blamed White unemployment and underemployment on quotas, and urged elimination of affirmative action.[61]

A third and related factor is the *loss of confidence* in the government and the concomitant rise of single-issue voter sentiment. This loss of confidence arose largely through citizen perceptions, especially emerging after the 1970s, that government programs have done little to solve such pressing issues as healthcare, education, welfare, crime, consumer protection, and infant and childcare, to name a few.[62] Not only has there been a general perception of government failure and incompetence in these areas, but also that this incompetence has come at a high price. Between 1970 and 1995, for example, government expenditures for healthcare have outpaced inflation by a 5 to 1 margin, for education by 3.5 to 1, and for criminal justice by 6 to 1.[63]

In a 1958 survey of Americans conducted by the National Elections Studies, Center for Political Studies, at the University of Michigan, one question that was asked measured citizen trust of government. The question was: "How much of the time do you trust government in Washington to do what is right – just about always, most of the time, or only some of the time?" In 1958, 73 percent of those polled responded either "just about always" or "most of the time" to the question, while only 23 percent responded "only some of the time." In 1970, the total percentage of persons that trusted government "just about always" or "most of the time" dropped to 53 percent. And in 1995, only 25 percent of those polled trusted the federal government "just about always" or "most of the time."[64]

It is interesting to note that this long-term decline in trust in government was reversed briefly in 2001 due to the terrorist attacks of 9/11. In the 2001 poll, conducted by ABC News and the *Washington Post*, 64 percent of those polled responded that they trusted the government "just about always" or "most of the time." By 2005, however, the level of trust had decline once again, with the figure standing at 31 percent.[65]

Many observers believed that with the election of President Barack Obama in 2008, citizens' faith and trust in government would be restored somewhat in light of what many perceived to be the misguided policies of the previous Bush Administration, especially with regard to the wars in Iraq and Afghanistan. However, this turned out not to be the case. A poll conducted by the Pew Research Center in 2010 found that only 22 percent of Americans trusted the government in Washington "almost always or most of the time."[66] The polls through 2019 continue to show a downward trend in trust in government. In 2014, only 19 percent of those polled trusted the government "always or most of the time." The figure dropped to 18 percent in 2015 through 2017, and in 2019 the figure dropped to 17 percent.[67]

This general collapse in government confidence has meant that citizen sentiment regarding the "good life" has fragmented into numerous single-issue or "hot button" agendas which produce rancorous partisan bickering among private citizens and at all levels of government, as portrayed through the media. Single-issue political agendas – whether abortion, the death penalty, getting tough on crime, funding and taxing issues, education, and victims' rights – tend to break down into an "us versus them" struggle, with one side claiming righteousness and virtuousness on the issue while portraying the other side as not only wrong or misguided but perhaps even as evil. Crime as a single-issue agenda is subject to this rancorous discourse and tends to be emotion-driven and in essence hijacked by a "moral majority" of concerned citizens who claim that politicians are "too soft" on crime and who thereby seek more retributive and punitive approaches toward offenders.

An example of such grassroots populism was the "three strikes and you're out" legislation that emerged out of Washington and then California which mandated life in prison without the possibility of parole on a defendant's third felony conviction, regardless of how serious that third offense actually was. Critics of three strikes legislation argued that penal policy ought not be decided in such a knee-jerk and emotional way, and that such legislation might likely send the California court and corrections systems into fiscal emergency because of the backlog of cases it will produce (e.g., defendants will have less incentive or be given no opportunity to plea bargain for a lesser charge), as well as a growth in the prison population because offenders will be given longer sentences.[68]

A fourth broad factor contributing to high incarceration rates is the *decline of the rehabilitative ideal*. Whereas the goal of retribution is to punish offenders because they *deserve* to be punished ("just deserts") since the assumption is made that they willfully violated the criminal law, the idea of rehabilitation is to discover *why* offenders break the law and to instill prosocial adjustments in these persons so that they will not offend again. Whereas retribution or just deserts favors determinate sentencing (equal sentences for similar crimes), rehabilitation favors *indeterminate sentences*, which means that an offender is kept in prison for treatment or other ameliorative measures only so long as it takes him or her to get "well." Once cured, the prisoner is released back to the community so he or she can become a productive member of society, rather than sitting in a jail or prison cell wasting taxpayers' dollars.

This rehabilitative ideal, a prominent feature of the criminal justice system from the 1890s through the early 1970s, was considered during this period to be both a laudable and attainable goal of the system. But for many of the reasons discussed above, by the early 1970s there was a loss of confidence in the ability to actually rehabilitate offenders within correctional facilities, and in light of this many urged a return to incarceration, not only because it was perceived to be more harsh and punitive but also because it was fairer. How could incarceration be viewed as both fairer *and* harsher than rehabilitation?

The rehabilitative model of justice had always adopted a medical case model for handling and processing clients. That is to say, under the auspices of the rehabilitative ideal, offenders who were earmarked for a treatment program upon the recommendations or mandate of the court, would be given a thorough assessment upon entry into the facility ("intake and assessment") and a unique treatment plan would be drawn up to meet the particular needs of the offender. During his or her period of incarceration, parole board members would be given reports as to the progress of the offender through the program, and at any point a determination could be made that the person no longer poses a threat to the community and should thereby be released.

Although putting this sort of discretion into the hands of health professionals for purposes of determining if and when a prisoner should be released would appear to meet the general spirit of the rehabilitative model and its therapeutic mode of sanctioning, the reality was that correctional discretion was often being used in a biased and prejudicial manner.

For example, studies clearly show that indigent persons and members of ethnic and racial minorities are less likely to be considered viable candidates for rehabilitation, and, even when they are placed into these programs, they are less likely to be granted parole in a timely manner when compared with their white counterparts. Indeed, the Report of the Working Party of the American Friends Service Committee entitled *Struggle for Justice*, published in 1971, fundamentally challenged the use of indeterminate sentencing within the criminal justice system. As David Garland notes, the authors of the report claimed that the criminal justice system's discriminatory use of the power to punish, particularly its use of imprisonment, was simply "a tool to repress blacks, the poor, the young and various cultural minorities."[69] Because of its hypocrisy and paternalism, and because of its naïve faith that rehabilitation could be both therapeutic and effective (which it was rarely shown to be), proponents of "progressive penology" were dealt a severe blow by a growing number of critics, and the rehabilitative ideal withered on the vine while the goals of retribution, deterrence, and incapacitation once again attained prominence.[70]

A fifth factor fueling the reemergence of punitive sanctions is the *return of the victim*, which is itself part of a broader cultural trend toward expressive justice. David Anderson defines *expressive justice* as "laws, policies, and practices that are designed more to vent communal outrage than to reduce crime."[71] Expressive justice is ancient, appearing first under conditions of mechanical solidarity and self-help as discussed by Durkheim. In modernity, however, order and justice were taken out of the hands of everyday citizens and placed under bureaucratic control through the work of criminal justice professionals such as police, prosecutors and judges, and corrections personnel. By doing this, justice would be decided on the basis of the facts of the case, thereby presumably protecting against the distortions of the irrationality and emotions of aggrieved victims.

Anderson believes the return of expressive justice appeared in earnest during the 1988 US presidential campaign between George H.W. Bush and Michael Dukakis. While Dukakis was governor of Massachusetts, an inmate who had been released on furlough went on to burglarize a house in Maryland, assaulted the homeowner, and raped the homeowner's fiancée. The republicans seized upon this unfortunate incident to make the case that Dukakis was soft on crime. They launched an aggressive advertising campaign which included mug shots of the perpetrator, Willie Horton, a Black man. Wittingly or unwittingly, the Willie Horton ad amounted to a new "politics of hysteria" in which fomenting moral panic among the public made good political sense.

According to Anderson, expressive justice is likely to emerge when crimes possess the following characteristics:

- the crimes were violent and produced injuries or deaths;
- the victims were usually white and middle class, while the perpetrator was an ethnic or racial minority;
- the victims were innocent, involved in no way in criminal or illicit activities which may have contributed to their victimization;
- perpetrators appeared to choose their victims randomly;
- perpetrators had a history of involvement with the criminal justice system.[72]

As discussed above, with the professionalization of policing and the promulgation of constitutional protections of criminal defendants in Britain, the United States, and other constitutional democracies, punishments were taken out of the hands of the members of the community and made the responsibility of the state. This meant that for the most part victims of crime were left on the sidelines while a specialized, professional coterie of formal control agents worked toward the collective goal of securing justice for crime victims. Over the last three decades, however, crime victims have become more visible both with regard to criminal court proceedings as well as media portrayals of especially poignant or compelling cases of victimization. In an interesting twist, therapeutic efforts have shifted away from perpetrators and are now focused more squarely on victims. This therapeutic ethos has now been translated into the new political imperative that "victims must be protected, their voices must be heard, their memory honoured, their anger expressed, their fears addressed."[73]

As Garland further notes, up until recently openly avowed expressions of vengeful sentiment were virtually taboo. Public officials connected with the prosecutor's office and the courts were expected to go about their business in a professional and sober manner, allowing procedural law to take its course and hopefully winning a conviction on the basis of the evidence presented. Now more than ever, however, public officials are openly expressing public anger and resentment over the plight of "helpless" victims and vowing to extract whatever vengeance is legally available. This expressive justice is an explicitly retributive discourse of victims' rights which provides impetus for politicians to support and lawmakers to enact increasingly draconian laws.[74]

The end of punitiveness?

Even given the bad news concerning US incarceration rates, there are signs of hope. Since 2000, the rate of growth of the prison population has slowed from a high of 6.5 percent in the 1990s to only 1.8 percent in 2008. By 2016, the US incarceration rate per 100,000 adults had declined to 860, the lowest rate since 1996, which equates to an incarceration rate of 0.09 percent.[75] At least part of this decline can be attributed to successful organizing in local communities and the work of nonprofit organizations formed specifically to address problems of violence. As Patrick Sharkey and colleagues explain, "When we model year-to-year changes in the prevalence of community nonprofits, we find that every 10 additional nonprofits per 100,000 residents leads to a 9 percent decline in the murder rate, a 6 percent decline in the violent crime rate, and a 4 percent decline in the property crime rate."[76] This also indicates one path which communities may follow to reclaim some modicum of informal control while resisting tendencies toward pathologization from the medical side or criminalization from the legal side.

There is also evidence that concerns with mass incarceration led to slow but steady policy innovations which contributed to the recent incarceration decline beyond those already discussed (e.g., probation and problem-solving courts). Two of the most prominent changes in law and policy since 2008 that have contributed to declines in incarceration are community corrections and reentry programs aimed at helping recently released prisoners make a successful transition back to civilian life.[77] Yet, even with the good news of a lowering of incarceration rates through community organizing and policy innovations, and with a seeming abandonment of the philosophy of punitiveness, the future of incarceration is still uncertain. For example, just as incarceration rates for adults in the criminal justice system have declined, the juvenile court continues to move in a punitive direction, as more juveniles are being tried as adults to assuage concerns that many youths are perpetrating serious, adult-like crimes. This has led to an unprecedented number of juveniles being given sentences of life without parole.[78] This parallels the continuing use of life sentences for adults even while overall crime rates and incarceration rates have declined or leveled off. Aging prison populations in both criminal justice and juvenile justice contexts will continue to pose challenges now and into the future.

In summary, the era of mass incarceration in the United States that began in earnest in the 1970s exhibited clear signs of subsiding beginning in the mid-1990s. Even as a consensus by that time began to emerge that the United States was imprisoning too many of its citizens, criminal prosecutors continued to act punitively and aggressively toward those charged with crimes. Heather Schoenfeld and colleagues argue that even as laws have been changing with regard to reducing or relaxing criminal sanctions, prosecutors have retained practices that still represent punitiveness, even going so far as to suggest that much prosecutorial discretion since the mid-1990s amounts to "overcriminalization."[79]

This has occurred as lawmakers continue to expand categories of criminal statutes even as crime and incarceration rates have declined, criminalizing more behaviors that are considered to be social problems. Such overcriminalization shows up by way of criminalizing such activities as driving with a suspended license, heightened punitiveness with regard to drug laws, DUI, or even selling a college term paper.[80] Another type of criminalization is moving toward more mandatory minimum sentences, thereby attempting to reduce judicial discretion through the enactment of mandatory sentencing grids. A third overcriminalization strategy is creating more sentencing enhancements, that is, penalties which increase the seriousness of specific crimes (examples include having possession of a firearm during a robbery although not used during the commissioning of the crime or, as we have seen, the case of hate crimes).

Schoenfeld and colleagues examined criminal case processing in Florida to determine whether prosecutorial discretion could be shown to be adding to overcriminalization. However, even as crime and incarceration rates have steadily declined over the last two decades, between 1998 and 2012, total filings per case (i.e., piling on charges per each criminal) rose from 19 percent to 25 percent of all cases. In addition, the number of criminal cases receiving only one charge decreased from 49 percent to 42 percent during this period. It also appears to be the case that the Great Recession of 2008 impacted police practices, largely through a push to reduce the state's corrections budget. In order to save money, resources were concentrated on a diminishing number of crime cases in order to get "best bang for the buck" via increased number of charges per case. Since the Great Recession there has been an increase in the inclusion of lesser-included crimes in criminal complaints, another indication of how prosecutors can "pile on sanctions" to fit changes in the political economy and perceived public support for punitiveness.

SUGGESTIONS FOR FURTHER READING

John Baugh, *Linguistics in Pursuit of Justice* (2018)
   In this book the author seeks ways to use insights from linguistics to ameliorate injustices in such areas as the history of slavery, linguistic profiling, witness testimony, identity discrimination, and abusive language, which the author terms "linguistic harassment."

Bill Bratton and Peter Knobler, *The Profession: A Memoir of Community, Race, and the Arc of Policing in America* (2021)
   Bill Bratton has served a long and distinguished career in law enforcement, having served as chief or police commissioner for departments in Boston, New York City, and Los Angeles since the 1980s. He was commissioner of the New York City Police Department and was given credit for the reduction of crime in the city during the 1990s, although the aggressive tactics employed by the police department (such as broken windows) drew criticism. In this memoir, Bratton reflects on the triumphs and travails of his work in policing and offers insights into current controversies such as defunding the police, community policing, and race and policing.

Ronnie A. Dunn and Wornie Reed, *Racial Profiling: Causes and Consequences* (2011)
   An excellent summary and overview of key issues in racial profiling. Topics covered include traffic ticketing, variations in the legislation of racial profiling by states, traffic violator surveys, and institutional racism.

Peter K. Enns, *Incarceration Nation: How the United States Became the Most Punitive Democracy in the World* (2016)

Enns pays close attention to how incarceration rates in the United States increased significantly in comparison to Canada and England beginning in the early 1980s, and that this divergence was due mainly to the strength of punitive public opinion in America at least through the early 2010s. He concludes that mass incarceration matters not only for those imprisoned but also for police officers, prison guards, and for those communities which have significant resources tied up in the housing of these inmates.

Ian Loader and Neil Walker, *Civilizing Security* (2007)

An analytically sophisticated examination of the various dimensions of security provision within modern Western society. How do states maintain legitimacy and the claim to be the essential providers of security in the face of multiple problems besetting them, including disparities of race, class, and gender in the processing of suspects through the criminal justice system? Even while acknowledging the persistence of these and other problems, the authors argue that states can indeed provide security fairly and equitably to all, thereby fulfilling the highest ideals of democratic governance.

DISCUSSION QUESTIONS

1. Two competing theories of police misconduct are "bad apples," which indicates that such misconduct is limited to a small handful of rogue cops, and institutional or systematic misconduct, which implicates the entirety of police organizations. Take a position on which one of these explanations of police misconduct is correct, and provide evidence for it.

2. Summarize the veil of darkness studies that have been used to measure the extent to which police engage in racial profiling. Is this a good approach for understanding the prevalence of racially-biased policing? Why or why not?

3. In the chapter, we discussed sentence enhancement laws connected with hate crimes. Are these enhancement laws needed, or are they a violation of the Equal Protection Clause of the Fourteenth Amendment?

4. For a long time in American society crime has been a wedge issue in partisan political debate. Discuss whether or to what extent crime has been a political issue since the election of President Barack Obama in 2008. If it has declined as a national wedge issue during this time, explain why.

5. What is expressive justice? How is expressive justice related to the concept of gonzo justice discussed in chapter 3?

Chapter 9
Terrorism and Social Control

Introduction

Terrorism is the most high-profile form of political violence in the world today, having been established on a day of infamy, September 11, 2001, when jihadist terrorists killed close to 3,000 people in simultaneous attacks on the World Trade Center and the Pentagon. These attacks were a shock not only to the United States but to the world community, as television coverage captured real-time footage of the hijacked planes crashing into both World Trade towers minutes apart, causing the collapse of both towers as well as numerous adjacent buildings. There were two additional hijacked planes, one which hit the Pentagon causing 42 deaths, while the other plane did not complete its mission as it crashed into a field in Somerset County killing all 44 people onboard, including the four hijackers. That fourth plane was headed for the White House and would have reached its destination had it not been for the bravery of some passengers onboard who brought down the plane.

This chapter will be concerned with providing a broad understanding of the nature and scope of international terrorism, seeking to explain why such acts are perpetrated and what measures could be taken to reduce or eliminate terror incidents. In the famous 1964 US Supreme Court case of *Jacobellis v. Ohio*, Justice Potter Stewart admitted that he could not formally define pornography, affirming only that "I know it when I see it."[1] We are similarly stymied in the case of terrorism. We certainly "know it when we see it;" the media industry gives it extensive coverage, and most of us hold taken-for-granted notions of what terrorism is. There have been numerous attempts to define terrorism over the years, but so far, a scientific consensus on a single preferred definition has not emerged. The best we can do is sort through the many available definitions and commit to one of them as we move forward in our discussion. We will use Brian Forst's definition of terrorism, which states that:

> Terrorism is the premeditated and unlawful use or threatened use of violence against a noncombatant population or target having symbolic significance, with the aim of either inducing political change through intimidation and destabilization or destroying a population defined as an enemy.[2]

Terrorism, then, is a form of political violence in general and a political crime against the state in particular.[3] Groups that come to be defined as terrorists admit that the violence they perpetrate, especially the targeting of innocent civilians, is indeed an atrocity, but it is viewed as a necessity and even a greater good as a form of payback against states which, they allege, are mercilessly oppressing their people and must be held accountable. Indeed, what distinguishes terrorism from crime is that the former is often acted upon for altruistic reasons aligning with an ideological or political philosophy, while crime is rarely seen as a form of helping behavior. In other words, most routine crime is engaged in for limited or personal reasons – for example, embezzling from your employer because you cannot make this month's rent – rather than as a means to achieving some larger political ends.[4]

Violent political extremism

Acknowledging the ways in which this political or ideological dimension can enter into the motivation for illicit activities, many terrorism scholars, policymakers, and analysts are using the term *violent political extremism* as a proxy for "terrorism." This reflects how the gap continues to close between thinking of terrorism as either an act of war – which is ultimately a political act – or a crime. However, even as a general scholarly consensus has emerged that terrorism is simultaneously both a criminal act and an act of war, there are still policy differences on whether such violent political extremism is best dealt with under the purview of the military (where perpetrators are treated as enemy combatants) or domestic law enforcement (where requirements of legal due process prevail). These questions come to the fore whenever US presidents authorize drone strikes against terrorist targets. When the strike is successful and ends in the death of the target – such as what happened in the killing of Anwar al-Awlaki by the Obama Administration in 2011 or Qasem Soleimani by the Trump Administration in 2020 – critics may claim that the United States has set itself up as an outlaw regime acting as "judge, jury, and executioner."

Because terrorists target civilian populations with the aim of changing the behavior of state actors, the atrocities of these acts and the collective trauma they cause readily lead to denouncements that terrorism is barbarism. In short, barbaric acts that shock the conscience of the civilized world deserve equally harsh, brutal, and destructive responses in return. Yet, these sort of "fight fire with fire," tit-for-tat responses on the part of modern states may, in turn, pull them into forms of barbarism which they claim to oppose.[5] Emblematic of this problem was the revelations of torture and other forms of brutalization that occurred at Abu Ghraib prison in Iraq, where terror detainees were being held in the early stages of the Iraq War during the Bush Administration.[6]

For many observers, the term violent political extremism may be preferable to terrorism because the latter was often associated with radical Islam and jihadism. This association became entrenched with the 9/11 attacks orchestrated against the United States by Osama bin Laden and al-Qaeda.[7] More recently, however, some 20 years after the horrific events of September 11, 2001, there has been an acknowledgment that violent political extremism need not be based solely on religion – however radical or unconventional the interpretation of that religious doctrine may be – but can appear as various forms of domestic terrorism motivated by racism (including white supremacism), authoritarianism, xenophobia or strong anti-immigrant sentiment, radical environmentalism, and various forms of anarchism including anti-government ideologies.

Domestic terrorism

It is worth noting that the FBI defines *domestic terrorism* as "Violent, criminal acts committed by individuals and/or groups to further ideological goals stemming from domestic influences, such as those of a political, religious, social, racial, or environmental nature."[8] A relatively new group of domestic terrorists are identified as *incels*, who are heterosexual men who fail at attracting persons of the opposite sex for intimate relations. Such men, stuck in a condition of involuntary celibacy, may turn their anger and resentment against women who spurn them into not only misogynistic thoughts or attitudes, but also physical assaults up to and including murder.[9] It is not clear, however, how real this incel category actually is, as it may be part of a moral panic that involves the demonization of heterosexual males along with their alleged toxic masculinity.

Individuals who engage in violent political extremism are thought to be radicalized into extremist ideologies through associations with other radicals either face-to-face or, even more likely, through the Internet and social media.[10] A recent study of the factors that predict involvement in violent political extremism found that:

- a history of stable employment significantly reduces involvement in violent political extremism;
- persons who have radical peers are more likely to engage in such violence;
- persons with a history of mental illness are more likely to engage in such violence;

- persons with criminal records have higher odds of engaging in such violence.[11]

For critics of the Trump Administration, this process of political extremism and radicalization affected followers of former president Trump, who on January 6, 2021 stormed the US capitol where five persons died and which caused upwards of $1.5 million in damage.[12] This event was the culmination of concerns critics had been voicing since Trump first made his appearance on the national political stage in 2015, namely, that Trump engenders a fascist populism tinged with xenophobia, racism, and authoritarianism.[13]

Connected with this, on June 1, 2021, President Joe Biden gave a talk on the 100th anniversary of the Tulsa race massacre – in which a white mob attacked persons, residents, and businesses in the predominately Black neighborhood of Greenwood in Tulsa, Oklahoma – and shared information from his new administration's intelligence community that terrorism associated with American white supremacy was the single most lethal threat to the homeland. Indeed, according to Biden's intelligence analysts, the threat from white supremacist domestic terrorists was greater than even that of ISIS or al-Qaeda.[14]

However, the rise of right-wing political violence and terrorism did not start with Trump but had been relatively long in the making since 2001, running through the presidencies of Bush and Obama before him.[15] Through 2017, the percentage of terror acts perpetrated in the United States by political or ideological affiliation were as follows:

- Far-right – 49.6%
- Far-left – 32%
- Jihadist-inspired – 18.3%[16]

As the data indicate, more recently far-right political extremism – which had been rising steadily since 2011 – is running ahead of both far-left and jihadist terrorism.[17] This serves to illustrate that terrorism is a term that has become both highly politically-charged and partisan, and it plays right into the hands of Schmitt's definition of the political as friends vs. enemies.

Anders Breivik

The deadliest domestic terror event occurred on July 22, 2011, in Oslo, Norway. A massive blast shook the prime minister's office – the heart of the Labour Party government – in the center of the city, killing eight people and injuring 209 more. The blast came from a car bomb detonated by Anders Behring Breivik, an extreme nationalist who was opposed to what he perceived to be the ongoing Islamization of Europe. The main problem from Breivik's point of view, and why he targeted the Labour

Party government, was their lax immigration policies and embrace of multiculturalism and the spirit of globalization.

But this was only the beginning of the carnage Breivik wrought that day. About an hour later, Breivik took a ferry from Oslo to the island of Utøya, located about 20 miles to the northwest. The ferryman saw that he was armed but allowed Breivik to board when he told him he was a police officer who was conducting an investigation into the Oslo bombing, word of which was just hitting the media. On that island that day were a number of young persons who were attending a youth camp organized by the Labour Party. They were all sitting ducks for Breivik, who, armed with a pistol, an automatic rifle, and multiple rounds of ammunition, began shooting people randomly. The first reports of shots on the island were made at 17:26, but a specialist SWAT unit did not arrive until about an hour later. The first police boat had sunk due to turbulent conditions, giving Breivik time to continue his carnage unabated. By the time officers arrived and Breivik surrendered to them, he had killed 69 people, mostly young persons attending the camp. The shooting spree lasted more than an hour.

There is no death penalty in Norway, so even if convicted of the mass killings Breivik would have spent about 23 years in prison. As a young man of 32 at the time of the killings, he would be only in his mid-50s by the time of his release. There was, however, the possibility of finding Breivik clinically insane, and if this were the case he could be held indefinitely under the policy of indeterminate (or open-ended) sentencing typical of a therapeutic or rehabilitative approach to criminality. After medical examinations, however, it was determined that Breivik was sane, that he knew what he was doing, and that he planned the attacks meticulously and with malice aforethought.[18] The findings of sanity and mental competence fulfilled the mens rea ("guilty mind") requirement of conviction under criminal law. In 2012, Breivik was convicted of the 77 murders he perpetrated that day and is currently being held in near-isolation in a prison in Skien. He was given the maximum sentence of 21 years under Norway's preventive detention law.[19]

Israel and Palestine

An example of this political dynamic is the longstanding conflict between Israel and Palestine, which since 1994 has generated more overt concerns about terrorism on the part of Palestine in the face of alleged state repression by Israel. Major grievances against the state of Israel and its supporters and sympathizers include:

- the United Nations' 1947 resolution which partitioned Palestine into Jewish and Arab states, but which effectively brought a Jewish state into being while dispossessing a large number of Palestinians of the lands they once occupied;

- the rise of a new reactionary philosophy of governance on the part of Israel, so-called Zionism, which preconceives a largely hostile reception and treatment of Palestinians in defense of Israeli statehood (the Nakab);
- Israel viewed as an apartheid state through the expropriation of land previously in the possession of the Palestinians, such as the continuing building of Jewish settlements in the Gaza Strip since 2005;
- and even beyond this pariah of an apartheid state, Israel's actions may be described as consistent with settler colonialism, such as limitations placed on Palestinians living in Occupied Territories to cross into pre-1967 borders;
- the use of the criminal justice system to punish dissent especially within the Green Line and Occupied Territories;
- the building of a partition wall in the West Bank, increasing state surveillance and militarized violence against Palestinians;
- Israeli hardline positions against Hamas (a former terrorist organization) which effectively took over the governance of Palestine after 2006 (with not only Israel but most of the West maintaining an embargo of non-negotiation with Hamas).[20]

Schmitt's friends vs. enemy distinction is clearly evident in the way that both sides of the Israeli–Palestine conflict charge each other with terrorism. As Igor Primoratz notes, "Every public debate about the conflict abounds in charges and countercharges of terrorism, indicating much confusion about who is and who is not a terrorist and just what terrorism is."[21] Other, more balanced and evenhanded analyses recognize that over the long history of the conflict both Israel and Palestine have engaged in morally-questionable actions that could be described as terrorism, specifically the component of targeting innocent civilians as a morally-justified defense of their homelands.[22] In this conflict, there is no true higher or moral ground. Rather, it is open to interpretation from partisan perspectives, with each side accusing the other side of terrorist atrocities.[23] Because of this, it is not clear how or if this conflict will ever be resolved.

As alluded to above, those actors or groups labeled terrorists typically invoke the ancient doctrine of necessity to justify their actions. Terrorists admit that what they are doing is illegal and often shock the conscience of the human community – such as ISIS releasing videos of graphic beheadings or burning people alive – but go on to explain that their carnage and mayhem are necessary to stave off even greater evils carried out by targeted nation-states (specifically, Israel and its Western allies in the United States and Europe).[24]

Because the nations of the world possess superior military power, and because terrorists are not as well organized and certainly not equipped with the weaponry needed to carry out large-scale combat, they must use means other than traditional warfare to take on militarily-superior adversaries. Conventional warfare, the type carried out by nations against other nations, is symmetrical insofar as combatants on both sides are armed with similar levels of equipment, organization, and training.[25] Conversely, terrorism is described as asymmetrical conflict because it pits members of terrorist organizations, who are typically less well organized and armed with far less lethal force, against well-organized and well-equipped national armies, navies, and air forces. Being outgunned and outmaneuvered by national military forces, terrorists cannot engage enemies on a battlefield as is the case for conventional warfare. Instead, they must remain dispersed and decentralized, lying in wait covertly and, when the time is right, launch attacks against civilian populations in crowded urban areas to inflict maximum damage.

The typical response to terrorism consists of "target-hardening" strategies which aim to make terror attacks less likely in the future. By target-hardening strategies, I am referring primarily to new or expanded federal law enforcement responses such as the establishment of the Department of Homeland Security, an expansion of routine public surveillance, expanded wiretap authority, shoring up security at border checkpoints, legislation aimed at facilitating tracking and monitoring of persons both in terms of migration and immigration, and a greater commitment to human assets in espionage. Many have decried that a number of these target-hardening strategies – especially those associated with changes in immigration and border policies – have contributed to the erosion of civil liberties and due process.[26] The USA PATRIOT Act has pushed to the limit the fragile balancing act between assuring citizens' freedom and civil liberties on the one hand, and maintaining order, public safety, and national security on the other. In the next section we will summarize some of the more important changes in the law that have taken place since the passage of the Act.

Changes in the law since 9/11

On October 26, 2001, President George W. Bush signed into law the USA PATRIOT Act (H.R. 3162), the full title of which is "Uniting and Strengthening America by Providing Appropriate Tools Required to Intercept and Obstruct Terrorism." The Act was pushed though without much legislative debate, passing the House easily on a 357 to 66 vote, while passing the Senate on a vote of 98 to 1. (Democratic senator Russ Feingold of Wisconsin cast the only no vote.) Several sections of the Act are especially controversial, and these will be discussed briefly.[27]

Under the title "Access to records and other items under the Foreign Intelligence Surveillance Act," Section 215 of the Act authorizes the government to seize personal records such as video rentals, books checked out from the library, medical and phone records, and information on the church, mosque, or synagogue one attends. Previous to the Act the government was required to produce a warrant and show probable cause to access private information of this sort. Indeed, under section 215 the government can now force third-party holders of personal records – such as libraries, schools, churches, or hospitals – to turn over this information. Even further, the holders of these records are barred from informing the person whose records were obtained that such a search of records ever took place. Just so long as the Department of Justice states that the investigation is needed to protect against "international terror," the record keepers are forced to comply with the request.

Another controversial part of the Act is section 802, titled "Definition of domestic terrorism." Domestic terrorism becomes a new category of crime, and is defined as "acts dangerous to human life that are a violation of the criminal laws of the United States" just so long as the actor's intent is to "influence the policy of a government by intimidation or coercion."[28] According to this definition, domestic terrorism could include various forms of protest that previously were not crimes in and of themselves such as environmental activism, abortion clinic protests, or even protests against the government staged, for example, in front of the White House, Pentagon, or other government buildings.

Sections 411 and 412 are titled respectively "Definitions relating to terrorism" and "Mandatory detention of suspected terrorists; habeas corpus; judicial review." Section 411 makes association with terrorist organizations a crime, even if the person who is claimed to be associated with the terror organization did not know about its terror activities. This is a dangerous form of "guilt by association" that is now codified into law for purposes of combating terrorism. Section 412 allows the Attorney General to detain aliens suspected of terrorist activities or association with terrorist organizations for a period of time without any prior showing or court ruling that the person is actually a threat. The effect of sections 411 and 412 is that aliens accused of terrorist actions or associations can either be deported or detained without judicial review (except for habeas corpus, which is not likely to be used in such cases).

The USA PATRIOT Act has effectively shifted greater discretionary powers to the president, more so than at any time in American history.[29] This is reflected as well in the way 9/11 changed the police response to terrorism. For example, in the months following 9/11, the FBI assigned 4,000 of its 11,500 special agents to counterterrorist activities.[30] And of course the passage of the USA PATRIOT Act and the creation of the Department of Homeland Security shortly after 9/11 meant that counterterrorist police work became more bureaucratized – that is, subject to administrative oversight, control, and regulation at the federal level, with the president acting as chief law enforcement officer – and as a consequence policing was placed more firmly under political scrutiny as well. In effect, 9/11 accelerated the militarization of the police, a trend that began in the late 1970s with the "war on drugs" and the continuing growth of an urban "underclass" which requires policing (see chapter 6).[31]

Even so, potential checks on the newly expanded discretionary powers of the executive branch, written into the PATRIOT Act itself, consisted of a number of sunset provisions which had to be reauthorized by Congress if they were to continue as law after December 31, 2005. The controversial sections of the PATRIOT Act discussed here (215, 411, 412, and 802), for example, were all sunset provisions, that is, they were due to expire at the beginning of 2006 unless reauthorized by Congress. Organizations such as the American Civil Liberties Union (ACLU) actively fought against real or perceived civil rights abuses built into these and other sunset provisions, and as of late 2005 the sentiment among Washington politicians and legislators seemed to be that many of them would indeed be allowed to expire.[32]

After a protracted period of bitter and often heated legislative wrangling over the issue, President Bush signed into law a renewal of the PATRIOT ACT on March 9, 2006. Many of the disputed sunset provisions were retained but with some modifications. For example, section 215 clarifies that most libraries are not subject to demands for information about suspected terrorists. It also gives libraries and other entities that receive subpoenas for information on terror suspects or terrorist organizations the right to challenge the requirement that they not inform anyone of the inquiry.[33]

From Bush to Obama

On May 26, 2011, President Barack Obama signed into law yet another extension of key provisions of the USA PATRIOT Act, including sections 215, 206 (use of roving wiretaps in terrorism investigations), and section 6001 of the Intelligence Reform and Terrorist Prevention Act of 2004. Section 6001, dubbed the "lone wolf" provision, closed a loophole in the original law which would have allowed persons working alone and not specifically affiliated with known terrorist organizations to escape Foreign Intelligence Act (or FISA) surveillance.[34]

There were two main areas that distinguished the terror policies of the Bush and Obama Administrations. First, the Bush Administration favored the utilization of human intelligence and military ground support in Iraq and Afghanistan in an attempt to capture enemy combatants alive and expose them to harsh interrogation tactics such as waterboarding – which the Obama Administration would later claim were forms of torture and hence illegal. By contrast, the Obama Administration favored the use of remote operations such as drone strikes to injure or kill enemy combatants wherever they operated. With its emphasis on taking enemy combatants alive so that useful information could be retrieved from them, the Bush Administration set up vast networks of detainment camps, at Guantanamo Bay, Cuba, and in Iraq and Afghanistan. Critics of the use of detention facilities by the Bush Administration were emboldened to speak in unanimity about the failure of its policies when news broke in 2004 about the abuse of prisoners at Abu Ghraib Prison in Iraq. From the photographs it was apparent that some of the prisoners had been beaten, sodomized and even killed. Others were forced into compromised and sexualized positions, as some of the prisoners were stripped naked and forced to lie upon each other in the shape of a pyramid. In many of the pictures American soldiers were gleefully posing with the prisoners, and this inhumanity and sadism led to international outcries against the Bush Administration terror-detainment policies.[35]

Trump and Biden

President Donald Trump took office in early 2017 and set about to undo or revise aspects of the terror policies of the Obama Administration. Candidate Trump had campaigned on ending the "endless wars" in Iraq and Afghanistan, and early on he sought input from the intelligence and military communities on how best to draw down troops in these and other terrorist hotspots. He also needed to develop a consistent strategy for dealing with ISIS, which emerged near the end of Obama's first term. Additionally, Trump expected to foster closer working relations with Israeli Prime Minister Netanyahu, who had a history of strained relations with President Obama. On this point, Husam Mohamad notes that

> Tensions between President Obama and Israeli Prime Minister Netanyahu were hard to conceal. Although Obama had on many occasions criticized the [Palestinian Authority], Netanyahu was not pleased with the Obama administration's policy towards Israel.[36]

Trump was open to utilizing a wide range of assets and strategies to contend with international terrorism. This means that he was open to bringing back Bush-era policies of harsh interrogation of terror prisoners or suspects, including waterboarding – which many observers decried as torture – while also utilizing Obama's preference for remote drone strikes. In addition to his strong backing of Israel, Trump's Middle East and counterterrorism policies emphasized the strengthening of military ties with Saudi Arabia as well as threatening Iran with sanctions and military confrontation.[37] Trump had long been critical of the Obama Administration's unwillingness to use terms such as "radical Islam" or "jihad" in their policy positions regarding the threat of international terrorism, and as a corrective he made free use of such terms in the official White House statement outlining the Administration's counterterrorism policies which was released in 2018. The Trump Administration's counterterrorism policy articulated four specific goals or end states, these being:

- eliminating the terrorist threat to the United States;
- securing US borders and all ports of entry against terrorist threats;
- ensuring that terrorism, including radical Islamist ideologies and other violent extremist ideologies, do not undermine the American way of life;
- helping foreign partners address terrorist threats so that the interests of the United States and its partners are not jeopardized.[38]

In addition, in 2020 Trump failed to reauthorize three provisions of the Foreign Intelligence Surveillance Act (FISA) which had been renewed under the USA Freedom Act of 2015. These three provisions were among the sunset provisions of earlier versions of the USA PATRIOT Act, namely section 215 covering business searches and roving wiretaps, while the third was the lone wolf provision (section 6001).[39] The reauthorization vote was canceled over President Trump's threat of veto because of alleged abuses of the FISA court in digging up dirt – the famous "pee dossier" containing salacious details of Trump's private life assembled by British former intelligence officer Christopher Steele – which was part of the Mueller Report and also implicated in Trump's first impeachment.[40] These allegations from the Trump Administration and conservative media of illegal spying on US citizens by the National Security Agency (NSA) and other intelligence organizations was part of a broader condemnation of a "deep state" of unelected bureaucrats pulling the strings of duly-elected political representatives. This claim of skullduggery on the part of a shadowy Deep State seemed to be confirmed by a warning Democratic Senator Chuck Schumer offered to Trump in 2017, where he said, "Let me tell you: You take on the intelligence community – they have six ways from Sunday at getting back at you."[41]

Joe Biden won the presidency in 2020 and began his term of office in early 2021, and because of his brief time in office (as of this writing) only a few observations about his Administration's counterterrorism policies can be made. One thing that can be said for certain is that Biden will return to Obama-era policies in whole or in part. However, with Benjamin Netanyahu ousted from his position as prime minister in June 2021, it is also likely that Biden will develop more amicable relations with Israel than was the case during the Obama years. In addition, the Biden Administration is seeking to reinstate the Iran Nuclear Deal which Trump had terminated during his presidency, signaling a possibly more conciliatory approach toward Iran. Connected with this, Biden intends for the United States to rejoin the Paris Climate Accord which Trump had also suspended.

Even with his relatively short time in office, Biden did make available an *Interim National Security Strategic Guidance* policy in March 2021.[42] Biden clearly wanted to get away from what was perceived as Trump's insular America First policies, and hence the document has many references to globalism, especially as indicated within the section on the global security landscape. The document emphasizes that new security threats do not respect walls or physical barriers – clearly a dig against Trump's border wall – but circulate globally and across sovereign borders. Hence, talk of terrorism is merged with pandemics and other biological risks, the escalating climate crisis, cyber and digital threats, international economic threats as well as humanitarian threats against migrants and refugees, and the proliferation of nuclear weapons. Amazingly, whereas Trump's counterterrorism policy document contains zero references to climate change, the Biden national security strategy document contains 28 instances of the term "climate change." For example, where the Trump policy spoke of the importance of general assistance to foreign partners in the war on terrorism, the Biden policy makes specific reference to helping Africa combat threats posed by "climate change and violent extremism," with climate change of course being listed first.

Martyrdom and suicide attacks

From 1990, the year that Iraqi forces led by Saddam Hussein invaded Kuwait, Osama bin Laden continued to expand al-Qaeda's global jihad, culminating in the suicide attacks of 9/11. After the 9/11 attack, bin Laden sent occasional audio and video messages to the media (most frequently the al-Jazeera network in Qatar) explaining various aspects of al-Qaeda's mission. His discussion of "martyrdom operations" is especially insightful.

> We stress the importance of the martyrdom operations against the enemy – operations that inflict harm on the United States and Israel that have been unprecedented in their history, thanks to Almighty God. We also point out that whoever supported the United States, including the hypocrites of Iraq or the rulers of Arab countries, those who approved their actions and followed them in this crusade war by fighting with them or providing bases and administrative support, or any form of support, even by words, to kill the Muslims in Iraq, should know that they are apostates and outside the community of Muslims. It is permissible to spill their blood and take their property. God says: "O ye who believe! Take not the Jews and the Christians for your friends and protectors: they are but friends and protectors to each other." And he amongst you that turns to them [for friendship] is of them. Verily, Allah guideth not a people unjust.[43]

Obviously bin Laden places great emphasis on martyrdom operations (otherwise known as suicide terrorism or suicide attacks) as perhaps the most effective strategy for realizing al-Qaeda's major political objectives. Even before the rise of bin Laden and al-Qaeda, however, the first known deployment of the strategy of suicide truck bombing occurred on November 11, 1982. A Sunni Palestinian terrorist organization known as Islamic Jihad, headed by sheikh Ahmed Qassir, detonated a bomb at the Israeli headquarters in Tyre, killing or injuring 141 people.[44]

Although it appears to be a highly irrational act, suicide terrorism possesses a strategic logic containing five major elements. First, suicide terrorism is typically not random or idiosyncratic, but carefully planned and executed. Rather than the random acts of desperate or depraved individuals, suicide attacks are orchestrated by an organized group to achieve specific political goals. Second, "the strategic logic of suicide terrorism is specifically designed to coerce modern democracies to make significant concessions to national self-determination."[45] The specific goal is often the withdrawal of the target state's military forces from a perceived national homeland (as typified in the Palestinian–Israeli conflict). Third, since 1980 the use of suicide terrorism has increased worldwide ostensibly because *it pays*. Some examples of government concessions to terrorist organizations following suicide bombing campaigns include:

- the retreat by American and French military forces from Lebanon in 1983;
- the retreat of Israeli forces from Lebanon in 1985;
- Israeli forces abandoning the Gaza Strip and the West Bank in 1994 and 1995;
- the Sri Lankan government's creation of an independent Tamil state beginning in 1990;
- the Turkish government's granting of autonomy to the Kurds in the late 1990s; and
- the forced evacuation by the Israeli government of Israeli settlers from the Gaza Strip in 2005.[46]

Suicide bombings are much more lethal than other types of attacks. For example, between 1980 and 2001, suicide attacks accounted for only 3 percent of all terrorist attacks but 48 percent of total deaths from terrorism.[47]

Fourth, although terrorist organizations have forced concessions from governments as indicated by the above list, the strategy of suicide terror may be approaching a point of diminishing returns. The exacting of moderate damage against a civilian population to force moderate concessions from governments may indeed work, but increasing the intensity of attacks and death counts will likely not lead to increased concessions on the part of target governments. Although many observers decry the potential civil rights abuses arising from the USA PATRIOT Act in response to the loss of close to 3,000 lives at the hands of al-Qaeda, the reality is that the United States has not yet become the tyrannical, repressive regime that al-Qaeda had hoped to produce. Fifth, although the strategy of suicide attacks poses a dilemma for modern democratic governments, perhaps the more effective response to such attacks is not heightened offensive military operations or the granting of more concessions, but investing in significant resources in border defenses and homeland security, just as the United States has done.

Granted also, that unlike the state of Israel or other governments that have been recent targets of suicide attacks (such as those of Great Britain and Spain), the United States is geographically large and spread out. Even a devastating attack on the United States that claims thousands of lives, such as happened on September 11 in New York, Pennsylvania, and Washington, DC, may not significantly impact other major American cities, at least not directly. For example, if a suicide bomber walked into a fruit market in Seattle, Washington, and managed to detonate explosives strapped to his body and kill 50 civilians, it would certainly be tragic and a major media event for the next several weeks, but life as most Americans know it would not be altered significantly. To be sure, for a while at least people even far away from the event would likely be more careful about being out and about in public places, they may change their short-term travel plans, and municipal and state governments may change certain operating procedures (e.g., more careful checking of packages or backpacks in public places and transportation venues).

Even with more emphasis placed on homeland security and border defense, it is hard to tell exactly how effective such "target-hardening" strategies really are. One could make the argument that since no major attacks have occurred since 9/11, then the new operating policies in place since the enactment of the USA PATRIOT Act have made a decisive difference. But one should also consider that in all the years previous to 9/11 there were no attacks close to that magnitude perpetrated either, and of course also during that time there was no Department of Homeland Security. In October 2005 President Bush announced that since 9/11 ten serious al-Qaeda plots had been foiled, three of them targeting the United States.[48] But again, it is difficult to determine whether the new safety procedures in place led to the foiling of these plots, or whether they would have likely been averted anyway with the old counterterrorism measures.

From the perspective of militant Islam, suicide is distinguished from martyrdom operations. A suicide puts one's life to an end for selfish reasons, and is therefore condemned, but martyrdom is a heroic act that has no connection to suicide. Therefore, from the perspective of militant Islam, it is a misnomer to refer to "suicide missions"; they are instead martyrdom missions.

Those who give themselves up for the greater goal of defeating the enemy whether infidels or apostates, and who carry out the missions successfully (rather than making it out alive or being captured) are referred to as shahids. The *shahid* (or martyr) who gives up his life in the jihad against a sworn enemy is promised grace or salvation in the afterlife.[49] The family of a shahid may also be compensated for the martyr's services. In Iraq while Saddam Hussein was in power, for example, families of shahids who successfully completed their suicide missions received $25,000 along with a personally worded "certificate of esteem."[50]

The "long hunt" and the death of bin Laden

Between 1998 and 2008, al-Qaeda, under the direction of bin Laden, was responsible for at least 84 terror attacks worldwide leading to the deaths of 4,300 individuals.[51] Because of this, since 9/11 American and foreign intelligence had been frantically following whatever leads were available in the attempt to track down bin Laden. All resources from mundane to high-tech were considered with the ultimate goal of bringing him to justice. One idea for the utilization of high-tech surveillance, for example, was the deployment of spy satellites which could identify shadows on the ground cast from someone walking. Although still in the preliminary stages of development, this so-called "gait analysis" was contemplated as a strategy for helping to find bin Laden.[52]

After the fall of the Taliban in Afghanistan, President George W. Bush stated in a press conference in 2002 that bin Laden was effectively "marginalized" and as a consequence there was not a great urgency to find him. The thinking was that the culture of jihad and hatred toward America among radical Islamic fundamentalists was so entrenched that it didn't matter much whether bin Laden was alive or not. The network of terror operatives in al-Qaeda and beyond was well trained and prepared to carry out jihad at the behest of any current leader or figurehead.

Nevertheless, by 2009 President Barack Obama had vowed to make it a priority once again to find bin Laden. The "long hunt" had returned in earnest.[53] On Monday, May 2, 2011, news broke around the world that special forces operations authorized by President Obama had located and killed bin Laden at a compound in Abbottabad, Pakistan the previous day.[54] It was an elite Navy SEAL team – SEAL Team Six to be exact – which was flown by American military helicopters from Afghanistan and dropped near the compound. Their orders were to kill bin Laden on sight, and after a brief gun battle bin Laden was indeed killed along with at least four others who were with him at the compound.

After news of the death of bin Laden spread, there was a clamoring for photographic evidence that bin Laden had actually been killed. There were long persistent rumors that bin Laden was already dead due to a chronic kidney condition. But after considering it for a while, President Obama decided against releasing pictures. He felt it may further inflame passions against the United States and needlessly put US servicemen and civilians in harm's way at the hands of terrorists seeking revenge for his death. In fact, the Obama Administration announced just shortly afterwards that bin Laden's body had already been buried at sea, which of course fueled further conspiracy theories in the blogosphere and elsewhere that it was all simply a ruse carefully calculated to bolster the sagging approval ratings of President Obama and his Administration.

The rise and decline of ISIS

Out of the remnants of al-Qaeda and the Taliban arose a powerful new terrorist organization going by the name of ISIS, or the Islamic State in Iraq and Syria. A variant on the organization's name was often used by President Barack Obama, namely ISIL (Islamic State in Iraq and the Levant). The Levant encompasses the geographical area of the old Ottoman Empire, stretching from Turkey in the eastern Mediterranean into the modern Middle East.[55] Obama preferred the name ISIL as a matter of policy, as he sought to move away from a narrow focus on Syria to a wider view of the whole of the Levantine Middle East.[56]

This wider view of the Levant allows for historical understanding of the origins of ISIS and its state-building aspirations, as it sought to establish a new caliphate through effective and ruthless acquisition of lands throughout the Middle East.[57] The movement for democratization across the Middle East beginning in 2010, which came to be known as the Arab Spring, led to a protracted civil war in Syria pitting Islamist factions against the defenders of traditional, secular institutional structures which had been held together, admittedly tentatively, since the 1950s.

ISIS and its leader, Abu Bakr al-Baghdadi, emerged as the leading force among the Islamist groups vying for supremacy amidst the chaos and displacement of the war with an eye toward establishing control militarily in Syria and beyond, much like what Hamas had accomplished in Palestine. And indeed, by 2014 ISIS had taken control of many of the areas in the region which they had targeted for establishment of their caliphate.[58]

As Syrian president Bashar al-Assad moved to quell the fighting in an effort to restore the civil peace in Syria, a wide range of international and regional actors imposed sanctions against the Assad regime, presumably for its targeting of protestors as part of the Arab Spring uprising. These sanctions, some of which were instigated by the United States in cooperation with European and Middle East partners, did little to deter the Assad regime, however. For example, the Assad regime continued to use chemical weapons against its people, and it was only later that the

Trump Administration gave teeth to the sanctions in 2017. Specifically, Trump ordered Tomahawk missile strikes against Syria for the chemical attacks, and one week later dropped the largest non-nuclear bomb in the possession of the US military – the so-called MOAB (or Massive Ordnance Air Blast, nicknamed the "mother of all bombs") – on a network of ISIS caves in Afghanistan. The bombing killed upwards of 95 ISIS fighters.[59] The continuing escalation of violence in the region led to a humanitarian crisis as many in Syria fled the fighting, producing multiple streams of refugees destined for Lebanon, Turkey, Jordan, and Iraq.[60] This led to further unrest across the region.

All told, from its beginnings with the Syrian conflict in 2011, ISIS pursued its goal of state-building and domination across the Levant largely through its willingness to commit atrocities which took terrorism to a new level altogether. Not only did ISIS develop a precise strategy for violent engagement, which is the mark of any effective terrorist group, it also wedded the unconventional warfare of terrorism with cutting-edge media technologies. For example, in 2015 not only did ISIS shoot down a plane on a mission of US-backed coalition forces in Syria, it captured the Jordanian pilot, Muath al-Kasasbeh, and filmed him being burned alive. To add further insult to the grotesqueness, a bulldozer was brought in to ground the cage and the pilot's charred remains down to ash, thereby leaving no body for a proper burial.[61] ISIS also released videos of other atrocities, including beheadings, rape, and torture. The distribution of professionally-made videos depicting ISIS atrocities was the embodiment of a full-spectrum propaganda of violent extremism which had never been seen before.[62]

Aside from carrying out atrocities against Jews and Christians, ISIS also perpetrated genocide against Shia Muslims. The split between the Sunni and Shia branches of Islam have to do with a longstanding doctrinal dispute within Islam of how the caliph, or the leader of the Muslims, shall be chosen. As Stern and Berger explain, "Sunnis believe that the caliph can be chosen by Muslim authorities. Shi'ites believe that the caliph must be a direct descendant of the Prophet [Muhammad] through his son-in-law and cousin Ali."[63] After consolidating control of Fallujah in western Iraq in late 2013, ISIS fashioned alliances with a number of Sunni Arab tribes in the region, and by June 2014 they had captured Mosul, a city of 1.5 million people in Iraq, and at any given moment upwards of 80 Sunni tribes were fighting alongside them. The conquering of Mosul, the site of Iraq's largest dam, was loudly proclaimed by ISIS as the fulfillment of the caliphate.[64]

With the capture of Mosul, ISIS seized Badoush Prison and separated the Shia inmates from Sunnis and Christians. They then walked the Shia prisoners to the edge of a ravine, opened fire and killed 600 of them.[65] ISIS's widespread use of beheadings was not only representative of their physical dominance across the caliphate, but also a symbolic gesture that the bodies of infidels or apostates chosen for execution could never be resurrected.[66] Beheadings also have enormous shock value, sending the message that ISIS is capable of anything and that nothing is beyond the pale or off the table. As discussed above, ISIS also developed a sophisticated media presence through the release of videos, the production of online periodical magazines, and posts from affiliated Twitter and Facebook accounts.[67] The self-proclaimed caliph and leader of ISIS, Abu Bakr al-Baghdadi, implored all Muslims to move to the new territory, and, through extensive social media outreach, many Westerners, including women, traveled to the region to join ISIS. The women who joined ISIS typically identifying themselves as *muhajirah*, that is, migrants from lands inhabited by infidels to Muslim lands for the ultimate purpose of contributing to jihad whether in supportive or direct combat modes.[68]

Through 2015 ISIS continued to expand its territory due in large part to its being perhaps the most well-funded terror organization in history. Some of the funding came from wealthy individuals from Persian Gulf countries – so-called "angel investors" – with the largest group of investors coming from Qatar.[69] In addition to private donations, ISIS also engaged in widespread criminal activity, including "millions of dollars it had seized from banks in the Iraqi cities and from other revenue streams, including taxation, extortion, oil sales, antiquities sales, and ransoms from kidnappings."[70] ISIS not only looted treasures and artifacts from museums in Iraq and Syria for later sale on the black market, they also destroyed irreplaceable cultural antiquities, presumably as a rejection of nationalism.[71]

During all this time ISIS had established a base in Libya in 2013 while minimizing al-Qaeda's influence there. And although ISIS tried to assert dominance in Libya much like it had in Iraq and Syria, its Libyan funding was inadequate and its fighting forces were stretched thin. By 2016, ISIS was in retreat not only in Libya, where it lost control of Sirte, but also in Iraq and Syria because of renewed attacks on ISIS strongholds carried out by United States and NATO forces.[72] In addition, since 2016 the flow of foreign fighters into Syria and other ISIS-controlled territories had dwindled steadily, contributing to the caliphate losing its robustness and vigor as a state and transitioning into a "small, lawless pocket" within the original host states, similar in ways to how the Taliban were configured in Pakistan before their decline.[73]

What became clear was that ISIS power centers simply failed to hold, that persons previously loyal to the cause abandoned their posts and dispersed to less dangerous areas, and that the planning necessary to keep funding flowing through various illicit pursuits fell into disarray as members of the control staff were either killed or ran for cover. With ISIS already in steep decline, on October 26, 2019, the United States, following up on tips provided to the CIA, launched a raid against a compound in northwest Syria where al-Baghdadi, the leader of ISIS, was staying. Special operations forces did indeed locate al-Baghdadi at the compound and, facing imminent capture or death, he detonated a suicide vest, killing himself and three of his children. President Donald Trump explained that al-Baghdadi had died "whimpering, screaming, and crying," gleefully emphasizing the fact that this was indeed a bad death.[74] This is of course symbolic payback for the atrocities ISIS had been carrying out under the direction of al-Baghdadi, including televised spectacles of beheadings and burning people alive.

Even in such a documented state of decline, however, ISIS is still able to influence others largely through the social media infrastructures, social connections, and loyalties it had cultivated, which are somewhat impervious to physical degradation concomitant to the dismantling of the caliphate. For example, the 2016 shooting rampage which left 49 dead at Pulse, a gay nightclub in Orlando, Florida, was perpetrated by Omar Mateen, a 29-year-old Afghani-American man. The killing spree was largely in retaliation for what Mateen perceived to be illicit US interference – including bombing raids on terrorist targets – in the Middle East. Mateen also announced his allegiance to ISIS, but even so, media coverage of the incident tended to portray him as a lone wolf terrorist while downplaying the possibility that this was a hate crime targeting the largely Latinx and LGBTQ patrons of the club.[75] The realization is that careful analysis of the motives and history of those who are labeled "lone wolf" terrorists reveals that they are not completely isolated or cut off from wider social influences whether online or offline, and that perhaps the lone wolf designation is not as useful a special category of terrorism or political extremism as previously assumed.[76]

Conclusion

Terrorism and counterterrorism activities have reduced societal reliance on informal control, to the extent that public trust has diminished, and with that, there is a greater reliance on general surveillance of the population, which assumes that everyone is at risk either of victimization or offending.[77] As discussed more fully in the final chapter, legal control in the wake of 9/11 has effectively blurred the boundaries between the military and the police, but also prodded the expansion of municipal and federal police forces. (Or if not actual expansion, municipal governments are being tasked with such federal mandates as the development of comprehensive evacuation plans, while police are expected to comply with federal guidelines regarding local law enforcement preparedness and response to terrorist threats.)

The terrorist emphasis on mass disruption and destruction of civil society means that not only are transportation and business enterprises targeted for attack, but also mass delivery systems such as mail and parcels, water, and energy. (Indeed, the first reaction of a number of observers upon news of the massive blackout that occurred in the northeastern United States in 2003 was that it was caused by terrorists.) For example, more and more municipal sewer districts are making the transition from a reliance on private security firms to the establishment of their own sworn police forces. In essence, municipal water and sewage districts are keen to turn their around-the-clock security guards into sworn police officers. State representative Jim Trakas of Independence, Ohio, who introduced a bill in 2005 to allow the formation of sewer district police forces, said "If you would have asked me on Sept. 10, 2001, I would have said that the sewer district does not need a police force. But in light of what we've learned, it's a matter of public safety and health."[78]

Finally, because terrorism operates without official or explicit state sponsorship, terrorists are everywhere and nowhere. Since terrorists are for the most part not bound together by geography, their social solidarity is assured by nontraditional means, through global networks of communication and media. This means that fighting terrorism will achieve only partial success if based on localized logics of target hardening, border defense, and homeland security. Since terrorism is a global phenomenon that transcends traditional understandings of time and place, successful counterterrorism measures must be global in nature as well.[79] As Karin Knorr Cetina explains,

> Countering terrorism will have to become a truly global effort involving a coalition of governments, extending to remote regions of the world, engaging the global struggle of ideas, and translating short-term concerns into long-term internal and external commitments.[80]

The Biden Administration's shift to a focus on domestic terrorism has the potential to lose sight of the ongoing threat of international terrorism. For example, there are reports that ISIS is retaking some lands in the Middle East and Africa, particularly Mozambique.[81] Additionally, President Biden's decision to withdraw US troops from Afghanistan in 2021 was met with the resurgence of the Taliban, which was responsible for bombings at Kabul airport which killed 13 US service personnel and which left untold numbers of Americans and other Westerners stranded and unable to flee the country. Indeed, the Taliban has now set itself up as the official government in Afghanistan.[82] This is the new reality confronting the Biden Administration, and for at least the short term, US counterterrorism policies will involve dual-track strategies for dealing simultaneously with international and domestic terrorism.

SUGGESTIONS FOR FURTHER READING

Peter Bergen, *United States of Jihad* **(2016)**

Bergen interviewed convicted terrorists as well as experts working in security and counterterrorism fields to create a profile of persons who are radicalized and possibly drawn into the role of enemy combatants. These persons are often unaffiliated and fit the profile of lone wolf terrorists.

James L. Gelvin, *The Israel-Palestine Conflict: A History* **(2021)**

Now in its fourth edition, this analysis by James Gelvin carefully traces out the Israel–Palestine conflict from ancient times to the present day. This includes more recently the abandonment by the Trump Administration of the Oslo Accords and how this imperils the two-state solution sought by previous US administrations.

Douglas V. Porpora, Alexander Nikolaev, Julia Hagemann May, and Alexander Jenkins, *Post-Ethical Society: The Iraq War, Abu Ghraib, and the Moral Failure of the Secular* **(2013)**

The authors gathered data and information from newspapers, television, and online commentary associated with the 2003 invasion of Iraq to gauge national sentiment concerning the war on terror and the naming of recognizable enemies (Muslims and those from the Middle East). The accounts of prisoner abuse at Abu Ghraib seemed to indicate, however, that it was not an isolated failure of military command or leadership, but a deeper cultural problem of declining ethical standards regarding respect for fellow human beings. National fervor attending to the war on terror gave rise to a post-ethical society whose guiding sentiment was that such torture and abuse of prisoners was deserved.

Lisa Stampnitzky, *Disciplining Terror: How Experts Invented "Terrorism"* **(2013)**

Drawing largely from Foucault's notion of disciplinary power, beginning in the 1970s concerns over terrorism produced an expert class of observers – in academia, the military, and policy thinktanks – which coalesced into a discipline which claimed objective understanding of an assumed stable and coherent terrorism field. Stampnitzky challenges this disciplining of terrorism, arguing that it was as much socially constructed or invented as it was discovered.

David J. Wasserstein, *Black Banners of ISIS: The Roots of the New Caliphate* **(2017)**

This book represents one of the best summaries of the rise and fall of ISIS. Wasserstein's book contributes to our understanding of how ISIS managed strategic violence, terror, and an effective media presence toward the establishment of a new caliphate. Within this analysis, Wasserstein is careful to distinguish between traditional Islam and the apocalyptic messianism of ISIS and similar Islamic terror groups.

DISCUSSION QUESTIONS

1. The Taliban restrengthened after the Biden Administration's decision to withdraw American troops from Afghanistan in early 2021. Discuss US options concerning dealing with terrorism and other issues in this part of the world.
2. Describe the incel. Is this a legitimate form of domestic terrorism? Why or why not?

3. How far can states go to respond to the barbarism of terrorism without in turn perpetrating their own forms of barbarism? In other words, how does the civilized world community adequately respond to the barbarism of terrorism?
4. Two notorious leaders of terrorist organizations, bin Laden (al-Qaeda) and al-Baghdadi (ISIS), have been killed on the orders of US presidents. Were these killings justified? Did they make Americans safer?
5. The Department of Homeland Security is one of the largest and most powerful administrative agencies in the United States. Some believe it is needed now more than ever, while others argue it has outlived its usefulness and should be disestablished. Explain which side of this debate you favor and provide evidence for your position.

Chapter 10
Conclusion: The Future of Social Control

Introduction: China's social credit system

The everyday lifeworld is populated by human beings pursuing their various life projects, utilizing whatever resources and personal attributes are available toward securing chosen ends. Most persons are free to choose their path in life just so long as they do not infringe on others' pursuit of their own satisfactions. For all this to work, society banks heavily on the informal system of socialization whereby competent agents – friends, families, school, churches, business, and so forth – guide persons toward activities which meet broad notions of propriety, legitimacy, or normalcy (as covered in chapter 3).

But it is also clear that, left to their own devices, some people make bad or disastrous choices and along the way harm themselves or others. If enough harm emerges from the actions of persons operating in the everyday lifeworld, certain patterns form which become visible to those within the system, and this can bring to bear intervention by agents of formal control whether medical, legal, or some combination of the two. From this systems perspective, one way of attacking this problem is to monitor various aspects of actors and their environments, including uses of various information technologies to probe into the affective or subjective dimensions of those persons categorized as at-risk. Indeed, modern states are systematically making greater and greater numbers of members of the population legible or visible to state functionaries, auditors, public health officials, criminal justice personnel, schools, businesses, and even fellow members of a community or neighborhood.

Since time immemorial human beings have utilized their senses – with vision and hearing being the most important – for purposes of monitoring the physical environment and its many features (including flora and fauna). This ancient form of watching is *natural surveillance*, that is, the direct monitoring of the surrounding world utilizing only the natural senses (sight, sound, smell, taste, and touch).[1] Although some individuals have better vision or hearing than others, and hence are better able to see or hear across greater distances, on balance the ancient condition of natural surveillance was one of mutual monitoring which gave no distinct advantages to any particular persons or groups.

Social advantages, particularly the emergence of political power, emerged later as particular clans or tribes developed technologies – better snares and strategies for capturing game, more lethal weapons, and better planning and organization for warfare – which put them in a position to prevail over nearby tribes or communities. Some of the earliest social planning was organizing for the war effort and, indeed, as Herbert Spencer noted, the military society far antedated the civil or industrial society. Society exists when people join together for some common purpose. We may follow Spencer again, as he observed that

> The motive for acting together, originally the dominant one, may be defense against enemies; or it may be the easier obtainment of food, by the chase or otherwise; or it may be, and commonly is, both of these. In any case, however, the units pass from the state of perfect independence to the state of mutual dependence; and as fast as they do this they become united into a society rightly so called.[2]

The state emerged within the transition from nomadic to sedentary life, and from the time of the ancient Greeks forward, this new political formation also informed ideas about the importance of learning to be tolerable to others – that is, civility – as a prerequisite for living peaceably within communities, towns, and cities. The state political apparatus – the premier imperatively coordinated association according to Weber[3] – varies according to how much power is shared between rulers and subjects. For example, the earliest models of statecraft, from ancient times through the last vestiges of the absolutist state – most mark this with the French Revolution of 1789[4] – endow kings with near limitless power who rule by decree over the mass of relatively powerless subjects.

New forms of government from 1789 through late modernity represented transitions from the raw and unbridled absolute rule of kings to some level of power sharing with subjects who are now described as citizens of a sovereign state or jurisdiction. For example, a *constitutional monarchy* is a type of mixed government in which a king or queen (the monarch) shares power with other established government figures (such as a prime minister and parliament) and in which citizens have voting rights.[5] A *constitutional democracy* emphasizes majoritarianism in which the will of the majority of voters can add or remove rights, while a *constitutional republic*, tracing from Natural Law, identifies certain laws as eternal, and any disputes that arise may be settled by judicial review.[6]

However, even in modern times and presumably into postmodernity and the foreseeable future, in some places the old absolutism of total rule by a single government head or small group of leaders is still active and viable. In its various forms, this is known as *autocracy* and it can exist on the political right (e.g., the fascism of Hitler's Germany and Mussolini's Italy) or the political left (e.g., various forms of communist or socialist dictatorships in Russia, China, Cuba, and elsewhere). There is also the possibility of a *theocracy*, namely, a state which rules, and whose laws are formulated and enacted, on the basis of religious doctrine. A list of currently active theocracies includes Iran and Saudi Arabia (Muslim) and the Vatican City in Rome (Catholicism).

The designated head of government – the king in the absolutist state, the executive in democracies (e.g., the president at the federal level or the governor at the state level), or the tyrant in dictatorships – is the sovereign. As Schmitt has pointed out, the sovereign or executive is "he who decides on the exception," especially under conditions described as an emergency.[7] Emergency conditions may lead the executive to declare martial law or to enact other provisions which effectively suspend the normal operations of the government, including the suspension of the freedom of citizens usually protected under law.[8] Recent examples of such curtailing of liberties for purposes of public safety are the measures put in place to protect citizens from terror attacks, and lockdowns during the Covid-19 pandemic in order to control the spread of the virus.

Beyond the case of constitutional democracies or republics, autocratic governments operate on the basis of perpetual lockdown insofar as the king or the dictator governs by fiat as there are no constitutional or other meaningful constraints on how they choose to rule. Such a condition of emergency and total state control is evident in China, which happened to be the country of origin of the Wuhan virus. Chinese journalist Liu Hu made a habit of pushing the boundaries of censorship in his country, and he did much of this work through a blog detailing misconduct of high government officials. In 2013 he was arrested by the Chinese government for "fabricating and spreading rumors" and was found guilty of defamation. He was fined and ordered to apologize on his social media account.[9]

By 2017, with the effects of that incident still lingering, Hu came to the realization that he had gotten caught up in an elaborate and all-encompassing surveillance system. Now known as the *social credit system*, this big-data surveillance project was launched by the Chinese government in the 1990s, the effects of which were not fully felt until 2013. In 2017 Lu was barred from buying an airline ticket on the basis of his being "not qualified," and he experienced other restrictions such as an inability to take out loans, buy property, or even travel by train. The social credit system was not only monitoring financial creditworthiness, but it was also providing scores of social trustworthiness, a subjective score which required deeper surveillance of all manner of social activities, especially those taking place on social media platforms. There was also a steady stream of reports to social credit authorities about him from friends, family, and neighborhood and business associates. Through this program, the Chinese government actually produced a blacklist of dishonest and untrustworthy people, which as of 2017 included some seven and half million Chinese citizens.

Ideally, the Internet is supposed to provide access to information on a relatively free and open basis, and platforms such as Facebook, Instagram, and Snapchat allow persons to come together to share in activities as they see fit. However, governments can and do monitor such activities and can restrict access according to covert or openly-stated needs (e.g., for national security or protecting against cyberattacks). For many critics, the social credit system gets close to an Orwellian, Big Brother surveillance apparatus which stifles dissent and limits freedom. China's current leader, Xi Jinping, has asserted total control of the Chinese Communist Party and with that, control of the Internet and the totality of digital technologies including big data, artificial intelligence, and the Internet of Things (or IoT, whereby computer chips are embedded in everyday products such as refrigerators and automobiles which allow for enhanced monitoring and control, all linked up to a network of such devices). For critics, this merging of Big Brother and big data represents an ominous development, something akin to a new type of digital totalitarianism.[10]

There is also a burgeoning use of new technologies for enhanced surveillance of populations, including the development of emotion recognition technologies utilizing artificial intelligence (AI) algorithms. Although the United States has been the leader in developing innovative AI technologies, China has been at the forefront in the application of such technologies to the monitoring of citizens in their everyday lives. Two surveillance projects in particular have positioned China as leader in the use of biometric, facial recognition, and emotion recognition surveillance. One is the Sharp Eye project, a nationwide effort to blanket the entirety of China's urban population with surveillance capabilities emphasizing license plate readers and facial recognition technologies. The second, which is coextensive with the social credit system discussed above, is the Fengqiao Experience, which is described as "a Mao Zedong-contrived practice in which ordinary Chinese citizens monitored and reported each other's improper behaviour to the authorities."[11]

Fengqiao is a type of governmentality, described by Foucault, which turns everyday citizens into agents of the state.[12] This is the acknowledgment that even with the most sophisticated and expansive surveillance systems, governments cannot monitor all persons at all places at all times. Because not all subjects are visible to the state at all times, one way of reducing their slipping through the surveillance web is to invite them to snitch on friends, neighbors, and acquaintances as part of civic duty. And this type of governmentality, which seeks to get close to a total surveillance state utilizing all resources whether technological or human, is not limited to only autocratic and dictatorial regimes but may also make appearances in democratic states under certain conditions. For example, as a result of the Covid-19 pandemic, when Los Angeles Mayor Eric Garcetti issued his first round of stay-at-home orders in March 2020, he announced that snitches would be rewarded for turning in neighbors who violated the orders.[13]

Emotion recognition, more broadly known as emotional biosensing, is an emerging technology utilized by many countries including the United States and China and expanding globally. The merging of big data, quantum computing, and biometrics has created a new field of affective computing which can recognize human emotions through utilization of both remote and wearable sensors.[14] For example, the CortiWatch is a wearable wristband that looks like a watch which measures cortisol levels of perspiration.[15] Cortisol is produced by the adrenal glands, and the measure of cortisol levels can be used as a stress indicator. These physiological indicators can eliminate the need to interact with surveillance subjects directly, thereby also bypassing the gap that exists between what persons say they are doing and what they are actually doing. Such technologies can also lead to heightened levels of self-monitoring, especially with the advent of smaller and more portable wearable sensors, such as with the wristband sensor Feel, dubbed as the "world's first emotion sensor and well-being advisor," which promises to make its wearers better human beings.[16] There is also an effacing of the distinctions between informal, legal, and medical controls, as persons are monitored by outside observers according to surveillance protocols while also willingly participating in their own surveillance through the donning of whichever wearable sensors are chosen according to the needs of the wearer. This gets us closer to Deleuze's notion of *societies of control* which, since 9/11 and as apparent during the Covid-19 pandemic, launches a new *security era* of interconnected surveillance regimes which collects a staggering amount of data on human populations.[17] The role of technology in enhancing natural surveillance will be explored further in the next section.

Technology and future attribute screening

When thinking about the future of social control, one is immediately reminded of the movie *Minority Report*. Set in the year 2054, the movie depicts a crime-free America where the government has made use of so-called Pre-Cogs, namely, gifted human psychics who can peer into the future and predict crimes before they happen. An elite Precrime law enforcement squad sits at the ready and can be sent into action against targets identified by the Pre-Cogs. Upon arrest a murder suspect is told something along the lines of "You are under arrest for the future murder of ...."

This seemingly fanciful scenario may not be as far out as it appears. The American government and its military have been flirting with the use of the psychic and paranormal since at least the 1960s. For example, a top-secret US military operation known as Star Gate investigated whether analysts could be trained in extrasensory perception (ESP) and remote viewing for purposes of spying on our enemies.[18] Newer approaches have eschewed the overtly psychic in favor of the development of technologies for sensing changes in physiological states which presumably are associated with intentions and/or state of mind. Since the 9/11 attacks, the United States has been actively engaged with high-tech firms to develop new and sophisticated technologies for identifying persons who may be planning to do something bad. The US Department of Homeland Security's Future Attribute Screening Technology (FAST) Project is one such effort to identify and neutralize persons harboring hostile intent. The main thrust of FAST is the development and validation of the Theory of Malintent. Malintent is defined as "the intent to cause harm."[19] The idea of malintent, which the FAST system is set up to detect, is that if persons are intending to do something bad – say, bring an explosive device into a crowded stadium – then they are likely to give off physiological clues which can be read by sensors and interpreted by trained human operators. These include voice stress indicators, heart rate and respiration monitors, remote eye tracking, thermal imaging, as well as monitors for measuring facial images and gestures which can be compared against a library of such images associated with stealth, determination, excitement, anticipation, and fidgetiness.

The program also utilizes mobile units which can be placed at entry points at borders or wherever large groups of individuals are gathered such as at sporting events, concerts, and airports. The mobile units monitor throughput, that is, the line of persons seeking entrance into the event, and is set up to measure persons' behavioral and psychophysical signals including eye movement, cardiovascular function, respiration, temperature, and skin chemistry.[20] Visual monitoring of face and bodily movements can be fed into an algorithm aided by artificial intelligence and quantum computing to crunch a potentially vast number of data points which produces profiles marking agitation, stealth, deep contemplation, concern, anticipation, all of which could trigger flags that would require them to be set aside by a human agent and asked questions about what they did that day and general plans.

A similar second generation biometric technology was developed in Europe, the aim of which was to protect EU citizens from terrorism, crime, and riots. The project, which concluded in 2013, was known as Automatic Detection of Abnormal Behaviour and Threats in Crowded Spaces (ADEBTS).[21] The project utilized closed-circuit television (CCTV) and other monitoring devices to gather data on the physical and human (or physiological) correlates to threat situations, with the goal of developing algorithms aided by artificial intelligence that could predict and hopefully reduce or eliminate such disruptions. Surveillance cameras and sensors can span wide geographical areas encompassing large segments of the globe (as in the case of geodesic satellites orbiting the earth), to entire cities (as in the case of London and a number of cities in China) or states (especially as this relates to "intelligent transportation systems" being used to monitor interstate commerce across the US federal highway system).[22]

Such algorithms for detecting abnormal behavior have found later application in seemingly benign pursuits, such as the establishment of smart home environments where the intelligent systems in place "learn" the tendencies and proclivities of home residents so as to better assist them with their day-to-day needs and activities.[23] An example of this is the voice-activated Cortana system of Microsoft which can act as a virtual assistant as needed by members of the household. This is related to developments in robotics engineering in which robotic pets or even humanoid androids can serve as human companions, with some of the more sophisticated ones being able to interact with their human hosts on an emotional level. For example, there is ongoing exploration of how social bonds evolve using minimally designed accompanying robots to "learn" the gestures and norms associated with successful bonding.[24] As we have seen throughout the book, the social bond is the focus of intense research from social, cultural, legal, medical, genetic, epigenetic, and technological perspectives. Students of social control should understand these various approaches to the social bond so that they are fully conversant with its function in preserving social order and under what circumstances it may break down or fail.

More on surveillance

In order to manage populations with the general goal of preserving the social order, governments must have at their disposal a wide range of surveillance resources for keeping tabs on the movement of citizens. On many levels, then, the study of social control is the study of surveillance, which David Lyon defines as "the focused, systematic and routine attention to personal details for purposes of influence, management, protection or direction."[25] We are all aware that different types of surveillance are monitoring our activities, whether by our neighbors in the community, parents at home, teachers in school, or police cruisers on the street. Included in this are the numerous activities of everyday life such as using an ATM to get cash, making a purchase and getting a store discount with your loyalty card, surfing the Internet, filing tax returns with your CPA or purchasing stocks through your broker, voting, or getting on a plane for a business trip. Although we may feel that the surveillance associated with all these activities is intrusive, on balance we are likely to feel some sense of calm or security simply knowing that watchfulness is built into the fabric of everyday life.

Yet, the continuing emphasis on surveillance and the fact that it is visible and palpable may also remind us that insecurities lurk around every corner. That is to say, even within the patchwork quilt of surveillance regimes operating in any community, insecurity is all around us. From ecological decline to terrorism, from Covid-19 to flash mobs, from economic instability to political polarization, there is a clamor to get these various risks under control through routine and continuous surveillance. Hence, even within the modern society of control there are possibilities for resistance, for countersurveillance, and for novel claims making against the holders of power (based on identity, citizenship, race, or expanding conceptions of human rights).[26]

As surveillance becomes more visible and accepted as a stable feature of everyday life, persons may go beyond their status as merely passive subjects of surveillance and actively participate in it. Indeed, persons can use their smartphones to record those who may be recording or monitoring their own activities, and this is called *sousveillance*. Examples of sousveillance include citizens recording police officers at traffic stops, customers recording shopkeepers, or even passersby on the street recording each other.[27] Surveillance technologies can also be employed by users to access images and messages for the sheer enjoyment of it, including making themselves available to others at social media sites and elsewhere. The love of watching and being watched is termed *scopophilia*, which is a pervasive feature of modern surveillance and media landscapes. There are many examples of this, including the proliferation of webcams depicting mundane activities; talk shows and reality shows; lifestyle showcases; personal histories and biographies; and self-posting abilities at numerous sites including YouTube, TikTok, Instagram, Spotify, Facebook, WhatsApp, Twitter, LinkedIn, Pinterest, Tumblr, Flickr, and a host of others. This represents the *synopticon*, a new version of the many watching the few – how many are watching depends on how many friends, followers, or subscribers one has – which promises to give everyone their own 15 minutes of fame.[28] Another indication of the use of surveillance for synoptic or scopophilic purposes is the development of the Glancephone. This app, which was originally designed to allow persons to see whether someone is available to be approached rather than rudely interrupting – replicating the subtle glances and considerations used in real life for sizing up this particular social situation – is instead much more likely to be used for the narrower purpose of drawing attention to oneself.[29]

Regardless of who is doing the surveilling and who or what the targets of surveillance may be, there are six basic strategies for controlling the physical and social environments within which persons carry out their activities. Many of these strategies are consistent with the perspectives of crime prevention through environmental design (CPTED), which emphasizes how criminal and deviant activities emerge and are sustained across space and time. Specific theories connected with CPTED are defensive space, routine activity theory, and broken windows.[30] Before moving on to a discussion of the six surveillance strategies, we will first summarize routine activity theory.

Routine activity theory

As initially developed by Lawrence Cohen and Marcus Felson in 1979, routine activity theory states that crime and other unwanted activities are more likely to occur when there is a convergence of three factors in space and time, namely, motivated offenders, suitable targets, and the absence of capable guardians.[31] *Motivated offenders* refers to the fact that in order for crime to take place, there must be human actors perpetrating acts that later come to be defined as violations of the criminal law. The concept of motivated offenders need never deal with the psychological endowment or subjectivity of actors falling under the category, but merely that their behaviors were later deemed to be criminal. Routine activity theory does not care about persons per se or whether or not they can be rehabilitated if they go bad. Indeed, the assumption is made that criminal temptation is situational, and if an opportunity arises even "good" people may go bad. For example, an otherwise law-abiding citizen may find a wallet on the street with $230 in cash, and he may decide to keep the cash and deposit the wallet and its contents – including credit cards and other potentially valuable items – in a nearby mailbox. The person realized cash is hard or impossible to trace so he kept it, while on the other hand credit cards could tie him to the owner of the wallet and so he decided to steer clear of them. This also means that it is fruitless to assume there are essential or observable features of persons or personalities which distinguishes them as normal or pathological.

Suitable targets refers to items which are deemed to be both valuable and accessible. There is also an implicit sliding scale of weight and value associated with the determination of the suitability of any target. This calculation is V/W, where V is the value of the item and W is its weight. This means the higher the V/W score, the more suitable or desirable the target. Hence, although refrigerators are valuable, they are also heavy and bulky and so we typically do not see burglary rings targeting major kitchen appliances. Lighter, more portable items are favored. Cash and jewelry are the premium items in the V/W calculation, and of course bills are preferred over coins. Bars of precious metals (gold and silver primarily) could be targets because of their value, but their sheer weight requires greater care and planning in order to pull off successful heists. Cars are both heavy and valuable, but because they are mobile they make much better criminal targets than other heavy objects.

Another important calculation regarding suitable targets is not only their accessibility but also the likelihood of escape after gaining access. Unless the item can be consumed on the spot – for example, a fully-cooked $150-a-pound A5 Wagyu steak – the perpetrator will need to plan escape routes and determine whether the odds of escaping with the valued item outweighs the risk of being caught. Items that are heavily guarded or difficult to access, even if they are valuable, will typically be rendered less suitable.

A third factor in the routine activity scheme is the presence or absence of *capable guardians*. The premier example of capable guardians are the police, but even the mere presence of individuals, such as passersby on the street or residents milling about their neighborhood, can act as effective guardians. For example, in the first few months of the lockdowns associated with Covid-19, residential burglaries declined significantly because people were in their homes and so were neighbors, all of whom were available on a consistent basis to monitor each other's homes. Conversely, burglaries in industrial and retail areas increased because people were not at work.[32]

The policy implications of routine activity theory are that crime reduction and prevention should focus more on targets and guardians and less on offenders because the pool of such offenders is relatively stable based upon the opportunity structures present in any locality. This perspective may also reflect a loss of faith in rehabilitation (as covered in chapter 8) insofar as focusing on individuals is not effective in reducing crime and deviance. Instead, crime reduction can be built into social and physical environments just so long as there is attention to populating key areas of concern with a critical mass of capable guardians.

Six strategies for designing out crime

Ecological orientations to reducing crime and deviance such as CPTED and routine activity theory have gained popularity over the last few decades and promise to remain dominant in policy and academic circles for the foreseeable future. We turn next to Gary Marx's discussion of six strategies for crime reduction within the built environment.[33]

The first strategy is *target removal* or disguise. Examples of this strategy include the move to a cashless society, furniture built into walls, and subway cars built with graffiti-resistant metals. And law enforcement may use deception to lure would-be criminals into exposing their criminal intentions, such as police sting operations which replace cocaine with harmless white powder or supplying fake explosives to a suspect who intends to detonate a bomb. Another example is painting gold bars black to hide their value.

A second strategy is *target devaluation* or spoilage. Radios and CD players in cars can be manufactured to be inoperable if they are removed from the dash, and Christmas trees can be sprayed with a foul-smelling substance until they are sold, at which time another spray is used to remove the odor. To deter bank robbery, dye packets can be dropped into bags of cash which explode upon being opened. Likewise, in order to deter theft in clothing stores, items can be tagged with alarms or dye packets which explode upon attempted removal. And to deter unaccompanied youth from entering shopping malls during certain hours, merchants can play classical music in front of their stores.

A third strategy is *target insulation*, which is also referred to as target hardening. With this most ancient practice, the target is visible but is protected in some way, such as locks which make it difficult to move, or perimeter maintenance through the use of moats, fences, or guard dogs. A variation of this is used in gated communities through the design of choke points where vehicle entry and exit must pass by a guard house which may be equipped with boom gates limiting access until identity is verified. And after gaining access, drivers may face further impediments such as speed bumps or dips to enforce posted minimum speed limits. And of course, all sorts of alarms can be employed to warn authorities if targets are moved or tampered with.

Fourth, there is the possibility of *offender weakening* or incapacitation, which constitutes various attempts to render their efforts harmless or ineffective. Radical examples of these are modifying the bodies of potential offenders, such as cutting off the hands of thieves or castrating sex offenders. Psychosurgeries such as lobotomy have been used to curb violence, and a judge may mandate that other violent offenders be required to take drugs to lower their serotonin levels. The police can utilize sensory weapons, such as powerful flashlights or acoustics, to disorient or restrain suspects, as well as nonlethal weapons such as handcuffs, mace, Tasers, smoke canisters, and nets for individual or crowd control. During high-speed chases, spikes can be scattered on the road to blow out tires. And for celebrities who are concerned with the unwanted encroachment of paparazzi, sensors can be utilized to detect the presence of digital cameras and, when detected, can send out a signal which disables them. This same technology can be used by musicians who want to stop audience members from making unauthorized recordings of their live concert performances.[34]

A fifth strategy is *exclusion*, which goes beyond merely weakening potential offenders. The classic example of this is incarceration of persons in prisons, jails, asylums, or penitentiaries, but other related ancient practices such as banishment and transportation physically remove persons from places they are not supposed to be. Technologies such as GPS electronic monitoring devices promise to locate persons and limit them to designated areas. As a result of the Covid-19 pandemic, there has been talk of mandatory vaccine cards which persons must show as proof of vaccination in order to travel or receive services in educational or business settings. And, of course, the ultimate exclusion strategy that states can employ is the death penalty.

Finally, a sixth strategy is *identification*, and this can be directed towards offenses, offenders, or targets. Even though not all crime or deviance can be prevented, it is still often desirable to know after the fact that such activities took place and to develop a sketch of the likely perpetrators. The development of forensic or biometric sciences has been all about tying physical or genetic evidence to individuals involved in acts which come to the attention of authorities. Many of these technologies have already been discussed, but beyond the hard skills utilized by law enforcement for purposes of crime prevention connected with these technologies, there is also greater attention to the soft skills of human relations training and outreach to members of the community to invite them to assist authorities for the securing of public safety. Hence, campaigns such as See Something Say Something, utilized by not only police but also neighborhood associations, businesses, schools, and universities, operate on the underlying principle of identification and the sifting through of more data rather than treating it as irrelevant background noise. This is called *dataveillance*, namely, electronic and digital surveillance which, because it is computer-based, can accommodate an extraordinarily large number of data points.[35] The result of this technological marvel is that all data can potentially be used in furtherance of some surveillance regime, which indicates that, if data can be collected on surveillance targets, it should be used or at least retained in digital storage. This also means that the big data bubble keeps expanding, and as it does so, the informal systems of decision-making utilizing local knowledge or even intuition (so-called "gut instinct") are rendered obsolete.[36] This also brings to bear an expert class of technicians who approach all things – social as well as physical and biological – as engineering problems that have the potential to be resolved through the correct algorithm or AI program guiding human decision-making.

Symbolic inflation

The continuing growth of surveillance and the technological refinement of big data merged with AI decision capabilities is part and parcel of a general expansion and inflation of the symbolic and communicative systems developed by human beings over the millennia. Beginning with the Industrial Revolution in the early 1800s, there was an acceleration of technological innovations (such as steam power, the railroads and telegraph, and the harnessing of electricity) which helped humanity gain greater control of the natural and built environment. With the emergence of computers in the 1950s and the later expansion of additional information technologies (especially the Internet and medical and genetic programming technologies), information itself became the basis of what James Beniger termed the new Control Revolution.[37]

As Max Weber has noted, one of the key features of the modern bureaucracy is the creation of an ongoing record of the activities of the organization and its personnel. Indeed, "The management of the modern office is based upon written documents (the 'files') which are preserved in their original or draft form, and upon a staff of subaltern officials and scribes of all sorts."[38] This activity, which emphasizes the written word over the spoken word – that is, textualization – is the central feature of bureaucracies which are now understood symbolically as "counting houses" (*Kontore*). This process of mandatory or required textualization has over time led to a proliferation of paperwork leading to such organizational pathologies as "red tape."[39]

In virtually all walks of life, both informal and formal, there is an expansion of recordkeeping for the sake of capturing more data and preserving it in files. For example, over the decades police reports have expanded enormously as greater detail is included in them, such as the requirement that sociodemographic characteristics of those involved in the incident be recorded.[40] And as a professor, I have observed over the years that my course syllabi have grown thicker and thicker not only because of requirements to include organizationally-mandated boilerplate language about plagiarism or disability accommodation, but also to guard against savvy students exploiting holes in grading policies for their own benefit. It is somewhat unnerving, and sadly indicative of the conditions of higher education, that I am compelled to include this additional statement in all my syllabi:

> Grades of A+, C–, D+, and D– are not reported at CSU. These grade ranges will be adhered to strictly. At the end of the semester there will invariably be a few students who are right at the border of the next highest grade, perhaps even only one point short. Well, those are the breaks. I will not be bumping up to the next grade students who are close, as this merely exacerbates the problem of grade inflation. And I will not go back to regrade quizzes, exams, or writing assignments to entertain your hopes of possibly squeezing out the additional points necessary to move you to the next grade level.

Another aspect of ongoing textualization is that more forms are being generated to memorialize all manner of activities, and social life in general takes on more of the characteristics of a legal contract. This is a type of rationalization called *information inflation* which has co-evolved with the advent of written language more than 50 centuries ago among the ancient Sumerians.[41] Both oral and written languages are symbol systems. Such symbol systems are used to transmit bits of information between speakers of the language; hence wherever information inflation occurs, it can be understood as a subset of symbolic inflation.

The primary way concepts of inflation and deflation have been used is with respect to money and monetary systems. For example, money as a medium is available to holders of the currency to exchange for valued items, and the amount of the currency should be somewhat stable with regard to price levels of consumer goods within the market or system. This idea, which embodies an equilibrium model, can be extended from monetary media such as money operating in markets to social or biological media such as blood, libido energy, self-esteem, influence, power, intelligence, and other cultural symbols operating in systems.[42] As Talcott Parsons and Gerald Platt explain, "An inflationary trend is a process by which the medium loses value relative to the valuable objects for which it is exchanged."[43] Governments can print money virtually out of thin air – or more precisely, they can buy government debt in the form of securities issued by the US Treasury and hope to repay it later, a policy utilized to bolster consumer spending and manufacturing which declined as a result of Covid-19 lockdowns – but the increase in the money supply means that too much money is chasing too few products, which reduces the buying power of the currency and which in turn can lead to inflation.

Orrin Klapp has argued that symbolic inflation occurs as a result of the operation of five distinct social magnifiers "which make things look bigger or more important than they really are."[44] The first of these is *overstatement*, which is the exaggeration of some area of life for some purpose deemed useful to the person or group making the inflated claim. Sometimes overstatement is benign, like such turns of phrase used for emphasis as "I could kill you!" or "The end of the world is nigh." Beyond this, overstatement is often used as a type of technique of neutralization for persons identified as members of a deviant or disvalued group. Persons who are labeled as deviant have a vested interest in claiming that they are not as odd or rare as critics make them out to be. This is consistent with the folk wisdom of "strength in numbers," such as the "neuro-tribes" of persons on the autism spectrum along with their defenders and supporters.[45] Indeed, the defense of deviance is a sort of numbers game, as in the example of the wildly different numbers quoted for the percentage of the population that is exclusively homosexual. Defenders of homosexuality who seek to normalize it use the higher figure of 10 percent of the population – derived largely from the Kinsey studies of sexuality of the 1950s – while others claim the true figure is closer to 1.5 to 3 percent. Whatever the percentage of homosexuality actually is, studies indicate that the public consistently overestimates the size of the gay population.[46]

A similar numbers game is playing out on the issue of the percentage of intersexed persons – those born with both male and female features, whether chromosomal, somatic, or some combination – in human populations. In her book *Sexing the Body*, Anne Fausto-Sterling claimed that about 1.7 percent of the population is intersexed, but later analysis revealed it is much rarer, accounting for only 0.018 percent of the population.[47] This is nearly 100 times lower than the figure claimed by Fausto-Sterling, a clear example of overstatement.

Another important aspect of overstatement is the well-documented phenomenon that human beings hold generally flawed understandings of their own abilities, including being overly optimistic about their future prospects. This indicates a persistent gap between self-perception and reality. For example, the correlation between people's judgment of their own intelligence and their performance on objective intelligence tests is typically a meager 0.20–0.30. People's beliefs in their ability to detect lying compared to others correlates at only 0.04 of their actual performance. And in the workplace, the correlation between how people expect to perform with regard to completing complex tasks compared to how they actually performed rarely rises above 0.20.[48] In short, flawed self-assessment is a relatively large contributor to symbolic inflation.

A second social magnifier is *crusading*, which Klapp describes as "the rhetorical inflation of a conflict into a war of good versus evil."[49] Those embarking on the crusade are angels purer than the driven snow, while those opposed or who are targets of the crusade are cast as evil and barely human. Crusades, then, are cut from the same cloth as Carl Schmitt's notion of the political as friends versus enemies. That is to say, partisan politics is always crusade-like.

A third social magnifier is *contagious communication*, which consists of highly-charged emotional claims that draw upon moral outrage as a source of solidarity for true believers. Such communications work best when they spread rapidly across a large group of people, similar to an infectious disease pandemic coursing through a population. Social media can be understood as a modern type of contagious communication, and it can effectively motivate large numbers of persons into simultaneous action much like the behavior of crowds or mobs. The "madness of crowds" can even instigate and sustain larger, mass movements such as in the case of ongoing concerns over gender, race, identity, or stolen elections.[50] Here, persons get on a soapbox and make the case that their concerns represent the most pressing issue of the day, in effect elevating the focal concern to a literal life-and-death struggle.

A fourth type of social magnifier is *self-expansion*, which is often accomplished through identification with others, especially those who are prominent, whether politicians, celebrities, or well-known fictional or historical figures. There is often a desire to appear larger-than-life and important, and one way of doing this is via emotional hitchhiking where one ties one's fortunes to select protagonists who have made a difference in the world and with whom the person seeks to be associated. Sometimes this attempt to live vicariously through the triumphs and travails of famous persons or dramatic personae goes bad, such as Mark David Chapman fancying himself as Holden Caulfield from *Catcher in the Rye*. Chapman, who assassinated John Lennon in 1980, is still incarcerated and will be coming up for parole for the eleventh time in 2022. Chapman stated in a recent interview that "I assassinated him … because he was very, very, very famous and that's the only reason and I was very, very, very, very much seeking self-glory. Very selfish."[51]

A fifth type of social magnifier is *oversupply*, and this covers an array of market-like features wherein culture symbols become devalued because of their abundance. For example, credentials inflation is the problem of too many people graduating with high honors (e.g., Summa Cum Laude), which waters down the value of the recognition. In sporting events, if everyone receives a trophy – even those on the losing team – does the trophy really mean anything? Tokens of approval, such as the standing ovation, used to be given rarely and highly selectively, to only the most high-achieving musical or dramatic performances. Lately, however, longstanding members of art and performance houses are appalled at the willingness with which audiences are leaving their seats to applaud average or even mediocre performances. There is also inflation of sentiments, seen most vividly in presidents now being expected to be Empathizers-in-Chief by making visible emotional displays at the site of disasters or with respect to other difficult national conversations, a characteristic which many persons believed was clearly lacking in President Trump. Trump was also prone to braggadocio (e.g., referring to himself as a "very stable genius") and hence also to overstatement.[52] Conversely, President Bill Clinton was famously associated with the line "I feel your pain."

Symbolic inflation may also afflict medical diagnosis, especially when the symptom checklist (or nosology) is vague or expansive. Examples of "alarming" increases in certain illnesses – such as fetal alcohol syndrome, fibromyalgia, chronic fatigue syndrome, and restless leg syndrome – can be accounted for as much by their overly expansive nosologies as on actual, putative increases in cases. Even autism, discussed in chapter 7, may be suffering from levels of diagnostic inflation. For example, before 1990, the frequency of autism diagnosis in human populations was 1 per 2,000–5,000 persons. By 2010, the CDC announced that the prevalence figure had increased to 1 in 150 children being diagnosed with the illness. More recently, the figure stands at 1 in 54 children. But across this time, the diagnostic criteria for autism have shifted and become more expansive. Gerald Grob and Allan Horwitz ask, "Is this increase real, or is the diagnosis now applied to children previously labeled as retarded or learning disabled when such terms have gone out of favor?"[53]

Allen Frances suggests that as a type of symbolic inflation, diagnostic inflation occurs because "most of the political and financial muscle is pushing abnormal" while "the forces pushing normal don't remotely counterbalance and aren't nearly forceful enough."[54] As previously discussed, "normal" itself has become a loaded term because of its association with privilege and the fear that those not labeled normal will face discrimination in some form or other. Additionally, with the seeming growth of all types of mental disorders, the concept "normal" may no longer make sense because the majority – or a large percentage – of the population could be categorized as ill. Over the last 20 years, in addition to the already discussed increase in the diagnosis of autism, the diagnosis of childhood bipolar disorder has increased 40-fold, while ADHD has tripled, and adult bipolar disorder has doubled.[55]

According to a recent Pew Research study, over 50 percent of liberal, white women under 30 have a mental health issue.[56] This is yet another indication of the broad problem of diagnostic inflation and the odd direction it can take when entangled with politics. For example, the study also finds that conservatives are less likely than liberals to have mental illnesses, so maybe those with aspirations of world-saving bear a heavy burden. Those on the political left may be convinced that they can somehow change the world for the better and end things like inequality, war, and all the -isms. And so, when they find out they can't, they are crushed, despondent, and hopeless, pretty much left to wringing hands over the walking wounded of neoliberalism. And since they are more likely to be atheists than those on the other side of the political aisle, they have no God to turn to for comfort. To occlude glimpses into the deep, dark abyss which is their life, with the pain of the masses of dispossessed and powerless internalized as their own pain, they may seek pharmaceutical relief in the form of tranquilizers, antidepressants, or whatever else is handy or available.

Responsibilization

Surveillance can take place within the context of informal control (via the employment of natural surveillance), legal control (largely by way of the criminal and juvenile justice systems), or medical control (especially by way of public health within the administrative state). Something of a tug of war has developed between legal, medical, and informal control, and it appears to be the case that on balance, informal control is losing out to the other two. As summarized in the previous chapter, informal social control appears to have waned significantly as a result not only of the threat of terrorism, but also of other long-term changes characteristic of the advent of the postmodern or postindustrial society. This has paved the way for the ascendancy of legal and medical control, and in some instances the boundaries between the three forms of control have become blurred.

Whereas police were set up as the specialized, legitimate agents of control within urban communities, which also thereby placed self-help into disrepute – giving rise to the concept of *vigilantism* where citizens take the law into their own hands – modern governments are now asking citizens to do their part to contribute to the maintenance of social order. In other words, governments are attempting to place more of the responsibility for community maintenance and order in the hands of citizens.[57] In Europe, David Garland has referred to this as the *responsibilization* strategy, and as he further explains,

> Instead of addressing crime in a direct fashion by means of the police, the courts and the prisons, this approach [responsibilization] promotes a new kind of indirect action, in which state agencies activate action by non-state organizations and actors. The intended result is an enhanced network of more or less directed, more or less informal crime control, complementing and extending the formal controls of the criminal justice state.[58]

In this sense, responsibilization is a sort of *contractual injunction* whereby police are empowered to act like brokers steering proper behavior indirectly through place managers who risk financial penalties for violating the "contract."[59] The equivalent in the United States is *third-party policing*, which is defined as "police efforts to persuade or coerce non-offending persons to take actions which are outside the scope of their routine activities, and which are designed to indirectly minimize disorder caused by other persons or to reduce the possibility that crime may occur."[60] Shop owners, landlords, and neighborhood associations are the kinds of persons and groups police are most likely to put pressure on to promote "collective responsibility" in targeted areas.

Under community policing, police departments inform local citizens that the crime problem is too vast and complex to be managed by the police alone, and it is within this context that they feel emboldened to ask for the help of citizens to be that extra set of eyes and ears, which was largely muted and deemed to be irrelevant during the second era of municipal policing (namely, professionalization and early reform). In ways, this is consistent with governmentality and the process of fanning out disciplinary mechanisms more broadly across the community. It is the condition of the "many watching the many."

This also represents the postmodern problem of boundary blurring: If everyone is responsible for crime control and disorder, meaningful distinctions between the police, government personnel, and non-governmental actors and organizations become harder and harder to draw. The blurring of boundaries also appears in the guise of the court's growing reliance on alternative or intermediate sanctions, including a whole host of community-based sanctions. Indeed, if punishments or treatments can be carried out successfully within communities rather than prisons or asylums, or if a person's home can serve as a prison as effectively as traditional correctional facilities, the strategy of social control shifts to an examination of how best to mix and merge informal, legal, and medical control resources. And of course, the enormous growth of privatization in both policing and corrections further blurs the boundaries between the roles of public and private organizations in social control.

Actuarial justice and the new penology

Another indication of changes in the relationship between legal, informal, and medical control is the emergence of what Jonathan Simon and Malcolm Feeley refer to as the *new penology*.[61] The authors argue that key changes since the Progressive Era (1890s through about 1910) have produced a new, "postmodern" way of thinking about crime and crime policy. Within the postmodern blurring of boundaries, there is a loss of faith in clearly distinguishing between the normal and the deviant, or the law-abiding citizen and the criminal, and applying legal sanctions accordingly. Instead, forward-looking risk profiles are employed – connected with the mass surveillance projects of both criminal justice and public health – hence actuarial notions of risk are employed with hopes of identifying and sanctioning deviants against the backdrop of the mass of anonymous others constituting the general public.

In addition, the gap between professional and public (or lay) discourses about crime has grown wider. There appears to be a declining consensus about what to do about crime and disorder, which is consistent with the theorized loss of certitude about the world that persons are experiencing under the postmodern condition. Consistent with this is the proliferation of a growing legion of "experts" – whether used in court to bolster a case, "talking heads" in the media, and policy think tanks servicing government and industry – ready to defend numerous positions about the nature of criminality. For example: "three strikes and you're out" was a grassroots movement, but professional discourses within criminology, law, and the social sciences have been highly critical. The same can be said of boot camps, lie detectors, random drug testing, Scared Straight programs, and so forth.[62]

Under modernity we had faith in the "scientific" approach to the problem of crime, especially during the Progressive Era (the heyday of the social sciences, where the birth of sociology and social work took place). In contrast, the new penology is content to conduct surveillance on whole populations because intervention at the individual level is now viewed as ineffective. This is of course consistent with the loss of faith in rehabilitation and the general position that "nothing works." In effect, there is no compelling vision with which to come to terms with the problems of crime and disorder. According to Simon and Feeley, it is now an administrative problem to be "managed." As a consequence, expediency runs rampant (e.g., judges tacking on drug testing as part of a probationary sentence when drugs were not part of the criminal complaint).

In sum, the major operational logic of the new penology is *actuarial justice*. Feeley and Simon describe its major characteristics as follows:

- actuarial justice relies on accounting procedures, such as the traditional measures of risk previously utilized in industry, finance, and medicine;
- it is concerned with techniques for identifying, classifying, and managing groups assorted by levels of dangerousness;
- it takes crime for granted;
- it accepts deviance as normal;
- it is skeptical that liberal interventionist crime control strategies do or can make a difference;
- its aim is not to intervene in individuals' lives for the purpose of changing them (rehabilitation) or punishing them (retribution); rather, it seeks to regulate groups as part of a strategy of managing danger.[63]

Dangerization

Hence, from the perspective of Simon and Feeley as well as a number of other scholars, Western governments are now primarily concerned with the management of risk and danger. By concentrating on risk in this way, governments are contributing to yet another "postmodern" blurring of boundaries. The most important boundary that has become blurred, according to Michalis Lianos, is the distinction between the normal and the deviant.[64] Under the traditional view, those who violated the community's norms deserved to be punished, and were identified and set aside for processing through the justice and penal systems. However, under the new condition which Lianos refers to as *dangerization*, individuals are not necessarily identified and responded to on the basis of their deviant acts. Instead, groups of persons, places, or events are identified as actually or potentially dangerous. In the postmodern condition, as more and more categories of persons, places, and events are identified as risky or dangerous, the entire society becomes identified as a "risk society," hence the notion of the "normal" as opposed to the occasionally deviant no longer makes sense.

Even within the condition of dangerization, social and economic exchanges continue to be facilitated by a growing reliance on constant and routine surveillance (such as the use of CCTV in urban areas). Rather than relying on the fallible perceptions of human beings, automated systems of surveillance can allow access to places and events through circuits of exclusion and inclusion.[65] In other words, rather than reacting to deviant acts that may take place, the goal is to manage environments by allowing or denying access to persons based on selected group factors, often facilitated through the use of searchable databases. Examples of this type of *social sorting* include loyalty cards at grocery stores and pharmacies; codes, passwords, and biometric scanning devices for electronic or physical access to buildings, products, or services; routine use of identification cards not only in business and government establishments but also increasingly in schools; and closely aligned with CPTED, physical alteration and modification of space, such as the erection of barriers, checkpoints, or other engineering designs which seek to allow access to persons who possess certain characteristics while keeping out those who do not possess the desired traits (as in the case of gated communities).[66]

This produces a new level of vigilance which citizens of the modern metropolis are obligated to engage in not only for their own protection, but also as a form of virtue signaling to others that they "have their backs." Lacking the type of regular face-to-face engagements characteristic of earlier forms of solidarity, neighbors are relying more and more on virtual engagement through electronic apps such as Nextdoor, Front Porch, and MyCoop, with the latter specifically designed for apartment dwellers.[67] Neighborhood Watch organizations are active as well, but have somewhat fallen out of favor since 2012 when Trayvon Martin was shot and killed by George Zimmerman in his role as a neighborhood watch coordinator for the gated community in which he lived.[68] Even so, dangerization moves forward and enlarges to the extent that fear of victimization is understood as a personal event within the atomization taking place across urban communities under neoliberalism.[69]

The colonization of the lifeworld

The current ascendancy of concepts such as social capital, responsibilization, and dangerization, as well as policies like community policing and third-party policing, is reflective of the recognition that the "invisible hand" of the market cannot solve persistent and chronic social problems such as crime, joblessness and unemployment, social isolation and marginalization of some groups, racism and sexism, or environmental degradation. When market forces can no longer be relied on to bond persons to conventional society, there is a tendency for these formal systems to encroach further into the realm of everyday life or the lifeworld. This attempt to steer lifeworld (or informal) activities by infusing them with oversight and directives from the formal realm (of law, medicine, the courts and the police) is what Jürgen Habermas has described as the *colonization of the lifeworld*. This is the problem of rationalization as discussed in chapter 1, but it goes even beyond Weber's original position.

In order to understand this, we must briefly cover the distinction Habermas makes between system and lifeworld.[70] Drawing from standard phenomenology, the *lifeworld* simply represents that part of society which is concerned with socialization, with face-to-face behavior, with family and other primary group relations, and with the development of self through close and ongoing contact with significant others. In this sense, the lifeworld is synonymous with everyday life (as discussed in chapter 3), and the primary form of control operating here is informal. By *system*, on the other hand, Habermas is referring to more formalized institutional settings, where other aspects of one's status-set become salient, such as worker, citizen, student, professor, customer, or patient.

Whereas the lifeworld is integrated through tacit understandings of one's obligations toward significant others such as family and friends, the system is integrated on the basis of the functional "needs" of the system. For example, in order for economic activity to work smoothly and efficiently, workers' actions have to be coordinated with others' actions with much greater precision than is the case for actions taking place in informal settings (such as between family members or friends). This means that formal guidelines tend to be promulgated for all members of a work group, and time pressures will be brought to bear to maximize the efficiency of workers' activities but also to minimize mutual interference. As a crucial aspect of modern social systems, norms of punctuality seek to ensure that vital actions will be dispersed across space and time in a predictable manner.

According to Habermas, however, with continuing societal rationalization, systems imperatives of efficiency and predictability tend to become parasitic on everyday lifeworld activities, thereby producing a variety of distortions. Instead of negotiating the conditions of their existence voluntarily within the context of shared lifeworlds, actors increasingly find more and a greater variety of "experts" ready and willing to step in to provide guidance about their everyday activities, be it dating, raising children, discussing and interpreting news of the day, how to do a wedding reception, or even how to throw a surprise birthday party. The colonization of the lifeworld by the system serves to mute everyday communicative action, and more than ever actors find themselves at the mercy of broader systems imperatives shaping and guiding – either through "strong" suggestions or outright coercion – their thoughts and actions. Even social control itself is less social than it once was, having been taken up as multiple and parallel projects by governments, institutions, workplaces, and schools, and much of which takes place virtually rather than face-to-face.[71]

Continuing concerns over shoring up informal control

What are we to do about this increasing encroachment of systems impera-tives into previously informally regulated areas of life? Are we fated to live in what Habermas has called an "expertocracy," where collective understandings of everyday life are replaced by the formalized rulings and recommendations of lawyers, bureaucrats, and the cost–benefit analyses of economists and organizational consultants?[72] Enlightenment and Progressive thinkers such as Lester Ward believed that science and reason would usher in an era of universal education where the errors of past thought would be corrected, thereby leading to the general improvement of society.[73] But it appears now that instrumental reason is being used more narrowly, as a technology to control various persons and groups that are seen as persistently incorrigible, disorderly, criminal, strange, or unpredictable.[74] Indeed, with the advent of more expansive and continuous surveillance technologies, we have moved from concentrating efforts on a relatively visible group of offenders or misfits, to now assuming that all persons within the camera's gaze are "bad." Since everyone is now poten-tially an offender, the police cannot hope to do the work of legal control alone, and hence everyone is asked to do their fair share.

Agents of legal control are faced with a peculiar juggling act: they must break the bad news that everyone is bad, but also ask these very same persons to watch over everyone else, in effect expecting citizens to act as auxiliary police officers in the service of their community. One way of dealing with this dilemma is for agents of control to cajole citizens, for example, by selling the notion that today's police are not only excellent communicators, but also more sensitive and compas-sionate toward citizens because of their training in soft skills and multiculturalism.[75] In addition, because they are better-educated, police should be trusted to take greater initiative, to solve problems, and to be a proactive rather than a merely reactive force.[76] In effect, the police are boundary-spanning multitaskers, a new hybrid role that is required in the postmodern metropolis where, sadly, nobody can be trusted, and where traditional measures have failed to distinguish the normal from the deviant.

Ultimately, then, citizens – who of course cannot be trusted – are being asked to take on more responsibility for the maintenance of the social system. Responsibilization takes many forms: traditional welfare programs have been transformed into welfare-to-work programs where the state divests its financial burden by using the social capital of families and the local community; municipal police are asking persons to draw upon neighborhood funds of information capital to assure social control; and the public school system, facing shrinking budgets and enrollments, is asking parent–teacher associations (PTAs), social services (especially its public health wing), the police, and even families (e.g., through home schooling) to pick up the slack.[77]

It appears that at least for the short term, local governance will continue to pursue strategies of responsibilization, and will continue to find ways to steer informal activities via the rhetoric of social capital, communitarianism, and community policing. Yet, however well-intentioned these programs and policies may be, there remain grave reservations about the formal sector's supervision and oversight of the informal realm because of the problems of the colonization of the lifeworld already discussed. In other words, there is an attempt to combine coercion with compassion in these varied hybrid undertakings – for example, community policing, intermediate sanctions, third-party policing, and a variety of so-called "problem-solving" courts such as drug courts, youth and family courts, mental health courts, and community courts – but the two simply do not mix very well.[78]

Under the community policing model, police are conceptualized more as generalists, hearkening back to the roles they originally occupied during the earliest, political spoils era (see chapter 5 for more on this). The vast array of service functions assigned to the police under community policing gives them entrée into the informal realm where they are simply not needed and, indeed, where they may do more harm than good. On this point I agree with Steve Herbert, who argues that "The police's coercive role means that they are not good community builders, and thus we fool ourselves – and harm communities – by holding onto the more elaborate rhetoric of community policing."[79] Indeed, much of the recent movement toward defunding of the police articulates this general concern, along, of course, with claims of institutionalized racism and bias of the entirety of the criminal justice system, especially as embodied in the Black Lives Matter movement.

In addition, the threat of terrorism in our global risk society has sent our brightest military minds into the realm of tracking "known unknowns."[80] Terrorists do not play by the rules of conventional warfare. These unconventional approaches, some of which were covered in chapter 9, are intended as much as anything to shock both civilian and military arenas, in effect making them incapable of mounting meaningful or reasonable responses. The idea of attempting to conceptualize the impossible or merely improbable is the military's attempt to stay one step ahead of terrorist perpetrators, and to prepare targeted societies for whatever terrors await if such plans were to be successfully carried out. This represents hyper-proactivity, or proactivity on steroids. Rather than putting a blue ribbon panel together after the fact to study why we were not prepared for the next big terrorist attack, why not put everything on the table, and conceptualize worst-case, perhaps nearly impossible scenarios which could be concocted by terrorists seeking to maximize damage to targeted populations?

This sort of thinking and planning lends itself to embracing futurist frameworks for counterterrorism both foreign and domestic. A 2017 publication of the Center for Homeland Defense and Security at the Naval Postgraduate School, titled "HSx: Futurist Thinking & Planning," admits that although the future cannot be predicted with certainty, it is possible to be systematic about what *could* happen in the future based upon extrapolations from past and recent terror events. The key futurist methodologies discussed are trend analysis, environmental scanning, scenario development, technological forecasting, and the Delphi method of assembling a panel of experts to reflect upon how well these various methodologies are integrated into the formation of coherent and plausible counterterrorism plans.[81]

Even so, these efforts are roadmaps for hypervigilance which feeds the incessant creep of legal control. It assumes the worst and looks for enemies under every rock, in every nook and cranny. Second-generation biometric technologies such as FAST also introduce a range of ethical questions which are not yet fully resolved, primarily because of how potentially intrusive they are, but also because they can operate without the awareness of those being targeted.[82] For better or worse, this is what we are stuck with in 2021 and beyond. But on the bright side, as medical and legal control continue to expand in new and innovative ways, both individually and in combination, perhaps persons will grow to appreciate and even nurture informal control within their everyday lives. Rather than seeking the intervention of third parties, which places an even greater premium on control-from-a-distance, maybe persons will strive to do more things face-to-face, to settle their differences amicably and agree to let the chips fall where they may. If these sorts of things happen, it will go some way toward halting or even reversing the colonization of the lifeworld. This was, after all, our birthright, and it still may be the best way to get things done.

SUGGESTIONS FOR FURTHER READING

Allen Frances, *Saving Normal* (2013)
> Frances, a doctor who was the chairman of the *DSM*-4 Task Force, offers an insider's view into the workings of the psychiatric profession and the steady stream of mental disorders appearing with each new edition of the *DSM*. His primary goal is to save normal and to move away from the profession's unhealthy fixation on the abnormal.

Jürgen Habermas, *Theory of Communicative Action*, 2 vols. (1984/1987)
> A landmark study in general theory. It is here that Habermas formulates his important concepts of distorted communication and the colonization of the lifeworld.

Orrin Klapp, *Inflation of Symbols: Loss of Values in American Culture* (1991)
> Klapp's book makes a profound contribution to the sociological study of value loss through the inflation of symbols in modern society. The areas of symbolic

inflation covered include tokens of approval, credentials, sentiments, fashion, and information.

Michalis Lianos, *The New Social Control: The Institutional Web, Normativity and the Social Bond* (2012)

Lianos argues that one of the primary results of the societal loss of faith in the criminal justice goal of rehabilitation is that we now treat all persons as potentially evil – facilitated through constant surveillance of public places – and hence no meaningful distinctions exist between the normal and the deviant. This trend toward "dangerization" has effectively turned the concept "deviance" into an empty signifier devoid of meaning.

Gary T. Marx, *Windows into the Soul: Surveillance and Society in an Age of High Technology* (2016)

This is a compendium of writings and observations on the newly developing field of surveillance studies. Topics include social processes in surveillance, ID chips, medical surveillance, resistance to surveillance, and the varieties of personal information that can be gleaned from individuals through various surveillance technologies.

DISCUSSION QUESTIONS

1. Describe the three elements of routine activities theory. Is this a useful theory for explaining crime? Why or why not?
2. Is China's social credit system a reasonable type of government surveillance, or does it go too far in its quest to gather data on many aspects of the lives of Chinese citizens?
3. Can malintent actually be detected and acted upon to thwart possible terror attacks as suggested by the Department of Homeland Security?
4. What is CPTED? Identify and discuss at least three strategies for designing out crime connected with this perspective.
5. Identify and discuss at least three social magnifiers that contribute to the problem of symbolic inflation.

Notes

Preface and Acknowledgments

1 Gordon et al. (2008).
2 See Vico (1982 [1724]).
3 This discussion of Vico can be found in modified form in Chriss (2021b).
4 See Ward (1883).
5 On the insatiability of human appetites, see Durkheim (1984 [1893]). On the concept of bare life, see Agamben (1998).
6 Patterson (1987, p. 210).
7 Ibid., p. 224.
8 Armstrong (2008, p. 95).
9 Patterson (1987, p. 225).
10 Ibid., p. 226.

Chapter 1: What Is Social Control?

1 Cohen (1985, p. 3).
2 Nadel (1953, p. 265).
3 MacIver and Page (1949, p. 137).
4 These figures are from https://ourworldindata.org/covid-deaths.
5 The emergence of the idea of social distancing as a result of the Covid-19 pandemic is indeed curious from a sociological perspective. In 1924 sociologist Emory Bogardus developed a so-called social distance scale, which purports to measure how close people are to others in their social relationships, studying how race, social class, gender, and income affect how close or distant such relations are (see Wark and Galliher, 2007). What is referred to as social distancing as applied to Covid-19 is not social distancing at all, but rather geographical or spatial distancing (that is, propinquity), which carries no specific sociological relevance.
6 This situation is discussed in a *Los Angeles Times* story. See https://www.latimes.com/food/story/2020-03-11/coronavirus-china-wet-markets.
7 A terse exchange on this controversy between Dr. Anthony Fauci and Senator Rand Paul is available at https://www.youtube.com/watch?v=fhr9o2nAa2E.
8 For more on the lab leak theory, see the story at https://www.cbsnews.com/news/covid-19-wuhan-lab-leak-theory/.
9 See Chriss (2021a, p. 23).
10 For more on this story, see https://abcnews.go.com/US/governor-urges-social-distancing-wisconsin-court-blocks-stay/story?id=70683102.

11 For more on this story, see https://www.nytimes.com/2020/12/01/opinion/supreme-court-Covid-19-religion.html.
12 Schmitt (2007).
13 Ibid.
14 Ross (1896). This and other articles on social control are collected in Ross (1901).
15 Ward (1883, 1893).
16 See, e.g., Rafter (2004).
17 See Ward (1893).
18 See Simmel (1950).
19 See Ross (1896, pp. 519–20).
20 Landis (1939, p. 21). Landis's work was brought to my attention upon reading Don Martindale's (1966) book *Institutions, Organizations, and Mass Society*, and it is the latter book by Martindale which stands as one of the greatest, sustained treatments of social control ever written.
21 See Spencer (1897a, pp. 505–48).
22 Spencer's analogy between nerves and government in the production of regulation was made explicit in Karl Deutsch's (1963) book *Nerves of Government* and subtitled "Models of Political Communication and Control."
23 Parts of this section appeared in Chriss (2004).
24 During the modern era, restitutive law – which Durkheim understood to mean civil law – emerged and operated alongside the longer-standing criminal law. Due to space constraints, civil law (or the law of torts) will not be covered in this book.
25 On postmodernity see, e.g., Agger (2002), Lyotard (1984), and Staples (2000).
26 Alpert (1939, p. 190).
27 For a thorough analysis of the sociodemographic data associated with the sinking of the Titanic, see Frey et al. (2011).
28 See, e.g., Freud (1927) and Parsons (1964).
29 A more thorough discussion of agents of socialization is provided in chapter 3.
30 For a good discussion of social control as socialization and the internalization of moral codes, see Ellwood (1925, pp. 157–87).
31 See, e.g., Best (1999), Chriss (1999b), Elliott et al. (1998), and Putnam (2000).
32 The concept of moral panics, initially developed by Stanley Cohen in 1972, has given rise to a vast secondary literature on the topic. For the original statement, see Cohen (1972).
33 I am drawing from Welch et al. (2002) for details of this case.
34 For a history of the term superpredator and a discussion of how it became one of the leading political issues of the 1990s, see Elikann (1999).
35 See Stratton (2015).
36 See, e.g., Altheide (2013). For a useful discussion of the role of the media in spreading moral panics, see Goode and Ben-Yehuda (2009).
37 For examples of social media facilitation of informal concerted actions, see Cross (2005), Hier (2008), Shih (2016), and Walsh (2020). Much of this can be subsumed under the general phenomenon of social media activism, which is covered in great detail by Swann (2019).
38 This is somewhat connected to the phenomenon of the "flash mob," the intentions of which can be either artistic or criminal. Members of flash mobs typically use social media platforms to organize the logistics of meeting up at a specific time and place. For more on flash mobs, see Chriss (2013).
39 Weissman (2019, p. 29). Interestingly, the term "blacklisting" has been blacklisted

by a number of social media providers because of its presumed racism. This gives fuel to critics who claim that political correctness, along with "wokeness" and "cancel culture," are running amok. For more on Twitter dropping use of the words "master," "slave," and "blacklist" on its platform, see the story at https://www.bbc.com/news/business-53273923.

40 Altheide (2013).
41 Weber (1968, p. 31).
42 Ibid., p. 53.
43 Ibid., pp. 215–16.
44 Ibid., p. 231.
45 Ibid., p. 241.
46 Weber (1978 [1922], p. 39).
47 Weber (1947, p. 156).
48 Giddings (1899, p. 203).
49 See especially Habermas (1996).
50 See Habermas (1975).
51 For more on the concept of the state as moral regulator, see Corrigan and Sayer (1985), Melossi (2004), and Ruonavaara (1997).
52 Weber (1968, p. 30).
53 Glassner (1990, p. 218).
54 See Alexander (1983, p. 63).
55 This discussion is taken from Scott (1998, pp. 64–71).
56 For a discussion of the invention of the passport, see Torpey (2000).
57 Scott (1998, p. 66).
58 Ibid., p. 69.
59 See, e.g., Go (2016).
60 For more on gift registries, see Bradford and Sherry (2013).

Chapter 2: A Typology of Social Control

1 See Black (1983).
2 See Phillips and Cooney (2005).
3 See Black (1998).
4 For more on the "gray zone" of police work during mental health encounters, see Wood et al. (2017).
5 For the classic statement of the important ways third parties alter dyadic (or two-person) social relations, see Simmel (1950). Donald Black (1998, 2011) has also made extensive use of this idea.
6 See Matza (1964). Note also that if we start with three pure or ideal forms of control (informal, legal, and medical), there is a possibility that these can combine into various hybrid forms. Indeed, there are four additional hybrid forms of control arising from the three pure types, namely informal-legal, informal-medical, legal-medical, and informal-legal-medical. It is left up to the reader to think about concrete cases aligning with these four hybrid forms, although some of them have been alluded to in the book.
7 See Chriss (2019).
8 Goffman (1967, p. 137).
9 For a comprehensive overview of neutralization research, see Maruna and Copes (2005).

10 Sykes and Matza (1957).
11 The first three items on this list are from Sykes and Matza (1957). For more on looting as a form of political protest or civil disobedience, see Osterweil (2020).
12 Sykes and Matza (1957, p. 668).
13 See, e.g., Gabay et al. (2020). For the definitive analysis of how victimization became a criminal defense, see Westervelt (1998).
14 Sykes and Matza (1957, p. 668).
15 For a summary, see Klingle and Chronopoulos (2018).
16 See Bittner (1970).
17 Ibid., p. 37.
18 See Chriss (2018a).
19 Bittner (1970).
20 Horne (2001, p. 4). For an excellent analysis of norm emergence and formation within families, particularly as this is related to the control of teen sex and pregnancy, see Mollborn (2017).
21 See Sumner (1906). For a useful summary of and commentary on Sumner's thought, see Philip Manning's (2015) edited volume.
22 Sumner (1906, p. 34).
23 See Horne and Mollborn (2020).
24 Ibid., p. 470.
25 Ibid., p. 473.
26 Hinshaw (2007, p. 8).
27 See Chriss (2011) and Stroshine et al. (2008).
28 Hannon et al. (2021, p. 869).
29 See Malinowski (1987 [1929]).
30 See Fee and Nusbaumer (2012), Griffiths et al. (2017), Hinshaw (2005), and Ravary et al. (2019).
31 Hatfield and Sprecher (1985).
32 See Smits (2012).
33 See Schiefenhövel (2013).
34 See Haslam (2005).
35 Unilever's announcement can be found at https://www.unilever.com/news/press-releases/2021/unilever-says-no-to-normal-with-new-positive-beauty-vision.html.
36 The key, early statement on the death of deviance is Sumner (1994). See also Goode (2004) and Horsely (2014).
37 See Braun (2021).
38 For a recent overview of neurosociology, see Franks (2019). For a discussion of implicit bias training for achieving diversity and inclusion goals within organizations, see Dover et al. (2020).
39 Merton (1968).
40 See Ellwood (1925, p. 454).
41 See Maclay (1990).
42 Mészáros (1971, pp. 64–5).
43 Roth and Mehta (2002, p. 132).
44 See Mead (1925).
45 See Heckathorn (1990).
46 For a definitive statement on social control as backward-looking, see Macy (1993).
47 For a discussion of meat eaters and grass eaters as applied to the problem of police corruption, see Nas et al. (1986).

48 See Bentham (1998 [1843]).
49 Hirschi and Gottfredson (2005, pp. 215–17).
50 Ibid., pp. 217–19.
51 For a useful summary of the labeling perspective, see Herman-Kinney (2003).
52 This Bureau of Justice Statistics document is available at https://bjs.ojp.gov/content/pub/pdf/18upr9yfup0514.pdf.
53 Houdek et al. (2021, p. 132).
54 For a definitive statement on the conditions under which punishments produce defiance rather than conformity, see Sherman (1993). In a later paper, Sherman (2017) compared experimental evidence of the strength of predictions of labeling, defiance, and restorative justice theories, and found the latter to be the more robust.
55 See De Coster and Lutz (2018).
56 Ditton (1979).
57 Ibid., p. 102.
58 Even so, employers do not need direct evidence that a candidate is an ex-convict to make hiring decisions because they can use race and gaps in one's employment history – knowing that Blacks as a group are overrepresented in the incarceration statistics – as informal indicators of criminality (Rafael, 2017, p. 255).
59 D'Alessio et al. (2015, p. 347).

Chapter 3: Informal Control

1 The concept of the "natural surrounding world" is taken from Gurwitsch (1979).
2 For a summary of the sociology of everyday life, or what is sometimes referred to as existential sociology, see Adler et al. (1987) and Gouldner (1975).
3 Ellwood (1925, pp. 193–4).
4 This discussion of the seven basic sources of socialization is a modification of the topic covered in Arnett (1995, pp. 619–24).
5 See Giddings (1899), Sumner (1906), and Ward (1903).
6 Hillery (1968, p. 245).
7 Spencer (1879, p. 73).
8 See Pearce et al. (2018).
9 For a summary of the diverse range of family surveillance, see Nelson and Garey (2009).
10 Clinton (1995).
11 For examples, see Arnett (1995, pp. 621–2).
12 See Hirschi (1969). For a discussion of the myth that peer pressure is overwhelmingly negative, see Jewell et al. (2019).
13 Harris (1998).
14 See Gouldner (1979).
15 Maume and Parrish (2021).
16 Hartmann and Massoglia (2007).
17 Gaither (2009, p. 342).
18 See Fontenelle-Tereshchuk (2021).
19 This discussion is taken from Chao et al. (1994).
20 See Bugdol (2018).
21 Ibid., p. 732.
22 See Kingston (2006).
23 Whereas Frank (2016) is writing for a general, albeit learned, audience, Sauder (2020)

is explicitly speaking to sociologists, making the point that they have seriously overlooked luck in their analyses of meritocracy.

24 See Chriss (1999d, pp. 107–10).

25 Adams (1982, p. 152). See also Chriss (2010b).

26 Marcuse (1964, p. 9).

27 See Spencer (1891, pp. 280–4). About 150 years before Spencer, Italian political philosopher Giambattista Vico made the point that the act of burying the dead effectively ties the living to familial ancestors. Vico took care to remind us that religion in Latin means to "tie" or "bind." In effect, burial represents the convergence of the informal controls of religion and the family (Cahnman 1981, p. 28). For a general treatment on the universal fear of death, see Moore and Williamson (2003).

28 See Tylor (1871). For authoritative overviews of the origins of the human species in general, and of religion in particular, see Murphy (1927) and Wallace (1966). We also observe the process of rationalization in the religious realm with the move from polytheism to monotheism (Stark 2001).

29 See Freud (1952 [1913]) and Durkheim (1965 [1915]).

30 Ellwood (1912, pp. 356–7).

31 This discussion owes in part to Hervieu-Léger (1998).

32 This summary of Durkheim is from Alpert (1939, pp. 199–203). The pertinent aspects of Durkheim's writings on religion are taken from Durkheim (1965 [1915]).

33 For a summary of this argument, see Stoddart (2011).

34 L'Engle et al. (2006).

35 See, e.g., Sariolghalam (2003) and Tsui (2005).

36 Altheide (1992, p. 70).

37 See, e.g., Lang and Lang (1981).

38 Kidd (1920, p. 124).

39 Castells (1996a, 1996b).

40 Gouldner (1979).

41 Castells (1996a, pp. 234–5).

42 See Ong (2002).

43 Gouldner (1976, p. 168).

44 See Gouldner (1976) and Habermas (1996).

45 See Luke (1989), Mayhew (1997), McLuhan (1964), Schaefer (1995), and Williams (1974).

46 Gouldner (1976, p. 95).

47 See Putnam (2000).

48 See Tenove (2020).

49 See Chriss (2018b). For the original study of news dissemination on Twitter, see Vosoughi et al. (2018).

50 See the story at https://www.politico.com/newsletters/morning-tech/2021/02/24/censorship-debate-rattles-house-hearing-793566.

51 See Sunstein (2020).

52 See Gelber (2012).

53 This summary of Lewin, Sherif, and Whyte is informed by Harrington and Fine (2006, pp. 8–9).

54 See Asch (1951, 1952).

55 See Simmel (1950).

56 Sunstein (2019).

57 Additionally, Garcia et al. (2021) found that less than 22 percent of vote switching during mock jury deliberation was attributable to changes in belief about the

evidence, which means that the vast majority of vote switching occurred as a result of group pressures to conform.

58 See especially Milgram (1963, 1965). These and other obedience experiments are summarized in Milgram (1974).

59 Goffman (1971, p. vii).

60 Spencer (1897b, p. 6).

61 Goffman served as President of the American Sociological Association in 1982, and his presidential address appropriately was titled "The Interaction Order" (Goffman 1983). However, Goffman was too ill to attend and did not deliver the paper himself.

62 Goffman (1983, p. 4).

63 Goffman (1959).

64 On the various elements comprising a competent lecture, see "The Lecture" in Goffman (1981).

65 See Scott (2010).

66 On the concept of interaction ritual, see Goffman (1967). On the concept of normal appearances, see Goffman (1971).

67 Civil inattention is discussed in Goffman (1963a, pp. 83–8).

68 Role distance is discussed most explicitly in Goffman (1961b).

69 For more on virtual versus authentic selves or identities, see Goffman (1963b, pp. 2–40).

70 An abridged version of this example of role distance was previously reported in Chriss (1999c).

71 A number of critics (see, e.g., Gouldner 1970; Habermas 1984; Wilshire 1982; Young 1990) have accused Goffman of having an overly cynical view of human behavior, one that amounts to a "con man" theory of everyday life. For a summary of these and other criticisms, see Chriss (1999c, 2003).

72 For the concept of fabricated frames, see Goffman (1974). For a brilliant discussion of secrecy, see Goffman (1959, pp. 141–66).

Chapter 4: Medical Control

1 The story of Cartwright and his drapetomania diagnosis is summarized in Armstrong (2003).

2 Conrad and Schneider (1980, p. 242).

3 See Fox (1959).

4 For more on the notion of normalizing discourses, see Foucault (1978).

5 Williams and Arrigo (2006, p. 6).

6 Foucault (1977).

7 See, e.g., Foucault (1965, 1973), Ward (2002), and Wingerter (2003).

8 This discussion is from Parsons (1951, pp. 436–9).

9 Zola (1972, p. 487, original emphasis).

10 Weisheit and Klofas (1998, p. 198).

11 The term "hygienization" is from Somers (1995), while "public healthification" is from Meyer and Schwartz (2000).

12 See, e.g., Welch et al. (2012).

13 See Adler and Adler (2006, p. 139). For an updated discussion of the provisional treatment of relational disorders in DSM-5, see Heyman and Slep (2019).

14 This listing of V codes can be found at https://www.psychdb.com/teaching/dsm-v-icd-z-codes.

15 See, for example, Herring (2019).
16 Kaul (2021).
17 For more on Mills' Harm Principle, see Chriss (2016).
18 The current situation regarding victimless crimes is murkier than ever, because the National Incident-Based Reporting System (NIBRS) of the Uniform Crime Reporting Program (UCR) is now officially referring to them as "crimes against society," a new category that joins the two traditional ones of crimes against persons and crimes against property. For more on this NIBRS classification, see https://ucr.fbi.gov/about-us/cjis/ucr/nibrs/2014/resource-pages/crimes_against_persons_property_and_society_f.pdf.
19 See Lund et al. (2015).
20 See Sundin et al. (2021).
21 Seid et al. (2015).
22 See, e.g., Ballard and Elston (2005).
23 See Conrad and Schneider (1980, pp. 172–214), Conrad (1992), and Kutchins and Kirk (1997, pp. 55–99) for discussions of homosexuality in relation to both medicalization and demedicalization.
24 See Conrad and Angell (2004).
25 These trends in demedicalization include: Grahame-Smith (2002), prescription drugs; Lin (2017), kinky sex; Torres (2014), lactation; Sobal (1995), obesity.
26 See especially Forth (2020).
27 Starr (1982).
28 See Clarke et al. (2003) and Halliwell (2013).
29 See Moynihan and Cassels (2005).
30 Furedi (2006).
31 On the concept of disease mongering, see Moynihan et al. (2002).
32 See Rogers and Mintzker (2016).
33 Klapp (1991, p. 2).
34 See Warner (1984) for a discussion of the yellow plague of 1878–84.
35 Skocpol (1992, pp. 302–4).
36 Eskin (2002, pp. 6–7).
37 Short (2006, pp. 204–5).
38 See, for example, Gideon's (2013) recommendations for bridging the gap between public health and criminal justice.
39 Chriss (2021a).
40 See Agamben (2021).
41 For more on these issues, see Chriss (2002), Fishbein (1991), Menninger (1968), Raine (1993), and Skodal (1998).
42 For discussions of the psychotherapeutic ethos and its relation to the therapeutic state, see Foucault (1976), Furedi (2004a), Moskowitz (2001), Nolan (1998, 1999), Rose (2003), and White (1998).
43 For more on the long history of the social control of sex in general and deviant sex in particular, see Chriss (2010a).
44 As Docheff and Conn (2004) explain, more recently some of the non-scoring policies have been implemented to keep the behavior of increasingly aggressive parents and spectators from getting out of hand. Keeping the scoreboard blank means no angry parents, the pressure is taken off the kids to perform, and everyone walks away happy.
45 See Schram (2000, p. 88).

46 Shoshana (2019).

47 See, e.g., Modell and Haggerty (1991).

48 Furedi (2004b, p. 20).

49 The National Center for PTSD's psychological first aid manual, as well as other disaster handouts and information, is available at https://www.ptsd.va.gov/professional/treat/type/psych_firstaid_manual.asp.

50 Furedi (2004b, p. 21).

51 This story is summarized at https://www.bbc.com/news/world-us-canada-38218247.

52 This story is at https://www.inspiremalibu.com/blog/dual-diagnosis/7-well-known-people-with-post-traumatic-stress-disorder-ptsd/.

53 For more on the issue of the growing sentiment that "meat is murder," see the story at https://www.dailymail.co.uk/news/article-6849177/Nearly-200-militant-vegans-chant-meat-murder-storm-cattle-farmers-property.html.

54 For more on this, see https://www.cnbc.com/2020/12/05/americans-are-spending-more-money-on-their-pets-during-the-pandemic.html.

55 See Kirk (2019).

56 See, e.g., Huss (2018).

57 More recently, tests have been conducted to see if dogs can detect Covid-19 in humans. Initial studies appear promising, but more large-scale testing is needed to confirm early findings. See Else (2020).

58 Compitus (2019, p. 119).

59 See, e.g., Heard-Garris et al. (2018). For an explicit analysis connecting microaggressions to victimhood culture, see Campbell and Manning (2018).

60 For more on victimhood nationalism, see Lerner (2020). For more on cultural and social trauma, see Alexander et al. (2004) and Hamburger (2021).

61 See Riska (2003).

62 Horwitz and Wakefield (2007).

63 Riska (2003, p. 74).

64 Ibid., p. 72.

65 For a useful discussion of the medicalization of aging and the redefining of sexual health among the elderly, see Marshall (2010).

66 This part of the discussion is informed by the American Psychiatric Association website dedicated to gender dysphoria. It is available at https://www.psychiatry.org/patients-families/gender-dysphoria/what-is-gender-dysphoria.

67 See, e.g., Hartman et al. (2019).

68 See Poteat et al. (2019, p. 8).

69 See. e.g., Nocka et al. (2021) and Poteat et al. (2019).

70 Gressgård (2010, pp. 539–40).

71 Dewey and Gesbeck (2017, p. 38).

72 Fox (1959).

73 See, e.g., Nocka et al. (2021).

74 This is one of the points discussed in a broader critique of medicalization developed by Conrad and Schneider (1980).

75 There are the occasional scientific treatments of crime and deviance that still take evil seriously. See, for example, Katz (1988).

76 For an FBI report on the prevalence of serial murder, see the document at https://www.fbi.gov/stats-services/publications/serial-murder.

77 Fox and Levin (1998). For an analysis that focuses specifically on sexual murderers, see James and Proulx (2014).

Chapter 5: Legal Control

1 These data are available at https://www.americanactionforum.org/research/the-economic-costs-of-the-u-s-criminal-justice-system/.

2 There are some activities that fall simultaneously under the categories of morality and law. For example, cheating on your spouse is broadly considered immoral, but in some jurisdictions adultery could also land you in legal hot water. Worldwide, however, there has been a trend of diminishing legal regulation of adultery and sodomy from 1945 through 2005 (Frank et al. 2010).

3 Interestingly, in reaction to Trump, the State of California attempted to pass a law which required that for presidential candidates to be put on the state ballot, they must publicly release their tax returns. But in 2019 the California Supreme Court struck down the law as unconstitutional because it illegitimately went beyond the minimal federal requirements for running for president (namely, natural born citizen, a resident for 14 years, and no younger than 35 years of age). For more on this decision, see https://calmatters.org/politics/california-election-2020/2019/11/california-trump-tax-return-law-struck-down/.

4 For an early and definitive statement on moral entrepreneurs, see Becker (1973, pp. 147–63).

5 See Hunt (1999) for an excellent summary of the history of moral regulation in Western society.

6 For information on medieval England and the later history of the criminal justice system in England and the United States, I am drawing primarily from Johnson and Wolfe (1996).

7 As Müller (2005) reports, the hue and cry was used not only against perpetrators, but often by victims as well.

8 For more on collective responsibility, the frankpledge system, and related systems of personal pledging that appeared in medieval England, see Feinberg (1968), Pimsler (1977), and Postles (1996).

9 McIntosh (1998, pp. 2–45).

10 Ibid., pp. 54–107.

11 See Warden (1978).

12 Siebert (1990, p. 8).

13 Ibid., p. 12.

14 Ibid., p. 21.

15 This section of the discussion of colonial America draws from Walker (1980, pp. 11–34).

16 Ibid., pp. 14–15.

17 See Friedman (1993, pp. 62–5).

18 Ibid., pp. 20–7.

19 For useful discussions of the Enlightenment as it relates to political, legal, and social changes beginning in the eighteenth century, see Lasch (1991), Meyer (1976), and Scott (1998).

20 Garland (1997, p. 24).

21 For a summary of Beccaria's thought, see Maestro (1973).

22 For more on utilitarianism and rational-choice theory, see Chriss (2016).

23 Cooper (1981, p. 678).

24 Sutherland and Cressey (1955, p. 274).

25 These points are summarized in Cooper (1976, pp. 78–80).

26 For an informative discussion of the history and ultimate passage of the Penitentiary Act, see Devereaux (1999).

27 Rothman (2002b [1970], p. 57).

28 Reid (1997). For more on policing on the American western frontier, see Chriss (2011, pp. 49–67).

29 Grimsted (1972, p. 372).

30 Broeker (1961).

31 Ibid., p. 372.

32 See Blomberg and Lucken (2000, pp. 48–61).

33 For a detailed exposition of this argument, see Rothman (2002b [1970]).

34 Monkkonen (1983, p. 126).

35 For this discussion of the first three eras of policing, I draw from Bittner (2003) and Kelling and Moore (1988). A fourth era, so-called post-9/11 policing, was added later by other writers.

36 See Upson (1929).

37 Hamilton and Sutton (1989).

38 Vollmer (1971 [1919]), p. 33.

39 Ibid.

40 Ibid., p. 35.

41 More recently, this wraparound services framework for children-at-risk has been established under the guise of multisystemic therapy, which is based on Urie Brofenbrenner's social ecological model of human development. For an overview as applied in clinical settings, see Henggeler and Schaeffer (2016).

42 These are examples of community policing programs at the Cleveland Police Department in Ohio.

43 For more on post-9/11 policing, see Chriss (2011).

44 See Loader and Walker (2007).

45 For an overview of how the development of post-9/11 policing is proceeding in selected police departments in Texas, see Stewart and Oliver (2021).

46 For a summary of the jury verdict, see https://fox8.com/news/jury-reaches-verdict-in-trial-of-ex-cop-derek-chauvin-in-george-floyds-death/.

47 https://www.npr.org/2022/02/21/1082219066/defense-rests-in-federal-trial-of-3-police-officers-in-george-floyds-killing

48 Radabe (2021, p. 232).

49 This document is located at https://www.ci.wheatridge.co.us/DocumentCenter/View/2300/Police-Customer-Survey?bidId=.

50 Abbott et al. (2020, p. 892).

51 Rose and Clear (2004, p. 232).

52 See Cohen (1985) for a useful treatment of net-widening.

53 Reiman and Leighton (2020).

54 Packer (1968).

55 See, e.g., Bagaric (2015, p. 3).

56 More information on California's Proposition 47 is available at https://www.courts.ca.gov/prop47.htm.

57 For this study, see Crodelle et al. (2021).

58 See, e.g., Agan et al. (2021).

59 For useful discussions of the goals of punishment, see Ashworth (1997) and Nolan (2001, pp. 156–64).

60 Garland (1991, p. 158).

61 For more on the "family crisis" thesis and its implications for informal social control, see Chriss (1999b), Garland (2001, pp. 82–4), Liska (1997), Meier (1982), and van Krieken (1986).
62 For his 1974 study in which he famously declared that "nothing works" in rehabilitation, see Martinson (1974).

Chapter 6: Informal Control: Housing Segregation, the Code of the Street, and Emerging Adulthood and Morality

1 Felson and Boba (2010, p. xii).
2 This section's discussion of the shifting bases of informal social control over the life course is informed by Sampson and Laub (1993, pp. 17–23).
3 Wang et al. (2005, pp. 307–9).
4 Werner Stark's (1976–87) sprawling six-volume *The Social Bond* is the definitive statement on the subject. For a summary and overview of Stark's published works, see Das and Strasser (2015).
5 Durkheim (1984 [1893], p. 238).
6 Thomson (2005, p. 422).
7 See Simmel (1950).
8 Musolf (2003).
9 Reiss (1951, p. 197).
10 Ibid., p. 198.
11 Ibid., p. 200.
12 Durkheim (1951 [1897]).
13 Hirschi (1969, p. 16). The quote is from Durkheim (1951 [1897], p. 209).
14 See especially Parsons (1951).
15 Hirschi (1969, p. 30).
16 Ibid., p. 23.
17 Ibid., p. 26.
18 Hirschi borrowed the concept of "stake in conformity" from Jackson Toby (1957).
19 Hirschi (1969, p. 20).
20 Ibid., pp. 83–109.
21 Ibid., p. 83.
22 Ibid., p. 92.
23 Ibid., p. 94.
24 See Simons et al. (2004).
25 Gottfredson and Hirschi (1990).
26 See, e.g., Taylor (2001).
27 Hirschi (2004, p. 540).
28 Hirschi and Gottfredson (1983).
29 Hirschi (2004, p. 541).
30 See, for example, Geis (2000) and Taylor (2001).
31 Gottfredson and Hirschi (1990, p. 89).
32 See Klipfel et al. (2017).
33 DeLisi et al. (2018).
34 DeLisi (2016).
35 DeLisi and Vaughn (2008).
36 For more on public harassment, see Gardner (1995).
37 See, e.g., Bastomski and Smith (2017).

38 Felson (1996).
39 See Rabe-Hemp and Schuck (2007).
40 See Brazil et al. (2018).
41 See Krupp et al. (2012).
42 Ibid., p. 7.
43 Pedersen (2004, p. 118).
44 Lara (2017, p. 367).
45 See Althaus et al. (2015), Swain et al. (2017), and Yamasue and Domes (2018). For more on autism, see chapter 7.
46 For an overview of Empathy Deficit Disorder, see Acho and Basilion (2018).
47 The research I am referring to here is the study by Unnever et al. (2006).
48 See Boisvert et al. (2012).
49 Wilson and Aponte (1985, p. 239).
50 Ibid., p. 247.
51 Cohen (1998, p. 224).
52 Marks (1991, p. 455).
53 This is the argument of Wilson (1987).
54 Wilson (1991, p. 594).
55 See Greene (1991, p. 240).
56 Wilson (2013).
57 Schelling (1978, p. 138). The italicized words in the quote are Schelling's. It is also the case that housing discrimination and segregation can operate as officially-sanctioned, or de jure, policies of government as documented in Rothstein (2017).
58 Boustan (2010, p. 417).
59 See Bonastia (2006, pp. 52–4).
60 Boustan (2010, pp. 418–19) goes on to explain that the destination for early migration from Mississippi was Chicago and St. Louis, while migrants from Alabama tended to choose Detroit and, to a lesser extent, Chicago and Cleveland. These migration streams had much to do with the railroad infrastructure available in each of these states.
61 For more on governmental strategies aimed at reducing white flight as well as housing and other forms of discrimination, see Bonastia (2006), Li (2009), Pais et al. (2009), and Withers et al. (2008).
62 Mulder (2015).
63 Everton (2015, p. 4).
64 Mulder (2015, p. 3).
65 Peterson and Krivo (2010).
66 Ibid., p. 124.
67 Light and Thomas (2019, p. 690).
68 Felson and Painter-Davis (2012).
69 See Anderson (1994, 1999).
70 Anderson (1999, p. 33).
71 See Hallwas (2008).
72 See Jacobs and Wright (2006).
73 See Parsons (1967).
74 Ibid., p. 342.
75 See Peterson and Krivo (2005) and Weiss and Reid (2005).
76 Portes (1998, p. 6).
77 See Putnam (2000).

78 Anderson (1999, pp. 72–3).
79 Ibid, pp. 68–9.
80 Ibid., p. 75.
81 Wolff et al. (2020).
82 Kubrin (2005).
83 For more on religion as social control, see Chriss (2020a).
84 For the definitive study of the early Puritans, see Erikson (1966).
85 See Wierzbicka (2004). For an overview of the history of moral regulation, see Hunt (1999).
86 Friedenberg (1969).
87 Barringer et al. (2020, p. 281).
88 See Weiss and Zhang (2020).
89 Smith (2011).
90 See Berger (1967).
91 Gouldner (1970, p. 78).
92 Matza (1961).
93 Smith (2011, p. 22).
94 Ibid., p. 28.
95 Chriss (1999d, p. 109).
96 Labaree (1997).
97 Saunders (2007).
98 Glanzer et al. (2018).
99 Ibid., pp. 722–3.
100 Ibid., p. 723.

Chapter 7: Medical Control: Selective Mutism, Autism, and Violence as a Disease

1 This information and other ASD-related material can be found at Autism Speaks, located at https://www.autismspeaks.org/autism-statistics-asd#:~:text=Autism%20 Prevalence,)%2C%20according%20to%202016%20data.&text=Boys%20are%20four%20 times%20more,diagnosed%20with%20autism%20than%20girls.
2 For representative works by these authors, see Foucault (1965), Goffman (1961a), Scheff (1966), and Szasz (1961, 1963). For an overview of the antipsychiatry movement, see Chriss (1999a).
3 Richert (2014).
4 See Markowitz (2006).
5 See Sumner (1994, pp. 214–19).
6 Skene (2002, p. 115).
7 For discussions of selective mutism, see Anstendig (1999), Gordon (2001), Kehle et al. (1998), Kumpulainen et al. (1998), Moldan (2005), and Rye and Ullman (1999).
8 See, e.g., Gordon (2001, p. 83).
9 For a general overview of selective mutism, see Wong (2010).
10 See Anstendig (1999, pp. 418–19).
11 For a general discussion of the medicalization of shyness beyond the specific case of selective mutism, see Scott (2006).
12 See Chriss (1999b, 2007b).
13 See, e.g., Kehle et al. (1998), Kumpulainen et al. (1998), Moldan (2005), and Rye and Ullman (1999).

14 This is from Gordon (2001, p. 86). The work cited in the quote is Kolvin and Fundudis (1981).

15 Anstendig (1999) and Moldan (2005).

16 This case is discussed in Rye and Ullman (1999, pp. 314–21).

17 For this discussion of Cho, I am drawing primarily from chapter IV, titled "The Mental Health History of Seung Hui Cho," from the 2009 document "Mass Shootings at Virginia Tech," available at http://scholar.lib.vt.edu/prevail/docs/April16ReportRev20100106. pdf.

18 This information is from the *New York Times* article, "Files Show University Gunman Denied Homicidal Thoughts," published in 2009 and available at http://www. nytimes.com/2009/08/20/us/20vtech.html.

19 For more on the spectrum concept in the diagnosis of mental illness, see Clark et al. (2017).

20 Johnson et al. (2016, p. 16).

21 This is from the Centers for Disease Control (CDC), located at https://www.cdc.gov/ ncbddd/autism/hcp-dsm.html.

22 Lunch Bunch is one among a range of social skills training programs for children with autism which can be integrated into school settings. See, e.g., Laushey et al. (2009).

23 Piaget (1963).

24 See Nitschke et al. (2020).

25 See Goffman (1971).

26 For more on the social control of food and sex, see Chriss (2010a). For a general overview of the difficulties of dining together for adults on the autism spectrum, see Kinnaird et al. (2019).

27 See Goldschmidt (2018).

28 See Ryan and Räisänen (2008).

29 See Zerbo et al. (2015) and Thom et al. (2019).

30 See Nogay et al. (2021) and Wasilewska and Klukowski (2015).

31 See Jenkinson et al. (2020).

32 See Rogers et al. (2018).

33 Zaboski and Storch (2018).

34 Wakefield (2002).

35 Ibid., pp. 154–5.

36 Ibid., p. 161.

37 Weisheit and Klofas (1998, p. 198).

38 See, e.g., Guetzloe (1992) and McMahon (2000).

39 See Chriss (2004).

40 Cornell (2018, p. 38).

41 See Kerr (2018, p. 95).

42 Newman (2004, pp. 14–15).

43 Prothrow-Stith (1993, p. 138).

44 See Starfield et al. (2008).

45 Cupler et al. (2021, p. 2).

46 Chriss (2015).

47 Guetzloe (1992).

48 McMahon (2000).

49 Guetzloe (1992, p. 8).

50 Szasz (2000, p. 4).

51 See, e.g., Cantor (2000), Montgomery (2000), and Pollack (2000).

52 McDonald (2000, p. 4).

53 Gilligan (2000, p. 1802). See also Hartling and Luchetta (1999).

54 Slutkin et al. (2018a, p. 48).

55 See Greene (2018).

56 Ibid., p. 513. For a rebuttal to Greene, see Slutkin et al. (2018b).

57 See Price-Huish (1997).

58 See Brunner et al. (1993).

59 Zhao et al. (2020, p. 2).

60 Krakowski (2003).

61 See Bernet et al. (2007, p. 1363).

62 Brunner (2006, p. 155).

63 Lorion (2001, pp. 97–8).

64 Ibid., p. 103.

65 See Durch et al. (1997, pp. 345–57).

66 See Dulmus and Hilarski (2002).

67 Fagan and Davies (2004, p. 129).

Chapter 8: Legal Control: Racial Profiling, Hate Crimes, and the Imprisonment Binge

1 Skolnick (1966).

2 Ibid., pp. 217–18.

3 See Holdaway (1983), as cited in Norris et al. (1992, pp. 217–18).

4 These data are available at https://www.census.gov/quickfacts/fact/table/US/PST045219 and https://www.ojjdp.gov/ojstatbb/crime/ucr.asp?table_in=2.

5 These data are from a Bureau of Justice Statistics publication available at https://bjs.ojp.gov/content/pub/pdf/Llgsfp.pdf.

6 Baumgartner et al. (2018, pp. 18–19).

7 See Katz (2019). For a similar argument, see Turner (2021).

8 For the extremely controversial data on IQ differentials by class and race, see Herrnstein and Murray (1994). In addition, see Kincheloe et al. (1996) for criticisms of the authors' interpretation of that data, especially its eugenicist policy implications.

9 Kitcher (1997, p. 280).

10 This position of Kitcher is summarized by Mercer (2020).

11 See Gouldner (1974).

12 This is Leo Strauss's (1965, p. 258) interpretation of Rousseau's view of science.

13 Although defunding the police is a "hot potato" issue, a balanced assessment of the controversy can be found in Bratton and Knobler (2021).

14 Davis (2003).

15 See, e.g., Bouza (2001), Eldredge (1998), Harris (2003), and Tonry (1996).

16 Batton and Kadleck (2004, p. 33).

17 Withrow (2004, p. 224). For an excellent overview and summary of the causes and consequence of racial profiling, see Dunn and Reed (2011).

18 Mac Donald (2003, p. 10).

19 See, e.g., Fredrickson and Siljander (2002) and Harris (2003).

20 Grogger and Ridgeway (2006).

21 These stops took place within the borders of the city of Oakland and hence did not include highway stops, which were the responsibility of the California Highway Patrol.

22 Grogger and Ridgeway (2006, p. 884).

23 Worden et al. (2012).

24 Ibid., p. 98.

25 Taniguchi et al. (2016, p. 1). Like other studies utilizing the veil of darkness method, this study found no evidence of racial profiling in the Greensboro, NC Police Department. A follow-up study of the Durham, NC Police Department (Taniguchi et al., 2017) found that officer-level factors accounted for roughly 10 percent of the variability in the rate of Black drivers stopped by the police.

26 Worden et al. (2012, p. 97).

27 Ibid., p. 102.

28 See Abrahams (2020).

29 See, e.g., Horrace and Rohlin (2016).

30 See Kalinowski et al. (2019).

31 Stacey and Bonner (2021).

32 See Regoeczi and Kent (2014).

33 For a summary of this argument, see Bloch (2021) and Welsh et al. (2021).

34 Regoeczi and Kent (2014, p. 201).

35 Linguistic profiling is engaging in discrimination against persons based upon their inferred race or other characteristics solely from hearing them speak, which is an illicit form of informal control. For studies of linguistic profiling in rental housing and insurance markets, see Massey and Lundy (2001) and Squires and Chadwick (2006). For a general overview of linguistic profiling, see Baugh (2018).

36 Even with the documented presence of hates groups, data indicate that the vast majority of hate crimes are perpetrated by individuals with no known connection to such hate groups. In effect, hate crime offenders tend to be "lone wolves." For a summary, see Ryan and Leeson (2011).

37 These incidents are reported in Levin and McDevitt (2002, pp. 5–6).

38 See Jenness and Grattet (2001).

39 Cogan (2002, p. 174).

40 Ibid.

41 These data are summarized in Perry (2001, pp. 252–3).

42 These data are available at https://www.justice.gov/hatecrimes/hate-crime-statistics.

43 These data are available at https://www.statista.com/statistics/737930/number-of-hate-crimes-in-the-us-by-motivation/.

44 See Disha et al. (2011).

45 See Dhanani and Franz (2020).

46 See Xu et al. (2021).

47 For more on this story, see https://www.nytimes.com/live/2021/03/17/us/shooting-atlanta-acworth.

48 For more on this story, see https://www.wsbtv.com/news/local/atlanta/da-seek-death-penalty-hate-crimes-charges-atlanta-spa-shootings/TSFCZFBZMRB7XNKV5TNRYAKPWA/.

49 Levin (1999, p. 11).

50 Abrahamson et al. (1994, p. 517).

51 See Levin (1999, pp. 12–19).

52 See Blumstein (2003).

53 Tonry and Farrington (2005).

54 These data are available at https://www.pewresearch.org/fact-tank/2021/08/16/americas-incarceration-rate-lowest-since-1995/#:~:text=At%20the%20end%20of%202019,custody%20of%20locally%20run%20jails.

55 Western et al. (2004, p. 1).
56 The term "imprisonment binge" to describe recent American penal philosophy and practice has been used by Austin et al. (2003).
57 See Pratt (2010).
58 Rothman (2002a [1980], p. 433).
59 Shelden (2004, p. 6).
60 For more on the drug treatment court, see Chriss (2002) and Nolan (2001).
61 Tonry (1999, p. 427).
62 See especially Caplow and Simon (1999).
63 Tonry (1999, p. 429).
64 Some speculate that trust in government declined precipitously beginning with the Watergate scandal of the Nixon Administration in 1974. But this speculation is not warranted. In 1968 the percentage of people who did not trust the government to "do the right thing" stood at 37 percent but shot up to 76 percent in 1972 (Gouldner 1979, p. 90). This increase predated the Watergate scandal by a good two years.
65 These survey data were summarized in Study#6056, and the 2005 data were gathered via interviews of 1,013 Americans that took place between September 9 and 12, 2005, conducted by NBC News and the *Wall Street Journal*. The full document may be found at http://online.wsj.com/public/resources/documents/poll20050914.pdf.
66 See http://www.npr.org/templates/story/story.php?storyId=126047343.
67 The figures from 2014 onward are from the Pew Research Center, located at https://www.pewresearch.org/politics/2019/04/11/public-trust-in-government-1958-2019/.
68 For examples of critical analyses of three strikes laws, see Austin et al. (1999) and Schmertmann et al. (1998).
69 Garland (2001, p. 55).
70 Ibid., p. 56.
71 Anderson (1995, p. 14).
72 Ibid., pp. 5–6.
73 Garland (2001, p. 11). See also Garland (2003, pp. 64–9). Although the rehabilitative ideal is in deep decline, there are still aspects of the therapeutic ethos evident within the operation of the criminal justice system, especially for those crimes that many consider to be illnesses such as drug use, excessive gambling, and other so-called addictions. For discussions of therapeutic justice as applied to the conceptualization and operation of drug courts, see Nolan (2001).
74 Garland (2001, p. 9).
75 These data are from the Pew Research Center, available at https://www.pewresearch.org/fact-tank/2018/05/02/americas-incarceration-rate-is-at-a-two-decade-low/.
76 Sharkey et al. (2017, p. 1215).
77 For a summary of these and other policy innovations, see Karstedt et al. (2019).
78 See Enns (2016, p. 163).
79 See Schoenfeld et al. (2019).
80 Ibid., p. 151.

Chapter 9: Terrorism and Social Control

1 See Andrews (2012).
2 Forst (2009, p. 5).
3 Skoll (2010, p. 65).
4 See Jensen et al. (2020).

5 For a summary of the "clash of barbarisms" which terrorism and state responses to it set in motion, see Achcar (2006).

6 For more on the Abu Ghraib scandal, see Keller (2006) and Skoll (2010).

7 See Stampnitzky (2013).

8 This definition is available at https://www.fbi.gov/investigate/terrorism.

9 For more on the incel phenomenon, see DeCook (2021) and Scaptura and Boyle (2020). As I was wrapping up writing in mid-2021, news broke of an incel plot being foiled which targeted female students at Ohio State University. For more on this story, see https://www.msn.com/en-us/news/crime/notes-found-in-ohio-home-of-self-described-incel-referenced-possible-mass-shooting-at-osu-court-records-say/ar-AAMpNNL?ocid=hplocalnews.

10 For more on the role of the Internet in political extremism and terrorism, see Conway (2017) and Meleagrou-Hitchins et al. (2017).

11 In addition, it is worth noting that LaFree et al. (2018, p. 252) found that "of all the independent variables, radical peers is the strongest predictor of violence."

12 See https://thehill.com/blogs/blog-briefing-room/news/556768-capitol-riot-caused-nearly-15-million-in-damage-federal.

13 See Evans and Giroux (2020).

14 More on this story is available at https://abcnews.go.com/Politics/biden-shine-light-tulsa-race-massacre-remarks-meeting/story?id=78020930.

15 See the report at https://www.washingtonpost.com/technology/2020/09/14/violent-antipolice-memes-surge/.

16 Silva et al. (2019).

17 See, e.g., Gruenewald (2011).

18 See Bangstad (2014), Borchgrevink (2013), and Jacobsen and Maier-Katkin (2015).

19 Laugerud and Langballe (2017).

20 The points of this list have been assembled from Anderson (2015), Muravchik (2014), and Rifkin (2017). Additionally, with its surprising win in the 2006 Palestinian Legislative Council elections, Hamas transitioned from a revolutionary terrorist organization to the political center as a recognized governmental entity for Palestine, more or less existing as a "state within a state" (Sela, 2015, p. 31).

21 Primoratz (2006, p. 27).

22 See, e.g., Gelvin (2021) and Slater (2015).

23 A good example of this is the spirited defense of Palestine against unwarranted Israeli aggression offered by Thomas Suarez (2017). Suarez goes so far as to argue that terrorism literally created the Israeli state and established a pernicious form of Zionism. This position is consistent with that of Anderson (2015).

24 For more on the necessity doctrine as used as a defense for terrorism, see Cohan (2006).

25 See the discussion in Chriss (2018a).

26 See, e.g., Baker (2002), Eland (2003), Hardin (2004), Mythen and Walklate (2006), and Welch (2003).

27 This discussion of controversial sections of the USA PATRIOT Act is informed by Krislov (2004) and Lithwick and Turner (2004).

28 Lithwick and Turner (2004, p. 100).

29 Crotty (2004, p. 199).

30 Deflem (2004, p. 80).

31 See Crowther (2000).

32 For a summary of these sunset provisions, see "USA PATRIOT Act Sunset: Provisions

that Expire on December 31, 2005," CRS Report for Congress. Document available at www.fas.org/sgp/crs/intel/RL32186.pdf.

33 Information from "Bush Signs Tempered USA Patriot Act," the *Plain Dealer*, p. A8, Friday, March 10, 2006.

34 For more on President Obama's reauthorization of these elements of the USA Patriot Act, see http://www.mainjustice.com/2010/02/27/obama-signs-patriot-act-reauthorization/.

35 For more on prisoner abuse at Abu Ghraib, see Porpora et al. (2013).

36 Mohamad (2019, p. 45).

37 Ibid., p. 27.

38 This is from the document titled *National Strategy for Counterterrorism of the United States of America*, which is available at https://www.dni.gov/files/NCTC/documents/news_documents/NSCT.pdf.

39 For more on this story, see https://www.businessinsider.com/house-cancels-vote-fisa-patriot-act-bill-trump-veto-2020-5.

40 All of this and more is summarized in Ramirez and Clem (2021).

41 For more on this story, see https://thehill.com/homenews/administration/312605-schumer-trump-being-really-dumb-by-going-after-intelligence-community.

42 This document is available at https://www.whitehouse.gov/briefing-room/statements-releases/2021/03/03/interim-national-security-strategic-guidance/.

43 bin Laden (2006, pp. 6–7).

44 This incident is described in Burleigh (2008, p. 348).

45 Pape (2003, p. 344).

46 Ibid.

47 Nunn (2004, p. 2).

48 "Bush Says 10 al-Qaida Plots Foiled since Sept. 11," *The Plain Dealer*, October 7, 2005, p. A12.

49 Shay (2004, pp. 1–33).

50 Ibid., p. 257.

51 These data are reported in a study titled "Background Report: The Fatal Terrorism of al-Qa'ida," published in May 2011 by the National Consortium for the Study of Terrorism and Responses to Terrorism. The study is available at http://www.start.umd.edu.

52 For more on gait analysis, see http://www.telegraph.co.uk/news/worldnews/northamerica/usa/2679057/Spy-satellites-could-analyse-shadows-from-space-to-help-identify-terrorists.html.

53 The phrase "long hunt" used in this section is from Peter Bergen (2011). Bergen (2011, pp. 335–49) provides a careful documentation of the decade-long hunt for bin Laden.

54 Information on the death of bin Laden was pieced together from http://www.msnbc.msn.com/id/42852700/ns/world_news-death_of_bin_laden/t/us-forces-kill-osama-bin-laden-pakistan/ and http://abcnews.go.com/US/osama-bin-laden-dead-navy-seal-team-responsible/story?id=13509739.

55 Mansel (2011).

56 See Siniver and Lucas (2016).

57 See Wasserstein (2017).

58 See Rath (2017).

59 Sylvester (2020).

60 Seeberg (2016, p. 102).

61 For a report on this incident, see https://www.cbsnews.com/video/isis-video-shows-jordanian-pilot-being-burned-to-death/.

62 For more on ISIS's use of media spectacle to shock the consciousness of the civilized world, see Baele (2020).

63 Stern and Berger (2015, pp. 19–20).

64 Ibid., pp. 44–5.

65 Hawley (2017, p. 160).

66 See Impara (2018).

67 Facebook has come under fire for the algorithm it uses to generate "likes" and friend recommendations for users of the platform. Victims of terrorism argue that, even unwittingly, Facebook facilitates outreach by terror organizations and may bring them into contact with such groups, thus potentially exposing them to ongoing terror investigations and possible criminal liability. For more on this issue, see Yost (2021).

68 See Macnair and Frank (2018) and Peresin and Cervone (2015).

69 For more on the Gulf "angel investors" providing private funding to ISIS, see the story at https://www.nbcncws.com/storyline/isis-terror/who-s-funding-isis-wealthy-gulf-angel-investors-officials-say-n208006.

70 See Bergen (2016, p. 250).

71 See Jones (2018).

72 See Ibrahim (2020, p. 50).

73 See Oosterveld and Bloem (2017, p. 15).

74 For a summary of this event, see the *Washington Post* report at https://www.washingtonpost.com/politics/whimpering-screaming-and-crying-a-beautiful-dog-trumps-bombastic-account-of-the-baghdadi-raid/2019/10/27/c50c3444-f8cc-11e9-9534-e0dbcc9f5683_story.html.

75 See Valcore and Buckler (2020).

76 For more on the problematics of the lone wolf designation even in light of the decline of ISIS and other terror organizations, see Beydoun (2018) and Schuurman et al. (2019).

77 Haggerty and Gazso (2005).

78 "Sewer District Wants Option of Armed Police," *The Plain Dealer*, Wednesday, June 29, 2005, p. B1.

79 See Beck (2002) and Spence (2005).

80 Knorr Cetina (2005, p. 213).

81 On the issue of a resurgent ISIS, see the story at https://www.wsj.com/articles/islamic-state-seeks-revival-in-christian-countries-11618498283.

82 On the Taliban's takeover of the Afghani government, see Giustozzi (2021).

Chapter 10: Conclusion: The Future of Social Control

1 Lyon (2007).

2 Spencer (1897b, p. 244).

3 Weber (1968).

4 See, e.g., Fukuyama (2011).

5 Both Great Britain and Canada are constitutional monarchies. For more on the Canadian Crown, see Jackson (2013).

6 See Chriss (2020b, p. 20).

7 See Schmitt (2005 [1922], p. 5).

8 See, e.g., Fatovic (2009).

9 This is from an online article updated on January 18, 2018, authored by Nathan Vanderklippe and published in the *Globe and Mail*, available at: https://www. theglobeandmail.com/news/world/chinese-blacklist-an-early-glimpse-of-sweeping-new-social-credit-control/article37493300/#comments.

10 Critics of the social credit system include Qiang (2019), Jiang and Fu (2018), Liang et al. (2018), and Economy (2019). Bing Song (2019, p. 35) warns that Western observers of China's social credit system may be overstating its dangers, suggesting that "Rather than instantly dismissing China's unconventional governance innovations, we need an open-minded discussion of the pros and cons – one that is sensitive to the challenges and priorities of different cultural and political contexts."

11 This is from Article 19, a human rights organization based in London that publishes a number of reports and policy positions. The article being cited here is titled "Emotional Entanglement: China's Emotion Recognition Market and Its Implications for Human Rights" (Article 19, 2021, p. 18). The website is https://www.article19.org/.

12 For a summary of Foucault's work on governmentality and biopolitics, see Dean (2013).

13 For more on this story, see https://losangeles.cbslocal.com/2020/03/31/coronavirus-los-angeles-eric-garcetti-snitches-get-rewards/.

14 See Marín-Morales et al. (2018).

15 Zamkah et al. (2020).

16 Howell et al. (2018, p. 2).

17 See Deleuze (1992) and Lyon and Haggerty (2012).

18 For more on Star Gate and other covert military operations exploring the world of the paranormal, see Smith (2004).

19 This information is taken from a 2008 document published by the Department of Homeland Security titled "Future Attribute Screening Technology (FAST) Project" (FAST, 2008).

20 See Egbert and Paul (2019, p. 109) and Piro et al. (2019).

21 A summary of this project is available at https://cordis.europa.eu/project/id/218197.

22 For more on intelligent transportation systems (ITS), see Monahan (2010, pp. 99–112).

23 See Chimamiwa et al. (2021).

24 See Youssef et al. (2015) and Youssef and Okada (2016).

25 Lyon (2007, p. 14).

26 For discussions of countersurveillance and various forms of resistance, see Foucault (1978) and Monahan (2010).

27 For more on sousveillance, see Thomsen (2019).

28 For more on scopophilia and synopticism, see Lyon (2006).

29 See Harper and Taylor (2009) and Harper (2010).

30 See Piroozfar et al. (2019).

31 Cohen and Felson (1979).

32 For more on this crime data, see https://econofact.org/crime-in-the-time-of-covid.

33 Marx (2015).

34 An *Atlantic* magazine article from 2016 goes into this in more detail. See https://www.theatlantic.com/technology/archive/2016/07/what-if-cameras-stopped-telling-the-truth/491150/.

35 For more on dataveillance and digital surveillance, see Gilliom and Monahan (2013), Marx (2016), and Parenti (2003).

36 For a collection of essays in defense of intuition-based decision-making, see Liebowitz (2015).

37 See Beniger (1986).

38 Weber (1968, p. 957).

39 Gouldner (1952).

40 See Baumgartner et al. (2018).

41 See Paul and Baron (2007). Connected with this, Klapp (1991, pp. 170–80) deals with the related issues of information overload and meaning lag.

42 See Farmer and Geanakoplos (2009).

43 Parsons and Platt (1973, p. 310).

44 Klapp (1991, p. 4). For an overview of Klapp's career and publications, see Best (2018).

45 See Silberman (2016). Indeed, numbers or the crowd is one of the key radiant points of social control according to Edward Ross (1900). For more on Ross's argument, see Chriss (2019).

46 See Haider-Markel and Joslyn (2018).

47 See Fausto-Sterling (2000). For the rebuttal to Fausto-Sterling's figures, see Sax (2002).

48 This data is summarized in Dunning et al. (2004).

49 Klapp (1991, p. 4).

50 See Murray (2019).

51 This story and interview are available at https://www.hawaiinewsnow.com/2020/12/08/denied-parole-times-john-lennons-killer-accepts-he-may-die-prison/.

52 This infamous quote was also used as the title of a book critical of Trump. See Rucker and Leonnig (2020).

53 Grob and Horwitz (2010, p. 23).

54 Frances (2013, p. 209).

55 Ibid., p. 104.

56 This study is discussed at https://www.eviemagazine.com/post/over-50-percent-white-liberal-women-under-30-mental-health-condition?fbclid=IwAR2qs9xSQuiZdMwgM1x1MZfw4d-gkufxZUv1Lny8V7__VG6EmOibV6-JlO8.

57 See, e.g., Brown (2004), Burney (2005), and Faulkner (2003).

58 Garland (2001, p. 124).

59 The idea of contractual injunction as it relates to the discourse of responsibilization was developed by McCarthy (2010).

60 Buerger and Mazerolle (1999, p. 402).

61 See Feeley and Simon (1994) and Simon and Feeley (2003).

62 Scared Straight is a juvenile awareness program in which at-risk youth are taken to prisons to meet face-to-face with adult prisoners. It is hoped that youth who meet up with these prisoners will be motivated to give up their delinquency for fear of becoming them. Evaluations (see, e.g., Petrosino et al., 2003) indicate that it has not been effective in reducing delinquency or later criminality among youth who participate in the program.

63 Feeley and Simon (1994, p. 173).

64 This discussion is taken from Lianos (2000).

65 See Rose (2000).

66 For further discussions of social sorting through the use of automated socio-technical environments, see Lianos (2000), Lyon (2003, 2004), Marx (1995), and Staples (2000).

67 For a discussion of various neighborhood apps and the role of smartphones in coordinating contacts and messaging, see Ceccato (2019). For a listing of these apps, see https://newdream.org/blog/top-10-neighborhood-platforms-for-connecting-and-collaborating.

68 For more on this incident, see Wright and Unah (2017).

69 Lianos (2012, p. 146).

70 For more on system versus lifeworld, see Chriss (1995) and Habermas (1984).

71 This position is similar to the desocialization of social control described by Lianos (2012) and Deleuze's (1992) society of control in which "dividuals" are caught in various webs and snarls in the transition from lifeworld to system and back again.

72 See Chriss (1999b, p. 195), Crossley (2003), and Habermas (1984).

73 See Ward (1903, 1906).

74 See Levin (2000, p. 17).

75 As opposed to earlier times when police for the most part relied on coercive force whenever engaging citizens during routine patrol, under community policing officers presumably act with more sensitivity and compassion. To what extent this is actually occurring has been investigated in Meliala (2001).

76 This new form of hybridity is best described as police playing the role of "contact men," with emphasis on police as boundary-spanning multitaskers trained in human relations to better serve an increasingly diverse client population. For more on this argument, see Chriss (2011).

77 See Somers (2005) for an excellent discussion of how the concept of social capital smuggles in aspects of responsibilization, such as the examples given in this paragraph.

78 For discussions of hybrid courts and similar undertakings which seek to combine compassion and coercion, see Chriss (2002), Dorf and Fagan (2003), and Nolan (2003). Squires (2006, p. 162) uses language similar to my own when he refers to the English anti-social behaviour ordinances (ASBOs) as "the blurring of care and control processes."

79 Herbert (2006, p. 139).

80 This idea of known unknowns, as the next step by which the US Department of Defense is conceptualizing possible future terrorist scenarios, however wild or fantastic they may be, has been developed in a provisional publication made available by the US Army War College (see Freier 2008). This is the ongoing project of refining AI algorithms to better predict crime, terrorism, disease pandemics, and other large-scale events (see King et al. 2020).

81 This document is available at https://www.hsdl.org.

82 This is the argument made by Sutrop and Laas-Mikko (2012).

References

Abbott, Jessica, Shelly A. McGrath, and David C. May. 2020. "The Effects of Police Effort on Victims' Fear of Crime." *American Journal of Criminal Justice* 45: 880–98.

Abrahams, Scott. 2020. "Officer Differences in Traffic Stops of Minority Drivers." *Labour Economics* 67: 1–11.

Abrahamson, Shirley S., Susan Craighead, and Daniel N. Abrahamson. 1994. "Words and Sentences: Penalty Enhancement for Hate Crimes." *University of Arkansas Little Rock Law Review* 16 (4): 515–42.

Achcar, Gilbert. 2006. *The Clash of Barbarisms: The Making of the New World Disorder*. Boulder, CO: Paradigm.

Acho, Jacqueline and Eva Basilion. 2018. *Empathy Deficit Disorder: Healing from Our Mix-Ups about Work, Home, and Sex*. Shaker Heights, OH: Acho Basilion Press.

Adams, Richard N. 1982. "The Emergence of the Regulatory Society." Pp. 137–63 in *Social Control: Views from the Social Sciences*, edited by J.P. Gibbs. Beverly Hills, CA: Sage.

Adler, Patricia A. and Peter Adler. 2006. "The Deviance Society." *Deviant Behavior* 27 (2): 129–48.

Adler, Patricia A., Peter Adler, and Andrea Fontana. 1987. "Everyday Life Sociology." *Annual Review of Sociology* 13: 217–35.

Agamben, Giorgio. 1998. *Homo Sacer: Sovereign Power and Bare Life*, translated by D. Heller-Roazen. Stanford, CA: Stanford University Press.

Agamben, Giorgio. 2021. *Where Are We Now? The Epidemic as Politics*, translated by V. Dani. London: Eris.

Agan, Amanda Y., Jennifer L. Doleac, and Anna Harvey. 2021. "Misdemeanor Prosecution." NBER Working Paper Series, Working Paper 28600. Cambridge, MA: National Bureau of Economic Research.

Agger, Ben. 2002. *Postponing the Postmodern: Sociological Practices, Selves and Theories*. Boulder, CO: Rowman and Littlefield.

Alexander, Jeffrey C. 1983. *The Modern Reconstruction of Classical Thought: Talcott Parsons*. Berkeley, CA: University of California Press.

Alexander, Jeffrey C., Ron Eyerman, Bernhard Giesen, Neil J. Smelser, and Piotr Sztompka. 2004. *Cultural Trauma and Collective Identity*. Berkeley, CA: University of California Press.

Alpert, Harry. 1939. *Emile Durkheim and His Sociology*. New York: Columbia University Press.

Althaus, M., Y. Groen, A.A. Wijers, H. Noltes, O. Tucha, and P.J. Hoekstra. 2015. "Oxytocin Enhances Orienting to Social Information in a Selective Group of High-Functioning Male Adults with Autism Spectrum Disorder." *Neuropsychologia* 79: 53–69.

Altheide, David L. 1992. "Gonzo Justice." *Symbolic Interaction* 15 (1): 69–86.

Altheide, David L. 2013. "Media Logic, Social Control, and Fear." *Communication Theory* 23: 223–38.

Anderson, David C. 1995. *Crime and the Politics of Hysteria*. New York: Random House.

Anderson, Elijah. 1994. "The Code of the Streets." *Atlantic Monthly* 273: 81–94.

Anderson, Elijah. 1999. *Code of the Street: Decency, Violence, and the Moral Life of the Inner City*. New York: Norton.

Anderson, Perry. 2015. "The House of Zion." *New Left Review* 96: 5–37.

Andrews, David. 2012. "Toward a More Valid Definition of 'Pornography.'" *Journal of Popular Culture* 45 (3): 457–77.

Anstendig, Karin D. 1999. "Is Selective Mutism an Anxiety Disorder? Rethinking Its DSM-IV Classification." *Journal of Anxiety Disorders* 13 (4): 417–34.

Armstrong, Dorsey. 2008. "Rewriting the Chronicle Tradition: The Alliterative *Morte Arthure* and Arthur's Sword of Peace." *Parergon* 25 (1): 81–101.

Armstrong, Thomas. 2003. "Attention Deficit Hyperactivity Disorder in Children: One Consequence of the Rise of Technologies and Demise of Play." Pp. 161–75 in *All Work and No Play: How Education Reforms Are Harming Our Preschoolers*, edited by S. Olfman. Westport, CT: Praeger.

Arnett, Jeffrey Jensen. 1995. "Broad and Narrow Socialization: The Family in the Context of a Cultural Theory." *Journal of Marriage and the Family* 57 (3): 617–28.

Article 19. 2021. "Emotional Entanglement: China's Emotion Recognition Market and Its Implications for Human Rights." A19/DIG/2021/001. London: Article 19. Available at: https://www.article19.org/wp-content/uploads/2021/01/ER-Tech-China-Report.pdf

Asch, Solomon E. 1951. "Effects of Group Pressure upon the Modification and Distortion of Judgments." Pp. 177–90 in *Groups, Leadership and Men: Research in Human Relations*, edited by H. Guetzkow. Pittsburgh, PA: Carnegie Press.

Asch, Solomon E. 1952. *Social Psychology*. Englewood Cliffs, NJ: Prentice-Hall.

Ashworth, Andrew. 1997. "Sentencing." Pp. 1095–135 in *Oxford Handbook of Criminology*, 2nd ed., edited by M. Maguire, R. Morgan, and R. Reiner. Oxford: Oxford University Press.

Austin, James, John Clark, Patricia Hardyman, and Henry D. Alan. 1999. "The Impact of 'Three Strikes and You're Out.'" *Punishment and Society* 1 (2): 131–62.

Austin, James, John Irwin, and Charles Kubrin. 2003. "It's About Time: America's Imprisonment Binge." Pp. 433–69 in *Punishment and Social Control*, enlarged 2nd edn., edited by T.G. Blomberg and S. Cohen. New York: Aldine de Gruyter.

Baele, Stephane J. 2020. "Introduction – Full-Spectrum Propaganda: Appraising the 'IS Moment' in Propaganda History." Pp. 1–19 in *ISIS Propaganda: A Full-Spectrum Extremist Message*, edited by S.J. Baele, K.A. Boyd, and T.G. Coan. New York: Oxford University Press.

Bagaric, Mirko. 2015. "Rich Offender, Poor Offender: Why It (Sometimes) Matters in Sentencing." *Minnesota Journal of Law & Inequality* 33 (1): 1–51.

Baker, Nancy V. 2002. "The Law: The Impact of Antiterrorism Policies on Separation of Powers: Assessing John Ashcroft's Role." *Presidential Studies Quarterly* 32 (4): 765–78.

Ballard, Karen and Mary Ann Elston. 2005. "Medicalisation: A Multi-dimensional Concept." *Social Theory and Health* 3 (3): 228–41.

Bangstad, Sindre. 2014. *Anders Breivik and the Rise of Islamophobia*. London: Zed Books.

Barringer, M.N., J.E. Sumerau, and David A. Gay. 2020. "Generational Variation in Young Adults' Attitudes toward Legal Abortion: Contextualizing the Role of Religion." *Social Currents* 7 (3): 279–96.

Bastomski, Sara and Philip Smith. 2017. "Gender, Fear, and Public Places: How Negative Encounters with Strangers Harms Women." *Sex Roles* 76: 73–88.

Batton, Candice and Colleen Kadleck. 2004. "Theoretical and Methodological Issues in Racial Profiling Research." *Police Quarterly* 7 (1): 30–64.

Baugh, John. 2018. *Linguistics in Pursuit of Justice*. Cambridge: Cambridge University Press.

Baumgartner, Frank R., Derek A. Epp, and Kelsey Shoub. 2018. *Suspect Citizens: What 20 Million Traffic Stops Tell Us about Policing and Race*. Cambridge: Cambridge University Press.

Beck, Ulrich. 2002. "The Terrorist Threat: World Risk Society Revisited." *Theory, Culture and Society* 19 (4): 39–55.

Becker, Howard S. 1973. *Outsiders: Studies in the Sociology of Deviance*. New York: Free Press.

Beniger, James R. 1986. *The Control Revolution: Technological and Economic Origins of the Information Society*. Cambridge, MA: Harvard University Press.

Bentham, Jeremy. 1998 [1843]. "Introduction to the Principles of Morals and Legislation." Pp. 23–39 in *Criminological Theory: Selected Classic Readings*, 2nd ed., edited by F.P. Williams III and M.D. McShane. Cincinnati, OH: Anderson Publishing.

Bergen, Peter. 2011. *The Longest War: The Enduring Conflict between America and al-Qaeda*. New York: Free Press.

Bergen, Peter. 2016. *United States of Jihad*. New York: Crown Publishers.

Berger, Bennett M. 1967. "Hippie Morality – More Old than New." *Transaction* 5 (2): 19–27.

Bernet, William, Cindy L. Vnencak-Jones, Nita Farahaney, and Stephen A. Montgomery. 2007. "Bad Nature, Bad Nurture, and Testimony Regarding *MAOA* and *SLC6A4* Genotyping at Murder Trials." *Journal of Forensic Sciences* 52 (6): 1362–71.

Best, Joel. 1999. *Random Violence: How We Talk about New Crimes and New Victims*. Berkeley, CA: University of California Press.

Best, Joel. 2018. "Outside the Interactionist Mainstream: The Contributions of Orrin E. Klapp." *Symbolic Interaction* 41 (4): 533–46.

Beydoun, Khaled A. 2018. "Lone Wolf Terrorism: Types, Stripes, and Double Standards." *Northwestern University Law Review* 112 (5): 1213–44.

bin Laden, Osama. 2006. "In His Own Words: Excerpts from Osama bin Laden's Messages." Pp. 1–8 in *Terrorism and Homeland Security*, edited by D.K. Gupta. Belmont, CA: Wadsworth.

Bittner, Egon. 1970. *The Functions of the Police in Modern Society*. Chevy Chase, MD: National Institute of Mental Health.

Bittner, Egon. 2003. "Staffing and Training Problem-Oriented Police." Pp. 151–8 in *Punishment and Social Control*, 2nd edn., edited by T.G. Blomberg and S. Cohen. Hawthorne, NY: Aldine de Gruyter.

Black, Donald. 1983. "Crime as Social Control." *American Sociological Review* 48 (1): 34–45.

Black, Donald. 1998. *The Social Structure of Right and Wrong*, revised edn. San Diego, CA: Academic Press.

Black, Donald. 2011. *Moral Time*. Oxford: Oxford University Press.

Bloch, Stefano. 2021. "Policing Car Space and the Legal Liminality of the Automobile." *Progress in Human Geography* 45 (1): 136–55.

Blomberg, Thomas G. and Karol Lucken. 2000. *American Penology: A History of Control*. Hawthorne, NY: Aldine de Gruyter.

Blumstein, Alfred. 2003. "Stability of Punishment: What Happened and What Next?" Pp. 255–69 in *Punishment and Social Control*, enlarged 2nd edn., edited by T.G. Blomberg and S. Cohen. New York: Aldine de Gruyter.

Boisvert, Danielle, Jamie Vaske, Justine Taylor, and John P. Wright. 2012. "The Effects of Differential Parenting on Sibling Differences in Self-Control and Delinquency among Brother-Sister Pairs." *Criminal Justice Review* 37 (1): 5–23.

Bonastia, Christopher. 2006. *Knocking on the Door: The Federal Government's Attempt to Desegregate the Suburbs*. Princeton, NJ: Princeton University Press.

Borchgrevink, Aage. 2013. *A Norwegian Tragedy: Anders Behring Breivik and the Massacre on Utøya*, translated by G. Puzey. Malden, MA: Polity Press.

Boustan, Leah Platt. 2010. "Was Postwar Suburbanization 'White Flight'? Evidence from the Black Migration." *Quarterly Journal of Economics* 125 (1): 417–43.

Bouza, Anthony V. 2001. *Police Unbound: Corruption, Abuse, and Heroism by the Boys in Blue*. Amherst, NY: Prometheus Books.

Bradford, Tonya Williams and John F. Sherry, Jr. 2013. "Orchestrating Rituals through Retailers: An Examination of Gift Registry." *Journal of Retailing* 89 (2): 158–75.

Bratton, Bill and Peter Knobler. 2021. *The Profession: A Memoir of Community, Race, and the Arc of Policing in America*. New York: Penguin.

Braun, Kathrin. 2021. *Biopolitics and Historic Justice: Coming to Terms with the Injuries of Normality*. Bielefeld: Transcript Verlag.

Brazil, I.A., J.D.M. van Dongen, J.H.R. Maes, R.B. Mars, and A.R. Baskin-Sommers. 2018. "Classification and Treatment of Antisocial Individuals: From Behavior to Biocognition." *Neuroscience and Biobehavioral Reviews* 91: 259–77.

Broeker, Galen. 1961. "Robert Peel and the Peace Preservation Force." *Journal of Modern History* 33 (4): 363–73.

Brown, Alison P. 2004. "Anti-Social Behaviour, Crime Control and Social Control." *The Howard Journal* 43 (2): 203–11.

Brunner, Han G. 2006. "MAOA Deficiency and Abnormal Behaviour: Perspectives on an Association." Pp. 155–67 in *Genetics of Criminal and Antisocial Behaviour*, vol. 194 of the Ciba Foundation Symposium, edited by G.R. Bock and J.A. Goode. Chichester, UK: Wiley.

Brunner, H.G., M. Nelen, X.O. Breakefield, H.H. Ropers, and B.A. van Oost. 1993. "Abnormal Behavior Associated with a Point Mutation in the Structural Gene for Monoamine Oxidase A." *Science* 262 (5133): 578–80.

Buerger, Michael E. and Lorraine Green Mazerolle. 1999. "Third-Party Policing: Theoretical Analysis of an Emerging Trend." Pp. 402–26 in *The Police and Society: Touchstone Readings*, 2nd edn., edited by V.E. Kappeler. Prospect Heights, IL: Waveland Press.

Bugdol, Marek. 2018. *A Different Approach to Work Discipline*. Cham: Palgrave Macmillan.

Burleigh, Michael. 2008. *Blood and Rage: A Cultural History of Terrorism*. Hammersmith, UK: Harper Press.

Burney, Elizabeth. 2005. *Making People Behave: Anti-Social Behaviour, Politics, and Policy*. Cullompton, UK: Willan.

Cahnman, Werner J. 1981. "Hobbes, Toennies, Vico: Starting Points in Sociology." Pp. 16–38 in *The Future of the Sociological Classics*, edited by B. Rhea. London: Allen and Unwin.

Campbell, Bradley and Jason Manning. 2018. *The Rise of Victimhood Culture: Microaggressions, Safe Spaces, and the New Culture Wars*. Cham: Palgrave Macmillan.

Cantor, Joanne. 2000. "Media Violence." *Journal of Adolescent Health* 27 (2): 30–4.

Caplow, Theodore and Jonathan Simon. 1999. "Understanding Prison Policy and Population Trends." *Crime and Justice: A Review of Research* 26: 63–120.

Castells, Manuel. 1996a. *The Information Age: Economy, Society and Culture. Volume I, The Rise of the Network Society*. Oxford: Blackwell Publishers.

Castells, Manuel. 1996b. "The Net and the Self: Working Notes for a Critical Theory of the Informational." *Critique of Anthropology* 16 (1): 9–38.

Ceccato, Vania. 2019. "Eyes and Apps on the Streets: From Surveillance to Sousveillance Using Smartphones." *Criminal Justice Review* 44 (1): 25–41.

Chao, Georgia T., Anne M. O'Leary-Kelly, Samantha Wolf, Howard J. Klein, and Philip D. Gardner. 1994. "Organizational Socialization: Its Content and Consequences." *Journal of Applied Psychology* 79 (5): 730–43.

Chimamiwa, Gibson, Marjan Alirezaie, Federico Pecora, and Amy Loutfi. 2021. "Multi-Sensor Dataset of Human Activities in a Smart Home Environment." *Data in Brief* 34: 106632.

Chriss, James J. 1995. "Habermas, Goffman, and Communicative Action: Implications for Professional Practice." *American Sociological Review* 60 (4): 545–65.

Chriss, James J. 1999a. "Introduction." Pp. 1–29 in *Counseling and the Therapeutic State*, edited by J.J. Chriss. New York: Aldine de Gruyter.

Chriss, James J. 1999b. "The Family under Siege." Pp. 187–98 in *Counseling and the Therapeutic State*, edited by J.J. Chriss. New York: Aldine de Gruyter.

Chriss, James J. 1999c. "Role Distance and the Negational Self." Pp. 64–80 in *Goffman and Social Organization*, edited by G.W.H. Smith. London: Routledge.

Chriss, James J. 1999d. *Alvin W. Gouldner: Sociologist and Outlaw Marxist*. Aldershot, UK: Ashgate.

Chriss, James J. 2002. "The Drug Court Movement: An Analysis of Tacit Assumptions." Pp. 189–213 in *Drug Courts in Theory and in Practice*, edited by J.L. Nolan, Jr. Hawthorne, NY: Aldine de Gruyter.

Chriss, James J. 2003. "Goffman as Microfunctionalist." Pp. 181–96 in *Goffman's Legacy*, edited by A.J. Treviño. Lanham, MD: Rowman and Littlefield.

Chriss, James J. 2004. "The Perils of Risk Assessment." *Society* 41 (4): 52–6.

Chriss, James J. 2007a. "The Functions of the Social Bond." *Sociological Quarterly* 48: 689–712.

Chriss, James J. 2007b. "Preface: Issue in the Juvenile Justice System." Pp. vii–xii in *Current Perspectives – Readings from InfoTrac College Edition: Juvenile Justice*, edited by J.J. Chriss. Belmont, CA: Wadsworth.

Chriss, James J. 2010a. "The Social Control of Sex and Food: A Brief Overview." Pp. 171–84 in *Social Control: Informal, Legal, and Medical*, edited by J.J. Chriss. Bingley, UK: Emerald.

Chriss, James J. 2010b. "Social Control Revisited." Pp. 1–16 in *Social Control: Informal, Legal, and Medical*, edited by J.J. Chriss. Bingley, UK: Emerald.

Chriss, James J. 2011. *Beyond Community Policing: From Early American Beginnings to the 21st Century*. Boulder, CO: Paradigm.

Chriss, James J. 2013. "Flash Mobs." Pp. 163–5 in *Encyclopedia of Street Crime in America*, vol. 6, edited by J.I. Ross. Thousand Oaks, CA: Sage.

Chriss, James J. 2015. "Social Marketing as Social Control." Pp. 151–74 in *Handbook of Persuasion and Social Marketing*, edited by D.W. Stewart. New York: Praeger.

Chriss, James J. 2016. "Influence, Nudging, and Beyond." *Society* 53: 89–96.

Chriss, James J. 2018a. "Political Violence in Historical Perspective." Pp. 1015–29 in *Sage Handbook of Political Sociology*, edited by W. Outhwaite and S.P. Turner. London: Sage.

Chriss, James J. 2018b. "Vico and the Divine Drama." *Berlin Journal of Critical Theory* 2 (3): 31–58.

Chriss, James J. 2019. "Social Control: History of the Concept." Pp. 9–22 in *Handbook of Social Control*, edited by M. Deflem. Hoboken, NJ: Wiley-Blackwell.

Chriss, James J. 2020a. "Religion as Social Control: Parsons and Foucault." *Interdisciplinary Journal of Research on Religion* 16 (7): 1–46.

Chriss, James J. 2020b. *Law and Society: A Sociological Approach*. Los Angeles, CA: Sage.

Chriss, James J. 2021a. "COVID-19 and Social Control." *Academicus* 23: 21–40.

Chriss, James J. 2021b. "Explorations in Philosophy and Theology: Agamben and Vico." *Berlin Journal of Critical Theory* 5 (2): 169–222.

Clark, Lee Anna, Bruce Cuthbert, Roberto Lewis-Fernández, William E. Narrow, and Geoffrey M. Reed. 2017. "Three Approaches to Understanding and Classifying Mental

Disorder: *ICD-11*, *DSM-5*, and the National Institute of Mental Health's Research Domain Criteria (RDoC)." *Psychological Science in the Public Interest* 18 (2): 72–145.

Clarke, Adele E., Laura Mamo, Jennifer R. Fishman, Janet K. Shim, and Jennifer Ruth Fosket. 2003. "Biomedicalization: Technoscientific Transformations of Health, Illness, and U.S. Biomedicine." *American Sociological Review* 68 (2): 161–94.

Clinton, Hillary Rodham. 1995. *It Takes a Village and Other Lessons Children Teach Us*. New York: Simon and Schuster.

Cockerham, William C. (ed.) 2021. *The Wiley Blackwell Companion to Medical Sociology*. Malden, MA: Wiley-Blackwell.

Cogan, Jeanine C. 2002. "Hate Crime as a Crime Category Worthy of Policy Attention." *American Behavioral Scientist* 46 (1): 173–85.

Cohan, John Alan. 2006. "Necessity, Political Violence and Terrorism." *Stetson Law Review* 35 (3): 903–81.

Cohen, Lawrence E. and Marcus Felson. 1979. "Social Change and Crime Rate Trends: A Routine Activity Approach." *American Sociological Review* 44 (4): 588–608.

Cohen, Philip N. 1998. "Black Concentration Effects on Black-White and Gender Inequality: Multilevel Analysis for U.S. Metropolitan Areas." *Social Forces* 77 (1): 207–29.

Cohen, Stanley. 1972. *Folk Devils and Moral Panics*. St. Albans, UK: Paladin.

Cohen, Stanley. 1985. *Visions of Social Control: Crime, Punishment and Classification*. Cambridge: Polity Press.

Compitus, Katherine. 2019. "Traumatic Pet Loss and the Integration of Attachment-Based Animal Assisted Therapy." *Journal of Psychotherapy Integration* 29 (2): 119–31.

Conrad, Peter. 1992. "Medicalization and Social Control." *Annual Review of Sociology* 18: 209–32.

Conrad, Peter and Alison Angell. 2004. "Homosexuality and Remedicalization." *Society* 41 (5): 32–9.

Conrad, Peter and Joseph W. Schneider. 1980. *Deviance and Medicalization: From Badness to Sickness*. St. Louis: C.V. Mosby Company.

Conway, Maura. 2017. "Determining the Role of the Internet in Violent Extremism and Terrorism: Six Suggestions for Progressing Research." *Studies in Conflict & Terrorism* 40 (1): 77–98.

Cooper, Robert Alan. 1976. "Ideas and Their Execution: English Prison Reform." *Eighteenth-Century Studies* 10 (1): 73–93.

Cooper, Robert Alan. 1981. "Jeremy Bentham, Elizabeth Fry, and English Prison Reform." *Journal of the History of Ideas* 42 (4): 675–90.

Cornell, Dewey G. 2018. "Threat Assessment." Pp. 37–52 in *Wiley Handbook of Violence in Education*, edited by H. Shapiro. Hoboken, NJ: Wiley-Blackwell.

Corrigan, Philip and Derek Sayer. 1985. *The Great Arch: English State Formation as Cultural Revolution*. Oxford: Basil Blackwell.

Crodelle, J., C. Vallejo, M. Schmidtchen, C.M. Topaz, and M.R. D'Orsogna. 2021. "Impacts of California Proposition 47 on Crime in Santa Monica, California." *PloS ONE* 16 (5): e0251199.

Cross, Simon. 2005. "Paedophiles in the Community: Inter-Agency Conflict, News Leaks and the Local Press." *Crime Media Culture* 1 (3): 284–300.

Crossley, Nick. 2003. "Even Newer Social Movements? Anti-Corporate Protests, Capitalist Crises and the Remoralization of Society." *Organization* 10 (2): 287–305.

Crotty, William. 2004. "On the Home Front: Institutional Mobilization to Fight the Threat of International Terrorism." Pp. 191–234 in *The Politics of Terror: The U.S. Response to 9/11*, edited by W. Crotty. Boston, MA: Northeastern University Press.

Crowther, Chris. 2000. "Thinking about the 'Underclass': Towards a Political Economy of Policing." *Theoretical Criminology* 4 (2): 149–67.

Cupler, Zachary A., Clinton J. Daniels, Derek R. Anderson, Michael T. Anderson, Jason G. Napuli, and Megan E. Tritt. 2021. "Suicide Prevention, Public Health, and the Chiropractic Profession: A Call to Action." *Chiropractic & Manual Therapies* 29 (14): 1–9.

D'Alessio, Stewart J., Lisa Stolzenberg, and Jamie L. Flexon. 2015. "The Effect of Hawaii's Ban the Box Law on Repeat Offending." *American Journal of Criminal Justice* 40: 336–52.

Das, Robin R. and Hermann Strasser. 2015. "The Sociologist from Marienbad: Werner Stark between Catholicism and Social Science." *Czech Sociological Review* 51 (3): 417–44.

Davis, Angela J. 2003. "Race, Cops, and Traffic Stops." Pp. 233–50 in *Crime Control and Social Justice: The Delicate Balance*, edited by D.F. Hawkins, S.L. Myers, Jr., and R.N. Stone. Westport, CT: Greenwood Press.

De Coster, Stacy and Jennifer Lutz. 2018. "Reconsidering Labels and Primary Deviance: False Appraisals, Reflected Appraisals, and Delinquency Onset." *Journal of Research in Crime and Delinquency* 55 (5): 609–48.

Dean, Mitchell. 2013. *The Signature of Power: Sovereignty, Governmentality and Biopolitics*. Los Angeles, CA: Sage.

DeCook, Julia R. 2021. "Castration, the Archive, and the Incel Wiki." *Psychoanalysis, Culture & Society* 26: 234–43.

Deflem, Mathieu. 2004. "Social Control and the Policing of Terrorism: Foundations for a Sociology of Counterterrorism." *American Sociologist* 35 (2): 75–92.

Deleuze, Gilles. 1992. "Postscript on the Societies of Control." *October* 59: 3–7.

DeLisi, Matt. 2016. *Psychopathy as Unified Theory of Crime*. New York: Palgrave Macmillan.

DeLisi, Matt and Michael Vaughn. 2008. "The Gottfredson-Hirschi Critiques Revisited: Reconciling Self-Control Theory, Criminal Careers, and Career Criminals." *International Journal of Offender Therapy and Comparative Criminology* 52 (5): 520–37.

DeLisi, Matt, Jennifer Tostlebe, Kyle Burgason, Mark Heirigs, and Michael Vaughn. 2018. "Self-Control Versus Psychopathy: A Head-to-Head Test of General Theories of Antisociality." *Youth Violence and Juvenile Justice* 16 (1): 53–76.

Deutsch, Karl. 1963. *Nerves of Government: Models of Political Communication and Control*. Glencoe, IL: Free Press.

Devereaux, Simon. 1999. "The Making of the Penitentiary Act, 1775–1779." *Historical Journal* 42 (2): 405–33.

Dewey, Jodie M. and Melissa M. Gesbeck. 2017. "(Dys) Functional Diagnosing: Mental Health Diagnosis, Medicalization, and the Making of Transgender Patients." *Humanity & Society* 41 (1): 37–72.

Dhanani, Lindsay Y. and Berkeley Franz. 2020. "Unexpected Public Health Consequences of the COVID-19 Pandemic: A National Survey Examining Anti-Asian Attitudes in the USA." *International Journal of Public Health* 65: 747–54.

Disha, Ilir, James C. Cavendish, and Ryan D. King. 2011. "Historical Events and Spaces of Hate: Hate Crimes against Arabs and Muslims in Post-9/11 America." *Social Problems* 58 (1): 21–46.

Ditton, Jason. 1979. *Controlology: Beyond the New Criminology*. London: Macmillan.

Docheff, D.M. and J.H. Conn. 2004. "It's No Longer a Spectator Sport – Eight Ways to Get Involved and Help Fight Parental Violence in Youth Sports." *Parks & Recreation* 39 (3): 62–70.

Dorf, Michael C. and Jeffrey A. Fagan. 2003. "Problem-Solving Courts: From Innovation to Institutionalization." *American Criminal Law Review* 40: 1501–11.

Dover, Tessa L., Cheryl R. Kaiser, and Brenda Major. 2020. "Mixed Signals: The Unintended Effects of Diversity Initiatives." *Social Issues and Policy Review* 14 (1): 152–81.

Dulmus, Catherine N. and Carolyn Hilarski. 2002. "Children and Adolescents Exposed to Community Violence." Pp. 129–47 in *Handbook of Violence*, edited by L.A. Rapp-Paglicci, A.R. Roberts, and J.S. Wodarski. New York: Wiley.

Dunn, Ronnie A. and Wornie Reed. 2011. *Racial Profiling: Causes and Consequences*. Dubuque, IA: Kendall Hunt.

Dunning, David, Chip Heath, and Jerry M. Suls. 2004. "Flawed Self-Assessment: Implications for Health, Education, and the Workplace." *Psychological Science in the Public Interest* 5 (3): 69–106.

Durch, Jane S., Linda A. Bailey, and Michael A. Stoto (eds.) 1997. *Improving Health in the Community*. Washington, DC: National Academy Press.

Durkheim, Emile. 1951 [1897]. *Suicide*, translated by J. Spaulding and G. Simpson. Glencoe, IL: Free Press.

Durkheim, Emile. 1965 [1915]. *Elementary Forms of the Religious Life*, translated by J.W. Swain. New York: Free Press.

Durkheim, Emile. 1984 [1893]. *The Division of Labor in Society*, translated by W.D. Halls. New York: Free Press.

Economy, Elizabeth. 2019. "Dissent is Not Dead." *Journal of Democracy* 30 (2): 57–63.

Egbert, Simon and Bettina Paul. 2019. "Preemptive 'Screening for Malintent': The Future Attribute Screening Technology (FAST) as a Double Future Device." *Futures* 109: 108–16.

Eland, Ivan. 2003. "Bush's War and the State of Civil Liberties." *Mediterranean Quarterly* 14 (4): 158–75.

Eldredge, Dirk C. 1998. *Ending the War on Drugs: A Solution for America*. Bridgehampton, NY: Bridge Works Publishing.

Elikann, Peter T. 1999. *Superpredators: The Demonization of Our Children by the Law*. New York: Insight Books.

Elliott, Delbert S., Beatrix A. Hamburg, and Kirk R. Williams (eds.) 1998. *Violence in American Schools: A New Perspective*. Cambridge: Cambridge University Press.

Ellwood, Charles A. 1912. *Sociology in Its Psychological Aspects*. New York: Appleton.

Ellwood, Charles A. 1925. *The Psychology of Human Society: An Introduction to Sociological Theory*. New York: Appleton.

Else, Holly. 2020. "Can Dogs Smell Covid? Here's What the Science Says." *Nature* 587: 530–1.

Enns, Peter K. 2016. *Incarceration Nation: How the United States Became the Most Punitive Democracy in the World*. Cambridge: Cambridge University Press.

Erikson, Kai T. 1966. *Wayward Puritans: A Study in the Sociology of Deviance*. New York: Wiley.

Eskin, Frada. 2002. "Public Health Medicine: The Constant Dilemma." *Journal of Public Health Medicine* 24 (1): 6–10.

Evans, Brad and Henry A. Giroux. 2020. "American Fascism: Fourteen Deadly Principles of Contemporary Politics." *symplokē* 28 (1–2): 181–205.

Everton, Sean F. 2015. "Networks and Religion: Ties that Bind, Loose, Build Up, and Tear Down." *Journal of Social Structure* 16 (10): 1–34.

Fagan, Jeffrey and Garth Davies. 2004. "The Natural History of Neighborhood Violence." *Journal of Contemporary Criminal Justice* 20 (2): 127–47.

Farmer, J. Doyne and John Geanakoplos. 2009. "The Virtues and Vices of Equilibrium and the Future of Financial Economics." *Complexity* 14 (3): 11–38.

Farrington, David P. and Joseph Murray (eds.) 2017. *Labeling Theory: Empirical Tests*. New York: Routledge.

FAST. 2008. "Privacy Impact Assessment for the Future Attribute Screening Technology (FAST) Project." Washington, DC: Department of Homeland Security.

Fatovic, Clement. 2009. *Outside the Law: Emergency and Executive Power*. Baltimore, MD: Johns Hopkins University Press.

Faulkner, David. 2003. "Taking Citizenship Seriously: Social Capital and Criminal Justice in a Changing World." *Criminal Justice* 3 (3): 287–315.

Fausto-Sterling, Anne. 2000. *Sexing the Body: Gender Politics and the Construction of Sexuality*. New York: Basic Books.

Fee, Holly R. and Michael R. Nusbaumer. 2012. "Social Distance and the Formerly Obese: Does the Stigma of Obesity Linger?" *Sociological Inquiry* 82 (3): 356–77.

Feeley, Malcolm M. and Jonathan Simon. 1994. "Actuarial Justice: The Emerging New Criminal Law." Pp. 173–201 in *The Futures of Criminology*, edited by D. Nelken. London: Sage.

Feinberg, Joel. 1968. "Collective Responsibility." *Journal of Philosophy* 65 (21): 674–88.

Felson, Marcus and Rachel Boba. 2010. *Crime and Everyday Life*, 4h edn. Los Angeles, CA: Sage.

Felson, Richard B. 1996. "Big People Hit Little People: Sex Differences in Physical Power and Interpersonal Violence." *Criminology* 34: 433–52.

Felson, Richard B. and Noah Painter-Davis. 2012. "Another Cost of Being a Young Black Male: Race, Weaponry, and Lethal Outcomes in Assaults." *Social Science Research* 41: 1241–53.

Fishbein, Diana H. 1991. "Medicalizing the Drug War." *Behavioral Sciences and the Law* 9: 323–44.

Fontenelle-Tereshchuk, Daniela. 2021. "'Homeschooling and the COVID-19 Crisis: The Insights of Parents on Curriculum and Remote Learning." *Interchange* 52 (2): 167–91.

Forst, Brian. 2009. *Terrorism, Crime, and Public Policy*. New York: Cambridge University Press.

Forth, Christopher E. 2020. "The Fat Imagery in Trump's America: Matter, Metaphor, and Animality." *Cultural Politics* 16 (3): 387–407.

Foucault, Michel. 1965. *Madness and Civilization*, translated by R. Howard. New York: Pantheon.

Foucault, Michel. 1973. *The Birth of the Clinic: An Archaeology of Medical Perception*, translated by A.M. Sheridan. London: Tavistock.

Foucault, Michel. 1976. *Mental Illness and Psychology*. New York: Harper Colophon.

Foucault, Michel. 1977. *Discipline and Punish: The Birth of the Prison*, translated by A. Sheridan. New York: Vintage Books.

Foucault, Michel. 1978. *The History of Sexuality*, translated by R. Hurley. New York: Pantheon Books.

Fox, James Alan and Jack Levin. 1998. "Multiple Homicide: Patterns of Serial and Mass Murder." *Crime and Justice* 23: 407–56.

Fox, Renée C. 1959. *Experiment Perilous: Physicians and Patients Facing the Unknown*. Glencoe, IL: Free Press.

Frances, Allen. 2013. *Saving Normal: An Insider's Revolt against Out-of-Control Psychiatric Diagnosis, DSM-5, Big Pharma, and the Medicalization of Ordinary Life*. New York: William Morrow.

Frank, David John, Bayliss J. Camp, and Steven A. Boutcher. 2010. "Worldwide Trends in the Regulation of Sex, 1945–2005." *American Sociological Review* 75 (6): 867–93.

Frank, Robert H. 2016. *Success and Luck: Good Fortune and the Myth of Meritocracy*. Princeton, NJ: Princeton University Press.

Franks, David D. 2019. *Neurosociology: Fundamentals and Current Findings*. Dordrecht: Springer.

Fredrickson, Darin D. and Raymond P. Siljander. 2002. *Racial Profiling: Eliminating the*

Confusion between Racial and Criminal Profiling and Clarifying What Constitutes Unfair Discrimination and Persecution. Springfield, IL: Charles C. Thomas.

Freier, Nathan. 2008. "Known Unknowns: Unconventional 'Strategic Shocks' in Defense Strategy Development." Carlisle, PA: US Army War College.

Freud, Sigmund. 1927. *The Ego and the Id*, translated by J. Riviere. London: Hogarth Press.

Freud, Sigmund. 1952 [1913]. *Totem and Taboo*. New York: Norton.

Frey, Bruno S., David A. Savage, and Benno Torgler. 2011. "Who Perished on the Titanic? The Importance of Social Norms." *Rationality and Society* 23 (1): 35–49.

Friedenberg, Edgar Z. 1969. "The Generation Gap." *Annals of the American Academy of Political and Social Science* 382 (1): 32–42.

Friedman, Lawrence M. 1993. *Crime and Punishment in American History*. New York: Basic Books.

Fukuyama, Francis. 2011. *The Origins of Political Order: From Prehuman Times to the French Revolution*. New York: Farrar, Straus, and Giroux.

Furedi, Frank. 2004a. *Therapy Culture: Cultivating Vulnerability in an Uncertain Age*. London: Routledge.

Furedi, Frank. 2004b. "The Silent Ascendancy of Therapeutic Culture in Britain." Pp. 19–50 in *Therapeutic Culture: Triumph and Defeat*, edited by J.B. Imber. New Brunswick, NJ: Transaction.

Furedi, Frank. 2006. "The End of Professional Dominance." *Society* 43 (6): 14–18.

Gabay, Rahav, Boaz Hameiri, Tammy Rubel-Lifschitz, and Arie Nadler. 2020. "The Tendency for Interpersonal Victimhood: The Personality Construct and Its Consequences." *Personality and Individual Differences* 165: 110134.

Gaither, Milton. 2009. "Homeschooling in the USA: Past, Present, and Future." *Theory and Research in Education* 7 (3): 331–46.

Garcia, Robert J., Emily V. Shaw, and Nicholas Scurich. 2021. "Normative and Informational Influence in Group Decision Making: Effects of Majority Opinion and Anonymity on Voting Behavior and Belief Change." *Group Dynamics: Theory, Research, and Practice* 25 (4): 319–33.

Gardner, Carol Brooks. 1995. *Passing By: Gender and Public Harassment*. Berkeley, CA: University of California Press.

Garland, David. 1991. "Sociological Perspectives on Punishment." *Crime and Justice: A Review of Research* 14: 115–65.

Garland, David. 1997. "Of Crimes and Criminals: The Development of Criminology in Britain." Pp. 11–56 in *Oxford Handbook of Criminology*, 2nd edn., edited by M. Maguire, R. Morgan, and R. Reiner. Oxford: Oxford University Press.

Garland, David. 2001. *The Culture of Control: Crime and Social Order in Contemporary Society*. Chicago, IL: University of Chicago Press.

Garland, David. 2003. "Penal Modernism and Postmodernism." Pp. 45–73 in *Punishment and Social Control*, enlarged 2nd edn., edited by T.G. Blomberg and S. Cohen. New York: Aldine de Gruyter.

Geis, Gilbert. 2000. "On the Absence of Self-Control as the Basis for a General Theory of Crime." *Theoretical Criminology* 4 (1): 35–53.

Gelber, Katharine. 2012. "'Speaking Back': The Likely Fate of Hate Speech Policy in the United States and Australia." Pp. 50–71 in *Speech and Harm: Controversies over Free Speech*, edited by I. Maitra and M.K. McGowan. Oxford: Oxford University Press.

Gelvin, James L. 2021. *The Israel-Palestine Conflict: A History*, 4th edn. Cambridge: Cambridge University Press.

Giddings, Franklin H. 1899. *The Elements of Sociology*. New York: Macmillan.

Gideon, Lior. 2013. "Bridging the Gap between Health and Justice." *Health & Justice* 1 (4): 1–9.

Gilligan, James. 2000. "Violence in Public Health and Preventive Medicine." *Lancet* 355 (9217): 1802–4.

Gilliom, John and Torin Monahan. 2013. *Supervision: An Introduction to the Surveillance Society*. Chicago, IL: University of Chicago Press.

Giustozzi, Antonio. 2021. "Afghanistan after the U.S. Withdrawal: Trends and Scenarios for the Future." *Asia Policy* 16 (3): 57–74.

Glanzer, Perry L., Jonathan P. Hill, and Jessica A. Robinson. 2018. "Emerging Adults' Conceptions of Purpose and the Good Life: A Classification and Comparison." *Youth & Society* 50 (6): 715–33.

Glassner, Barry. 1990. "Fit for Postmodern Selfhood." Pp. 215–43 in *Symbolic Interaction and Cultural Studies*, edited by H.S. Becker and M.M. McCall. Chicago, IL: University of Chicago Press.

Go, Julian. 2016. *Postcolonial Thought and Social Theory*. New York: Oxford University Press.

Goffman, Erving. 1959. *Presentation of Self in Everyday Life*. New York: Anchor Doubleday.

Goffman, Erving. 1961a. *Asylums: Essays on the Social Situation of Mental Patients and Other Inmates*. Garden City, NY: Doubleday Anchor.

Goffman, Erving. 1961b. *Encounters: Two Studies in the Sociology of Interaction*. Indianapolis, IN: Bobbs-Merrill.

Goffman, Erving. 1963a. *Behavior in Public Places: Notes on the Social Organization of Gatherings*. New York: Free Press.

Goffman, Erving. 1963b. *Stigma: Notes on the Management of Spoiled Identity*. Englewood Cliffs, NJ: Prentice-Hall.

Goffman, Erving. 1967. *Interaction Ritual: Essays on Face-to-Face Behavior*. Chicago, IL: Aldine.

Goffman, Erving. 1971. *Relations in Public: Microstudies of the Public Order*. New York: Harper Torchbooks.

Goffman, Erving. 1974. *Frame Analysis: An Essay on the Organization of Experience*. Boston, MA: Northeastern University Press.

Goffman, Erving. 1981. *Forms of Talk*. Philadelphia, PA: University of Pennsylvania Press.

Goffman, Erving. 1983. "The Interaction Order." *American Sociological Review* 48: 1–17.

Goldschmidt, Janice. 2018. "A Broad View: Disordered Eating on the Autism Spectrum." *Eating Disorders Review* 29 (3): n.p.

Goode, Erich. 2004. "Is the Sociology of Deviance Still Relevant?" *American Sociologist* 35 (4): 46–57.

Goode, Erich and Nachman Ben-Yehuda. 2009. *Moral Panics: The Social Construction of Deviance*. Oxford: Wiley-Blackwell.

Gordon, Bob, Bruce Anderson, Ken Daurio, Cinco Paul, Jimmy Hayward, Steve Martino, John Powell, et al. 2008. *Dr. Seuss' Horton Hears a Who!* Beverly Hills, CA: Twentieth Century Fox Film Corp.

Gordon, Neil. 2001. "Mutism: Elective or Selective, and Acquired." *Brain and Development* 23: 83–7.

Gottfredson, Michael R. and Travis Hirschi. 1990. *A General Theory of Crime*. Stanford, CA: Stanford University Press.

Gouldner, Alvin W. 1952. "Red Tape as a Social Problem." Pp. 410–18 in *Reader in Bureaucracy*, edited by R.K. Merton, A.P. Gray, B. Yockey, and H.C. Selvin. Glencoe, IL: Free Press.

Gouldner, Alvin W. 1970. *The Coming Crisis of Western Sociology*. New York: Basic Books.

Gouldner, Alvin W. 1974. "Marxism and Social Theory." *Theory and Society* 1 (1): 17–35.

Gouldner, Alvin W. 1975. "Sociology and the Everyday Life." Pp. 417–32 in *The Idea of Social Structure*, edited by L.A. Coser. New York: Harcourt Brace Jovanovich.

Gouldner, Alvin W. 1976. *The Dialectic of Ideology and Technology*. New York: Oxford University Press.

Gouldner, Alvin W. 1979. *The Future of Intellectuals and the Rise of the New Class*. New York: Seabury Press.

Grahame-Smith, D.G. 2002. "The Demedicalization of Prescribing." *International Journal of Pharmaceutical Medicine* 16: 233–8.

Greene, Michael B. 2018. "Metaphorically or Not, Violence is Not a Contagious Disease." *AMA Journal of Ethics* 20 (5): 513–15.

Greene, Richard. 1991. "Poverty Concentration Measures and the Urban Underclass." *Economic Geography* 67 (3): 240–52.

Gressgård, Randi. 2010. "When Trans Translates into Tolerance – Or Was it Monstrous? Transsexual and Transgender Identity in Liberal Humanist Discourse." *Sexualities* 13 (5): 539–61.

Griffiths, Scott, Stuart B. Murray, Aimee Medeiros, and Aaron J. Blashill. 2017. "The Tall and the Short of It: An Investigation of Height Ideals, Height Preferences, Height Dissatisfaction, Heightism, and Height-Related Quality of Life Impairment among Sexual Minority Men." *Body Image* 23: 146–54.

Grimsted, David. 1972. "Rioting in Its Jacksonian Setting." *American Historical Review* 77 (2): 361–97.

Grob, Gerald N. and Allan Horwitz. 2010. *Diagnosis, Therapy, and Evidence: Conundrums in Modern American Medicine*. New Brunswick, NJ: Rutgers University Press.

Grogger, Jeffrey and Glen Ridgeway. 2006. "Testing for Racial Profiling in Traffic Stops from behind a Veil of Darkness." *Journal of the American Statistical Association* 101 (475): 878–87.

Gruenewald, Jeff. 2011. "A Comparative Examination of Homicides Perpetrated by Far-Right Extremists." *Homicide Studies* 15 (2): 177–203.

Guetzloe, Eleanor. 1992. "Violent, Aggressive, and Antisocial Students: What Are We Going To Do With Them?" *Preventing School Failure* 36 (3): 4–9.

Gurwitsch, Aron. 1979. *Human Encounters in the Social World*, translated by F. Kersten. Pittsburgh, PA: Duquesne University Press.

Habermas, Jürgen. 1975. *Legitimation Crisis*, translated by T. McCarthy. Boston, MA: Beacon Press.

Habermas, Jürgen. 1984. *Theory of Communicative Action*, vol. 1, translated by T. McCarthy. Boston, MA: Beacon Press.

Habermas, Jürgen. 1987. *Theory of Communicative Action*, vol. 2, translated by T. McCarthy. Boston, MA: Beacon Press.

Habermas, Jürgen. 1996. *Between Facts and Norms: Contributions to a Discourse Theory of Law and Democracy*, translated by W. Rehg. Cambridge, MA: MIT Press.

Haggerty, Kevin D. and Amber Gazso. 2005. "Seeing beyond the Ruins: Surveillance as a Response to Terrorist Threats." *Canadian Journal of Sociology* 30 (2): 169–87.

Haider-Markel, Donald P. and Mark R. Joslyn. 2018. "Not Threat, But Threatening: Potential Causes and Consequences of Gay Innumeracy." *Journal of Homosexuality* 65 (11): 1527–42.

Halliwell, Martin. 2013. *Therapeutic Revolutions: Medicine, Psychiatry, and American Culture, 1946–1970*. New Brunswick, NJ: Rutgers University Press.

Hallwas, John E. 2008. *Dime Novel Desperadoes: The Notorious Maxwell Brothers*. Urbana, IL: University of Illinois Press.

Hamburger, Andreas. 2021. "Social Trauma: A Bridging Concept." Pp. 3–15 in *Social Trauma – An Interdisciplinary Textbook*, edited by A. Hamburger, C. Hancheva, and V.D. Volkan. Cham: Springer.

Hamilton, Gary G. and John R. Sutton. 1989. "The Problem of Control in the Weak State: Domination in the United States, 1880–1920." *Theory and Society* 18 (1): 1–46.

Hannon, Lance, Malik Neal, and Alex R. Gustafson. 2021. "Out-of-Place and In-Place Policing: An Examination of Traffic Stops in Racially Segregated Philadelphia." *Crime & Delinquency* 67 (6–7): 868–90.

Hardin, Russell. 2004. "Civil Liberties in the Era of Mass Terrorism." *Journal of Ethics* 8 (1): 77–95.

Harper, Richard. 2010. *Texture: Human Expression in the Age of Communications Overload*. Cambridge, MA: MIT Press.

Harper, Richard and Stuart Taylor. 2009. "Glancephone – An Exploration of Human Expression." Pp. 1–10 in *MobileHCI'09: Proceedings of the 11th International Conference on Human-Computer Interaction with Mobile Devices and Services*. New York: ACM Press.

Harrington, Brooke and Gary Alan Fine. 2006. "Where the Action Is: Small Groups and Recent Developments in Sociological Theory." *Small Group Research* 37 (1): 4–19.

Harris, David A. 2003. *Profiles in Injustice: Why Racial Profiling Cannot Work*. New York: New Press.

Harris, Judith R. 1998. *The Nurture Assumption*. New York: Free Press.

Hartling, Linda M. and Tracy Luchetta. 1999. "Humiliation: Assessing the Impact of Derision, Degradation, and Debasement." *Journal of Primary Prevention* 19 (4): 259–78.

Hartman, Laura, Guy Widdershoven, Annelou de Vries, Annelijn Wensing-Kruger, Martin den Heijer, Thomas Steensma, and Bert Molewijk. 2019. "Integrative Clinical Ethics Support in Gender Affirmative Care: Lessons Learned." *HEC Forum* 31 (3): 241–60.

Hartmann, Douglas and Michael Massoglia. 2007. "Reassessing the Relationship between High School Sports Participation and Deviance: Evidence of Enduring, Bifurcated Effects." *Sociological Quarterly* 48: 485–505.

Haslam, Nick. 2005. "Dimensions of Folk Psychiatry." *Review of General Psychology* 9 (1): 35–47.

Hatfield, Elaine and Susan Sprecher. 1985. *Mirror, Mirror: The Importance of Looks in Everyday Life*. Albany, NY: SUNY Press.

Hawley, Emily. 2017. "ISIS Crimes against the Shia: The Islamic State's Genocide against Shia Muslims." *Genocide Studies International* 11 (2): 160–81.

Heard-Garris, N.J., M. Cale, L. Camaj, M.C. Hamati, and T.P. Dominguez. 2018. "Transmitting Trauma: A Systematic Review of Vicarious Racism and Child Health." *Social Science & Medicine* 199: 230–40.

Heckathorn, Douglas D. 1990. "Collective Sanctions and Compliance Norms: A Formal Theory of Group-Mediated Social Control." *American Sociological Review* 55: 366–84.

Heitmeyer, Willhelm, Simon Howell, Sebastian Kurtenbach, Abdul Rauf, Muhammad Zaman, and Steffen Zdun. 2019. *Codes of the Street*. Cham: Springer International.

Henggeler, Scott W. and Cindy M. Schaeffer. 2016. "Multisystemic Therapy®: Clinical Overview, Outcomes, and Implementation Research." *Family Process* 55 (3): 514–28.

Herbert, Steve. 2006. *Citizens, Cops, and Power: Recognizing the Limits of Community*. Chicago, IL: University of Chicago Press.

Herman-Kinney, Nancy J. 2003. "Deviance." Pp. 695–720 in *Handbook of Symbolic Interactionism*, edited by L.T. Reynolds and N.J. Herman-Kinney. Lanham, MD: Altamira Press.

Herring, Jonathan. 2019. *Law and the Relational Self*. Cambridge: Cambridge University Press.

Herrnstein, Richard J. and Charles Murray. 1994. *The Bell Curve: Intelligence and Class Structure in American Life*. New York: Free Press.

Hervieu-Léger, Danièle. 1998. "The Transmission and Formation of Socioreligious Identities in Modernity: An Analytical Essay on the Trajectories of Identification." *International Sociology* 13 (2): 213–28.

Heyman, Richard E. and Amy M. Smith Slep. 2019. "Relational Disorders and Beyond." Pp. 19–34 in *APA Handbook of Contemporary Family Psychology, Vol. 3: Family Therapy and Training*, edited by B.H. Fiese, M. Celano, K. Deater-Deckard, E.N. Jouriles, and M.A. Whisman. Washington, DC: American Psychological Association.

Hier, Sean P. 2008. "Thinking beyond Moral Panic: Risk, Responsibility, and the Politics of Moralization." *Theoretical Criminology* 12 (2): 173–90.

Hillery, George A., Jr. 1968. *Communal Organizations: A Study of Local Societies*. Chicago, IL: University of Chicago Press.

Hinshaw, Stephen P. 2005. "The Stigmatization of Mental Illness in Children and Parents: Developmental Issues, Family Concerns, and Research Needs." *Journal of Child Psychology and Psychiatry* 46 (7): 714–34.

Hinshaw, Stephen P. 2007. *The Mark of Shame*. New York: Oxford University Press.

Hirschi, Travis. 1969. *Causes of Delinquency*. Berkeley, CA: University of California Press.

Hirschi, Travis. 2004. "Self-Control and Crime." Pp. 537–52 in *Handbook of Self-Regulation: Research, Theory, and Applications*, edited by R.F. Baumeister and K.D. Vohs. New York: Guilford Press.

Hirschi, Travis and Michael R. Gottfredson. 1983. "Age and the Explanation of Crime." *American Journal of Sociology* 89: 552–84.

Hirschi, Travis and Michael R. Gottfredson. 2005. "Punishment of Children from the Perspective of Control Theory." Pp. 214–22 in *Corporal Punishment of Children in Theoretical Perspective*, edited by M. Donnelly and M.A. Straus. New Haven, CT: Yale University Press.

Holdaway, Simon. 1983. *Inside the British Police: A Force at Work*. London: Blackwell.

Horne, Christine. 2001. "Sociological Perspectives on the Emergence of Norms." Pp. 3–34 in *Social Norms*, edited by M. Hechter and K. Opp. New York: Russell Sage Foundation.

Horne, Christine and Stefanie Mollborn. 2020. "Norms: An Integrated Framework." *Annual Review of Sociology* 46: 467–87.

Horrace, William C. and Shawn M. Rohlin. 2016. "How Dark is Dark? Bright Lights, Big City, Racial Profiling." *Review of Economics and Statistics* 98 (2): 226–32.

Horsely, Mark. 2014. "The 'Death of Deviance' and Stagnation of 20th-Century Criminology." Pp. 85–107 in *Death and Resurgence of Deviance*, edited by M. Dellwing, J.A. Kotarba, and N.W. Pino. London: Palgrave Macmillan.

Horwitz, Allan V. and Jerome C. Wakefield. 2007. *The Loss of Sadness: How Psychiatry Transformed Normal Sorrow into Depressive Disorder*. Oxford: Oxford University Press.

Houdek, Petr, Petr Koblovský, and Marek Vranka. 2021. "The Challenge of Human Psychology to Effective Management of the COVID-19 Pandemic." *Society* 58: 131–4.

Howell, Noura, John Chuang, Abigail De Kosnik, Greg Niemeyer, and Kimiko Ryokai. 2018. "Emotional Biosensing: Exploring Critical Alternatives." In *Proceedings of the ACM on Human-Computer Interaction, vol. 2*. New York: ACM Press.

Hunt, Alan. 1999. *Governing Morals: A Social History of Moral Regulation*. Cambridge: Cambridge University Press.

Huss, Rebecca J. 2018. "Canines in the Classroom: Issues Relating to Service Animals in

Primary and Secondary Educational Institutions after *Fry v. Napoleon Community Schools.*" *Animal Law Review* 24 (1): 53–76.

Ibrahim, Azeem. 2020. *Rise and Fall? The Rise and Fall of ISIS in Libya.* Carlisle, PA: US Army War College Press.

Impara, Elisa. 2018. "A Social Semiotics Analysis of Islamic State's Use of Beheadings: Images of Power, Masculinity, Spectacle and Propaganda." *International Journal of Law, Crime and Justice* 53: 25–45.

Jackson, D. Michael. 2013. "Introduction: The Enduring Canadian Crown." Pp. 1–14 in *Canada and the Crown: Essays on Constitutional Monarchy*, edited by D.M. Jackson and P. Lagassé. Montreal: McGill-Queen's University Press.

Jacobs, Bruce A. and Richard Wright. 2006. *Street Justice: Retaliation in the Criminal Underworld.* Cambridge: Cambridge University Press.

Jacobsen, Colin and Daniel Maier-Katkin. 2015. "Breivik's Sanity: Terrorism, Mass Murder, and the Insanity Defense." *Human Rights Quarterly* 37: 137–52.

James, Jonathan and Jean Proulx. 2014. "A Psychological and Developmental Profile of Sexual Murderers: A Systematic Review." *Aggression and Violent Behavior* 19: 592–607.

Jenkinson, Richard, Elizabeth Milne, and Andrew Thompson. 2020. "The Relationship between Intolerance of Uncertainty and Anxiety in Autism: A Systematic Literature Review and Meta-Analysis." *Autism* 24 (8): 1933–44.

Jenness, Valerie and Ryken Grattet. 2001. *Making Hate a Crime: From Social Movement to Law Enforcement.* New York: Russell Sage Foundation.

Jensen, Michael A., Aaron Safer-Lichenstein, Patrick A. James, and Gary LaFree. 2020. "The Link between Prior Criminal Record and Violent Political Extremism in the United States." Pp. 121–46 in *Understanding Recruitment to Organized Crime and Terrorism*, edited by D. Weisburd, E.U. Savona, B. Hasisi, and F. Calderoni. Cham: Springer.

Jewell, Jeremy D., Michael I. Axelrod, Mitchell J. Prinstein, and Stephen Hupp. 2019. *Great Myths of Adolescence.* Hoboken, NJ: Wiley-Blackwell.

Jiang, Min and King-Wa Fu. 2018. "Chinese Social Media and Big Data: Big Data, Big Brother, Big Profit?" *Policy & Internet* 10 (4): 372–92.

Johnson, Herbert A. and Nancy Travis Wolfe. 1996. *History of Criminal Justice.* Cincinnati, OH: Anderson.

Johnson, Norah L., Karen Burkett, Judy Reinhold, and Margaret W. Bultas. 2016. "Translating Research to Practice for Children with Autism Spectrum Disorder: Part I: Definition, Associated Behaviors, Prevalence, Diagnostic Process, and Interventions." *Journal of Pediatric Health Care* 30 (1): 15–26.

Jones, Brian J. 2019. *Social Capital in American Life.* Cham: Palgrave Macmillan.

Jones, Christopher W. 2018. "Understanding ISIS's Destruction of Antiquities as a Rejection of Nationalism." *Journal of Eastern Mediterranean Archaeology and Heritage Studies* 6 (1–2): 31–58.

Kalinowski, Jesse J., Matthew B. Ross, and Stephen L. Ross. 2019. "Now You See Me, Now You Don't: The Geography of Police Stops." *AEA Papers & Proceedings* 109: 143–7.

Karstedt, Susanne, Tiffany Bergin, and Michael Koch. 2019. "Critical Junctures and Conditions of Change: Exploring the Fall of Prison Populations in U.S. States." *Social & Legal Studies* 28 (1): 58–80.

Katz, Jack. 1988. *Seductions of Crime: Moral and Sensual Attraction in Doing Evil.* New York: Basic Books.

Katz, Jack. 2019. "Hot Potato Criminology: Ethnographers and the Shame of Poor People's Crimes." *Annual Review of Criminology* 2: 21–52.

Kaul, Volker. 2021. "Communities and the Individual: Beyond the Liberal-Communitarian Divide." *Philosophy and Social Criticism* 47 (4): 392–401.

Kehle, Thomas J., Melissa R. Madaus, Victoria S. Baratta, and Melissa A. Bray. 1998. "Augmented Self-Modeling as a Treatment for Children with Selective Mutism." *Journal of School Psychology* 36 (3): 247–60.

Keller, Allen S. 2006. "Torture in Abu Ghraib." *Perspectives in Biology and Medicine* 49 (4): 553–69.

Kelling, George L. and Mark H. Moore. 1988. "The Evolving Strategies of Policing," in *Perspectives on Policing, No. 1*. Washington, DC: National Institute of Justice.

Kerr, Selina E.M. 2018. *Gun Violence Prevention? The Politics behind Policy Responses to School Shootings in the United States*. Cham: Palgrave Macmillan.

Kidd, Benjamin. 1920. *The Science of Power*, 9th edn. London: Methuen & Co.

Kincheloe, Joe L., Shirley R. Steinberg, and Aaron D. Gresson III (eds.) 1996. *Measured Lies: The Bell Curve Examined*. New York: St. Martin's Press.

King, Thomas C., Nikita Aggarwal, Mariarosaria Taddeo, and Luciano Floridi. 2020. "Artificial Intelligence Crime: An Interdisciplinary Analysis of Foreseeable Threats and Solutions." *Science and Engineering Ethics* 26 (1): 89–120.

Kingston, Paul W. 2006. "How Meritocratic is the United States?" *Research in Social Stratification and Mobility* 24 (2): 111–30.

Kinnaird, Emma, Caroline Norton, Caroline Pimblett, Catherine Stewart, and Kate Tchanturia. 2019. "Eating as an Autistic Adult: An Exploratory Qualitative Study." *PloS ONE* 14 (8): e0221937.

Kirk, Colleen P. 2019. "Dogs Have Masters, Cats Have Staff: Consumers' Psychological Ownership and Their Economic Valuation of Pets." *Journal of Business Research* 99: 306–18.

Kitcher, Philip. 1997. "An Argument about Free Inquiry." *Noûs* 31 (3): 279–306.

Klapp, Orrin E. 1991. *Inflation of Symbols: Loss of Values in American Culture*. New Brunswick, NJ: Transaction.

Klingle, Matthew and Themis Chronopoulos. 2018. "Police Misconduct, Community Opposition, and Urban Governance in New York City, 1945–1965." *Journal of Urban History* 44 (4): 643–68.

Klipfel, Kristen M., Carlo Garofalo, and David S. Kosson. 2017. "Clarifying Associations between Psychopathy Facets and Personality Disorders among Offenders." *Journal of Criminal Justice* 53: 83–91.

Knorr Cetina, Karin. 2005. "Complex Global Microstructures: The New Terrorist Societies." *Theory, Culture and Society* 22 (5): 213–34.

Kolvin, I. and T. Fundudis. 1981. "Elective Mute Children: Psychological Development and Background Factors." *Journal of Child Psychology and Psychiatry* 22: 219–32.

Krakowski, Menahem. 2003. "Violence and Serotonin: Influence of Impulse Control, Affect Regulation, and Social Functioning." *Journal of Neuropsychiatry and Clinical Neurosciences* 15 (3): 294–305.

Krislov, Daniel. 2004. "Civil Liberties and the Judiciary in the Aftermath of 9/11." Pp. 134–59 in *The Politics of Terror: The U.S. Response to 9/11*, edited by W. Crotty. Boston, MA: Northeastern University Press.

Krupp, Daniel Brian, Lindsay A. Sewall, Martin L. Lalumière, Craig Sheriff, and Grant T. Harris. 2012. "Nepotistic Patterns of Violent Psychopathy: Evidence for Adaptation?" *Frontiers in Psychology* 3 (article 305): 1–8.

Kubrin, Charis E. 2005. "Gangstas, Thugs, and Hustlas: Identity and Code of the Street in Rap Music." *Social Problems* 52 (3): 360–78.

Kumpulainen, K., E. Räsänen, H. Raaska, and V. Somppi. 1998. "Selective Mutism among Second-Graders in Elementary School." *European Child and Adolescent Psychiatry* 7: 24–9.

Kutchins, Herb and Stuart A. Kirk. 1997. *Making Us Crazy: DSM: The Psychiatric Bible and the Creation of Mental Disorders*. New York: Free Press.

Labaree, David F. 1997. *How to Succeed in School without Really Learning*. New Haven, CT: Yale University Press.

LaFree, Gary, Michael A. Jensen, Patrick A. James, and Aaron Safer-Lichtenstein. 2018. "Correlates of Violent Political Extremism in the United States." *Criminology* 56 (2): 233–68.

Landis, Paul H. 1939. *Social Control: Social Organization and Disorganization in Process*. Philadelphia, PA: Lippincott.

Lang, Gladys Engel and Kurt Lang. 1981. "Mass Communications and Public Opinion: Strategies for Research." Pp. 653–82 in *Social Psychology: Sociological Perspectives*, edited by M. Rosenberg and R.H. Turner. New York: Basic Books.

Lara, Francisco. 2017. "Oxytocin, Empathy and Human Enhancement." *Theoria* 32 (3): 367–84.

Lasch, Christopher. 1991. *The True and Only Heaven: Progress and Its Critics*. New York: Norton.

Laugerud, Solveig and Åse Langballe. 2017. "Turning the Witness Stand into a Speaker's Platform: Victim Participation in the Norwegian Legal System as Exemplified by the Trial against Anders Behring Breivik." *Law & Society Review* 51 (2): 227–51.

Laushey, Kelle M., L. Juane Heflin, Margaret Shippen, Paul A. Alberto, and Laura Fredrick. 2009. "Concept Mastery Routines to Teach Social Skills to Elementary Children with High Functioning Autism." *Journal of Autism and Development Disorders* 39: 1435–48.

L'Engle, Kelly Ladin, Jane D. Brown, and Kristin Kenneavy. 2006. "The Mass Media Are an Important Context for Adolescents' Sexual Behavior." *Journal of Adolescent Health* 38: 186–92.

Lerner, Adam B. 2020. "The Uses and Abuses of Victimhood Nationalism in International Politics." *European Journal of International Relations* 26 (1): 62–87.

Levin, Brian. 1999. "Hate Crimes: Worse by Definition." *Journal of Contemporary Criminal Justice* 15 (1): 6–21.

Levin, Jack and Jack McDevitt. 2002. *Hate Crimes Revisited: America's War on Those Who Are Different*. Boulder, CO: Westview Press.

Levin, Miriam R. 2000. "Contexts of Control." Pp. 13–39 in *Cultures of Control*, edited by M.R. Levin. Amsterdam: Harwood.

Li, Mingliang. 2009. "Is There 'White Flight' into Private Schools? New Evidence from High School and Beyond." *Economics of Education Review* 28: 382–92.

Liang, Fan, Vishnupriya Das, Nadiya Kostyuk, and Muzammil M. Hussain. 2018. "Constructing a Data-Driven Society: China's Social Credit System as a State Surveillance Infrastructure." *Policy & Internet* 10 (4): 415–53.

Lianos, Michalis. 2000. "Dangerization and the End of Deviance." *British Journal of Criminology* 40 (2): 261–78.

Lianos, Michalis. 2012. *The New Social Control: The Institutional Web, Normativity and the Social Bond*, translated by R. Nice. Ottawa: Red Quill Books.

Liebowitz, Jay. (ed.) 2015. *Bursting the Big Data Bubble: The Case for Intuition-Based Decision Making*. Boca Raton, FL: CRC Press.

Light, Michael T. and Julia T. Thomas. 2019. "Segregation and Violence Reconsidered: Do Whites Benefit from Residential Segregation?" *American Sociological Review* 84 (4): 690–725.

Lin, Kai. 2017. "The Medicalization and Demedicalization of Kink: Shifting Contexts of Sexual Politics." *Sexualities* 20 (3): 302–23.

Liska, Allen E. 1997. "Modeling the Relationships between Macro Forms of Social Control." *Annual Review of Sociology* 23: 39–61.

Lithwick, Dahlia and Julia Turner. 2004. "A Guide to the Patriot Act." Pp. 94–103 in *Homeland Security*, edited by N. Smith and L.M. Messina. New York: H.W. Wilson.

Loader, Ian and Neil Walker. 2007. *Civilizing Security*. Cambridge: Cambridge University Press.

Lorion, Raymond P. 2001. "Exposure to Urban Violence: Shifting from an Individual to an Ecological Perspective." Pp. 97–113 in *Integrating Behavioral and Social Sciences with Public Health*, edited by N. Schneiderman, M.A. Speers, J.M. Silva, H. Tomes, and J.H. Gentry. Washington, DC: American Psychological Association.

Luke, Timothy W. 1989. *Screens of Power: Ideology, Domination, and Resistance in Informational Society*. Urbana, IL: University of Illinois Press.

Luke, Timothy W. 2021. *The Travails of Trumpification*. Candor, NY: Telos Press.

Lund, Ingunn Olea, Erica Sundin, Carolien Konijnenberg, Kamilla Rognmo, Priscilla Martinez, and Andrea Fielder. 2015. "Harm to Others from Substance Use and Abuse." *Substance Abuse* 9 (S2): 119–24.

Lyon, David. 2003. "Surveillance as Social Sorting: Computer Codes and Mobile Bodies." Pp. 13–30 in *Surveillance as Social Sorting: Privacy, Risk and Digital Discrimination*, edited by D. Lyon. London: Routledge.

Lyon, David. 2004. "Technology vs. 'Terrorism': Circuits of City Surveillance since September 11, 2001." Pp. 297–311 in *Cities, War, and Terrorism: Towards an Urban Geopolitics*, edited by S. Graham. Malden, MA: Blackwell.

Lyon, David. 2006. "9/11, Synopticon, and Scopophilia: Watching and Being Watched." Pp. 35–54 in *The New Politics of Surveillance and Visibility*, edited by K.D. Haggerty and R.V. Ericson. Toronto: University of Toronto Press.

Lyon, David. 2007. *Surveillance Studies: An Overview*. Cambridge: Polity.

Lyon, David and Kevin D. Haggerty. 2012. "The Surveillance Legacies of 9/11: Recalling, Reflecting on, and Rethinking Surveillance in the Security Era." *Canadian Journal of Law and Society* 27 (3): 291–300.

Lyotard, Jean-François. 1984. *The Postmodern Condition: A Report on Knowledge*, translated by G. Bennington and B. Massumi. Minneapolis, MN: University of Minnesota Press.

Mac Donald, Heather. 2003. *Are Cops Racist?* Chicago, IL: Ivan R. Dee.

MacIver, Robert M. and Charles Page. 1949. *Society*. New York: Rinehart and Co.

Maclay, George R. 1990. *The Social Organism: A Short History of the Idea that a Human Society May Be Regarded as a Gigantic Living Creature*. Croton-on-Hudson, NY: North River Press.

Macnair, Logan and Richard Frank. 2018. "The Mediums and the Messages: Exploring the Language of Islamic State Media through Sentiment Analysis." *Critical Studies on Terrorism* 11 (3): 438–57.

Macy, Michael W. 1993. "Backward-Looking Social Control." *American Sociological Review* 58 (6): 819–36.

Maestro, Marcello. 1973. *Cesare Beccaria and the Origins of Penal Reform*. Philadelphia, PA: Temple University Press.

Malinowski, Bronislaw. 1987 [1929]. *The Sexual Lives of Savages*. Boston, MA: Beacon Press.

Manning, Philip D. (ed.) 2015. *On Folkways and Mores: William Graham Sumner Then and Now*. New Brunswick, NJ: Transaction.

Mansel, Philip. 2011. *Levant: Splendour and Catastrophe on the Mediterranean*. New Haven, CT: Yale University Press.

Marcuse, Herbert. 1964. *One-Dimensional Man: Studies in the Ideology of Advanced Industrial Society*. Boston, MA: Beacon Press.

Marín-Morales, Javier, Juan Luis Higuera-Trujillo, Alberto Greco, Jaime Guixeres, Carmen Llinares, Enzo Pasquale Scilingo, Mariano Alcañiz, and Gaetano Valenza. 2018. "Affective Computing in Virtual Reality: Emotion Recognition from Brain and Heartbeat Dynamics Using Wearable Sensors." *Nature Scientific Reports* 8: 13657.

Markowitz, Fred E. 2006. "Psychiatric Hospital Capacity, Homelessness, and Crime and Arrest Rates." *Criminology* 44 (1): 45–72.

Marks, Carole. 1991. "The Urban Underclass." *Annual Review of Sociology* 17: 445–66.

Marshall, Barbara L. 2010. "Science, Medicine and Virility Surveillance: 'Sexy Seniors' in the Pharmaceutical Imagination." *Sociology of Health and Illness* 32 (2): 211–24.

Martindale, Don. 1966. *Institutions, Organizations, and Mass Society*. Boston, MA: Houghton Mifflin.

Martinson, Robert. 1974. "What Works? Questions and Answers about Prison Reform." *Public Interest* 35: 22–54.

Maruna, Shadd and Heith Copes. 2005. "What Have We Learned from Five Decades of Neutralization Research?" *Crime and Justice: A Review of Research* 32: 221–320.

Marx, Gary T. 1995. "The Engineering of Social Control: The Search for the Silver Bullet." Pp. 225–46 in *Crime and Inequality*, edited by J. Hagan and R.D. Peterson. Stanford, CA: Stanford University Press.

Marx, Gary T. 2015. "Technology and Social Control." Pp. 117–24 in *International Encyclopedia of the Social & Behavioral Sciences*, vol. 24, 2nd edn., edited by J.D. Wright. London: Elsevier.

Marx, Gary T. 2016. *Windows into the Soul: Surveillance and Society in an Age of High Technology*. Chicago, IL: University of Chicago Press.

Massey, Douglas S. and Garvey Lundy. 2001. "Use of Black English and Racial Discrimination in Urban Housing Markets: New Methods and Findings." *Urban Affairs Review* 36 (4): 452–69.

Matza, David. 1961. "Subterranean Traditions of Youth." *Annals of the American Academy of Political and Social Science* 338: 102–18.

Matza, David. 1964. *Delinquency and Drift*. New York: John Wiley & Sons.

Maume, David J. and Michael Parrish. 2021. "Heavy-Contact Sport Participation and Early Adolescent Delinquency." *Social Currents* 8 (2): 126–44.

Mayhew, Leon H. 1997. *The New Public: Professional Communication and the Means of Social Influence*. Cambridge: Cambridge University Press.

McCarthy, Daniel J. 2010. "Self-Governance or Professionalized Paternalism? The Police, Contractual Injunctions and the Differential Management of Deviant Populations." *British Journal of Criminology* 50 (5): 896–913.

McDonald, David. 2000. "Violence as a Public Health Issue." *Trends and Issues in Crime and Criminal Justice* 163: 1–6.

McGann, P.J. and David Hutson (eds.) 2011. *Sociology of Diagnosis*. Bingley, UK: Emerald.

McIntosh, Marjorie Keniston. 1998. *Controlling Misbehavior in England, 1370–1600*. Cambridge: Cambridge University Press.

McLuhan, Marshall. 1964. *Understanding Media: The Extensions of Man*. New York: McGraw-Hill.

McMahon, Pamela M. 2000. "The Public Health Approach to the Prevention of Sexual Violence." *Sexual Abuse* 12 (1): 27–36.

Mead, George H. 1925. "The Genesis of the Self and Social Control." *International Journal of Ethics* 35 (3): 251–77.

Meier, Robert F. 1982. "Perspectives on the Concept of Social Control." *Annual Review of Sociology* 8: 35–55.

Meleagrou-Hitchins, Audrey Alexander, and Nick Kaderbhai. 2017. "The Impact of Digital

Communications Technology on Radicalization and Recruitment." *International Affairs* 93 (5): 1233–49.

Meliala, Adrianus. 2001. "The Notion of Sensitivity in Policing." *International Journal of the Sociology of Law* 29: 99–111.

Melossi, Dario. 2004. "Theories of Social Control and the State between American and European Shores." Pp. 32–48 in *The Blackwell Companion to Criminology*, edited by C. Sumner. Malden, MA: Blackwell.

Menninger, Karl. 1968. *The Crime of Punishment*. New York: Viking.

Mercer, Mark. 2020. "Why Scholars Won't Research Group Difference." *Academic Questions* 33: 581–5.

Merton, Robert K. 1968. *Social Theory and Social Structure*, enlarged edn. New York: Free Press.

Mészáros, István. 1971. *The Necessity of Social Control*. London: Merlin Press.

Meyer, D.H. 1976. "The Uniqueness of the American Enlightenment." *American Quarterly* 28 (2): 165–86.

Meyer, Ilan H. and S. Schwartz. 2000. "Social Issues as Public Health: Promise and Peril." *American Journal of Public Health* 90 (8): 1189–91.

Milgram, Stanley. 1963. "Behavioral Study of Obedience." *Journal of Abnormal and Social Psychology* 67: 371–8.

Milgram, Stanley. 1965. "Some Conditions of Obedience and Disobedience to Authority." *Human Relations* 18: 56–76.

Milgram, Stanley. 1974. *Obedience to Authority: An Experimental View*. New York: Harper and Row.

Modell, John and Timothy Haggerty. 1991. "The Social Impact of War." *Annual Review of Sociology* 17: 205–24.

Mohamad, Husam. 2019. "U.S. Policy and Israeli-Palestinian Relations." *Journal of South Asian and Middle Eastern Studies* 43 (1): 26–56.

Moldan, Marian B. 2005. "Selective Mutism and Self-Regulation." *Clinical Social Work Journal* 33 (3): 291–307.

Mollborn, Stefanie. 2017. *Mixed Messages: Norms and Social Control around Teen Sex and Pregnancy*. New York: Oxford University Press.

Monahan, Torin. 2010. *Surveillance in the Time of Insecurity*. New Brunswick, NJ: Rutgers University Press.

Monkkonen, Eric H. 1983. "The Organized Response to Crime in Nineteenth- and Twentieth-Century America." *Journal of Interdisciplinary History* 14 (1): 113–28.

Montgomery, Kathryn. 2000. "Youth and Digital Media: A Policy Research Agenda." *Journal of Adolescent Health* 27 (2): 61–8.

Moore, Calvin C. and John B. Williamson. 2003. "The Universal Fear of Death and the Cultural Response." Pp. 3–13 in *Handbook of Death and Dying, vol. 1*, edited by C.D. Bryant. Thousand Oaks, CA: Sage.

Moskowitz, Eva S. 2001. *In Therapy We Trust: America's Obsession with Self Fulfillment*. Baltimore, MD: Johns Hopkins University Press.

Moynihan, Ray and Alan Cassels. 2005. *Selling Sickness: How the World's Biggest Pharmaceutical Companies are Turning Us All into Patients*. New York: Nation Books.

Moynihan, Ray, Iona Heath, and David Henry. 2002. "Selling Sickness: The Pharmaceutical Industry and Disease Mongering." *British Medical Journal* 324 (13): 886–90.

Mulder, Mark. 2015. *Shades of White Flight: Evangelical Congregations and Urban Departure*. New Brunswick, NJ: Rutgers University Press.

Müller, Miriam. 2005. "Social Control and the Hue and Cry in Two Fourteenth-Century Villages." *Journal of Medieval History* 31: 29–53.

Muravchik, Joshua. 2014. *Making David into Goliath: How the World Turned against Israel*. New York: Encounter Books.

Murphy, John. 1927. *Primitive Man: His Essential Quest*. London: Oxford University Press.

Murray, Douglas. 2019. *The Madness of Crowds: Gender, Race and Identity*. London: Bloomsbury Continuum.

Musolf, Gil Richard. 2003. "The Chicago School." Pp. 91–117 in *Handbook of Symbolic Interactionism*, edited by L.T. Reynolds and N.J. Herman-Kinney. Lanham, MD: Altamira.

Mythen, Gabe and Sandra Walklate. 2006. "Criminology and Terrorism: Which Thesis? Risk Society or Governmentality?" *British Journal of Criminology* 46: 379–98.

Nadel, S.F. 1953. "Social Control and Self-Regulation." *Social Forces* 31 (3): 265–73.

Nas, Tevfik F., Albert C. Price, and Charles T. Weber. 1986. "A Policy-Oriented Theory of Corruption." *American Political Science Review* 80 (1): 107–19.

Nelson, Margaret K. and Anita Ilta Garey (eds.) 2009. *Who's Watching? Daily Practices of Surveillance among Contemporary Families*. Nashville, TN: Vanderbilt University Press.

Newman, Katherine S. 2004. *Rampage: The Social Roots of School Shootings*. New York: Basic Books.

Nitschke, Amanda, Raywat Deonandan, and Anne T.M. Konkle. 2020. "The Link between Autism Spectrum Disorder and Gut Microbiota: A Scoping Review." *Autism* 24 (6): 1328–44.

Nocka, Christen, Madeline C. Montgomery, Ana Progovac, Carly E. Guss, Philip A. Chan, and Julia Raifman. 2021. "Primary Care for Transgender Adolescents and Young Adults in Rhode Island: An Analysis of the All Payers Claims Database." *Journal of Adolescent Health* 68: 472–9.

Nogay, Nalan Hakime, Jennifer Walton, Kristen M. Roberts, Marcia Nahikian-Nelms, and Andrea N. Witwer. 2021. "The Effect of the Low FODMAP Diet on Gastrointestinal Symptoms, Behavioral Problems and Nutrient Intake in Children with Autism Spectrum Disorder: A Randomized Controlled Pilot Trial." *Journal of Autism and Developmental Disorders* 51 (8): 2800–11.

Nolan, James L., Jr. 1998. *The Therapeutic State: Justifying Government at Century's End*. New York: New York University Press.

Nolan, James L., Jr. 1999. "Acquiescence or Consensus? Consenting to Therapeutic Pedagogy." Pp. 107–29 in *Counseling and the Therapeutic State*, edited by J.J. Chriss. New York: Aldine de Gruyter.

Nolan, James L., Jr. 2001. *Reinventing Justice: The American Drug Court*. Princeton, NJ: Princeton University Press.

Nolan, James L., Jr. 2003. "Redefining Criminal Courts: Problem-Solving and the Meaning of Justice." *American Criminal Law Review* 40: 1541–65.

Norris, Clive, Nigel Fielding, Charles Kemp, and Jane Fielding. 1992. "Black and Blue: An Analysis of the Influence of Race on Being Stopped by the Police." *British Journal of Sociology* 43 (2): 207–24.

Nunn, Sam. 2004. "Thinking the Inevitable: Suicide Attacks in America and the Design of Effective Public Safety Policies." *Journal of Homeland Security and Emergency Management* 1 (4): 1–21.

O'Mahony, Charles and Aisling de Paor. 2017. "The Use of Behavioural Genetics in the Criminal Justice System: A Disability & Human Rights Perspective." *International Journal of Law and Psychiatry* 54: 16–25.

Ong, Walter J. 2002. *Orality and Literacy: The Technologizing of the Word*, 2nd edn. New York: Routledge.

Oosterveld, Willem Theo and Willem Bloem. 2017. *The Rise and Fall of ISIS: From Evitability to Inevitability*. The Hague: Hague Centre for Strategic Studies.

O'Reilly, Michelle, Jessica Nina Lester, and Tom Muskett (eds.) 2017. *A Practical Guide to Social Interaction Research in Autism Spectrum Disorders*. London: Palgrave Macmillan.

Osterweil, Vicky. 2020. *In Defense of Looting: A Riotous History of Uncivil Action*. New York: Bold Type Books.

Packer, Herbert L. 1968. *The Limits of the Criminal Sanction*. Stanford, CA: Stanford University Press.

Pais, Jeremy F., Scott J. South, and Kyle Crowder. 2009. "White Flight Revisited: A Multiethnic Perspective on Neighborhood Out-Migration." *Population Research and Policy Review* 28 (3): 321–46.

Pape, Robert A. 2003. "The Strategic Logic of Suicide Terrorism." *American Political Science Review* 97 (3): 343–61.

Parenti, Christian. 2003. *The Soft Cage: Surveillance in America, from Slavery to the War on Terror*. New York: Basic Books.

Parsons, Talcott. 1951. *The Social System*. Glencoe, IL: Free Press.

Parsons, Talcott. 1964. *Social Structure and Personality*. Glencoe, IL: Free Press.

Parsons, Talcott. 1967. "On the Concept of Political Power." Pp. 297–354 in *Sociological Theory and Modern Society*, T. Parsons. New York: Free Press.

Parsons, Talcott and Gerald M. Platt. 1973. *The American University*. Cambridge, MA: Harvard University Press.

Patterson, Lee. 1987. *Negotiating the Past: The Historical Understanding of Medieval Literature*. Madison, WI: University of Wisconsin Press.

Paul, George L. and Jason R. Baron. 2007. "Information Inflation: Can the Legal System Adapt?" *Richmond Journal of Law and Technology* 13 (3): 1–41.

Pearce, Lisa D., George M. Hayward, Laurie Chassin, and Patrick J. Curran. 2018. "The Increasing Diversity and Complexity of Family Structures for Adolescents." *Journal of Research on Adolescence* 28 (3): 591–608.

Pedersen, Cort. 2004. "Biological Aspects of Social Bonding and the Roots of Human Violence." *Annals of the New York Academy of Sciences* 1036 (1): 106–27.

Peresin, Anita and Alberto Cervone. 2015. "The Western *Muhajirat* of ISIS." *Studies in Conflict & Terrorism* 38: 495–509.

Perry, Barbara. 2001. *In the Name of Hate: Understanding Hate Crimes*. New York: Routledge.

Peterson, Ruth D. and Lauren J. Krivo. 2005. "Macrostructural Analyses of Race, Ethnicity, and Violent Crime: Recent Lessons and New Directions for Research." *Annual Review of Sociology* 31: 331–56.

Peterson, Ruth D. and Lauren J. Krivo. 2010. *Divergent Social Worlds: Neighborhood Crime and the Racial-Spatial Divide*. New York: Russell Sage Foundation.

Petrosino, Anthony, Carolyn Turpin-Petrosino, and John Buehler. 2003. "Scared Straight and Other Juvenile Awareness Programs for Preventing Juvenile Delinquency: A Systematic Review of the Randomized Experimental Evidence." *Annals of the American Academy of Political and Social Science* 589: 41–62.

Phillips, Scott and Mark Cooney. 2005. "Aiding Peace, Abetting Violence: Third Parties and the Management of Conflict." *American Sociological Review* 70 (2): 334–54.

Piaget, Jean. 1963. *Origins of Intelligence in Children*, translated by M. Cook. New York: Norton.

Pimsler, Martin. 1977. "Solidarity in the Medieval Village? The Evidence of Personal Pledging at Elton, Huntingdonshire." *Journal of British Studies* 17 (1): 1–11.

Piro, Benoît, Giorgio Mattana, and Vincent Nöel. 2019. "Recent Advances in Skin Chemical Sensors." *Sensors* 19 (20): 1–41.

Piroozfar, Poorang, Eric. R.P. Farr, Emmanuel Aboagye-Nimo, and Janet Osei-Berchie.

2019. "Crime Prevention in Urban Spaces through Environmental Design: A Critical UK Perspective." *Cities* 95: 1–11.

Pollack, William S. 2000. *Real Boys' Voices*. New York: Random House.

Porpora, Douglas V., Alexander Nikolaev, Julia Hagemann May, and Alexander Jenkins. 2013. *Post-Ethical Society: The Iraq War, Abu Ghraib, and the Moral Failure of the Secular*. Chicago, IL: University of Chicago Press.

Portes, Alejandro. 1998. "Social Capital: Its Origins and Applications in Modern Sociology." *Annual Review of Sociology* 24: 1–24.

Postles, David. 1996. "Personal Pledging: Medieval 'Reciprocity' or 'Symbolic Capital'?" *Journal of Interdisciplinary History* 26 (3): 419–35.

Poteat, Tonia, Katherine Rachlin, Sean Lare, Aron Jannsen, and Aaron Dever. 2019. "History and Prevalence of Gender Dysphoria." Pp. 1–24 in *Transgender Medicine: A Transdisciplinary Approach*, edited by L. Poretsky and W.C. Hembree. Cham: Humana Press.

Pratt, Travis C. 2010. *Addicted to Incarceration: Corrections Policy and the Politics of Misinformation in the United States*. Los Angeles, CA: Sage.

Price-Huish, Cecilee. 1997. "Born to Kill? 'Aggression Genes' and Their Potential Impact on Sentencing and the Criminal Justice System." *SMU Law Review* 50 (2): 603–26.

Primoratz, Igor. 2006. "Terrorism in the Israeli-Palestinian Conflict: A Case Study in Applied Ethics." *Jerusalem Philosophical Quarterly* 55: 27–48.

Prothrow-Stith, Deborah. 1993. *Deadly Consequences*. New York: Harper Perennial.

Putnam, Robert D. 2000. *Bowling Alone: The Collapse and Revival of American Community*. New York: Simon and Schuster.

Qiang, Xiao. 2019. "President Xi's Surveillance State." *Journal of Democracy* 30 (1): 53–67.

Rabe-Hemp, Cara and Amie Schuck. 2007. "Violence Against Police Officers: Are Female Officers at Greater Risk?" *Police Quarterly* 10 (4): 411–28.

Radabe, Patrick. 2021. "Racist Cop or Product of a Racist Police Academy?" *Journal of Black Studies* 52 (3): 231–47.

Rafael, Steven. 2017. "The Effects of Conviction and Incarceration on Future Employment Outcomes." Pp. 237–62 in *Labeling Theory: Empirical Tests*, edited by D.P. Farrington and J. Murray. New York: Routledge.

Rafter, Nicole. 2004. "The Unrepentant Horse-Slasher: Moral Insanity and the Origins of Criminological Thought." *Criminology* 42 (4): 979–1008.

Raine, Adrian. 1993. *The Psychopathology of Crime: Criminal Behavior as a Clinical Disorder*. San Diego, CA: Academic Press.

Ramirez, Deborah and Greer Clem. 2021. "Fortifying the Rule of Law: Filling the Gaps Revealed by the Mueller Report and Impeachment Proceedings." *Northeastern University Law Review* 13 (1): 1–40.

Rath, Saroj Kumar. 2017. "Searching a Political Solution for Syria." *India Quarterly* 73 (2): 180–95.

Ravary, Amanda, Mark W. Baldwin, and Jennifer A. Bartz. 2019. "Shaping the Body Politic: Mass Media Fat-Shaming Affects Implicit Anti-Fat Attitudes." *Personality and Social Psychology Bulletin* 45 (11): 1580–9.

Regoeczi, Wendy and Stephanie Kent. 2014. "Race, Poverty, and the Traffic Ticket Cycle: Exploring the Situational Context of the Application of Police Discretion." *Policing* 37 (1): 190–205.

Reid, John Phillip. 1997. *Policing the Elephant: Crime, Punishment, and Social Behavior on the Overland Trail*. San Marino, CA: Huntington Library.

Reiman, Jeffrey and Paul Leighton. 2020. *The Rich Get Richer and the Poor Get Prison: Thinking Critically about Class and Criminal Justice*, 12th edn. Abingdon, UK: Taylor & Francis.

Reiss, Jr., Albert J. 1951. "Delinquency as the Failure of Personal and Social Controls." *American Sociological Review* 16 (2): 196–207.

Richert, Lucas. 2014. "'Therapy Means Political Change, Not Peanut Butter': American Radical Psychiatry, 1968–1975." *Social History of Medicine* 27 (1): 104–21.

Rifkin, Mark. 2017. "Indigeneity, Apartheid, Palestine: On the Transit of Political Metaphors." *Cultural Critique* 95: 25–70.

Riska, Elianne. 2003. "Gendering the Medicalization Thesis." Pp. 59–97 in *Gender Perspectives on Health and Medicine*, edited by M. Texler Segal, V. Demos, and J.J. Kronenfeld. Bingley, UK: Emerald.

Rogers, Jacqui, Renska Herrema, Emma Honey, and Mark Freeston. 2018. "Towards a Treatment for Intolerance of Uncertainty for Autistic Adults: A Single Case Experimental Design Study." *Journal of Autism and Developmental Disorders* 48 (8): 2832–45.

Rogers, Wendy A. and Yishai Mintzker. 2016. "Getting Clearer on Overdiagnosis." *Journal of Evaluation in Clinical Practice* 22 (4): 580–7.

Rose, Dina R. and Todd R. Clear. 2004. "Who Doesn't Know Someone in Jail? The Impact of Exposure to Prison on Attitudes toward Formal and Informal Controls." *Prison Journal* 84 (2): 228–47.

Rose, Nikolas. 2000. "Government and Control." *British Journal of Criminology* 40: 321–39.

Rose, Nikolas. 2003. "Neurochemical Selves." *Society* 41 (1): 46–59.

Ross, Edward A. 1896. "Social Control." *American Journal of Sociology* 1 (5): 513–35.

Ross, Edward A. 1900. "The Radiant Points of Social Control." *American Journal of Sociology* 6 (2): 238–47.

Ross, Edward A. 1901. *Social Control: A Survey of the Foundations of Order*. New York: Macmillan.

Roth, Wendy D. and Jal D. Mehta. 2002. "The Rashomon Effect: Combining Positivist and Interpretivist Approaches in the Analysis of Contested Events." *Sociological Methods and Research* 31 (2): 131–73.

Rothman, David J. 2002a [1980]. *Conscience and Convenience: The Asylum and Its Alternatives in Progressive America*, revised edn. Hawthorne, NY: Aldine de Gruyter.

Rothman, David J. 2002b [1970]. *The Discovery of the Asylum*, revised edn. Hawthorne, NY: Aldine de Gruyter.

Rothstein, Richard. 2017. *The Color of Law: A Forgotten History of How Our Government Segregated America*. New York: Liveright Publishing.

Rucker, Philip and Carol Leonnig. 2020. *A Very Stable Genius: Donald J. Trump's Testing of America*. New York: Penguin Press.

Ruonavaara, Hannu. 1997. "Moral Regulation: A Reformulation." *Sociological Theory* 15 (3): 277–93.

Ryan, Matt E. and Peter T. Leeson. 2011. "Hate Groups and Hate Crime." *International Review of Law and Economics* 31: 256–62.

Ryan, Sara and Ulla Räisänen. 2008. "'It's Like You Are Just a Spectator in this Thing': Experiencing Social Life the 'Aspie' Way." *Emotion, Space and Society* 1 (2): 135–43.

Rye, Mark S. and Douglas Ullman. 1999. "The Successful Treatment of Long-Term Selective Mutism: A Case Study." *Journal of Behavior Therapy and Experimental Psychiatry* 30: 313–23.

Sampson, Robert J. and John H. Laub. 1993. *Crime in the Making: Pathways and Turning Points through Life*. Cambridge, MA: Harvard University Press.

Sariolghalam, Mahmood. 2003. "Understanding Iran: Getting Past Stereotypes and Mythology." *Washington Quarterly* 26 (4): 69–82.

Sauder, Michael. 2020. "A Sociology of Luck." *Sociological Theory* 38 (3): 193–216.

Saunders, Daniel. 2007. "The Impact of Neoliberalism on College Students." *Journal of College & Character* 8 (5): 1–9.

Sax, Leonard. 2002. "How Common is Intersex? A Response to Anne Fausto-Sterling." *Journal of Sex Research* 39 (3): 174–78.

Scaptura, Maria N. and Kaitlin M. Boyle. 2020. "Masculinity Threat, 'Incel' Traits, and Violent Fantasies among Heterosexual Men in the United States." *Feminist Criminology* 15 (3): 278–98.

Schaefer, Richard J. 1995. "National Information Infrastructure Policy: A Theoretical and Normative Approach." *Internet Research: Electronic Networking Applications and Policy* 5 (2): 4–13.

Scheff, Thomas J. 1966. *Being Mentally Ill: A Sociological Theory*. Chicago, IL: Aldine.

Schelling, Thomas C. 1978. *Micromotives and Macrobehavior*. New York: Norton.

Schiefenhövel, Wulf. 2013. "Biased Semantics for *Right* and *Left* in 50 Indo-European and Non-Indo-European Languages." *Annals of the New York Academy of Sciences* 1288 (1): 135–52.

Schmertmann, Carl P., Adansi A. Amankwaa, and Robert D. Long. 1998. "Three Strikes and You're Out: Demographic Analysis of Mandatory Prison Sentencing." *Demography* 35 (4): 445–63.

Schmitt, Carl. 2005 [1922]. *Political Theology: Four Chapters on the Concept of Sovereignty*, translated by G. Schwab. Chicago, IL: University of Chicago Press.

Schmitt, Carl. 2007. *The Concept of the Political*, expanded edn., translated by G. Schwab. Chicago, IL: University of Chicago Press.

Schoenfeld, Heather, Rachel M. Durso, and Kat Albrecht. 2019. "Maximizing Charges: Overcriminalization and Prosecutorial Practices during the Crime Decline." Pp. 145–79 in *After Imprisonment*, edited by A. Sarat. Bingley, UK: Emerald.

Schram, Sanford F. 2000. "In the Clinic: The Medicalization of Welfare." *Social Text* 18 (1): 81–107.

Schuurman, Bart, Lasse Lindekilde, Stefan Malthaner, Francis O'Connor, Paul Gill, and Noémie Bouhana. 2019. "End of the Lone Wolf: The Typology that Should Not Have Been." *Studies in Conflict & Terrorism* 42 (8): 771–8.

Scott, James C. 1998. *Seeing Like a State: How Certain Schemes to Improve the Human Condition Have Failed*. New Haven, CT: Yale University Press.

Scott, Susie. 2006. "The Medicalisation of Shyness: From Social Misfits to Social Fitness." *Sociology of Health and Illness* 28 (2): 133–53.

Scott, Susie. 2010. "How to Look Good (Nearly) Naked: The Performative Regulation of the Swimmer's Body." *Body and Society* 16 (2): 143–68.

Seeberg, Peter. 2016. "The Crisis in Syria, International and Regional Sanctions, and the Transformation of the Political Order in Syria." Pp. 101–22 in *The Levant in Turmoil*, edited by M. Beck, D. Jung, and P. Seeberg. Houndmills, UK: Palgrave Macmillan.

Seid, Abdu K., Ulrike Grittner, Thomas K. Greenfield, and Kim Bloomfield. 2015. "To Cause Harm and to be Harmed by Others: New Perspectives on Alcohol's Harms to Others." *Substance Abuse* 9 (S2): 13–22.

Sela, Avraham. 2015. "From Revolution to Political Participation: Institutionalization of Militant Islamic Movements." *Contemporary Review of the Middle East* 2 (1&2): 31–54.

Shapiro, Harvey (ed.) 2018. *Wiley Handbook of Violence in Education*. Hoboken, NJ: Wiley-Blackwell.

Sharkey, Patrick, Gerard Torrats-Espinosa, and Delaram Takyar. 2017. "Community and the Crime Decline: The Causal Effect of Local Nonprofits on Violent Crime." *American Sociological Review* 82 (6): 1214–40.

Shay, Shaul. 2004. *The Shahids: Islam and Suicide Attacks*, translated by R. Lieberman. New Brunswick, NJ: Transaction.

Shelden, Randall G. 2004. "The Imprisonment Crisis in America: Introduction." *Review of Policy Research* 21 (1): 5–12.

Sherman, Lawrence W. 1993. "Defiance, Deterrence, and Irrelevance: A Theory of the Criminal Sanction." *Journal of Research in Crime and Delinquency* 30 (4): 445–73.

Sherman, Lawrence W. 2017. "Experiments in Criminal Sanctions: Labeling, Defiance, and Restorative Justice." Pp. 149–76 in *Labeling Theory: Empirical Tests*, edited by D.P. Farrington and J. Murray. New York: Routledge.

Shih, Elena. 2016. "Not in My 'Backyard Abolitionism.'" *Sociological Perspectives* 59 (1): 66–90.

Short, John Rennie. 2006. *Urban Theory: A Critical Assessment*. Basingstoke: Palgrave Macmillan.

Shoshana, Avihu. 2019. "Seeing Like a DSM: Therapeutic Governance, Welfare, and Social Workers." *Sociological Forum* 34 (1): 181–200.

Siebert, Donald T. 1990. "The Aesthetic Execution of Charles I: Clarendon to Hume." Pp. 7–27 in *Executions and the British Experience from the 17th to the 20th Century: A Collection of Essays*, edited by W.B. Thesing. Jefferson, NC: McFarland and Co.

Silberman, Steve, 2016. *Neurotribes: The Legacy of Autism and the Future of Neurodiversity*. New York: Avery.

Silva, Jason R., Celinet Duran, Joshua D. Frielich, and Steven M. Chermak. 2019. "Addressing the Myths of Terrorism in America." *International Criminal Justice Review* 30 (3): 302–24.

Simmel, Georg. 1950. *The Sociology of Georg Simmel*, translated and edited by K.H. Wolff. New York: Free Press.

Simon, Jonathan and Malcolm M. Feeley. 2003. "The Form and Limits of the New Penology." Pp. 75–115 in *Punishment and Social Control*, enlarged 2nd edn., edited by T.G. Blomberg and S. Cohen. New York: Aldine de Gruyter.

Simons, Leslie Gordon, Ronald L. Simons, Rand D. Conger, and Gene H. Brody. 2004. "Collective Socialization and Child Conduct Problems: A Multilevel Analysis with an African American Sample." *Youth and Society* 35 (3): 267–92.

Singh, Ilina, Walter P. Sinnott-Armstrong, and Julian Savulescu (eds.) 2014. *Bioprediction, Biomarkers, and Bad Behavior: Scientific, Legal, and Ethical Challenges*. Oxford: Oxford University Press.

Siniver, Asaf and Scott Lucas. 2016. "The Islamic State Lexical Battleground: U.S. Foreign Policy and the Abstraction of Threat." *International Affairs* 92 (1): 63–79.

Skene, Allyson. 2002. "Rethinking Normativism in Psychiatric Classification." Pp. 114–27 in *Descriptions and Prescriptions: Values, Mental Disorders, and the DSMs*, edited by J.Z. Sadler. Baltimore, MD: Johns Hopkins University Press.

Skocpol, Theda. 1992. *Protecting Soldiers and Mothers: The Political Origins of Social Policy in the United States*. Cambridge, MA: Belknap Press.

Skodal, Andrew E. (ed.) 1998. *Psychopathology and Violent Crime*. Washington, DC: American Psychiatric Press.

Skoll, Geoffrey R. 2010. *Social Theory of Fear: Terror, Torture, and Death in a Post-Capitalist World*. New York: Palgrave Macmillan.

Skolnick, Jerome H. 1966. *Justice without Trial: Law Enforcement in Democratic Society*. New York: Wiley.

Slater, Jerome. 2015. "Terrorism and the Israeli-Palestinian Conflict." *Middle East Policy* 22 (3): 79–99.

Slutkin, Gary, Charles Ransford, and Daria Zvetina. 2018a. "How the Health Sector Can Reduce Violence by Treating it as a Contagion." *AMA Journal of Ethics* 20 (1): 47–55.

Slutkin, Gary, Charles Ransford, and Daria Zvetina. 2018b. "Response to 'Metaphorically or Not, Violence is Not a Contagious Disease.'" *AMA Journal of Ethics* 20 (5): 516–19.

Smith, Christian. 2011. *Lost in Transition: The Dark Side of Emerging Adulthood.* Oxford: Oxford University Press.

Smith, Paul H. 2004. *Reading the Enemy's Mind: Inside Star Gate – America's Psychic Espionage Program.* New York: Forge Books.

Smits, Rik. 2012. *The Puzzle of Left-Handedness.* London: Reaktion Books.

Sobal, Jeffrey. 1995. "The Medicalization and Demedicalization of Obesity." Pp. 67–90 in *Eating Agendas*, edited by D. Maurer and J. Sobal. New York: Aldine de Gruyer.

Somers, A. 1995. "W(h)ither Public Health?" *Public Health Reports* 110: 657–61.

Somers, Margaret R. 2005. "Beware Trojan Horses Bearing Social Capital: How Privatization Turned Solidarity into a Bowling Team." Pp. 233–74 in *The Politics of Method in the Human Sciences*, edited by G. Steinmetz. Durham, NC: Duke University Press.

Song, Bing. 2019. "The West May Be Wrong about China's Social Credit System." *New Perspectives Quarterly* 36 (1): 33–5.

Spence, Keith. 2005. "World Risk Society and War against Terror." *Political Studies* 53: 284–302.

Spencer, Herbert. 1879. *The Data of Ethics.* Lovell, Coryell & Co.

Spencer, Herbert. 1891. *Principles of Sociology, vol. 1.* New York: Appleton.

Spencer, Herbert. 1897a. *Principles of Sociology, vol. I-2.* New York: Appleton.

Spencer, Herbert. 1897b. *Principles of Sociology, vol. II-1.* New York: Appleton.

Squires, Gregory D. and Jan Chadwick. 2006. "Linguistic Profiling: A Continuing Tradition of Discrimination in the Home Insurance Industry?" *Urban Affairs Review* 41 (3): 400–15.

Squires, Peter. 2006. "New Labour and the Politics of Antisocial Behaviour." *Critical Social Policy* 26 (1): 144–68.

Stacey, Michele and Heidi S. Bonner. 2021. "Veil of Darkness and Investigating Disproportionate Impact in Policing: When Researchers Disagree." *Police Quarterly* 24 (1): 55–73.

Stampnitzky, Lisa. 2013. *Disciplining Terror: How Experts Invented "Terrorism."* Cambridge: Cambridge University Press.

Staples, William G. 2000. *Everyday Surveillance: Vigilance and Visibility in Postmodern Life.* Lanham, MD: Rowman and Littlefield.

Starfield, B., J. Hyde, J. Gérvas, and I. Heath. 2008. "The Concept of Prevention: A Good Idea Gone Astray?" *Epidemiology & Community Health* 62 (7): 580–3.

Stark, Rodney. 2001. *One True God: Historical Consequences of Monotheism.* Princeton, NJ: Princeton University Press.

Stark, Werner. 1976–1987. *The Social Bond: An Investigation into the Bases of Law-Abidingness*, 6 vols. New York: Fordham University Press.

Starr, Paul. 1982. *The Social Transformation of American Medicine.* New York: Basic Books.

Stern, Jessica and J.M. Berger. 2015. *ISIS: The State of Terror.* New York: HarperCollins.

Stewart, Daniel M. and Willard M. Oliver. 2021. "The Adoption of Homeland Security Initiatives in Texas Police Departments: A Contextual Perspective." *Criminal Justice Review* 46 (1): 80–98.

Stoddart, Eric. 2011. *Theological Perspectives on a Surveillance Society: Watching and Being Watched.* Farnham, UK: Ashgate.

Stratton, Greg. 2015. "Transforming the Central Park Jogger into the Central Park Five: Shifting Narratives of Innocence and Changing Media Discourse in the Attack on the Central Park Jogger, 1989–2014." *Crime Media Culture* 11 (3): 281–97.

Strauss, Leo. 1965. *Natural Right and History*. Chicago, IL: University of Chicago Press.

Stroshine, Meghan, Geoffrey Alpert, and Roger Dunham. 2008. "The Influence of 'Working Rules' on Police Supervision and Discretionary Decision Making." *Police Quarterly* 11 (3): 315–37.

Suarez, Thomas. 2017. *State of Terror: How Terrorism Created Modern Israel*. Northampton, MA: Olive Branch Press.

Sumner, Colin. 1994. *The Sociology of Deviance: An Obituary*. New York: Continuum.

Sumner, William Graham. 1906. *Folkways*. Boston, MA: Ginn and Co.

Sundin, Erica, Maria Rosario Galanti, Jonas Landberg, and Mats Ramstedt. 2021. "Severe Harm from Others' Drinking: A Population-based Study on Sex Differences and the Role of One's Own Drinking Habits." *Drug and Alcohol Review* 40: 263–71.

Sunstein, Cass. 2019. *Conformity*. New York: New York University Press.

Sunstein, Cass. 2020. "Falsehoods and the First Amendment." *Harvard Journal of Law & Technology* 33 (2): 387–426.

Sutherland, Edwin H. and Donald R. Cressey. 1955. *Principles of Criminology*, 5th edn. Chicago, IL: J.B. Lippincott Co.

Sutrop, Margit and Katrin Laas-Mikko. 2012. "From Identity Verification to Behavior Prediction: Ethical Implications of Second Generation Biometrics." *Review of Policy Research* 29 (1): 21–36.

Swain, Marissa Sakaguchi, Rumiko Okada and Erin O'Callaghan. 2017. "The Social Implications of Oxytocin with Autism Spectrum Disorder: A Review of the Literature." *Journal of Behavioral and Social Sciences* 4: 305–14.

Swann, Patricia. 2019. *Cases in Public Relations Management: The Rise of Social Media and Activism*. New York: Routledge.

Sykes, Gresham M. and David Matza. 1957. "Techniques of Neutralization: A Theory of Delinquency." *American Sociological Review* 22 (6): 664–70.

Sylvester, Judith. 2020. "President Trump and the Mother of All Bombs: Quickly Forgotten." *Athens Journal of Mass Media and Communications* 6 (1): 23–42.

Szasz, Thomas. 1961. *The Myth of Mental Illness*. New York: Dell.

Szasz, Thomas. 1963. *Law, Liberty, and Psychiatry*. New York: Collier.

Szasz, Thomas. 2000. "Second Comment on 'Aristotle's Function Argument.'" *Philosophy, Psychiatry, and Psychology* 7 (1): 3–16.

Taniguchi, Travis, Josh Hendrix, Brian Aagaard, Kevin Strom, Alison Levin-Rector, and Stephanie Zimmer. 2016. "A Test of Racial Disproportionality in Traffic Stops Conducted by the Greensboro Police Department." RTI Project Number 0290184.003.284. Research Triangle Park, NC: RTI International.

Taniguchi, Travis, Josh Hendrix, Alison Levin-Rector, Brian Aagaard, Kevin Strom, and Stephanie Zimmer. 2017. "Extending the Veil of Darkness Approach: An Examination of Racial Disproportionality in Traffic Stops in Durham, NC." *Police Quarterly* 20 (4): 420–48.

Taylor, Claire. 2001. "The Relationship between Social and Self-Control: Tracing Hirschi's Criminological Career." *Theoretical Criminology* 5 (3): 369–88.

Tenove, Chris. 2020. "Protecting Democracy from Disinformation: Normative Threats and Policy Responses." *International Journal of Press/Politics* 25 (3): 517–37.

Thom, Robyn P., Christopher J. Keary, Michelle L. Palumbo, et al. 2019. "Beyond the Brain: A Multi-System Inflammatory Subtype of Autism Spectrum Disorder." *Psychopharmacology* 236: 3045–61.

Thomsen, Frej Klem. 2019. "The Concepts of Surveillance and Sousveillance: A Critical Analysis." *Social Science Information* 58 (4): 701–13.

Thomson, Irene Taviss. 2005. "The Theory that Won't Die: From Mass Society to the Decline of Social Capital." *Sociological Forum* 20 (3): 421–48.

Toby, Jackson. 1957. "Social Disorganization and Stake in Conformity: Complementary Factors in the Predatory Behavior of Hoodlums." *Journal of Criminal Law and Criminology* 48: 12–17.

Tonry, Michael. 1996. "Racial Politics, Racial Disparities, and the War on Crime." Pp. 165–86 in *Race, Crime, and Justice*, edited by B.A. Hudson. Brookfield, VT: Dartmouth University Press.

Tonry, Michael. 1999. "Why Are U.S. Incarceration Rates So High?" *Crime and Delinquency* 45 (4): 419–37.

Tonry, Michael and David P. Farrington. 2005. "Punishment and Crime across Space and Time." Pp. 1–39 in *Crime and Punishment in Western Countries, 1980–1999*, edited by M. Tonry and D.P. Farrington. Chicago, IL: University of Chicago Press.

Torpey, John C. 2000. *The Invention of the Passport: Surveillance, Citizenship, and the State.* Cambridge: Cambridge University Press.

Torres, Jennifer M.C. 2014. "Medicalizing to Demedicalize: Lactation Consultants and the (De)medicalization of Breastfeeding." *Social Science & Medicine* 100: 159–66.

Tsui, Lokman. 2005. "Introduction." *China Information* 19 (2): 181–8.

Turner, Stephen. 2021. "Explaining Away Crime: The Race Narrative in American Sociology and Ethical Theory." *European Journal of Social Theory* 24 (3): 356–73.

Tylor, Edward B. 1871. *Primitive Culture*. London: Murray.

Unnever, James D., Francis T. Cullen, and Robert Agnew. 2006. "Why is 'Bad' Parenting Criminogenic? Implications from Rival Theories." *Youth Violence and Juvenile Justice* 4 (1): 3–33.

Upson, Lent D. 1929. "The International Association of Chiefs of Police and Other American Police Organizations." *Annals of the American Academy of Political and Social Science* 146 (1): 121–7.

Valcore, Jace L. and Kevin Buckler. 2020. "An Act of Terror and an Act of Hate: National Elite and Populace Newspaper Framing of Pulse Nightclub Shooting." *Criminal Justice Studies* 33 (3): 276–96.

van Krieken, Robert. 1986. "Social Theory and Child Welfare: Beyond Social Control." *Theory and Society* 15 (3): 401–29.

Vico, Giambattista. 1982 [1724]. *Vico: Selected Writings*, edited and translated by L. Pompa. Cambridge: Cambridge University Press.

Vollmer, August. 1971 [1919]. "The Policeman as a Social Worker." Pp. 32–8 in *Proceedings of the Annual Conventions of the International Association of Chiefs of Police, 1913–1920*, vol. III. New York: Arno Press.

Vosoughi, Soroush, Deb Roy, and Sinan Aral. 2018. "The Spread of True and False News Online." *Science* 359: 1146–51.

Wakefield, Jerome C. 2002. "Values and the Validity of Diagnostic Criteria: Disvalued versus Disordered Conditions of Childhood and Adolescence." Pp. 148–64 in *Descriptions and Prescriptions: Values, Mental Disorders, and the DSMs*, edited by J.Z. Sadler. Baltimore, MD: Johns Hopkins University Press.

Walker, Samuel. 1980. *Popular Justice: A History of American Criminal Justice*. New York: Oxford University Press.

Wallace, Anthony F.C. 1966. *Religion: An Anthropological View*. New York: Random House.

Walsh, James P. 2020. "Social Media and Moral Panics: Assessing the Effects of Technological Change on Societal Reaction." *International Journal of Cultural Studies* 23 (6): 840–59.

Wang, Xia, Thomas G. Blomberg, and Spencer D. Li. 2005. "Comparison of the Educational

Deficiencies of Delinquent and Nondelinquent Students." *Evaluation Review* 29 (4): 291–312.

Ward, Lester F. 1883. *Dynamic Sociology*, 2 vols. New York: Appleton.

Ward, Lester F. 1893. *Psychic Factors of Civilization*. Boston, MA: Ginn and Company.

Ward, Lester F. 1903. *Pure Sociology: On the Origins and Spontaneous Development of Society*. New York: Macmillan.

Ward, Lester F. 1906. *Applied Sociology: A Treatise on the Conscious Improvement of Society by Society*. Boston, MA: Ginn and Company.

Ward, Steven C. 2002. *Modernizing the Mind: Psychological Knowledge and the Remaking of Society*. Westport, CT: Praeger.

Warden, G.B. 1978. "Law Reform in England and New England, 1620 to 1660." *William and Mary Quarterly* 35 (4): 668–90.

Wark, Colin and John F. Galliher. 2007. "Emory Bogardus and the Origins of the Social Distance Scale." *American Sociologist* 38: 383–95.

Warner, Margaret. 1984. "Local Control versus National Interest: The Debate over Southern Public Health, 1878–1884." *Journal of Southern History* 50 (3): 407–28.

Wasilewska, Jolanta and Mark Klukowski. 2015. "Gastrointestinal Symptoms and Autism Spectrum Disorder: Links and Risks – A Possible New Overlap Syndrome." *Pediatric Health, Medicine and Therapeutics* 6: 153–66.

Wasserstein, David J. 2017. *Black Banners of ISIS: The Roots of the New Caliphate*. New Haven, CT: Yale University Press.

Weber, Max. 1947. *The Theory of Social and Economic Organization*, translated by A.M. Henderson and T. Parsons, and edited by T. Parsons. New York: Free Press.

Weber, Max. 1968. *Economy and Society*, translated and edited by Guenther Roth and Claus Wittich. New York: Bedminster Press.

Weber, Max. 1978 [1922]. "Excerpts from Wirtschaft und Gesellschaft." Pp. 33–42 in *Weber: Selections in Translation*, translated by E. Matthews, edited by W.G. Runciman. Cambridge: Cambridge University Press.

Weisheit, Ralph A. and John M. Klofas. 1998. "The Public Health Approach to Illicit Drugs." *Criminal Justice Review* 23 (2): 197–207.

Weiss, David and Xin Zhang. 2020. "Multiple Sources of Aging Attitudes: Perceptions of Age Groups and Generations from Adolescence to Old Age across China, Germany, and the United States." *Journal of Cross-Cultural Psychology* 51 (6): 407–23.

Weiss, Harald E. and Lesley Williams Reid. 2005. "Low-Quality Employment Concentration and Crime: An Examination of Metropolitan Labor Markets." *Sociological Perspectives* 48 (2): 213–32.

Weissman, Jeremy. 2019. "P2P Surveillance in the Global Village." *Ethics and Information Technology* 21 (1): 29–47.

Welch, Michael. 2003. "Ironies of Social Control and the Criminalization of Immigrants." *Crime, Law and Social Change* 39 (4): 319–37.

Welch, Michael, Eric A. Price, and Nana Yankey. 2002. "Moral Panic over Youth Violence: Wilding and the Manufacture of Menace in the Media." *Youth & Society* 34 (1): 3–30.

Welch, Rosie, Samantha McMahon, and Jan Wright. 2012. "The Medicalisation of Food Pedagogies in Primary Schools and Popular Culture: A Case for Awakening Subjugated Knowledges." *Discourse: Studies in the Cultural Politics of Education* 33 (5): 713–28.

Welsh, Megan, Joshua Chanin, and Stuart Henry. 2021. "Complex Colorblindness in Police Processes and Practices." *Social Problems* 68: 374–92.

Western, Bruce, Mary Pattillo, and David Weiman. 2004. "Introduction." Pp. 1–18 in *Imprisoning America: The Social Effects of Mass Incarceration*, edited by M. Pattillo, D. Weiman, and B. Western. New York: Russell Sage Foundation.

Westervelt, Saundra Davis. 1998. *Shifting the Blame: How Victimization became a Criminal Defense*. New Brunswick, NJ: Rutgers University Press.

White, Susan. 1998. "Interdiscursivity and Child Welfare: The Ascent and Durability of Psycho-legalism." *Sociological Review* 46 (2): 264–92.

Wierzbicka, Anna. 2004. "The English Expressions *Good Boy* and *Good Girl* and Cultural Models of Child Rearing." *Culture and Psychology* 10 (3): 251–78.

Williams, Christopher R. and Bruce A. Arrigo. 2006. "Introduction: Philosophy, Crime, and Theoretical Criminology." Pp. 1–38 in *Philosophy, Crime, and Criminology*, edited by B.A. Arrigo and C.R. Williams. Urbana, IL: University of Illinois Press.

Williams, Raymond. 1974. *Television, Technology and Cultural Form*. London: Fontana.

Wilshire, Bruce W. 1982. *Role Playing and Identity: The Limits of Theatre as Metaphor*. Bloomington, IN: Indiana University Press.

Wilson, William Julius. 1987. *The Truly Disadvantaged: The Inner City, the Underclass, and Public Policy*. Chicago, IL: University of Chicago Press.

Wilson, William Julius. 1991. "The Truly Disadvantaged Revisited: A Response to Hochschild and Boxill." *Ethics* 101 (3): 593–609.

Wilson, William Julius. 2013. "Combating Concentrated Poverty in Urban Neighborhoods." *Journal of Applied Social Science* 7 (2): 135–43.

Wilson, William Julius and Robert Aponte. 1985. "Urban Poverty." *Annual Review of Sociology* 11: 235–58.

Wingerter, J. Richard. 2003. *Science, Religion, and the Meditative Mind*. Lanham, MD: University Press of America.

Withers, Suzanne Davies, William A.V. Clark, and Tricia Ruiz. 2008. "Demographic Variation in Housing Cost Adjustments with US Family Migration." *Population, Space and Place* 14: 305–25.

Withrow, Brian L. 2004. "Race-Based Policing: A Descriptive Analysis of the Wichita Stop Study." *Police Practice and Research* 5 (3): 223–40.

Wolff, Kevin T., Jonathan Intravia, Michael T. Baglivio, and Alex R. Piquero. 2020. "Adherence to the Street Code Predicts an Earlier Anticipated Death." *Journal of Research in Crime and Delinquency* 57 (2): 139–81.

Wong, Priscilla. 2010. "Selective Mutism: A Review of Etiology, Comorbidities, and Treatment." *Psychiatry* 7 (3): 23–31.

Wood, Jennifer D., Amy C. Watson, and Anjali J. Fulambarker. 2017. "The 'Gray Zone' of Police Work during Mental Health Encounters: Findings from an Observational Study in Chicago." *Police Quarterly* 20 (1): 81–105.

Worden, Robert E., Sarah J. McLean, and Andrew P. Wheeler. 2012. "Testing for Racial Profiling with the Veil of Darkness Method." *Police Quarterly* 15 (1): 92–111.

Wright, Valerie and Isaac Unah. 2017. "Media Exposure and Racialized Perceptions of Inequities in Criminal Justice." *Social Sciences* 6 (3): 1–22.

Xu, Jianhua, Guyu Sun, Wei Cao, Wenyuan Fan, Zhihao Pan, Zhaoyu Yao, and Han Li. 2021. "Stigma, Discrimination, and Hate Crimes in Chinese-Speaking World amid Covid-19 Pandemic." *Asian Journal of Criminology* 16: 51–74.

Yamasue, Hidenori and Gregor Domes. 2018. "Oxytocin and Autism Spectrum Disorders." Pp. 449–65 in *Behavioral Pharmacology of Neuropeptides: Oxytocin*, edited by R. Hurlemann and V. Grinevich. Cham: Springer.

Yost, Ellen Smith. 2021. "Social Support for Terrorists: Facebook's 'Friend Suggestion'

Algorithm, Section 230 Immunity, Material Support for Terrorists, and the First Amendment." *Santa Clara High Technology Law Journal* 37 (3): 301–36.

Young, T.R. 1990. *The Drama of Social Life: Essays in Post-Modern Social Psychology*. New Brunswick, NJ: Transaction Books.

Youssef, Khaoula and Michio Okada. 2016. "Exploring the Social Bonding that Evolves between a Human and a Minimally Designed Accompanying Robot." *Information and Media Technologies* 11: 250–63.

Youssef, Khaoula, P. Ravindra De Silva, and Michio Okada. 2015. "Exploring the Four Social Bonds Evolvement for an Accompanying Minimally Designed Robot." Pp. 337–47 in *Social Robotics*, ICSR 2015, Lecture Notes in Computer Science, vol. 9388, edited by A. Tapus, E. André, J.C. Martin, F. Ferland, and M. Ammi. Cham: Springer.

Zaboski, Brian A. and Eric A. Storch. 2018. "Comorbid Autism Spectrum Disorder and Anxiety Disorders: A Brief Review." *Future Neurology* 13 (1): 31–27.

Zamkah, Abdulaziz, Terence Hui, Simon Andrews, Nilanjan Dey, Fuqian Shi, and R. Simon Sherratt. 2020. "Identification of Suitable Biomarkers for Stress and Emotion Detection for Future Personal Affective Wearable Sensors." *Biosensors* 10 (40): 1–15.

Zerbo, Ousseny, Albin Leong, Lisa Barcellos, Pilar Bernal, Bruce Fireman, and Lisa A. Croen. 2015. "Immune Mediated Conditions in Autism Spectrum Disorders." *Brain, Behavior, and Immunity* 46: 232–6.

Zhao, Bao, Yanmiao Cao, Liang Zhang, and Wenzin Zhang. 2020. "Parental Practices and Adolescent Effortful Control: MAOA T941G Gene Polymorphism as a Moderator." *Frontiers in Psychology* 11 (60): 1–9.

Zola, Irving K. 1972. "Medicine as an Institution of Social Control." *Sociological Review* 20 (4): 487–504.

Index

CPSIA information can be obtained
at www.ICGtesting.com
Printed in the USA
JSHW051123180423
40469JS00003B/16